Transforming Occupation in the Western Zones of Germany

An American armoured car attracts a crowd of young Germans in Berlin, 1946 (Getty Images).

Transforming Occupation in the Western Zones of Germany

Politics, Everyday Life and Social Interactions, 1945–55

Edited by
Camilo Erlichman and Christopher Knowles

BLOOMSBURY ACADEMIC
LONDON • NEW YORK • OXFORD • NEW DELHI • SYDNEY

BLOOMSBURY ACADEMIC
Bloomsbury Publishing Plc
50 Bedford Square, London, WC1B 3DP, UK

BLOOMSBURY, BLOOMSBURY ACADEMIC and the Diana logo are trademarks of Bloomsbury Publishing Plc

First published in Great Britain 2018
Paperback edition published 2020

A catalogue record for this book is available from the British Library.

A catalog record for this book is available from the Library of Congress.

ISBN: HB: 978-1-3500-4922-2
PB: 978-1-3501-5132-1
ePDF: 978-1-3500-4923-9
eBook: 978-1-3500-4924- 6

Typeset by Newgen KnowledgeWorks Pvt. Ltd., Chennai, India

Contents

Illustrations

Contributors

Andrew H. Beattie is Senior Lecturer in European Studies and German at the University of New South Wales, Sydney, Australia.

Douglas Bell is a doctoral candidate at Texas A&M University, USA.

Bettina Blum completed her PhD at the University of Münster. She is now responsible for the research and exhibition project 'The British in Westphalia' at the City of Paderborn, Germany.

Rebecca Boehling is Professor of History; Director, Global Studies Program; and Director, Judaic Studies Program at the University of Maryland, Baltimore County (UMBC), USA.

Susan L. Carruthers is Professor in American History at the University of Warwick, UK.

Daniel Cowling is a doctoral candidate at the University of Cambridge, UK.

Heather L. Dichter is Associate Professor in the Leicester Castle Business School and International Centre for Sports History and Culture at De Montfort University, UK.

Camilo Erlichman is Assistant Professor in the Institute of History, Leiden University, The Netherlands.

Ann-Kristin Glöckner is a doctoral candidate at the University of Halle-Wittenberg, Germany.

Nadja Klopprogge is a doctoral candidate at the John F. Kennedy Institute's Graduate School of North American Studies at the Freie Universität, Berlin.

Christopher Knowles is a visiting research fellow at King's College London and Archives By-Fellow at Churchill College, Cambridge, UK.

Johannes Kuber is a doctoral candidate at RWTH Aachen University, Germany.

Dominik Rigoll is a research fellow at the Zentrum für Zeithistorische Forschung, Potsdam, Germany.

Caroline Sharples is Senior Lecturer in European History at the University of Roehampton, London, UK.

Peter M. R. Stirk is Senior Lecturer in the School of Government and International Affairs, and Director of the Centre for the History of Political Thought at Durham University, UK.

Michael Wala is Professor of North American History at Ruhr University Bochum, Germany.

Acknowledgements

The idea for this book originated at a conference on 'The Allied Occupation of Germany Revisited: New Research on the Western Zones of Occupation', held in September 2016 at the German Historical Institute, London. We would like to thank the German Historical Institute, the German History Society, the Society for the Study of French History, the Royal Historical Society and the Beyond Enemy Lines project at King's College London, funded by the European Research Council, for supporting the conference. We are grateful to all those who participated in and gave papers at the conference for stimulating discussions on a new framework for research on the post-war occupation of Germany, and for contributing ideas on the significance of the occupation period within the broader history of post-war Europe. We are particularly indebted to Andreas Gestrich and Michael Schaich, director and deputy director, respectively, of the German Historical Institute, for their support, as well as to Felix Römer and Bernd Weisbrod for chairing two of the sessions. We are also grateful to the three anonymous peer reviewers of this book for their helpful comments and suggestions. Finally, we should like to thank Alexandra Paulin-Booth for compiling the index with much attention to detail. What follows is intended as a novel exploration of a subject that is now in need of urgent rediscovery by historians, but we owe a large intellectual debt to earlier generations of scholars who have worked on the occupation period. We hope that the approaches presented here will contribute towards a more comprehensive and contextualized understanding of the post-war occupation of Germany, and that this book will act as a stimulus to others seeking novel ways of engaging with the period.

Abbreviations

ACC	Allied Control Council
AMGOT	Allied Military Government of Occupied Territories (in Italy)
BAOR	British Army of the Rhine
BJV	*Bayerischer Jagdschutz & Jägerverband* (Bavarian Hunting Organization)
BND	*Bundesnachrichtendienst* (German federal intelligence agency)
BVP	*Bayerische Volkspartei* (Bavarian People's Party)
CCG (BE)	Control Commission for Germany (British Element)
CDU	*Christlich Demokratische Union* (Christian Democratic Union)
FRG	Federal Republic of (West) Germany
GDR	German Democratic Republic
ICRC	International Committee of the Red Cross
IMT	International Military Tribunal (at Nuremberg)
JCS	Joint Chiefs of Staff (USA)
KRO	Kreis Resident Officer
MCC	Ministerial Collecting Center
NAACP	National Association for the Advancement of Colored People
NAAFI	Navy, Army and Air Forces Institutes
NSDAP	Nationalsozialistische Deutsche Arbeiterpartei (National Socialist German Workers' Party, the official name of the Nazi Party)
OMGUS	Office of Military Government, United States
OSS	Office of Strategic Services (USA)
PMGO	Provost Marshal General's Office (USA)
POW	prisoner of war
SA	*Sturmabteilung* (Nazi stormtroopers)
SD	*Sicherheitsdienst* (an intelligence arm of the SS)
SHAEF	Supreme Headquarters Allied Expeditionary Force
SLRU	Special Legal Research Unit (UK)
SMG	School of Military Government (USA)
SPD	*Sozialdemokratische Partei Deutschlands* (Social Democratic Party of Germany)
SS	*Schutzstaffel* (a Nazi internal security and paramilitary organization)
UNRRA	United Nations Relief and Rehabilitation Agency
USFET	(Headquarters of the) United States Forces in the European Theater
YMCA	Young Men's Christian Association

Part One

Contextualizing Occupation

1

Introduction: Reframing Occupation as a System of Rule

Camilo Erlichman and Christopher Knowles

In 2003, amidst blurry TV images of the night-time bombing of Baghdad, the Allied occupation of Germany after the Second World War experienced a remarkable comeback. In its search for justifications for the invasion of Iraq, the Bush administration issued various statements that sought to legitimize the military interventions of the present by reference to the successes of 'democratization' through occupation in the past. In a speech in March 2003, President Bush proclaimed that 'there was a time when many said that the cultures of Japan and Germany were incapable of sustaining democratic values. They were wrong. Some say the same of Iraq today. They, too, are mistaken.'[1]

Bush's statement was just one of many similar pronouncements made at the time. Leading members of his administration had been floating such comparisons for a while, making frequent declarations that established a range of analogies between post-war Germany and contemporary Iraq. If post-war reconstruction had turned Western Germany from a country in ruins into a prosperous market economy and liberal democracy, they proclaimed, American post-war efforts in Iraq would surely turn the country from a 'failed state' into a beacon of political and economic stability in the region. Intellectual ammunition for such arguments was provided by think tanks close to the US government, who produced various studies using the fashionable label of 'nation building', drawing up catalogues with 'lessons' from the successful occupations of Germany and Japan for the present-day occupations in the Middle East. One such publication by the RAND Corporation, tellingly entitled *America's Role in Nation-Building: From Germany to Iraq*, contained a glowing endorsement by Paul Bremer, the top civilian administrator of the Coalition Provisional Authority in Iraq. For Bremer, the RAND publication that traced America's history of 'nation building' since 1945 represented 'a marvellous "how to" manual for post-conflict stabilization and reconstruction'.[2]

Professional historians, particularly in the United States, were quick to protest at such historical simplifications. Writing in the *Los Angeles Times*, Atina Grossmann and Mary Nolan, two leading US experts on German history, accused the US administration of 'ransack[ing] history for successful precedents', using 'facile historical comparisons' that 'distort the postwar situation and blind Americans to the challenges ahead in Iraq'.[3] Other scholarly interventions were quick to follow, most of which highlighted that there were many more differences than similarities between the cases of Germany and Iraq.[4] Meanwhile, historians of the American occupation of Japan expressed similar despair, emphasizing how the occupation of Iraq lacked legitimacy, not only among the victors but most importantly among the local population.[5] But if historians were quick to call into question the irresponsible use of the 'good occupations'[6] of Germany and Japan as a blueprint for future military operations designed to achieve 'regime change' and 'nation building', the analytical question of how the occupation of Germany by the Western Allies fits within a broader historical framework remains essentially unresolved.

The occupation of Germany, it would seem, is still generally understood by historians as a unique and exceptional case, with most scholars regarding the subject as a story of post-war transition internal to German history, with passing reference to the national history of the four occupiers.[7] Alternatively, historians have focused on how the division of Germany into four zones of occupation exacerbated tensions between the Western Allies and the Soviet Union, thereby contributing to the emergence of a Cold War Europe divided between East and West, and the integration of the Federal Republic of Germany within the Western Alliance.[8] A third historiographical strand has explored the occupation as part of a broad 'post-war' narrative that analyses the challenges faced by people across Europe after the mass violence, death and destruction following the Second World War and the legacies of the Third Reich and the Holocaust, with some approaching the immediate post-war history of Germany as a story of post-conflict reconstruction.[9] None of these approaches, however, discuss military occupation as a subject in its own right, or engage with the question of how the ruling strategies of the three Western Allies, together with the outcomes and legacies of occupation, can best be placed within a broader transnational or comparative framework.[10] The present volume is conceived as a response to this gap in the historiographies of post-war Germany and Europe.

The title of this book, *Transforming Occupation in the Western Zones of Germany*, seeks to capture a three-fold approach to the subject. First, it contributes to an evaluation of the impact of the occupation upon German society, exploring the extent to which daily life, politics, society and culture were transformed during the occupation period. Our conception of transformation, however, does not seek to suggest that the experience of occupation changed everything in German society.[11] It rather follows the recent suggestion by Simon Jackson and A. Dirk Moses that the most productive analytical question for historians of occupation is to explore the specific '"usages and practices" through which occupation *transforms*'.[12] To use a musical analogy, one might regard transformation as a process of modulation, a change from one key into another that contains elements of both. Second, *Transforming Occupation* reflects and follows an increased focus by historians on studying ruling techniques, social interactions and everyday life. These subjects have transformed historical approaches to the history of the mid-twentieth century, but are still marginal to the historiography of the post-war occupation of Germany.[13] Third, the present volume aims to transform our understanding of the place of the occupation period within German and European history, arguing that the occupation needs to be understood and studied as a distinct period in modern German history that can be explored using similar approaches to those adopted to analyse other cases of military occupation.

Military occupation as a dynamic power relationship

In addressing these questions, this volume starts from the assumption that military occupation is a discrete *system of rule*,[14] in which the power relationships between rulers and ruled are different from those in other modern hierarchical societies, such as parliamentary or presidential democracies, absolute or constitutional monarchies, dictatorships or other forms of authoritarian government. The defining feature of military occupation is the combination of *foreign* rule with the dependence, in the last resort, on the use of threat or force. Most rulers, even domestic military dictators, can draw on various forms of legitimacy derived from their pre-existing relationship with the local population and are in that sense rooted within local society and its current values.[15] Military occupation, on the other hand, normally begins life without intrinsic legitimacy, though the severity of the problem of legitimacy always depends on the historical context, and in particular on whether the occupation is perceived by the population as liberation from oppression, as conquest or subjugation following defeat in war by a foreign enemy, or as an illegitimate form of more long-term foreign control. In practice, this means that most occupation regimes need to find ways of legitimizing their hold on power and so induce the population to accept their authority, at least if they wish to stabilize their rule and achieve their political objectives.[16] This quest for legitimacy and stability prompts occupiers to develop and apply a number of ruling techniques that seek to preserve their authority and power, making the most efficient use of the resources available to them and, if possible, circumventing the need to apply violent forms of coercion.[17]

The fundamental concept underlying this volume is therefore that the occupation of the western zones of Germany, as a system of rule, can best be understood as a dynamic power relationship between the three Western Allies and the local German population. The unequal and ever-changing balance of power between occupiers and occupied affected all aspects of society and operated at different levels, including the structure of national, regional and local government; the relative status and influence of social, economic, political and generational groups; and the everyday life and personal relationships of individuals. Occupation affected people in different ways depending on their citizenship, social class, gender, ethnicity, geographical location, previous history and personal beliefs.

The following chapters demonstrate the complexity and diversity of occupation, providing examples of how the Western Allies planned for occupation and how they attempted to manage the legacy of war and the crimes committed during the Third Reich. Some of the chapters explore aspects of everyday life under occupation, with case studies on the application of occupation policies on the ground, on social encounters, on personal relationships and on the legacies of occupation. The Soviet Zone, however, has not been included in this volume. This is not intended to deter future comparative evaluations, but it seemed necessary to gain a greater understanding of similarities and differences within and between the western zones before extending the comparisons to include the Soviet Zone. If this is not done first, it can be all too easy to revert to a simplistic binary divide between East and West, in which the Cold War functions as the *deus ex machina* that persuaded the Western Allies, and the United States in particular, to promote German rehabilitation, while ignoring significant differences between policies, ruling strategies and conditions in the western zones.

Collectively, the case studies presented in this volume illustrate the dynamic and shifting reality of power relations under occupation rule. Although the Allies had won the war with the total defeat of the Third Reich, occupied the entire country and faced hardly any resistance that seriously challenged their rule, in the case of occupied Germany their power was never absolute. This led to complex processes of conflict and cooperation with the local population, to the application of diverse strategies of rule that sought to take into account local interests and expectations, to discussions and debates between occupiers and occupied over specific policies, and to a wide range of social encounters and personal relationships that ranged from street brawls and rape to friendship and marriage. To be sure, the balance of power was always unequivocally tilted towards the side of the occupiers who held the monopoly of force and could always resort to repressing threats to their authority with harsh measures, which in the initial phase of the occupation they often did. Power relations, however, changed subtly over time, as the occupiers devolved responsibility progressively to German officials and newly created German administrations, and the role of the occupiers changed from maintaining order, deterring any possible resistance and managing the legacy of the Nazi past, to promoting economic reconstruction, political renewal and personal reconciliation.[18]

The changing dynamics of power affected both the ability of the Western Allies, at all levels of the occupation hierarchy, to realize their objectives and the nature of the German response. While the occupation lasted, the power of the Allies penetrated many spheres of everyday life, impacting on the life of Germans across all strata of society and altering social relations. In doing so, military occupation functioned as a highly disruptive force within daily life, breaking up daily routines and habits and imposing severe material pressures and privations. The occupation may in that sense be regarded as a 'state of emergency', an extraordinary moment that produced novel forms of behaviour among a population that needed to adapt or find new strategies to survive.[19] At the same time, it confronted the population not only with the question of how to cope with extraordinary social and political circumstances, but also with the vexed problem of how to respond to the presence of a foreign ruler. As a result, it forced individuals as well as larger social groups to make difficult choices about how they should relate to the occupiers, producing a range of often highly ambiguous attitudes that fell somewhere between the two extremes of collaboration and resistance. Echoing the work of Michel de Certeau and James C. Scott who have conceptualized daily life as a sphere in which populations can counteract the demands of those in power, studying everyday life then becomes an investigation of the strategies and practices chosen by those facing occupation to respond to a changing power framework that was not of their own making, but which they were able to mould through their own attitudes and responses.[20] Exploring social interactions on the ground is therefore also part of an attempt to restore a degree of agency to all those affected by the occupation, instead of treating them as mere recipients of policies dictated from above.

From high politics to social interactions: Historiography

Placing the question of how occupation *functions* in practice at the heart of this volume implies a redirection of attention away from the high politics of the occupation. With the gradual declassification of archival sources on the occupation period in the 1970s and 1980s, historians started producing an impressive body of scholarship that broadly conceived the occupation as a diplomatic wrestling match between the three Western Allies and the Soviet Union, in which geopolitical rivalries were fought out within the increasingly conflictual framework of the early Cold War. The actors in this story were often the policy makers at the top of the Allies' foreign policy establishments who interacted with German political leaders, an approach most successfully demonstrated in Hans-Peter Schwarz's classic, meticulously researched and still unsurpassed study of the politics of the occupation, *Vom Reich zur Bundesrepublik*.[21] Here, and in other political histories of the period that focused on either international relations or on internal German politics, the occupation gained its broader historical significance from the fact that it served as a point of crystallization for the pursuit of major diplomatic and economic interests by the Allies, the development of German political structures and institutions, and ultimately as a mirror of the broader ideological battles of the period.[22]

One legacy of this extensive body of work is that the Cold War still features prominently as a major paradigm within more recent general interpretations of the era.[23] As a result, many historians have tended to assign to it explanatory centrality for understanding the policies of the occupiers, while side-stepping a deeper engagement with relations between the occupiers and the occupied. Similarly, seeking to explain the long-term partition of Germany into two separate states in 1949, many historians tended to approach the occupation primarily as part of the 'pre-history' of the two Germanies, and thus as a period that put in place the institutional and political structures that prefigured the shape of the two subsequent states.[24] As such, the legacies of the occupation period were not thought to be found by exploring the sociopolitical changes wrought by the occupation upon German society, but rather traced at the level of constitutional structures and the formal political process.

At the same time, with a growing specialization and compartmentalization of historical research on the period since the late 1980s and 1990s, an extensive historiography emerged that examined and reassessed the implementation of big Allied reform projects such as the Potsdam 'four Ds', including democratization (and its twin concept of 're-education'), denazification, decartelization and demilitarization.[25] Again, while much of this work has increased our understanding of the various occupiers' objectives and interests in Germany, it tended to concentrate on *policies* rather than on ruling strategies and social interactions between the occupiers and the occupied, often tracing in detail the rationalities behind the occupiers' decision-making process, but ignoring the German responses. Some pioneering steps towards a study of interactions under occupation were, however, made at an early stage. This included, most notably, John Gimbel's path-breaking 1961 study of the city of Marburg under American occupation, which explored the sociopolitical impact of the occupation, though it could only draw on a highly limited number of archival documents as most of the primary sources remained classified at the time.[26] In the last three decades, other major contributions that provide granular analyses of interactions at the local level have been published, including Rebecca Boehling's seminal study of three cities under US occupation, Adam Seipp's highly innovative micro-history of the transformation of a rural community during the occupation, as well as the monumental history of the American occupation in 1945 by Klaus-Dietmar Henke.[27]

So far, however, this effort has mostly concentrated on the US Zone, while there have been few comparable bottom-up approaches for the French and British Zones.[28] This is particularly evident in the way historians have approached the history of social relations, gender and race under occupation. While scholars such as Petra Goedde, Elizabeth Heineman, Maria Höhn, Atina Grossmann, Heide Fehrenbach and Timothy Schroer have contributed to the emergence of a rich historiography on the US Zone that pays attention to interactions between Germans and Americans on the ground, no similarly extensive and sophisticated work exists for the other zones of occupation.[29] This lack of balance and the concomitant privileging of work on the US Zone, however, is characteristic for the historiography of the occupation of Western Germany as a whole. The literature is shaped by a clear emphasis on what happened in the US Zone, with developments in the other western zones often treated as mere addenda to US policies, or as insignificant within the broader story of post-war Germany. Very often, there is an implicit assumption that American policies were simply carried out in the other zones as well, neglecting in the process zonal differences in ruling strategies and local experiences, as well as the wider consequences of the three occupiers' different approaches for relations between occupiers and occupied on the ground. The result is a marginalization of the diversity of the experience of occupation in the western zones, which are often mistakenly treated as a monolithic bloc. That might be regarded as one of the more durable intellectual legacies of the Cold War, the most unfortunate consequence of which is the current lack of archival studies on the occupation that engage in inter-zonal comparisons.[30]

The privileging of the US Zone in writing on the occupation is also connected to the more general problem of how historians assess the broader significance and legacies of the period. A heated debate took place in the 1970s, encouraged by the emergence of a new critical generation of left-wing historians who, motivated largely by concerns at a supposed lack of democracy in the Federal Republic, questioned the degree to which the Allied occupation had produced real change in Western Germany. Rather than identifying occupation as the precursor to a successful process of democratization, as postulated by both the Western Allies and the German government, these historians emphasized the 'restoration' of authoritarian attitudes and practices within government and society, and the extent to which political, social and economic structures prevalent in both Nazi Germany and the Weimar Republic had been re-established in the post-war period. Calling into question the widespread notion of a *Stunde Null* (zero hour) and a fundamental break with the past after the end of National Socialism, they emphasized continuities with the preceding decades and stressed the fundamental role the Western Allies had played in re-establishing a capitalist system in Germany, while suppressing what in their view was a general desire among the population for wide-ranging social, political and economic reforms.[31] In this interpretation, the Western Allies emerged as the oppressors of German grassroot movements that advocated revolutionary change, such as the anti-fascist (*Antifa*) committees that had emerged in the immediate aftermath of the war. According to this narrative, it was, therefore, the Allies, led by the United States, the anti-Communist superpower, who were responsible for blocking any fundamental transformation of German society.[32]

These were in many respects highly politicized debates, and in the more recent historiography, the juxtaposition of the two binaries of 'new start or restoration' (*Neuanfang oder Restauration*) no longer determines the shape of historical writing on the occupation period, with most scholars sharing the rather unspectacular view that, as with most historical periods of transition, the immediate post-war era contained elements of both continuity and renewal.[33] This historiographical consensus, however, leaves the question open as to what were the most significant outcomes of the occupation period, and what forms of change did take place in the post-war era. As a response to this problem, an influential literature has emerged which locates the legacies of the occupation mainly in the gradual *Americanization* of Germany, emphasizing the impact of the US presence upon German businesses, culture, gender relations, media, consumption patterns and broader sociopolitical attitudes.[34] A related but somewhat more inclusive interpretation that gives more credit to the contribution of other western states has been articulated around the notion of *Westernization*, which emphasizes the circulation of ideas and values in the first three post-war decades and the transformation of Germany as a result of the adoption of sociopolitical ideas and economic practices from both the United States and Britain.[35] In this interpretation, however, the transformation of Germany is not related primarily to the effects of occupation rule in itself, but rather to the broader transfer and interchange of liberal democracy, capitalism and anti-Communist attitudes in the Western Bloc and within the general framework of the Cold War. Once more, the durable sociopolitical legacies of the three western zones of occupation remain elusive.

While this volume draws on the growing and diverse literature on the occupation, it seeks to depart from existing approaches in several important respects. In particular, the following chapters approach occupation as a system of rule by exploring power relations on the ground through case studies of ruling techniques, social interactions and daily life. The history of everyday life under occupation during the mid-twentieth century has only in recent years moved to the centre of historiographical attention, reflecting a growing awareness among historians that occupations often had major social, material, political and cultural repercussions amidst 'ordinary people', away from the major corridors of power.[36] In the case of occupied Germany, however, studies of daily life have so far remained limited. In exploring this relatively novel field, this volume builds upon the pioneering work of Lutz Niethammer on the social history of the immediate post-war period.[37] By interpreting Allied rule as a 'liberal occupation dictatorship' (*liberale Besatzungsdiktatur*), Niethammer approached the occupation as a power framework that was top-down in nature, but encouraged various forms of interaction with the occupied population and in doing so had significant repercussions on the texture of German society.[38] As his work on daily life also suggests, tracing interactions between the occupiers and the occupied should not be regarded as an ultimately futile exercise in recounting anecdotes of exotic encounters, but should rather be seen as a crucial component in any wider attempt to understand how the occupation affected life among both the occupiers and the occupied, allowing one 'to grasp the multiplicity of experience and individuals' attempts to order and make sense of their everyday lives'.[39]

Five perspectives on the occupation of the western zones

This volume is structured around a conceptual framework that places the occupation of the western zones of Germany firmly within the context of the study of military occupation generally, rather than treating the subject either as a unique and exceptional 'interregnum period' in the history of post-war Germany, or as part of an equally exceptional phase in the history of post-war Europe. The key elements of the framework are fourfold. First, they include an examination of the origins and longer-term lineages that contributed to military occupation as the eventual outcome. These causal factors will vary from case to case, but will always have to be managed and will strongly influence the aims and policies of the occupiers and the responses of the occupied. Second, they entail a detailed analysis of how the occupation functioned as a system of rule, including the various techniques applied by the occupiers to maintain their power and authority, the response of the occupied and the diverse ways in which occupation affected everyday lives. Third, they involve an exploration of the nature of interactions between occupiers and occupied at many different levels, from official contacts in town and city administrations to violent disputes and protests, intimate encounters and personal friendships. Finally, the framework includes an assessment of the diverse legacies of occupation, of its impact upon the future political, social, economic and cultural structures of the occupied territory, and, in particular, of how the occupation affected the long-term social position and power of those individuals and groups that acted as social intermediaries between the occupiers and the occupied.

Transforming Occupation in the Western Zones of Germany is divided into five parts that provide different perspectives structured in accordance with this conceptual approach. Part One seeks to place the occupation of Western Germany within a wider historical context, demonstrating how the occupiers' policies and ruling techniques were shaped by their previous experiences of occupation, and how the challenges they faced in Germany in turn influenced the subsequent international law and practice of occupation. In her chapter on American planning for the post-war occupation of Germany, Susan Carruthers shows how previous occupations undertaken by the United States were discursively ignored or disregarded, following the widely accepted but incorrect view that the United States, as a presumably anti-imperialist power, did not engage in military occupation. Yet at the same time, US experiences of the 'Yankee' occupation of the confederate states after the American Civil War and of the short-lived US participation in the occupation of Rhineland after the First World War, as well as more recent US experiences in ruling Italy, all influenced both the training of occupation personnel at the School of Military Government in Charlottesville and subsequent policy and practice in occupied Germany.

Echoing the theme of diversity in how occupation was defined and interpreted in different contexts, Peter Stirk describes in his chapter how the British and Americans claimed that their presence in Germany was not actually an occupation at all or, alternatively, that it was a special *sui generis* case and therefore not subject to the international rules of war agreed in the Hague Regulations of 1899/1907. At the Geneva Convention of 1949, however, all the participants, including those from the United States, Britain and France, had recent experiences of occupation very much in mind as they debated proposed clauses on issues such as the obligation of an occupier to feed the defeated enemy, a practice that was subsequently translated into international law, albeit in a highly qualified form. As Stirk demonstrates, however, the practice of 'regime transformation' and the occupiers' ability to change the laws of an occupied country, as the Western Allies had done in Germany, did not find full expression in international law and remains controversial today.

Part Two takes these threads contextualizing the occupation of Germany further, but applies them to the ruling techniques of the occupiers on the ground and, in particular, to their attempts at managing the political, social, mental as well as physical and symbolic legacies of National Socialism in the immediate post-war period. This can be seen as a story that has an obvious specificity and internal relevance to the history of mid-twentieth-century Germany. However, while the occupation of Germany had distinct antecedents in that it followed the Nazi dictatorship, the Holocaust and a total war that unleashed extraordinary levels of destruction, it is also possible to use it as a case study that allows one to obtain insights that apply to occupation, the aftermath of war and 'regime change' more generally.

In her contribution, Rebecca Boehling uses the comparative lens of transitional justice to analyse denazification policies in the US Zone of Germany, examining how the occupiers established special courts and tribunals to judge actions that individuals had performed earlier under a legal, social and political system that was entirely shaped by the Nazi government. The questions of what legal framework should be used in such instances, what sanctions and punishments should be applied, who should police and enforce them and what compensation should be offered to the victims, especially during the transitional period before a new legal system is established, remain contested issues. More broadly, those involved in processes of transitional justice in post-conflict situations tend to operate within a difficult tension between, on the one hand, the desire to produce deep sociopolitical change and transform broader societal perceptions, prejudices and beliefs that may have led to the murder of millions and, on the other hand, the more pragmatic need to create order and get things running again in a devastated country. As her chapter demonstrates, in the German case that tension was often resolved to the benefit of technocratic figures who were appointed by the Allies to influential positions despite their activities during the Third Reich, leading to

Figure 1.1 A denazification tribunal meeting in Berlin, 1946 (Getty Images).

a protracted process in which the demands of victims for truth were muted and their suffering took many decades to reach recognition among broader society.

Similarly, Andrew Beattie's discussion of extrajudicial internment as a means of undertaking a political purge and securing regime change raises issues about the use of nonjudicial measures that are by no means unique to post-war Germany. Beattie's interzonal analysis of internment questions widespread narratives that present the western powers as primarily benevolent occupiers, emphasizing instead the highly coercive strategies of rule utilized by the three occupiers to enforce their security interests. By demonstrating the durability of internment, Beattie is able to show that the familiar assumption that the Cold War produced a sudden abandonment of punitive policies in Germany requires substantial revision. More generally, however, his analysis highlights how a ruling strategy such as internment produced interactions between the occupiers and the occupied, leading to a range of responses among different German groups, some of whom chose to cooperate with the occupiers, while others criticized the policy and, in doing so, called into question the legitimacy of occupation rule.

Caroline Sharples, in the third chapter in Part Two, explores the porous boundaries between public and private rights, duties and obligations, in the specific case of the disposal of the bodies of Nazi war criminals condemned to death and executed. Is a punishment complete when a person is executed, or does it extend to the treatment of the dead body? For the three Western Allies, the issue presented a great challenge, prompting extensive debates about the best course of action, taking into account the broader symbolism of the matter, social and cultural norms prevalent among the population, and the intricate problem of how to deal with the threat posed by right-wing groups using the real or imaginary burial sites for their own political purposes. Most significantly perhaps, Sharples's chapter raises important questions about the temporality of the occupation and its long-term legacies, as the incarceration of war criminals in Allied prisons continued well after the Federal Republic became a sovereign state in 1955, with Allied debates about the disposal of the Nazi corpse lingering on until the demise of the last imprisoned war criminal in 1987, and speculation within German society about the location of Nazi graves persisting well after the formal end of occupation.

Part Three explores the manifold contradictions that emerged when specific occupation policies were applied on the ground. The three cases presented here illustrate a significant gulf between the self-image of the various occupiers as benevolent rulers and the actual perception of their activities by the German population. That clash between image and reality was often the result of the occupiers' bold self-confidence about the superiority of the model of democracy practiced in their own countries and the advantages of their broader sociocultural values, leading to numerous instances of incomprehension, miscommunication and indeed outright conflict between the occupiers and the occupied.

As Bettina Blum demonstrates in her analysis of British requisitioning policies in Westphalia, the occupiers' policy of requisitioning German homes to accommodate British officers, and in particular their ongoing refusal to return empty German properties to their previous owners, produced a highly emotional response among the local German population, who, in a manner that the British often found entirely stupefying, saw themselves as the innocent victims of the war, disregarding any links between their current plight and the war of aggression launched by Germany, while ignoring the suffering of people elsewhere in Europe. Conflicts between the occupiers and the occupied gravitating around material issues often resulted in proxy debates about much larger issues, in which Germans articulated notions of victimhood and attempted to regain the moral high ground by accusing the occupiers of not living up to their own democratic standards. Such discourses culminated in the recurring accusation that the British were behaving in the manner of colonial rulers and treated Germans like 'natives'. At the same time, however, such conflicts also bore the potential for a rapprochement between German and British people, with the occupiers seeking to involve German officials to resolve the housing problem and find joint solutions.

Heather Dichter shows how the occupiers dissolved the national youth and sports organizations created by the Nazis and replaced them with others operating on supposedly more 'democratic' principles, often with input from 'experts' recruited from Britain, the United States or France. Quite what 'democracy' – that omnipresent concept of the immediate post-war period – meant in such contexts remained highly ambiguous, with the occupiers alluding to a vague set of principles around fair play, teamwork, sportsmanship and opportunities based on meritocracy, while implementing institutional reforms that sought to root out the Nazi leadership principle and make internal decision-making structures more democratic. Of equal, if not greater, importance, however, was their broader attempt to reshape German society through a top-down emphasis on transforming the attitudes and behaviour of

German 'youth leaders' through designated leadership schools and programmes, and creating exchange and travel programmes so that these future elites would adopt the occupiers' respective model of democracy as well as embrace related conceptions of engaged 'good citizenship' by observing such practices in action. Here and elsewhere, for the three Western Allies, 'doing occupation' often meant working through social, political and economic elites and trying to influence Germans more widely by interfering selectively at the higher levels of society.

Elite cooperation, however, did not always proceed as smoothly as the occupiers might have wished. Such clashes between the occupiers and social elites are the theme of Douglas Bell's analysis of American policies vis-à-vis hunting, a sphere in which more long-term German and American understandings of nature as well as concomitant notions of how to relate to the environment collided. Bell shows how the American occupation of the environment, and in particular the indiscriminate and highly destructive shooting of game by American personnel, produced significant unrest among Bavarian groups that thought that long-standing German approaches towards wildlife and the environment were threatened. For many American officials, by contrast, German hunters as a social group as well as German hunting laws more specifically represented vestiges of authoritarianism and Nazism that required fundamental change. Even such seemingly specialized debates about the right approach towards nature and the adoption of novel hunting laws were always part of broader negotiations between the occupiers and the occupied, gravitating around competing conceptions of sovereignty and contrasting sociocultural attitudes. As Bell suggests, such discussions ultimately contributed to the re-emergence of civil society in Germany, as German groups acquired a novel space to voice and debate their views and concerns.

Part Four explores everyday life during the occupation through examining social encounters and personal relationships between occupiers and occupied. Each of the chapters in this section focuses on life as experienced by a particular social group or selected individuals in one of the three western zones, highlighting the complexity and ambivalence of the relations between occupiers and occupied from different analytical perspectives. Despite the fraternization ban imposed by the Commanders-in-Chief in the US and British Zones at the start of the occupation, personal encounters between occupiers and occupied were widespread. Some encounters occurred through people acting in an official capacity, such as between Allied and German officials responsible for the administration of towns and local districts. Many other encounters were unofficial, ranging from street brawls, unprovoked attacks and conflicts over living accommodation, to more friendly encounters, such as joint trips to the countryside, sightseeing or walking holidays and personal friendships. Personal and intimate encounters between men and women ranged across a wide spectrum, from instances of rape and violent assault to more friendly encounters and longer-term consensual partnerships, including marriage.

In her chapter on the politics of cross-racial sexual relationships in the US Zone, Nadja Klopprogge adopts a spatial approach to explore what she terms the 'intimate landscape' of post-war Germany, highlighting how personal relationships between African American GIs and white German women in three historically significant spaces in post-war Germany were interpreted by individual soldiers and the black press in the United States to create their own image of Germany as a venue for the struggle for social justice at home in the United States.

Similarly, Ann-Kristin Glöckner also adopts a spatial approach, together with concepts from gender studies, to examine a wide range of interactions between occupiers and occupied in the French Zone. In doing so, she explores how the balance of power shifted subtly from place to place and over time. Everyday interactions were part of a broader power struggle that encompassed gender, race and nationality. As Glöckner's examples indicate, the field of interpersonal relations was a power framework in which the occupiers, despite their presumed monopoly of force, were not always in the stronger position.

The impact of occupation on the occupier is also explored in Daniel Cowling's chapter on the everyday subjective experiences of two British women, as related in personal letters and photographs sent home from Germany. Such 'ego-documents' on the life of members of the occupation authorities in the British Zone contrast markedly with more familiar images of misery, destruction and desolation in post-war Europe. In these narratives, the occupation emerges as a life-enhancing and fulfilling experience that provided manifold personal opportunities and a sense of individual freedom, new friendships, adventures that had been unthinkable at home, and long-lasting memories.

The final section, Part Five, looks to the diverse legacies of the post-war occupation of the western zones of Germany, including studies of social groups that acted as intermediaries between occupiers and occupied. It shows how certain German groups emerged as beneficiaries of the occupation, playing a significant part in the subsequent history of the Federal Republic and thereby shaping the more durable legacy of occupation. In his study of Catholic priests in the archdiocese of Freiburg, Johannes Kuber discusses the local parish clergy's response to occupation based on hundreds of contemporary reports submitted by Catholic priests to the Archbishop. The archdiocese covered parts of both the US and French Zones, and the reports reveal significant differences in how the priests perceived two Allied occupying forces. Kuber highlights the various functions the priests took up at local level, filling a gap that had been opened following the collapse of the central German government. Their roles ranged from peace negotiators and temporary informal advisors to the occupying forces, to advocates for the civilian population, mediators and self-appointed protectors of the interests of their parishioners and their local communities. He concludes that the situation of change and uncertainty enabled the Catholic parish priests to temporarily pause a long-term trend of decreasing social significance and ensure that their influence, at least in rural parishes, remained significant well into the 1960s.

Perhaps most remarkable, however, were the successful efforts of a few highly influential German government officials recruited by the Allies and given senior roles in the new political and administrative structures established after 1945, despite their having worked in similarly responsible positions throughout the Third Reich. This is the theme of Dominik Rigoll's chapter exploring the diverse career trajectories of functional elites who subsequently took over key positions as government administrators in the Federal Republic of Germany. While this continuity of personnel, facilitated by the Western Allies, did not signify a simple 'restoration' of the old regime, it did contribute to a particular kind of authoritarian democracy established in the western zones that typified the early years of the Federal Republic.

A similar, though more extreme process is described by Michael Wala in his chapter on former members of the SS, SA and *Wehrmacht* who worked in close collaboration with western intelligence agencies during the early Cold War. Using their supposed knowledge of Soviet intelligence activities acquired during the Second World War, former members of the SS and Gestapo were able to not only avoid prosecution but also obtain, often with Allied support, positions in the emerging security and intelligence services of the newly formed Federal Republic. They subsequently worked closely with US, British and French secret services and, though only ever half-trusted by their new allies, were accepted by and fully embedded within the western Cold War intelligence community, thereby contributing to the Adenauer government's goal of becoming an integral part of the Western Alliance. The legacies of occupation lasted long after its formal end in 1955.

A comparative approach to the study of military occupation

With hindsight, the creation of the Federal Republic in 1949 and its subsequent development over the next four decades into a remarkably stable, capitalist, liberal democracy might appear to have been an almost inevitable consequence of occupation and defeat in war, as economic and political structures and institutions prevalent in the United States, Britain and France were adopted in Germany. This, however, was not a foregone conclusion in 1945. National Socialism was discredited after the war, but many Germans believed that liberal democracy and the particular model of capitalism that had prevailed during the Weimar Republic had failed them as well. The German central state had collapsed and suffered a tremendous loss of legitimacy, having failed to protect its citizens from physical and economic hardships. There was a severe lack of the most basic resources, including food, living accommodation and fuel, affecting the daily lives of those who had survived the war and causing great uncertainty as to how, or even where, they would live, work and rebuild their future lives. The reconstruction of the German state after twelve years of Nazi dictatorship and the return of sociopolitical stability after the uncertainties of both the Nazi and Weimar periods were, however, achieved remarkably quickly. Exploring the making of that post-war stability and the specific dynamics that shaped it, both in Germany and elsewhere in Europe, amidst a broader context of social and political uncertainty, therefore deserves further historical investigation.[40]

When viewed from the perspective of the Allies, a favourable outcome seemed equally unlikely at the end of the war. For at least the first year of the occupation, the British, Americans and French disagreed profoundly over various aspects of their policies towards Germany. The French vetoed the formation of central administrations that could have enabled the four zones to be administered as a single entity, while promoting economic separation of the Rhineland and Ruhr. The British and Americans disagreed over many issues, including economic policy, the level of industry discussions in late 1945 and early 1946, the 'socialization' of industry, and the devolution of power to regional German administrations in the US Zone, which the British considered recklessly premature.[41] Moving the lens from these matters of high politics to focus on issues of ruling strategies, social interactions and everyday life under occupation, as has been attempted in this volume, reveals similarities as well as differences in approach between the three Western Allies in areas such as internment policies and practice, youth and sports programmes, and the willingness of American, British and French occupation officials to work together with German administrators, initially at local and regional levels, and then with federal politicians and senior civil servants. Several of the case studies presented here include suggestions of how the diverse experiences of occupation in the three western zones helped to shape the social and political texture of the Federal Republic.

Wherever possible, issues have been examined across more than one of the zones, although this was necessarily limited by the current state of research, which has generally treated developments in each of the zones separately. As the chapters in this volume demonstrate, internal power dynamics within the western zones encouraged cooperation, discussion and debate between occupiers and occupied. Compromises were found over contentious issues such as requisitioning, or over particular behaviour by Allied soldiers that antagonized the local population. Influential individuals and members of social and political elites on both sides, such as the clergy, senior civil servants, local officials, the intelligence services and, to some extent, even the military, identified a common interest and were willing to cooperate to maintain and indeed often solidify aspects of the pre-existing social order, such as the privileged position of certain elites within society, the protection of property rights, adherence to a set of sociocultural norms and modes of behaviour, as well as the continuity of the state bureaucracy. More generally, strategic considerations around how to run an occupation efficiently were similar among the three Western Allies, all of whom worked in conjunction with German social intermediaries, recognized that German interests would have to be taken into consideration to avert significant conflict with the local population, and developed increasingly determined policies to block the rise of Communism. These shared policies converged to produce what one historian of the occupation has aptly described as pragmatic *Stabilisierungsbündnisse* – tacitly understood pacts between the occupiers and the occupied based on a shared recognition of the need for sociopolitical stability in a period of political and social upheaval.[42]

From a historical perspective, if the post-war occupation of Germany was unique or *sui generis* in some ways, it is also clearly recognizable as a distinct case of military occupation. This is evident from the legal arguments made to justify the authority of the Allies, the language used in proclamations, ordinances and laws, and the more general power structures established nationally and locally, comprising Military Governors (later rebranded as High Commissioners), resident officers and district officials. Power was now in the hands of foreign rulers, and this reality structured social relations on the ground. Everyday life in the western zones of Germany under Allied rule was evidently not subject to the same risk of indiscriminate imprisonment, torture, deportation, forced labour, collective reprisals, mass murder and genocide that characterized, for example, much of German-occupied eastern Europe during the war, but many aspects of daily life were still affected by the presence of the occupiers.

A better historical understanding of the history of the western zones of Germany needs to be framed, in our view, not only as the aftermath of the war, the Holocaust and Nazi dictatorship, or as the prehistory of the Federal Republic, or even as a response to the emerging Cold War between the new global superpowers, but as a distinct period of military occupation. The conceptual framework used in this volume highlights the complexity of occupation, how people tried to manage the legacy of a violent and disruptive past, the diverse ruling strategies of the occupiers, the responses of the occupied, the role of social intermediaries, conflict and cooperation, everyday life and personal relationships, and the diverse legacies of occupation. Above all, it emphasizes the need to place any one case of military occupation within the broader context of the longer-term lineage of foreign rule. The framework used in this volume is, however, not the only possible model. Extending the field of enquiry through exploring comparatively different cases of military occupation would allow one to situate the case of the occupation of Germany within a broader history of foreign rule and so trace apparently contradictory factors that are common across different instances of occupation, such as continuity and change, cooperation and conflict, reconciliation and justice, privilege and deprivation, winners and losers, rhetoric and substance, perception and reality, 'doing occupation' through direct action or ruling indirectly through intermediaries, managing the past and preparing for the future.[43]

Military occupation always involves at least two countries. In the case of post-war Germany, it involved many more. Studying the subject of occupation takes us beyond a traditional framework for studying national history and leads us towards embracing transnational and comparative approaches. All occupations are different. Some were oppressive and based on the application of brute force; others were less violent, generally benevolent and constructive. Some were short and some much longer. Some were very limited in scope and aspirations; others affected all aspects of economic, social, political and personal life. Occupation and rule by a former enemy, after military defeat, is an emotive subject, and different conclusions have been drawn in different countries from their experience of occupation. One may, of course, question if it is possible to make valid comparisons between different occupations and if, for example, the oppressive German occupations of France, Denmark or Norway, let alone the extremely violent German occupations in eastern Europe during the Second World War, shared any common features with the relatively benign post-war occupations of Germany by the Western Allies.[44] On the other hand, it could be argued that broader comparisons should be made, for example, between occupation and imperial rule, following the observation that imperial experiences had a major impact on the Western Allies' practice of occupation in Germany.[45] Yet as these examples show, whatever view one takes on a specific case, military occupation is always a transnational phenomenon. This volume has proposed some issues that were significant for the history of post-war Germany and Europe, but which, in our view, also need to be addressed in any other comparative study of military occupation and foreign rule.

Military intervention and occupation is back on the agenda, though under different names, such as regime change or nation building. Occupation, often invoked under the more agreeable label of liberation, has been presented and legitimized in public discourse as contributing to internal stability, as essential for maintaining national security or even survival, or as necessary for protecting threatened minorities and spreading democracy globally. Yet at the same time, recent experiments with occupation have been abject failures in bringing about the type of change, democratization and stability that policy makers often refer to when they advocate military intervention. In the UK, the Chilcot Enquiry, after years of collecting evidence, castigated the government for 'wholly inadequate' preparations for the aftermath of war and occupation of Iraq.[46] This volume aims to show that historical research can provide an important corrective to simplistic understandings of what the experience of occupation may entail, by demonstrating some of the paradoxes and intricacies inherent in occupation and highlighting the ambiguities that policies of stabilization and top-down democratization often carry with them. Revisiting what is often seen as the model, benevolent and successful occupation of Germany by the Western Allies after the war is important in its own right, in helping us understand the transition from war to peace in Germany and in post-war Europe generally. But it is also part of the process of gaining a better understanding of occupation generally and is now more relevant than ever.

Notes

1 President's radio address, 1 March 2003. Available online: https://georgewbush-whitehouse.archives.gov/news/releases/2003/03/text/20030301.html (accessed 28 October 2017).

2 See Bremer's endorsement on the back cover of James Dobbins, John G. McGinn, Keith Crane, Seth G. Jones, Rollie Lal, Andrew Rathmell, Rachel Swanger and Anga Timilsina, *America's Role in Nation-Building: From Germany to Iraq* (Santa Monica: RAND, 2003). The fascination with discovering a golden formula that accounts for success in military occupation, with Germany as a pre-eminent example, has also percolated into political science writing. See, for example, David M. Edelstein, *Occupational Hazards: Success and Failure in Military Occupation* (Ithaca: Cornell University Press, 2010).

3 Atina Grossmann and Mary Nolan, 'Germany Is No Model for Iraq', *Los Angeles Times*, 16 April 2003. Available online: http://articles.latimes.com/2003/apr/16/news/war-oegross16 (accessed 28 October 2017).

4 In November 2003, for example, the German Historical Institute Washington and the Friedrich Ebert Foundation organized a conference to discuss the recent invocations of the occupation by the Bush administration. See Robert Gerald Livingston, 'How Valid Are Comparisons? The American Occupation of Germany Revisited', *Bulletin of the German Historical Institute* 34 (2004): 205–7. A follow-up panel was convened at the GSA annual conference in September 2005: Rebecca Boehling, 'American Occupations: Germany 1945–1949, Iraq 2003–2005', *Bulletin of the German Historical Institute* 38 (2006): 153–5. For a British response, see Christopher Knowles, 'The British

Occupation of Germany, 1945–49: A Case Study in Post-Conflict Reconstruction', *RUSI Journal* 158, no. 6 (December 2013): 78–85; Christopher Knowles, 'Germany 1945–1949: A Case Study in Post-Conflict Reconstruction', *History & Policy* (January 2014). Available online: www.historyandpolicy.org/policy-papers/papers/germany-1945-1949-a-case-study-in-post-conflict-reconstruction (accessed 30 October 2017).

5 John Dower, 'A Warning from History: Don't Expect Democracy in Iraq', *Boston Review* (February/March 2003). Available online: http://bostonreview.net/world/john-w-dower-warning-history (accessed 28 Oct 2017); John Dower, 'Don't Expect Democracy This Time: Japan and Iraq', *History and Policy* (1 April 2003). Available online: www.historyandpolicy.org/policy-papers/papers/dont-expect-democracy-this-time-japan-and-iraq (accessed 28 October 2017).

6 See Susan L. Carruthers, *The Good Occupation: American Soldiers and the Hazards of Peace* (Cambridge, MA: Harvard University Press, 2016), and her chapter in this volume.

7 Konrad H. Jarausch, *After Hitler: Recivilizing Germans, 1945–1995* (Oxford and New York: Oxford University Press, 2006); Richard Bessel, *Germany 1945: From War to Peace* (London: Simon & Schuster, 2009); Ulrich Herbert (ed.), *Wandlungsprozesse in Westdeutschland: Belastung, Integration, Liberalisierung 1945–1980* (Göttingen: Wallstein, 2002).

8 A typical example of this approach is the appropriately titled work by Noel Annan, *Changing Enemies: The Defeat and Regeneration of Germany* (London: Harper Collins, 1995). For a revisionist slant questioning the 'old orthodoxy' that it was the Soviets who forced partition, see Carolyn Eisenberg, *Drawing the Line: The American Decision to Divide Germany, 1944–1949* (Cambridge, New York, Melbourne: Cambridge University Press, 1996).

9 Notable examples include three influential survey histories of post-war Europe: Eric Hobsbawm, *Age of Extremes* (London: Abacus, 1995); Tony Judt, *Postwar: A History of Europe since 1945* (London: William Heinemann, 2005); Mark Mazower, *Dark Continent: Europe's Twentieth Century* (London: Allen Lane, 1998). See also Richard Bessel and Dirk Schumann (eds), *Life after Death: Approaches to a Cultural and Social History of Europe during the 1940s and 1950s* (Cambridge: Cambridge University Press, 2003); Frank Biess and Robert G. Moeller (eds), *Histories of the Aftermath: The Legacies of the Second World War in Europe* (New York and Oxford: Berghahn, 2010); Mark Mazower, Jessica Reinisch and David Feldman (eds), *Post-War Reconstruction in Europe: International Perspectives, 1945–1949* (Past and Present Supplement 6) (Oxford: Oxford University Press, 2011).

10 The comparative work of Peter Stirk is a welcome exception: *The Politics of Military Occupation* (Edinburgh: Edinburgh University Press, 2012).

11 For a recent exploration of the related concept of 'transformative occupation', see Simon Jackson and A. Dirk Moses, 'Transformative Occupations in the Modern Middle East', *Humanity* 8, no. 2 (2017): 231–46. An extensive literature has emerged around the normative question of whether the international law of occupation allows occupiers to make significant transformations to the constitution, politics, society and economy of an occupied country. From the many contributions in this debate, see, for example, Eyal Benvenisti, *The International Law of Occupation*, 2nd edn (Oxford: Oxford University Press, 2012) and Gregory H. Fox, 'The Occupation of Iraq', *Georgetown Journal of International Law* 36, no. 2 (2005): 195–297. Peter Stirk's chapter in this volume explores the issue in more detail.

12 Jackson and Moses, 'Transformative Occupations', 234 (emphasis in original).

13 Influential examples of this literature include Detlev J. K. Peukert, *Inside Nazi Germany: Conformity, Opposition, and Racism in Everyday Life* (New Haven: Yale University Press, 1987); Sheila Fitzpatrick, *Everyday Stalinism: Ordinary Life in Extraordinary Times: Soviet Russia in the 1930s* (New York and Oxford: Oxford University Press, 2000); R. J. B. Bosworth, *Mussolini's Italy: Life under the Fascist Dictatorship, 1915–1945* (New York: Penguin, 2007). See also, more recently, Nicholas Stargardt, *The German War: A Nation under Arms, 1939–45* (London: Vintage, 2016).

14 This approach to occupation is developed more extensively in Camilo Erlichman, 'Strategies of Rule: Cooperation and Conflict in the British Zone of Germany, 1945–1949' (PhD diss., University of Edinburgh, 2015), esp. 32–36.

15 This understanding of legitimacy owes much to Martin Conway and Peter Romijn (eds), *The War for Legitimacy in Politics and Culture 1936–1946* (Oxford and New York: Berg, 2008), esp. 1–27, as well as to the work of David Beetham, *The Legitimation of Power*, 2nd edn (Basingstoke: Palgrave Macmillan, 2013), 3–41.

16 On the problem of legitimacy and foreign rule, see Michael Hechter, *Alien Rule* (Cambridge: Cambridge University Press, 2013).

17 For a broader theory of occupation rule and its variations, see Cornelis J. Lammers, 'Occupation Regimes Alike and Unlike. British, Dutch and French Patterns of Inter-Organizational Control of Foreign Territories', *Organization Studies* 24, no. 9 (2003): 1379–403, esp. 1379–86, and Cornelis J. Lammers, 'Levels of Collaboration. A Comparative Study of German Occupation Regimes during the Second World War', *Netherlands' Journal of Social Sciences* 31 (1995): 3–31.

18 Christopher Knowles, *Winning the Peace: The British in Occupied Germany, 1945–1948* (London: Bloomsbury Academic, 2017), 179–88.

19 Robert Gildea and the team, 'Introduction', in *Surviving Hitler and Mussolini: Daily Life in Occupied Europe*, ed. Robert Gildea, Olivier Wieviorka and Anette Warring (Oxford: Berg, 2006), 1–15, esp. 6–9.

20 Michel de Certeau, *The Practice of Everyday Life* (Berkeley: University of California Press, 1988); James C. Scott, *Weapons of the Weak: Everyday Forms of Peasant Resistance* (New Haven and London: Yale University Press, 1985).

21 Hans-Peter Schwarz, *Vom Reich zur Bundesrepublik: Deutschland im Widerstreit der außenpolitischen Konzeptionen in den Jahren der Besatzungsherrschaft 1945–1949*, 2nd edn (Stuttgart: Klett-Cotta, 1980). There is still no scholarly interzonal survey of the occupation period available in English.

22 Hermann Graml, *Die Alliierten und die Teilung Deutschlands: Konflikte und Entscheidungen, 1941–1948* (Frankfurt a. M.: Fischer, 1988); Josef Foschepoth (ed.), *Kalter Krieg und deutsche Frage: Deutschland im Widerstreit der Mächte 1945–1952* (Göttingen: Vandenhoeck & Ruprecht, 1985). For a diplomatic history from a British perspective, see Anne Deighton, *The Impossible Peace: Britain, the Division of Germany and the Origins of the Cold War* (Oxford: Clarendon, 1990). For the French Zone, see Dietmar Hüser, *Frankreichs 'doppelte Deutschlandpolitik': Dynamik aus der Defensive – Planen, Entscheiden, Umsetzen in gesellschaftlichen und wirtschaftlichen, innen- und außenpolitischen Krisenzeiten, 1944–1950* (Berlin: Duncker & Humblot, 1996); Geneviève Maelstaf, *Que faire de l'Allemagne? Les responsables français, le statut international de l'Allemagne et le problème de l'unité allemande (1945–1955)* (Paris: Direction des Archives Ministère des Affaires Étrangères, 1999).

23 For a broader critique of the heuristic value and limits of writing post-war history through the lens of the Cold War, see Holger Nehring, 'What Was the Cold War?', *English Historical Review* 127, no. 527 (2012): 921–49. Martin Conway, 'The Rise and

Fall of Western Europe's Democratic Age, 1945–1973', *Contemporary European History* 13, no. 1 (2004): 67–88, suggests how one might write the history of post-war Europe without pressing the period into the explanatory 'straightjacket' of the Cold War.

24 Theodor Eschenburg, *Jahre der Besatzung: 1945–1949* (Mannheim: Dt. Verlagsanst; Brockhaus, 1983); Christoph Kleßmann, *Die doppelte Staatsgründung: Deutsche Geschichte, 1945–1955*, 5th ed. (Bonn: Bundeszentrale für politische Bildung, 1991). See also the many publications by Wolfgang Benz: for example, Wolfgang Benz, *Auftrag Demokratie: Die Gründungsgeschichte der Bundesrepublik und die Entstehung der DDR 1945–1949* (Berlin: Metropol, 2009).

25 Influential works include James F. Tent, *Mission on the Rhine: Reeducation and Denazification in American-Occupied Germany* (Chicago: University of Chicago Press, 1982); Nicholas Pronay and Keith M. Wilson (eds.), *The Political Re-education of Germany and Her Allies after World War II* (London: Croom Helm, 1985); Clemens Vollnhals (ed.), *Entnazifizierung: Politische Säuberung und Rehabilitierung in den vier Besatzungszonen 1945–1949* (Munich: Deutscher Taschenbuch Verlag, 1991).

26 John Gimbel, *A German Community under American Occupation* (Stanford: Stanford University Press, 1961).

27 Rebecca L. Boehling, *A Question of Priorities: Democratic Reforms and Recovery in Postwar Germany* (New York and Oxford: Berghahn, 1996); Adam R. Seipp, *Strangers in the Wild Place: Refugees, Americans, and a German Town, 1945–1952* (Bloomington: Indiana University Press, 2013); Klaus-Dietmar Henke, *Die amerikanische Besetzung Deutschlands*, 2nd ed. (Munich: R. Oldenbourg Verlag, 1996).

28 The best academic survey on the British Zone is still Ian D. Turner (ed.), *Reconstruction in Post-War Germany: British Occupation Policy and the Western Zones 1945–55* (Oxford, New York and Munich: Berg; St. Martin's Press, 1989), but this contains relatively little on everyday life. See however the work on Hamburg: Michael Ahrens, *Die Briten in Hamburg: Besatzerleben 1945–58*, 2nd ed. (Munich: Dölling und Galitz Verlag, 2011); Frances A. Rosenfeld, 'The Anglo-German Encounter in Occupied Hamburg, 1945–1950' (PhD thesis, Columbia University, 2006). Historians of the French Zone have only recently started to discover the subject. See, for example, the ongoing research project by Karen H. Adler (University of Nottingham) on the social and cultural history of the French Zone, and her article 'Selling France to the French. The French Zone of Occupation in Western Germany, 1945–c.1955', *Contemporary European History* 21, no. 4 (2012): 575–95.

29 Petra Goedde, *GIs and Germans: Culture, Gender, and Foreign Relations: 1945–1949* (New Haven: Yale University Press, 2003); Elizabeth D. Heineman, *What Difference Does a Husband Make? Women and Marital Status in Nazi and Postwar Germany* (Berkeley and London: University of California Press, 1999); Maria Höhn, *GIs and Fräuleins: The German-American Encounter in 1950s West Germany* (Chapel Hill: University of North Carolina Press, 2002); Atina Grossmann, *Jews, Germans, and Allies: Close Encounters in Occupied Germany* (Princeton: Princeton University Press, 2007); Heide Fehrenbach, *Race after Hitler: Black Occupation Children in Postwar Germany and America* (Princeton: Princeton University Press, 2007); Timothy L. Schroer, *Recasting Race after World War II: Germans and African Americans in American-Occupied Germany* (Boulder: University Press of Colorado, 2007). For a more impressionistic account, see Werner Sollors, *The Temptation of Despair: Tales of the 1940s* (Cambridge, MA: The Belknap Press of Harvard University Press, 2014).

30 For one recent exception, however, see Jessica Reinisch, *The Perils of Peace: The Public Health Crisis in Occupied Germany* (Oxford: Oxford University Press, 2013).
31 Characteristic examples of the so-called restoration literature include Eberhard Schmidt, *Die verhinderte Neuordnung 1945–1952: Zur Auseinandersetzung um die Demokratisierung der Wirtschaft in den westlichen Besatzungszonen und in der Bundesrepublik Deutschland* (Frankfurt a. M.: Europäische Verlangsanstalt, 1970); Ute Schmidt and Tilman Fichter, *Der erzwungene Kapitalismus: Klassenkämpfe in den Westzonen 1945–1948* (Berlin: Wagenbach, 1971); Ernst-Ulrich u.a Huster, *Determinanten der westdeutschen Restauration* (Frankfurt a. M.: Suhrkamp, 1972).
32 Lutz Niethammer, Ulrich Borsdorf and Peter Brandt (eds.), *Arbeiterinitiative 1945: Antifaschistische Ausschüsse und Reorganisation der Arbeiterbewegung in Deutschland* (Wuppertal: Hammer, 1976).
33 For an early attempt to arrive at a more nuanced interpretation, see Jürgen Kocka, '1945: Neubeginn oder Restauration', in *Wendepunkt deutsche Geschichte 1848–1945*, ed. Carola Stern and Heinrich August Winkler (Frankfurt a. M.: Fischer, 1979), 141–90.
34 From this extensive literature, see, for example, Volker Berghahn, *The Americanisation of West German Industry, 1945–1973* (Cambridge and New York: Cambridge University Press, 1986); Uta G. Poiger, *Jazz, Rock, and Rebels: Cold War Politics and American Culture in a Divided Germany* (Berkeley: University of California Press, 2000); Heide Fehrenbach and Uta G. Poiger (eds.), *Transactions, Transgressions, Transformations: American Culture in Western Europe and Japan* (New York: Berghahn Books, 2000); Ralph Willett, *The Americanization of Germany, 1945–1949* (London: Routledge, 1992).
35 Anselm Doering-Manteuffel, *Wie westlich sind die Deutschen? Amerikanisierung und Westernisierung im 20. Jahrhundert* (Göttingen: Vandenhoeck & Ruprecht, 1999).
36 See, for example, Robert Gildea, Olivier Wieviorka and Anette Warring (eds.), *Surviving Hitler and Mussolini: Daily Life in Occupied Europe* (Oxford: Berg, 2006); Tatjana Tönsmeyer and Krijn Thijs, 'Introduction: Dealing with the Enemy. Occupation and Occupied Societies in Western Europe', *Francia* 44 (2017): 349–58.
37 Lutz Niethammer (ed.), '*Hinterher merkt man, daß es richtig war, daß es schief gegangen ist*': *Nachkriegserfahrungen im Ruhrgebiet* (Berlin and Bonn: Dietz, 1983); Lutz Niethammer, 'Rekonstruktion und Desintegration. Zum Verständnis der deutschen Arbeiterbewegung zwischen Krieg und Kaltem Krieg', in *Politische Weichenstellungen im Nachkriegsdeutschland: 1945–1953*, ed. Heinrich August Winkler (Göttingen: Vandenhoeck & Ruprecht, 1979), 26–43; Lutz Niethammer, 'Zum Wandel der Kontinuitätsdiskussion', in *Westdeutschland 1945–1955: Unterwerfung, Kontrolle, Integration*, ed. Ludolf Herbst (Munich: Oldenbourg, 1986), 65–83.
38 Lutz Niethammer, *Die Mitläuferfabrik: Die Entnazifizierung am Beispiel Bayerns* (Berlin: Dietz, 1982), 653.
39 Lutz Niethammer, '"Normalization" in the West: Traces of Memory Leading Back into the 1950s', in *The Miracle Years: A Cultural History of West Germany, 1949–1968*, ed. Hanna Schissler (Princeton and Oxford: Princeton University Press, 2001), 238.
40 The call to treat the making of post-war stability as a serious research topic has been articulated forcefully in Charles S. Maier, 'The Two Postwar Eras and the Conditions for Stability in Twentieth-Century Western Europe', *American Historical Review* 86, no. 2 (1981): 327–52.

41 On French proposals for the separation of Rhineland and Ruhr, and British plans for the socialization of industry, see Rolf Steininger, *Ein neues Land am Rhein und Ruhr: Die Ruhrfrage 1945–6 und die Entstehung Nord Rhein-Westfalens* (Cologne: Verlag W. Kohlhammer, 1990). On the level of industry discussions, see B.U. Ratchford and Wm. D. Ross, *Berlin Reparations Assignment: Round One of the Berlin Peace Settlement* (Chapel Hill: University of North Carolina Press, 1947) and Alec Cairncross, *A Country to Play With: Level of Industry Negotiations in Berlin 1945–46* (Gerrards Cross: Colin Smythe, 1987). On British views of premature devolution by the United States, see Knowles, *Winning the Peace,* 69.

42 Henke, *Amerikanische Besetzung*, 32, 986–96.

43 The novel field of comparative occupation studies is just beginning to emerge, with historically inclined studies still very limited. See Stirk, *Politics of Military Occupation*; Peter M. R. Stirk, *A History of Military Occupation from 1792 to 1914* (Edinburgh: Edinburgh University Press, 2016); Günther Kronenbitter, Markus Pöhlmann and Dierk Walter (eds.), *Besatzung: Funktion und Gestalt militärischer Fremdherrschaft von der Antike bis zum 20. Jahrhundert* (Paderborn, München and Wien: Schöningh, 2006).

44 The question of the validity of such comparisons was at the heart of the workshop 'Foreign Rule in Western Europe: Towards a Comparative History of Military Occupation, 1940–1949', University of Cologne, 17–18 January 2015. See the conference report: Peter Ridder, 'Tagungsbericht: Foreign Rule in Western Europe: Towards a Comparative History of Military Occupations 1940–1949'. Available online: www.hsozkult.de/conferencereport/id/tagungsberichte-5934 (accessed 31 October 2017).

45 Erlichman, 'Strategies of Rule', esp. chs 1 and 2.

46 Sir John Chilcot's public statement, 6 July 2016. Available online: www.iraqinquiry.org.uk/the-inquiry/sir-john-chilcots-public-statement/ (accessed 20 September 2017).

2

Preoccupied: Wartime Training for Post-War Occupation in the United States, 1940–5

Susan L. Carruthers

In 1943, Yale historian Ralph Henry Gabriel lamented a worrisome blind spot that he dubbed an 'American paradox'. US military personnel had occupied numerous territories over the span of the nation's existence. Citing Library of Congress information specialist, Benjamin Akzin, Gabriel referenced no less than twenty-one 'principal instances': a total that put the United States in second place behind only the UK in a global league table of occupying powers. Yet Americans seemed to retain no memory of this history, exhibiting little inclination to acknowledge a national propensity for occupation. This amnesia troubled Gabriel less because of what it revealed of his fellow citizens' evasiveness about the past than because of its implications for the future. If Americans refused to acknowledge an extended national tradition of Military Government, they might well hesitate to accept the necessity for long-term occupation of Axis territory after the war ended. And in 1943, despite the recent entry of the United States into the Second World War, protracted Allied rule over defeated enemy states already formed a fixed point in many military planners' projections of a post-war *Pax Americana*.[1]

Sixty years later, in 2003, Americans continued to exhibit jitteriness about occupation, hesitating to utter the 'O-word'. This revealingly jocular formulation was coined by Paul Bremer, who headed the Coalition Provisional Authority in Iraq during its yearlong existence from 2003 to 2004. The term, he said, had an 'ugly sound' to American ears.[2] Yet, even as they sought refuge in synonyms and circumlocutions, President George W. Bush and other key advocates of 'Operation Iraqi Freedom' persistently evoked America's post-war rehabilitation of Germany and Japan during the six-month run-up to the invasion of Iraq in March 2003.[3] Their intent in impressing history into service was evidently to reassure sceptics that the United States had an exemplary record in the business of 'extreme makeover'. If such noxious foes as Nazi Germany and imperial Japan could be remade in short order as pacific and prosperous allies, then it would surely be – in the argot of the day – a 'cakewalk' to depose Saddam Hussein and remodel Iraq as an exemplary Middle Eastern democracy. US troops would be greeted on the streets of Baghdad with 'sweets and flowers', or so vice president Dick Cheney predicted.[4]

Not all Americans shared this optimism. Several eminent historians warned that the Bush administration's preferred historical analogy failed to withstand inspection. An invaded and occupied Iraq would utterly fail to resemble Germany or Japan exhausted by long years of ruinous war. With hindsight, the warnings of scholars such as John Dower, author of a Pulitzer Prize-winning portrait of occupied Japan, *Embracing Defeat*, have come to appear all the more prescient.[5] Fifteen years on, with Iraq in ruins – its fragmented population depleted, disordered, or departed – it is hard to find American admirers of 'Operation Iraqi Freedom'. But while diagnoses of what went wrong diverge, one common motif is that the remaking of Iraq, unlike the 'good occupations' of Germany and Japan sixty years earlier, was hopelessly shoddy in its planning: a *Fiasco* in the title of journalist Thomas Ricks' best-selling account.[6] During the Second World War, by contrast, years of careful preparation laid the groundwork for occupational success, or so many recent authors have claimed. Meticulous long-range planning has thus come to appear foundational to the 'good occupation'.[7] As a result, faith in extensive preparation joins the tangled web of American ideas about occupation, conceived variously as something the country has never done; something that the United States has done often but keeps forgetting it has ever done; or as something Americans have done so very well – so generously and selflessly – that it really deserves a more melodious descriptor.

Strikingly, however, few uniformed Americans who participated in the occupations of Italy, Germany, Japan, Korea and other territories subject to US military rule after the Second World War felt themselves adequately prepared or considered those ventures to have been ably executed.[8] Their judgements suggest that the mystique of training requires interrogation. This chapter offers a critical account of preparation for occupation undertaken in the wartime United States. It takes as its point of departure a contention that the mobilization of resources for Military Government was a two-fold project. Planning for the war's aftermath demanded both ideological reorientation and practical preparation. Americans had to reckon with their previous experiences of occupation in order to embrace this mission and to conceptualize what exactly the business of post-war reordering entailed. Yet this turn to the past for lessons and inspiration was a fraught undertaking. Occupation was inescapably entwined with thorny questions of national history and self-image, particularly with regard to imperialism overseas and the Civil War and Reconstruction at home. Uncomfortable issues of race and empire inclined many Americans to think evasively about occupation, with significant consequences for the practical dimensions of training.

Civilians or soldiers? The origins of the School of Military Government

Ralph Gabriel, who decried the 'American paradox' of occupational amnesia in 1943, was not only a professor of history at Yale but also an instructor at the newly established School of Military Government (SMG). This training academy for occupation officers, hosted by the University of Virginia in Charlottesville and operating under the aegis of the Provost Marshal General's Office (PMGO), opened for business in May 1942, followed some months later by a network of Civil Affairs Training Schools established at other campuses across the country. The Charlottesville School's inauguration marked a victory for the military in a long-running internecine battle that had roiled Franklin D. Roosevelt's cabinet, with the warring parties sparring over whether civilians or men in uniform should assume control over post-war reconstruction.[9]

When deliberations over post-war policy began in earnest in 1941, many of FDR's advisers urged that the leading role in reorienting the Axis territories, and those liberated from German and Japanese control, should be assigned to civilian agencies. Advocates of this position stressed that the agents of reconstruction, whatever punitive functions they might have to discharge, would be required to deliver food, clothing and shelter to refugee populations in extremis. In the longer term, occupation authorities would also have to oversee the reconstitution of defeated polities along more democratic lines. These humanitarian and rehabilitative objectives were surely better entrusted to civilians with expertise in welfare and municipal administration than to the armed forces. Trained to fight wars, soldiers lacked the appropriate skills and mentality to rekindle life in the aftermath of catastrophe. Such arguments were advanced by prominent New Dealers such as Secretary of the Interior Harold Ickes and Vice President Henry Wallace. FDR himself, famously mercurial in his preferences, weighed in on the civilian-oriented side of the debate.[10]

Inter-agency wrangling was intense and protracted. But the armed forces won the day, stressing that no civilian organization yet existed with the administrative machinery, personnel and powers of compulsion that the military possessed. In the first instance, US occupation forces would be required to serve the cause of victory as their first responsibility, securing the rear lines to ensure that defeated populations remained quiescent as the juggernaut of combat rumbled on. Only men in uniform – men, that is, with guns – would be able to extinguish the embers of conflict; and without some semblance of law and order, however rudimentary, there could be no delivery of aid or any start to reconstructive operations, material or political. These were powerful arguments, particularly since planning for the United Nations Relief and Rehabilitation Agency (UNRRA), the nascent multinational organization envisioned as the key provider of assistance to refugees, remained rudimentary in 1942. UNRRA simply lacked the personnel, machinery and logistical clout to undertake the ensemble of roles envisioned for occupation personnel.[11]

While the opening of the SMG in Charlottesville institutionalized the military's triumph in the battle for post-war primacy, it did not end sniping from hostile civilians. The loudest shots rang out from the headlines of the *Chicago Tribune*, a newspaper that eased its habitual isolationist stance only grudgingly and partially during the war. According to the *Tribune*, Charlottesville was a 'School for Gauleiters': an educational innovation 'borrowed … from Adolf Hitler'.[12] Likening American officer trainees to the 'despised' Wehrmacht overlords of occupied Europe was a stinging insult. More telling, though, was the paper's insistence that the 'whole idea of this school' ran 'contrary to the instincts of the American people and the principles of our government'. And since Military Government was so utterly un-American, it ought not to be undertaken. 'The notion that our soldiers will be available for long-term occupation of foreign soil is absurd and it follows that the training of officers for this kind of pro-consular work abroad is absurd,' the *Tribune* scoffed, offering no alternative prescription for Germany's post-war treatment.[13]

This editorial line tapped into a deep seam of American suspicion over large standing armies, viewed as the potential instrument of tyranny. According to this familiar construction, the United States had achieved independence thanks to the efforts of citizen militias that seamlessly merged back into civilian life after defeating British colonial rule. Thereafter, the United States had favoured conscript armies mobilized hastily for war-waging rather than maintaining a sizable military establishment.[14] In comparison with the major European powers, the US military on the eve of the Second World War was indeed strikingly small. However, the *Tribune*'s critique obscured the extent to which the United States was no stranger to rule over foreign territory. To decry the prospect of a post-war military imperium overseas, which the paper anticipated would portend the stifling of self-rule in the United States itself, was to overlook the extent to which Washington *already* exercised suasion over various territories from Central America and the Caribbean to China and the Pacific islands. Empire had become an engrained 'way of life', not a temptation to which the United States might one day succumb.[15] But this was a difficult truth to acknowledge. Since anti-colonialism was foundational to America's self-understanding as a nation that had repelled oppressive British rule to establish itself as a shining beacon of republican liberty, imperialism was a mantle more often shrugged off than donned unabashedly. Empire – like occupation – grated on American ears.

With more progressive critics like Ickes also protesting that a 'germ of imperialism' lurked within the SMG, the top brass bristled. Their defensiveness assumed various forms. One rhetorical stratagem was to insist that civilians' fears of 'rule by the sword' were a hysterical fantasy that should be laughed off. 'The best to do is to keep our sense of humor. There is no military caste in this country', insisted Undersecretary of War Robert Patterson, who was equally adamant that there was nothing *imperial* about occupation. The former implied a protracted project of dominance, whereas Military Government would be as short-lived as circumstances permitted. Men in uniform would step aside just as soon as UNRRA was ready to step in.[16] Provost Marshal General Allen Gullion was even more empathic when he castigated the 'error' of regarding imperialism and Military Government as 'practically indistinguishable'.[17] To underscore the depth of their distaste for the long-term task of post-war reconstruction, senior officers and War Department personnel stressed that, despite having performed this function before, the military never retained any institutional memory of its previous efforts. As a result, the services began each war having to reinvent the doctrinal wheel of post-war occupation. 'In the past, American armed forces have participated in a surprisingly large number of military and quasi-military governments', observed a War Department memorandum presented to FDR in November 1942. 'In not a single instance, however, was the mission undertaken with a personnel having the slightest advance knowledge of the task involved. This was even true of the American occupation of the Rhineland, our latest and perhaps, best conducted job of military government.'[18]

Prominent military figures repeated these claims with the incantatory consistency of a mantra. However, the assertion that the Army had never trained for occupation in the past was simply not true. The Army's official post mortem into the US occupation of Germany after the First World War, known as the Hunt Report and later touted by instructors at Charlottesville as the 'bible' of officer-trainees, itself lamented a lack of prior training.[19] Arguably, Hunt overstated the case. But whatever had or had not been done in the way of training before the Great War, army officers certainly versed themselves in the extended history of US occupation during the interwar years. Indeed, it would be surprising had they altogether neglected to do so, given the number of occupations US forces carried out in the early decades of the twentieth century, including interventions in Mexico, Nicaragua, Haiti, the Dominican Republic and Siberia. The Army's pedagogical efforts left a clear paper trail. In 1920, Harry A. Smith (another officer who had served in the Rhineland) produced a primer entitled *Military Government.* This was one of several volumes used by student committees at the Army War College. These working parties generated further studies on Military Government, including a 1934 guide for post-war occupation entitled *Basic Manual for Military Government by US Forces*. And this in turn laid the basis for the Army's *FM 27-5: Basic Field Manual, Military Government* issued in 1940, and then revised in 1943.[20]

By the time *FM 27-5* appeared in 1940, the US military had developed a discrete body of doctrine relating to the practice of Military Government. The most durable precept to crystallize in US military legal thought prior to the Second World War related to a foundational normative issue. Could an occupying power legitimately seek to change the politico-legal system and cultural mores of an occupied territory?[21] To this question key American legal theorists and military practitioners answered a resounding 'no'. Every significant army statement on military occupation reiterated this axiomatic principle. No attempt to change the culture of an occupied territory should be made. Wherever possible, American officers should work with and through existing legal and governmental structures, so long as operational security was not jeopardized in so doing.[22]

'It is better to leave all laws, civil and criminal, in effect and their enforcement to the local officials ... Do not try to make over the people, to change their habits or customs, or bind them to our way of thinking', cautioned Harry Smith's 1920 primer.[23] For Smith this seemed to be a matter more of racialized common sense than cultural sensitivity; hence his warning, 'There should be no attempt to Anglo-Saxonize what cannot be Anglo-Saxonized.'[24] Twenty years later, the prohibition was elaborated in *FM 27-5* as a matter of both principle and expediency:

> The existing laws, customs, and institutions of the occupied country have been created by its people, and are presumably those best suited to them. They and the officers and employees of their government are familiar with them, and any changes will impose additional burdens upon the military government. Therefore, it follows from the basic policies of welfare of the governed (par. 9d) and economy of effort (par. 9d) that the national and state laws and local ordinances of the occupied territory should be continued in force, the habits and customs of the people respected, and their governmental institutions continued in operation, except insofar as military necessity (par. 9a) or other cogent reasons may require a different course.[25]

This insistence on respecting local cultures matched international law's delineation of military occupation as a temporary sequestration of sovereignty that neither amounted to, nor portended, annexation, a principle codified in Article 43 of the Hague Regulations of 1899/1907. As trustees, not conquerors, occupying powers incurred responsibilities towards the population over whom they exercised dominion for a finite period only. Occupation, the PMGO repeated, was a purely *administrative* function: a 'super-structure erected over the local set-up'.[26]

Since the Army *had* in fact elaborated doctrine to guide its practice of occupation, why insist otherwise? Assertions of reluctance to take on a post-war proconsular role attest the military's eagerness to scotch critics' warnings against an 'imperial' institution intent on usurping civilian agencies' rightful authority at home and overseas. They further hint at the distaste felt by some men in uniform for a mission that might smack of the humanitarian: an ascription that seemingly diminished martial masculinity. Thus Colonel Hardy Cross Dillard, who ran the SMG, admonished new entrants: 'You are not rehabilitation experts going out to build four-lane highways all over the world. Your job is a tough Army job with as its primary goal helping the Army win the war.'[27] At a more implicit level, these too fervent and too frequent claims of occupational ignorance betray unease with the historical experiences that informed doctrine. Together these vectors of ambivalence converged to produce a normative conception of occupation as something simultaneously short-term and 'hands-off'. Yet the historical record suggests something quite different. US occupations prior to the 1940s had often been both protracted in duration and profound in their imprint on local polities and populations. To understand the chasm between the putative ideal and embodied experience thus requires a deeper appreciation of prior experience, and of the selective way in which instructors at Charlottesville tried to create a 'usable' past to inspire and inform Military Government trainees.

Charlottesville and the shadow of Reconstruction

Officers who attended the SMG came from various walks of life to attend a four-month course of instruction in the theory and practice of occupation. Lawyers, civil engineers, university professors and others (including regular army officers who, it was widely rumoured, had not excelled as leaders of men in the field) found themselves on the bucolic campus of the university founded by Thomas Jefferson, where they attended lectures on international law, the history of occupation, and the human geography and psychology of the Axis powers.[28] A substantial element of the curriculum was practically oriented. Officers worked in small groups to solve 'problems' in occupation which had them poring over the blueprints of cities in Italy, Germany, and Japan that the Army anticipated they would preside over when the war ended.

Trainees at the SMG could hardly fail to appreciate the *southernness* of their temporary home in Charlottesville. As Harold Callender noted in a feature story for the *New York Times Magazine*, the town was dotted with 'Confederate heroes standing about in bronze'.[29] If officers who hailed from the northern states did not appreciate this before arriving, they soon became aware that Ralph Gabriel's diagnosis of national memory loss about occupation was somewhat misplaced. In the South, Americans remembered very vividly that the United States had a long history of exercising military rule over subjugated populations. Generations of white Southerners had kindled an aggrieved consciousness of tyrannous 'Yankee bayonets' wielded over unregenerate parts of the Confederate South during and after the Civil War.[30]

For several areas of the South, occupation by Union troops was not coterminous with defeat but central to the experience of war itself. As soon as the Civil War began, Lincoln placed the border states of Maryland, Kentucky and Missouri under Military Government. This preventive measure offered a rough template for the form of martial authority that would be exercised over expanding regions as Union troops reclaimed rebel territory.[31] By the following spring, Union troops had occupied several parts of Virginia; points along the North Carolina coast, South Carolina and Florida; southeastern Louisiana; middle and western Tennessee; portions of northern Mississippi and northern Alabama.[32] Since Military Government in the Secessionist south was, as A. H. Carpenter put it in 1901, 'an instrument of war to hold in subjection conquered territory', its primary preoccupation was with compelling obedience to Federal authority and punishing acts of defiance.[33] Union troops arrested and imprisoned those who gave voice to, or were suspected of harbouring, secessionist sentiments. Teachers, preachers, newspaper editors and myriad others found themselves thrown into jail for seditious speech acts. Thousands more whose loyalty was deemed questionable were kept under surveillance, prevented from voting and 'in other ways made innocuous'.[34] These included pervasive recourse to capital punishment.

Soldiers' participation in remaking patterns of land ownership, labour and race relations left an indelible imprint on the South. To freedmen and women, Union troops appeared (at least initially) as heralds of emancipation. But to defenders of the old order, men in blue were harbingers of the apocalypse, 'military despotism' ushering in what one jaundiced diarist in Beaufort, North Carolina decried as the 'dark reign of Niggerism'.[35] Far from protecting whites' property rights, Union soldiers assisted (or turned a blind eye to) freedmen and women as they laid claim to the land or possessions of their former masters. Astonishingly, in the eyes of such spectators, federal troops permitted freedmen – and sometimes even freedwomen – to offer testimony against white alleged wrongdoers in military courts, finding in the plaintiffs' favour on occasion. Worst of all, they encouraged the enlistment of black men, arming them and licensing them to kill upholders of the secessionist cause: 'an element of the war more horrible than anything that has yet been let loose upon us', one confederate supporter fumed.[36]

After the Confederacy's defeat, Military Government continued during the era of Reconstruction (1866–77) for varying amounts of time in different areas. Federal troops were charged with overseeing the political reconstitution of power in recalcitrant Southern states, and tasked (at least on paper) with protecting newly emancipated African Americans from the retaliatory violence of white supremacists as the Ku Klux Klan gathered force.[37] Predictably, many white southerners' accounts played down the ferocity of the supremacist backlash against the Civil War's verdict. Instead, Reconstruction loomed as a time of terrible suffering imposed on the South by vengeful occupying troops, along with an invasion of larcenous Northerners (unflatteringly dubbed 'carpetbaggers') eager to exploit dispossessed plantation owners' distress and to siphon Federal funds for reconstruction into their own pockets. Meanwhile, the extension of the franchise to former slaves – culminating in the election of a number of black lawmakers to state legislatures – appeared, to appalled white conservatives, as a monstrous inversion of the proper racial order of things.

Since visions of African American political incapacity were widely shared by white Northerners, many of whom sympathized more with the perpetrators of white supremacist terrorism than with its victims, the 'tragic' version of Reconstruction as abomination soon achieved the status of *national* common sense.[38] Northern historians played a key role in substantiating and propagating the hegemonic interpretation of Reconstruction as 'the nadir of national disgrace'. Led by Columbia University's William A. Dunning, whose *Reconstruction, Political and Economic, 1865–1877* appeared in 1907, this school dominated the field for decades.[39] Military government, in this telling, existed primarily to force 'negro suffrage' on the South.[40] But propagating this narrative of white 'martyrdom' was not the esoteric preserve of Ivy League scholars alone. In the South, much energy was expended to keep the 'Yankee bayonets' of folk memory honed to a fine point, with organizations like the United Daughters of the Confederacy promoting this viewpoint in schools, pageants and other forms of popular commemorative activity.[41]

Their endeavours were aided by popular novelists like Thomas Nelson Page and Thomas Dixon, and electrified by the emergent medium of motion pictures. In the early twentieth century, no cultural production did more to disseminate the 'tragic' vision of Reconstruction, with its accompanying glorification of Klan violence, than D. W. Griffith's *The Birth of a Nation* (1915). The ballyhoo that boosted Griffith's film drowned out the NAACP's appeals that this incendiary material should be banned at a time when the flames of racial prejudice were already stoked high. Far from being condemned, though, *The Birth of a Nation* received the ultimate accolade of a private screening at the White House attended by President Wilson, a graduate school friend of Thomas Dixon, on whose novels *The Leopard's Spots* (1902) and *The Clansman* (1905) it was based. Wilson's own *History of the American People* (1902) was quoted in the film to validate its claim that 'this is an historical presentation of the Civil War and Reconstruction'.[42]

That the first Southern president elected since the Civil War should have possessed strong views on the subject of Reconstruction is hardly surprising. Although Woodrow Wilson was only six years old at the time of Emancipation, he grew up steeped in the confederate folklore of his home state, Virginia. In an essay on Reconstruction published in *The Atlantic Monthly*'s first issue of 1901, Wilson railed against the 'extraordinary and very perilous state of affairs' brought about by Lincoln's Proclamation:

> Here was a vast 'laboring, landless, homeless class', once slaves, now free; unpracticed in liberty, unschooled in self-control; never sobered by the discipline of self-support, never established in any habit of prudence; excited by a freedom they did not understand, exalted by false hopes; bewildered and without leaders, and yet insolent and aggressive; sick of work, covetous of pleasure, – a host of dusky children untimely put out of school.[43]

Sharing the dominant view that Reconstruction effected a disastrous upending of racial hierarchy, Wilson reviled the South's treatment under Radical Reconstruction. The former Confederate states had been presided over by military commanders who were, in his view, 'practically absolute rulers', while 'carpetbagger regimes' misgoverned and looted portions of the South under their control.[44] This interpretation directly informed his approach to the occupation of Germany after its defeat in 1918. Taking Reconstruction to illustrate 'the dangerous intoxication of an absolute triumph upon the side which won the war', Wilson cautioned against an excessively punitive approach towards Germany under the influence of a similar inebriation. According to political scientist Gideon Rose, 'the minister's son would do unto the beaten Germans as he wished others had done unto the beaten confederates'.[45]

The US occupation of the Rhineland, which lasted from 1918 to 1923, was duly conceived along what its architects regarded as benign lines: an exercise in administrative supervision over German bureaucrats and politicians, rather than wholesale transformation or larcenous expropriation from a defeated enemy. Occupying the moral high ground above all else, the victors would resist claiming the spoils. They would not repeat the presumed errors of the past. The critique of Reconstruction espoused by Wilson thus cast a long shadow over how American civil and military leaders thought about post-war occupation. At Charlottesville, the Dunning School formed the official line, with Ralph Gabriel teaching SMG officers that nothing positive could be gleaned from the Federal army's attempt during and after the Civil War to secure the civil rights of newly emancipated men and women. Rather, this debacle yielded only dire warnings about the perilous consequences of attempting to 'change the culture' of a society at gunpoint, as federal troops had ostensibly done in occupied areas of the South where they ousted the white plantocracy and empowered former slaves. This, warned Gabriel, had been an exercise 'founded on vindictiveness and hatred'.[46]

The idea that occupying forces should be respectful of local customs, traditions and mores – written into *FM 27-5* and drummed insistently into SMG trainees – reiterated a powerful lesson extracted from the American past, but it increasingly failed to accord with how Allied leaders envisioned the future. At successive meetings of the Big Three during the latter years of the war, Roosevelt, Churchill and Stalin committed the United Nations (as the Allied nations styled themselves) to draconian plans for the Axis powers' post-war chastisement and reconstitution. Germany and Japan were to be thoroughly stripped of their capacity to wage war. This goal would require that enemy states were not only disarmed but also deindustrialized. Without coal mines and steel plants, without munitions factories and shipyards, Germany and Japan would be incapable of sending millions of uniformed men on the path of conquest ever again. Reducing the Axis powers to a condition of perpetual impotence was the shared aspiration of American, British and Soviet leaders.[47]

At their most far-reaching, post-war projections envisioned a root-and-branch ideological reorientation of German and Japanese societies. The 'four Ds' enshrined in the basic policy blueprint for post-war Germany issued to General Eisenhower in April 1945, Joint Chiefs of Staff Directive 1067, included democratization as the positive counterpoint to demilitarization, denazification and deindustrialization.[48] Fascistic and militaristic ideas would be replaced with more pacific and egalitarian notions. And since inscribing new patterns of thought on the tabula rasa effected by the Axis powers' total defeat would require patience, the timeline envisioned for occupation was protracted. When the war ended in 1945, this critical issue of duration remained uncertain. But in the United States, many wartime leaders – along with prominent opinion formers – talked in terms of years, decades, or even generations.[49]

Such sweeping visions were hard to square with the circumscribed precepts being inculcated at Charlottesville. 'Best gov't is least gov't', student Richard Van Wagenen dutifully scribbled down, although there was nothing minimalist about Allied plans to reshape Axis societies and economies from top to bottom. This gulf between theory and practice was not, however, the only paradox to mark US Military Government training.[50] The notion that US occupiers had only once attempted to 'change the culture' of the occupied – in the postbellum South – offered an insufficient description of history all around. Viewed from a different perspective, Radical Reconstruction had not gone nearly far enough in extirpating pervasive ideas of racial hierarchy that undergirded white supremacism; nor had Federal troops systematically intervened to thwart Ku Klux Klan terrorism. For African Americans and progressive critics, white Southerners' practices and precepts remained far too *little* disturbed by the turmoil of the Civil War and the hastily terminated experiment in Radical Reconstruction that followed it.[51]

What, then, of the other 'principal instances' of occupation that instructors at Charlottesville turned to as they fashioned a valorous tradition of Military Government 'lite'? Closer scrutiny suggests that US forces *never* in fact remained thoroughly aloof and respectful of local traditions. Whatever military doctrine may have decreed, occupation was invariably a transformative venture. Several of the instances enumerated by Akzin in his inventory for the Library of Congress referred to territories that had subsequently been incorporated into the United States, such as California and New Mexico. Other countries or regions had been subject to long-running US military interventions. Haiti, for instance, was occupied by the US Marine Corps from 1915 to 1934. While Haitians notionally still controlled their own government, Americans determined the composition of the Haitian parliament, who held the presidency and what policies were implemented. Meanwhile, Haitian banks and customs houses were directly overseen by Americans. Far from respecting local customs and legal norms, US occupation forces strove to stamp out religious and cultural practices of which they disapproved. They also imposed a new constitution, which FDR in 1920 bragged that he had written as assistant secretary of the Navy.[52] Although he later denied authorship, the fact remained that this American-authored document was foisted onto Haiti's parliament at gunpoint. Nor did occupation as practiced in the Philippines, after US forces ousted the Spanish in 1899, find local laws and culture 'best suited' to the islands' inhabitants. Had indigenous practices been deemed satisfactory there would hardly have been any need for Filipinos' 'benevolent assimilation' and all the violent unmaking that American aspiration entailed: an extended colonial project ruptured only by the invasion of Japanese troops in 1941.[53]

Just one experience of occupation roughly adhered to the 'hands offism' edict: that undertaken in the Rhineland after the First World War.[54] In their zone around Koblenz,

US Army officers did indeed work largely with and through local German municipal authorities. But it was hardly the case that Americans played no role in shaping a foreign political landscape. Pretending to a lofty apoliticism, occupation personnel assisted local elites in quashing the revolutionary upsurge of 1919. US military personnel had no more time for workers' councils than their reactionary German counterparts.[55] If occupation was a 'carapace' stretched over existing arrangements, this setup facilitated the restoration of conservative hegemony in Germany. Moreover, while War Department personnel and the PMGO extolled the Rhineland as the 'best run' of US occupations past, this operation had self-evidently failed in what, by the latter phase of the Second World War, was conceived as occupation's key function: preventing a defeated power from embarking on a revanchist campaign to reverse the verdict of battle.

Officers at Charlottesville and the larger network of Civil Affairs Training Schools thus received a bewildering array of mixed messages about the mission for which they were training. If they listened to their instructors, they believed their job was to tread as lightly as possible in the countries they occupied; but if they followed political developments, they would understand that their task was to alter the Axis powers beyond all recognition. If they heeded Undersecretary of War Patterson or Provost Marshal General Gullion, they believed there was nothing imperial about occupation. Yet their lecturers, seeking examples of 'good governance' to offset the irredeemable occupation of the Confederate South, turned to the United States' imperial past. Students of Military Government were tutored in the virtues of Winfield Scott, who had governed California as it was wrested from Mexico, and Leonard Wood, surgeon and general, whose efforts had done much to 'sanitize' Cuba after war with Spain of 1898. The implicit, and sometimes more explicit, message that instructors like Gabriel hoped to impart was that US interventions effected such modernizing transformations as not to constitute imperialism at all: an exceptionalist self-understanding that, ironically, reprised a rationalization of empire shared by European colonial powers.[56]

Privileged fictions

Faced with such contradictory cues about whether the purpose of occupation was primarily punitive or rehabilitative, over who was best placed to undertake this work and how long it would take, it is perhaps no wonder that officer trainees – and civilians more broadly – who wanted to understand the war in progressive internationalist terms should have turned to a work of fiction for reassurance that Americans in uniform could reform and redeem defeated Axis populations. The novel in question was John Hersey's *A Bell for Adano*. Undoubtedly the most popular representation of occupation to emerge from the Second World War, the novel was dashed off in three weeks of 'angry haste' after the twenty-nine-year-old journalist returned to the United States fresh from a week spent reporting on the Allied occupation of Sicily in July 1943.[57]

The rage that galvanized Hersey's creativity stemmed from his indignation over General George S. Patton's leadership in Sicily. Incidents that official censorship debarred Hersey from reporting as journalist for *Time* and *Life* – such as Patton's

Figure 2.1 John Hersey, author of *A Bell for Adano*, driving a jeep (Getty Images).

insistence that a mule be shot when it failed to move out of his convoy's path with sufficient alacrity – could be relayed in thinly veiled fictional form. *A Bell for Adano* duly featured an intemperate martinet, General Marvin, quite obviously modelled on Patton. Drawing attention to the General's brutishness, a 'bad man, something worse than what our troops were trying to throw out', Hersey stressed that rank insensitivity to the local population could undo the regenerative purposes of occupation. But the novel's more inspirational message was that the United States *did* in fact possess occupation personnel capable of transforming former enemies into future allies. The hero of Hersey's novel, Major Victor Joppolo, is a first-generation Italian American whose bilingualism and cultural savoir-faire help him appreciate that what the residents of Adano desire most urgently is a new church bell, the old one having been melted down for munitions. In a bluntly didactic foreword, Hersey stressed the necessity of Americans putting faith in men like Joppolo, who represented 'our future in the world'.[58]

Hersey restaged the clash between 'civilian values' and the dictates of 'military necessity' that had splintered FDR's cabinet. In the novel, Joppolo's humanitarian impulses prevail – albeit at the expense of his career. Disciplined for having countermanded General Marvin's order debarring mules from the streets of Adano, the major is sent away just as the first chimes ring out from the bell he has artfully procured for the extravagantly appreciative townsfolk. Joppolo may have been demoted, but Hersey's promotion of the ideals his endearing hero embodied struck a deeply responsive chord with American readers. Within months of publication in 1944, *A Bell for Adano* had been transformed into a smash hit Broadway play, with a Twentieth Century Fox film adaptation following in 1945. The book not only won its youthful author a Pulitzer Prize but also elicited as much popular adulation as critical acclaim. Hundreds of effusive readers, from Albert Einstein to teenage schoolchildren, wrote to congratulate Hersey on his moving depiction of a war-ravaged Italian town brought back to life under the compassionate guidance of an Italian American major.[59]

The novel's admirers included army officers and enlisted men in training for occupation duty. 'Many of us are headed for Military Government, and the picture of Major Joppolo will remain a vivid guide to use when we hit our particular Adanos', Corporal Sam Pillsbury assured Hersey, writing from Camp Reynolds, Pennsylvania.[60] Likeminded soldiers, eager to voyage overseas and start tackling the epic job of post-war reordering, no doubt warmed to Joppolo's impatience with Military Government training. Just a few pages into the novel, Hersey has his protagonist tear up his lecture notes. Instead, the major relies on 'notes to Joppolo by Joppolo': a compendium of commonsensical propositions about handling Italians amassed through experience. This cavalier gesture anticipated a conundrum that would continue to vex, and divide, uniformed Americans during the war and after: whether one could in fact *train* for the mission of occupation.

According to one school of thought, nothing could adequately prepare soldiers for what they would encounter in the immediate wake of war. Besieged by hungry, desperate people, amid the ruins of collapsed political regimes, what could soldiers do but respond 'on the hoof' to rapidly shifting emergency conditions? Some American personnel thus maintained that sheer force of personality and an ability to improvise were the qualities good military administrators required, since 'post-war' – in all its unpredictable extremity and chaos – defied attempts at planning. Individuals either possessed the requisite traits of empathy, flexibility, and a sense fair play or they did not. No amount of lecturing on law and history could impart them in men liable to be incapacitated by chronic disorder or overwhelmed by raw human distress.[61]

Other officers, however, felt that faith in 'muddling through' was itself constitutive of the problems encountered by Military Government: a rationalization of administrative sloppiness. This view was forcefully articulated by Maurice Neufeld, who served with the occupation in Sicily and was notably unimpressed by *A Bell for Adano*. Hersey, Neufeld pointed out to his wife, had spent just a week in Licata, the town on which Adano was modelled, shadowing Frank Toscani (the officer on whom Joppolo was loosely based). The Italian American officer 'could never teach Licatans or any Italians about democracy in three weeks', Neufeld insisted. 'Teaching them democracy, besides, at this stage of the game, is not the important job, and it's not taught as such'.[62] Eager to dispel Hersey's romanticism, he pointed out that Military Government was not about finding new church bells and delivering homilies on democratization, but meeting much more urgent needs like providing food, repressing Allied soldiers' sexual violence, and attempting to restore prefascist institutions. Acknowledging the radical contingency of emergency conditions, Neufeld nevertheless regarded trained administrators as superior executors of Military Government – not officers oozing can-do optimism.[63]

Neufeld's conviction that planning for occupation was essential did not mean that he believed his own preparation had been adequate or that Sicily, as the first real test of Allied Military Government of Occupied Territories (AMGOT), vindicated the Army's training programme. On the eve of his departure from Sicily for Salerno in January 1944, Neufeld grimly concluded that 'AMGOT has a C record and no more'.[64] He was not alone in his negativity. Many uniformed Americans who served in post-war Europe or Asia deemed their training deficient, particularly in the area of language skills.[65]

Those who felt more positive about the value of their SMG education nevertheless noted that the unforeseen speed of post-war demobilization, as the White House and War Department buckled under intense public pressure to 'bring the boys home', ensured that few officers trained to assume control over particular municipalities or regions actually reached their intended destinations. Even if they did, the helter-skelter pace of demobilization often meant that those men – and the handful of women belatedly permitted to attend the SMG – did not remain in place long enough to achieve administrative efficiency. One unanticipated outcome of protracted preparation in the United States for the war's aftermath was that men who had sought commissions early for the SMG often had enough 'points' (according to the computational scale that determined eligibility for demobilization) to guarantee return to the United States within weeks of the war's end. And it soon became clear that officers who had trained for the mission of post-war reordering were just as susceptible to the virus of homesickness as other Americans in uniform, adding their voices to the clamour pressing for a swift return to the United States in the fall of 1945 and early 1946.[66]

The pervasive demoralization that afflicted the American armies of occupation in both Europe and Asia lends a rather ironic ring to more recent calls for a SMG to be resuscitated and to widely repeated claims that, once upon a time, the United States knew how to plan a good occupation.[67] If the reconstruction of Germany and Japan turned out to Americans' long term satisfaction, this did not occur without a good deal of short-term consternation – or full-blown outrage – over how poorly managed and squalidly transactional these ventures were on a day-to-day basis. What made the occupation troops' presence tolerated was the total defeat of populations exhausted by long years of all-out war. And what later made the occupations appear successful – the reorientation of former foes as stalwart allies – was initiated by the great geopolitical reversal that swiftly followed the war's end. Once an apocalyptic showdown with the USSR loomed as a vivid possibility in many Americans' minds, making common cause with a rearmed West Germany appeared a much wiser path than insisting on all the 'Ds' enshrined in the Potsdam Agreement and the first US Directive on Military Government, JCS 1067. In short, the occupations became 'good' more by chance than design. Advocates of longer and better training for US military control over foreign populations might do well to consider the unexpectedness of this outcome.

Notes

1 Professor R. H. Gabriel, 'Preliminary Survey of American Experience with Military Government', 7 February 1944, Folder 12, Box 8, Ralph Henry Gabriel Papers, Sterling Memorial Library, Yale University. See also Ralph H. Gabriel, 'American Experience with Military Government', *American Political Science Review* 37 (1943): 417–38;

'American Experience with Military Government', *American Historical Review* 49 (1944): 630–43. Benjamin Akzin, *Data on Military Government in Occupied Areas, with Special Reference to the United States and Great Britain* (Washington, DC: Library of Congress, Legislative Reference Service, 1942). How long the occupation would last was a vexed question, but planners envisioned that it would last a minimum of two years. Senior army personnel repeatedly warned against the dangers of 'premature withdrawal' from hostile territory, an error they argued the United States had made in the Philippines in the early twentieth century. For correspondence illustrating these tensions, see Official File OF 5130, Armed Forces May 1944–1945, Box 3, Franklin D. Roosevelt Library, Hyde Park, New York.

2 Scott Wilson, 'Bremer Adopts Firmer Tone for US Occupation of Iraq', *Washington Post*, 26 May 2003, A13.

3 David E. Sanger and Eric Schmitt, 'U.S. Has a Plan to Occupy Iraq, Officials Report', *New York Times*, 11 October 2002, A1. 'President George W. Bush Speaks at AEI's Annual Dinner', 28 February 2003. Available online: www.aei.org/publication/president-george-w-bush-speaks-at-aeis-annual-dinner/ (accessed 20 September 2017).

4 Ken Adelman, 'Cakewalk in Iraq', *Washington Post*, 13 February 2002, A27. George Packer attributes the 'sweets and flowers' phrase to Kanan Makiya, whose projections coloured Cheney's claim that US troops would be 'greeted as liberators'; *The Assassins' Gate: America in Iraq* (New York: Farrar, Straus, and Giroux, 2005), 96–8.

5 John W. Dower, *Embracing Defeat: Japan in the Wake of World War II* (New York: W. W. Norton, 1999); John Dower, 'A Warning from History: Don't Expect Democracy in Iraq', *Boston Review* (February/March 2003).

6 Thomas E. Ricks, *Fiasco: The American Military Adventure in Iraq* (New York: Penguin Press, 2006); Larry Jay Diamond, *Squandered Victory: The American Occupation and the Bungled Effort to Bring Democracy to Iraq* (New York: Times Books, 2005); James M. Fallows, *Blind into Baghdad: America's War in Iraq* (New York: Vintage Books, 2006). The British government's Chilcot Inquiry reached the same verdict in 2016, concluding that planning and preparations for 'Iraq after Saddam Hussein' were 'wholly inadequate'. See www.iraqinquiry.org.uk/the-inquiry/sir-john-chilcots-public-statement/ (accessed 20 September 2017).

7 I explore the conceit of the 'good occupation' more thoroughly elsewhere; Susan L. Carruthers, *The Good Occupation: American Soldiers and the Hazards of Peace* (Cambridge, MA: Harvard University Press, 2016).

8 Carruthers, *Good Occupation*, passim.

9 This chapter concentrates on the Charlottesville school because it offered the first training programme to be inaugurated by the PMGO, and because it continued throughout the war to be conceived (by the PMGO at least) as the most elite 'postgraduate' institution for officer trainees. For more on SMG and Civil Affairs Training Schools, see Carruthers, *Good Occupation*, ch. 1; *History of Military Government Training* (Washington, DC: PMGO, 1945); Harry L. Coles and Albert K. Weinberg, *Civil Affairs: Soldiers Become Governors* (Washington, DC: Office of the Chief of Military History, Department of the Army, 1964); Karl-Ernst Bungenstab, 'Die Ausbildung der amerikanischen Offiziere für die Militärregierung nach 1945', *Jahrbuch für Amerikastudien* 18 (1973): 195–212; Rebecca Boehling, *A Question of Priorities: Democratic Reforms and Economic Recovery in Postwar Germany: Frankfurt, Munich, and Stuttgart under U.S. Occupation, 1945–1949* (Providence, RI: Berghahn Books, 1996), 31–6; Walter M. Hudson, *Army Diplomacy: American Military*

Occupation and Foreign Policy after World War II (Lexington: University Press of Kentucky, 2015), 61–93.

10 This privately expressed opinion also circulated in political gossip columns; Drew Pearson, 'Roosevelt Skeptical of Army Rule', *Washington Post*, 5 January 1943, B7.

11 Jessica Reinisch, 'Internationalism in Relief: The Birth (and Death) of UNRRA', in *Post-War Reconstruction in Europe: International Perspectives, 1945–1949*, ed. Mark Mazower, Jessica Reinisch and David Feldman (Oxford: Oxford University Press, 2011), 258–89.

12 'Army Training "Pro-Consuls" – Not Gauleiters', *Chicago Daily Tribune*, 30 May 1943, 3.

13 'American Gauleiters', *Chicago Daily Tribune*, 8 January 1943, 12.

14 Arthur Ekirch, *The Civilian and the Military: A History of the American Anti-Militarist Tradition* (New York: Oxford University Press, 1956).

15 William Appleman Williams, *Empire as a Way of Life: An Essay on the Causes and Character of America's Present Predicament Along with a Few Thoughts about an Alternative* (New York: Oxford University Press, 1980).

16 Associated Press, 'Army Trains War Governors', *Christian Science Monitor*, 30 December 1942, 6.

17 Maj. Gen. Allen W. Gullion, 'Postwar Occupation Plans Revealed for United States', *Washington Post*, 22 November 1942, B4.

18 War Department, Memorandum for FDR, November 1942, PMGO, *History of Military Government Training*, reel 1.

19 *American Military Government of Occupied Germany, 1918–1920: Report of the Officer in Charge of Civil Affairs, Third Army and American Forces in Germany* (Washington, DC: United States Army, 1943).

20 Hudson, *Army Diplomacy*, 37–70; *War Department, Basic Field Manual on Military Government – Field Manual 27-5* (Washington, DC: Government Printing Office, 1940).

21 On the broader problem of 'regime transformation', see Peter Stirk's chapter in this volume.

22 Maj. Gen. Allen W. Gullion, 'Military Government', *Cavalry Journal* 52 (March–April 1943): 59–60. An emphasis on 'justice, honor, and humanity' – along with 'economy of effort' – characterizes the account offered by Brig. Gen. C. W. Wickersham, 'Military Government', *Federal Bar Association Journal* 43 (1943–44): 43–7. The preamble to the PMGO's *History of Military Government Training* (issued in 1945) notes that 'the ideal Military Government is one which can integrate the local laws, customs, institutions and economy of an occupied areas and … superimposed military control with a minimum of disturbance to the former and a maximum of control by the latter'; reel 1.

23 Colonel H. A. Smith, *Military Government* (Fort Leavenworth: General Service Schools Press, 1920), 9–10.

24 Ibid., 80.

25 *FM 27-5*, section II, paragraph 10, d, 5–6.

26 Doris Appel Graber, *The Development of the Law of Belligerent Occupation 1863–1914: A Historical Survey* (New York: Columbia University Press, 1949); PMGO, *History of Military Government Training*, reel 1.

27 'Outline of Objectives', 15 May 1943, Folder 'School of Military Government Memos (1942)', Box 41, Hardy Cross Dillard Papers, Arthur J. Morris Law Library, University of Virginia, Charlottesville.

28 Joseph P. Harris, 'The Selection and Training of Civil Affairs Officers', *Public Opinion Quarterly* 7 (Winter 1943): 694–706.
29 Harold Callender, 'Trained to Govern: The Army Looks Ahead', *New York Times Magazine*, 2 May 1943, 11.
30 Bruce E. Baker, *What Reconstruction Meant: Historical Memory in the American South* (Charlottesville: University of Virginia Press, 2007).
31 A. H. Carpenter, *Military Government of Southern Territory, 1861–1865* (Washington, DC: Government Printing Office, 1901), 470–1.
32 Stephen V. Ash, *When the Yankees Came: Conflict and Chaos in the Occupied South, 1861–1865* (Chapel Hill: University of North Carolina Press, 1995), 16.
33 Carpenter, *Military Government*, 477.
34 William Russ, 'Administrative Activities of the Union Army during and after the Civil War', *Mississippi Law Journal* 17 (May 1945): 73.
35 James Rumley, diary entry for 25 March 1862, in *The Southern Mind under Union Rule: The Diary of James Rumley, Beaufort, North Carolina, 1862–1865*, ed. Judkin Browning (Gainesville: University Press of Florida, 2009), 62.
36 Ibid., 62. On the experiences of black soldiers in occupied Germany, see Nadja Klopprogge's chapter in this volume.
37 Gregory P. Downs, *After Appomattox: Military Occupation and the Ends of War* (Cambridge, MA: Harvard University Press, 2015).
38 David W. Blight, *Race and Reunion: The Civil War in American Memory* (Cambridge, MA: Belknap/Harvard University Press, 2001), 117.
39 Dunning's interpretation, however influential, was not pioneering. He tapped the same vein as James Ford Rhodes's *History of the United States* (1893–1906) and John W. Burgess's *Reconstruction and the Constitution, 1866–1877* (1902). For a succinct overview of the 'tragic legend', see Kenneth M. Stampp, *The Era of Reconstruction 1865–1877* (New York: Vintage Books, 1965), 3–23.
40 William A. Dunning, 'Military Government during Reconstruction', in *Essays on the Civil War and Reconstruction* (Gloucester, MA: Peter Smith, 1969; first published 1897), 139.
41 W. Fitzhugh Brundage, *The Southern Past: A Clash of Race and Memory* (Cambridge, MA: Belknap/Harvard University Press, 2005).
42 Lloyd E. Ambrosius, 'Woodrow Wilson and *The Birth of a Nation*: American Democracy and International Relations', *Diplomacy and Statecraft* 18 (2007): 690.
43 Woodrow Wilson, 'The Reconstruction of the Southern States', *Atlantic Monthly* (January 1901): 6. For a larger consideration of the Civil War's place in Wilson's thought, see Anthony Gaughan, 'Woodrow Wilson and the Legacy of the Civil War', *Civil War History* 43, no. 3 (September 1997): 225–42.
44 Wilson, 'Reconstruction of the Southern States', 9, 10.
45 Gideon Rose, *How Wars End: Why We Always Fight the Last Battle* (New York: Simon & Schuster, 2010), 32.
46 Gabriel, 'American Experience with Military Government', 639.
47 Melissa Willard-Foster, 'Planning the Peace and Enforcing the Surrender: Deterrence in the Allied Occupations of Germany and Japan', *Journal of Interdisciplinary History* 40 (2009): 33–56; Merle Fainsod, 'The Development of American Military Government Policy during World War II', in *American Experiences in Military Government in World War II*, ed. Carl J. Friedrich et al. (New York: Rinehart, 1948), 23–51.
48 Carl J. Friedrich, 'Military Government and Democratization: A Central Issue of American Foreign Policy', in *American Experiences in Military Government in World War II*, 3.

49 James F. Tent, *Mission on the Rhine: Reeducation and Denazification in American-Occupied Germany* (Chicago: University of Chicago Press, 1982).

50 Richard V. Van Wagenen, Lecture Notes on Major Barber, 3 May 1943, Box 1, Richard V. Van Wagenen Papers, US Army Military History Institute, Carlisle, Pennsylvania.

51 This revisionist perspective informed an extremely popular wartime novel set in South Carolina during the era of Radical Reconstruction – Howard Fast's *Freedom Road* (New York: Crown, 1969; first published 1944). Fast expressly conceived his novel as a warning about the dangers of premature withdrawal of troops charged with expunging fascism with implications for the US occupation of Germany.

52 Hans Schmidt, *The United States Occupation of Haiti, 1915–1934* (New Brunswick: Rutgers University Press, 1995), 111.

53 Paul A. Kramer, *The Blood of Government: Race, Empire, the United States and the Philippines* (Chapel Hill: University of North Carolina Press, 2006).

54 I borrow the 'hands offism' coinage from Hardy C. Dillard, 'Power and Persuasion: The Role of Military Government', *Yale Review* 42 (1953): 216.

55 Ernst Fraenkel, *Military Occupation and the Rule of Law: Occupational Government in the Rhineland 1918–1923* (New York: Oxford University Press, 1944), 29–34. On the paradoxical character of US imperial ideology, see Paul Kramer, 'Empires, Exceptions, and Anglo-Saxons: Race and Rule between the British and United States Empires, 1880–1910', *Journal of American History* 88, no. 4 (March 2002): 1315–53.

56 Gabriel, 'American Experience with Military Government', 420.

57 John Hersey, *A Bell for Adano* (New York: Alfred A. Knopf, 1944); Susan L. Carruthers, '"Produce More Joppolos": John Hersey's *A Bell for Adano* and the Making of the "Good Occupation"', *Journal of American History* 100 (2014): 1086–113.

58 Hersey, *A Bell for Adano*, vii.

59 Carruthers, 'Produce More Joppolos'.

60 Margaret Clement to Hersey, 2 March 1944, Box 27; Cpl. Sam Pillsbury to Hersey, Box 19, John Hersey Papers, Beinecke Library, Yale University.

61 Carruthers, *Good Occupation*, 46–8.

62 Maurice to Hinda Neufeld, 7 May 1944, Folder 1, Box 6, Maurice F. Neufeld Papers, Library of Congress.

63 Maurice F. Neufeld, 'The Failure of AMG in Italy', *Public Administration Review* 6 (1946): 137–48.

64 Maurice Neufeld Diary, 6 January 1944, Folder 1, Box 1, Neufeld Papers.

65 George Fitzpatrick et al., *A Survey of the Experience and Opinion of US Military Government Officers in World War II* (Chevy Chase, MD: Operations Research Office, Johns Hopkins University, 1956).

66 Carruthers, *Good Occupation*, ch. 6.

67 Brent C. Bankus and James O. Kievit, 'Reopen a Joint School of Military Government and Administration?', *Small Wars & Insurgencies* 19 (March 2008): 137–43.

3

Benign Occupations: The Allied Occupation of Germany and the International Law of Occupation

Peter M. R. Stirk

There have only been two waves of the international codification of the laws of wars (with the law of military occupation forming a subset of those) since the attempt was first made in 1874 to bring the theory and practice of military occupation within the scope of international law. The first wave lasted from the Brussels Conference of 1874 to the Hague Conference of 1907.[1] The ensuing Hague Regulations survived the cauldron of the First World War in the sense that the war failed to induce any serious effort to revise the Regulations, though there was provision for improved protection for 'Wounded and Sick in Armies in the Field and Prisoners of War' in the two Geneva Conventions of 27 July 1929.[2]

The second wave of codification followed immediately after the Second World War culminating in the Geneva Conventions of 1949, especially the Fourth Convention dealing with 'The Protection of Civilian Persons in Time of War'. This Convention is typically seen as a response to the horrors of the Second World War, notably to the practices of Nazi Germany and its Allies and Japan in the Far East.[3] This chapter, by contrast, seeks to show the extent to which the making of international law has been influenced not by these 'malign' occupations, but by the supposedly 'benign' post-war occupations of Germany by the three victorious Western Allies – the United States, Britain and France. More precisely, it focuses upon how during the occupation and the negotiations of the Geneva Convention in 1949 the Western Allies struggled to bring their interests and practices as occupiers within the scope of international law.

The term 'benign occupation' has to be used with some qualification because firstly, occupations are never perceived as benign by those subject to them and often not even by those imposing them, and secondly, the Allied occupations at the end of the Second World War have been reinvented and reinterpreted as benign by subsequent historians and commentators. Recent research has questioned such uncritical assessments.[4] It will be suggested, however, that the term 'benign' is not wholly without merit. At the same time, the following comments attempt to locate those occupations within the wider history of military occupation and the law of occupation, by identifying some of the changes in the practice and normative evaluation of military occupation that were considered as a result of Allied experience in post-war Germany. Given the impossibility of surveying the full range of the law of occupation, reference is made to three areas or practices which stood out as significant in the experiences of both occupiers and occupied during the military occupation of Germany. These areas are the taking and execution of hostages, the provision of food, and regime transformation. All three areas have been central to the experience of military occupation both in post-war Germany and elsewhere and presented challenges of varying difficulty to their attempted regulation in the international law of occupation.

Hostages

In practice, of course, the contrast between the two sets of occupation, the malign and the benign, is inescapable. The taking and execution of hostages served as a prominent distinguishing mark. German willingness to take hostages was often presented by politicians, lawyers and commentators as a product of a specifically Germanic tradition, traced back to the days of the Franco-German war, with contemporary German defence of the practice by reference to international law criticized as nothing more than self-exculpation.[5] The view of hostage taking as something uniquely German overlaps with an emphasis, shared by many historians after the Second World War, upon the extent to which more specifically Nazi views of race fed into the selection and execution of hostages, and the way in which those views were held by the *Wehrmacht* as well as by the SS and the Nazi police apparatus.

Condemnation of German designation of hostages and their subsequent execution emerged early, with US President Franklin D. Roosevelt invoking the spectre of 'fearful retribution' in October 1941 in protest against the execution of hostages. 'Civilized peoples,' the president proclaimed, 'long ago adopted the basic principle that no man should be punished for the deed of another.'[6] A more wide ranging protest from exiled European governments followed in January 1942, calling for war crimes trials for the 'regime of terror characterized in particular by imprisonments, mass expulsions, execution of hostages and massacres'.[7] Similarly, participation in the selection of hostages was one of the prime charges against Pierre Pucheu in North Africa. Pucheu was the first high profile Vichy minister to stand trial and be condemned to death, a sentence he could not escape despite the fact that he had turned against Vichy and had sought to join its opponents.[8] From the vantage point of 1948, Lord Wright, a distinguished British lawyer and Chairman of the United Nations War Crimes Commission, drew an explicit contrast between Germanic understanding and practice of hostage taking and wider international approaches. Thus, in an article entitled 'The Killing of Hostages as a War Crime',[9] published in *The British Yearbook of International Law*, he argued that recurring condemnation of the practice could be traced back to the days of Hugo Grotius in the seventeenth century. Wright invoked Article 6b of the London Charter of the Nuremberg International Military Tribunal listing the 'killing of hostages' as a war crime. He confidently asserted that it 'is clear that no custom or usage has been established to justify the killing of innocent hostages. The unilateral practice of one nation, Germany, cannot establish a valid custom'.[10] Noting some discrepancy between his views and the treatment of hostages in the American *Rules of Land Warfare*, which provided for the possibility that hostages might be taken and executed, he seized on the assertion in paragraph 259 that 'when a hostage is accepted he is treated as a prisoner of war' as being inconsistent with the permissibility of ever executing hostages as provided for in paragraph 258 and concluded that the American manual 'could only be material as evidence of the army's practice, and it is clear that the United States forces have not followed that practice'.[11]

On the grounds of law and practice, however, the position was actually more equivocal than Wright suggested. On the grounds of practice he was correct in asserting that there had been no resort to hostage taking by the Americans in the Second World War. However, as Melissa Willard–Forster has emphasized, the Americans had specifically provided for the taking of hostages in both Germany and Japan, along with a series of other punitive measures, in the event of resistance to their occupation forces.[12] In the case of Japan, the provision for taking hostages was set out in the *Basic Outline Plan for 'Blacklist' Operations to Occupy Japan Proper and Korea after Surrender or Collapse*. The Outline started from the supposition that it 'is probable that there will be some resistance in some form or another'.[13] Under the heading 'Hostages' it then set out the following:

> Hostages may be taken as a further means of enforcing group or community obedience to terms of surrender or compliance with the Laws of War … The execution of hostages is not regarded with favour and requires the specific authority of the Commander-in-Chief, U.S. Army Forces, Pacific, in each case.[14]

In the European theatre the taking of hostages was included in SHAEF's *Handbook for Unit Commanders* of 15 February 1945 and in the document, *Combating the Guerrilla* of 1 May 1945.[15] The revised *Handbook* of February 1945 included a new chapter, 'Measures for the protection of Allied forces in their relations with the civil population in occupied Germany', which also provided for hostage taking, alongside a wider set of reprisals, including destruction or seizure of property, compulsory evacuation, destruction of communities, and devastation of territory. There was no specific reference to killing hostages or refraining from such, though further directives were to be issued 'in the event resort to reprisals and sanctions becomes necessary'.[16] Hostages could be seized by the occupying force 'to ensure compliance with its instructions, or as security for the good behaviour of the inhabitants'.[17] The highly contentious use of hostages on trains to deter attacks by guerrillas was specifically mentioned as one possibility.[18] The provisions of *Combating the Guerrilla* for hostage taking were perfunctory, merely listing it as one of the 'stern measures' that 'may include curfew, limitations on assembly and movement, forced labor, and the taking of hostages'.[19] The earlier *Manual of Military Government and Civil Affairs*, FM-27-5 of December 1943, had listed hostage taking along with collective fines and reprisals, though it contained the warning that 'such actions are usually an indication of weakness of the occupying forces and of ineffective control of the inhabitants. Careful consideration should be given to the question of determining whether such devices will serve as a deterrent or aggravate an already difficult situation'.[20] That element of caution was pragmatic, neither detracting from the willingness in principle to resort to such methods nor calling into question their legitimacy.

That such devices were nevertheless being held in readiness reflects, of course, the fear and uncertainty of the Allied forces. An Appendix, dated 12 September 1944, to the SHAEF *Handbook* warned that 'German hatred may be far deeper and more universal than in 1918' and that the 'occupying forces must be prepared for civil disorders, including sniping and assaults on individuals, sabotage, provoked riots, perhaps even organized raids'.[21] *Combating the Guerrilla* also anticipated resistance, noting that there 'are indications that German attempts at underground or guerrilla activity may increase'.[22] As Allied Forces invaded Germany such anxieties were maintained and even inflamed by speculation on Hitler's retreat to an Alpine redoubt, guerrilla warfare, and the Werewolf phenomenon. Although the significance of Werewolf and the wider prospect of guerrilla warfare has its defenders, the security concerns of the Allies have been condemned by Christa Horn as amounting to a veritable 'hysteria of the occupying power'.[23] Klaus-Dietmar Henke also quotes a Military Government report covering May and June 1945, describing the Werewolf phenomenon as a 'hallucination, a hallucination of the Germans as well as of their enemies', but adds that months after the capitulation, the 'Werewolf hysteria' persisted'.[24] Similarly, Christina von Hodenberg writes of an 'American myth of "Hitler's werewolves" '.[25]

It turned out that there was no need to invoke the provisions for the seizure of hostages. The Allies did have sufficient forces to overawe a heavily defeated enemy in both Germany and Japan. There were isolated incidents and some embarrassment when the French General Leclerc threatened to seize and execute hostages, especially because he indicated that he would draw hostages from POWs if necessary, which would have amounted to a clear violation of the 1929 Geneva Convention.[26] That, as the American and British press put it, was 'the dangerous part of the proclamation' for the 'rules of war permit the execution of hostages so long as they are not prisoners of war'.[27] Such qualifications could later fade from view and General Eisenhower, pressed by defence counsel for the accused in the so-called Hostages Trial in Nuremberg in 1947, could affirm confidently that he had not issued orders for the execution of hostages.[28]

But that still left the question of the legality of the practice. Contrary to Lord Wright's claim, the taking of hostages had been regarded by the military forces of all the major powers as a long-established custom, albeit of varying form and application. There was not always great clarity about what constituted hostage taking. The original customary meaning of someone offered as surety for the performance of a treaty had died out in all but name. There was a distinction between hostages, meaning people seized in order to prevent or deter the commission of some act, and people subject to reprisals for acts already committed; though in both cases it was innocents who were held vicariously liable for the acts.[29] In some accounts the hostage seems to have elicited more sympathy than the victim of reprisals. It is noteworthy here that the German compulsion of Frenchmen to travel on French railway engines during the Franco-German war of 1870–1, or more typically in fact in the carriages, elicited great indignation on part of French lawyers and publicists, even though there seems to be no record of any of these hostages losing their life as a result of this practice. Moreover, the subsequent claims that hostage taking was a peculiarly German custom were not true.[30] It was a sensitive issue, however, and this sensitivity was probably the reason for the lack of discussion of hostage taking at the Brussels Conference of 1874 and at either of the Hague Conferences. As the British delegate to the Brussels Conference, Sir Alfred Horsford, reported concerning the provisions for reprisals in the Russian draft: 'it was almost impossible to enter upon any discussion of the matter without opening the door to recriminations. It seemed to be the general feeling that occasions on which reprisals of a severe character had been executed were of far too recent a date to allow the practice to be discussed calmly'.[31] The drafters of the later Oxford Manual, a text of 1880 produced by the Institute for International Law and intended as a model for national military manuals, had the courage to address the wider issues of reprisals, seeking to set limits to both their incidence and severity, but did not specifically address the figure of the hostage. As for the Hague Conference of 1899, as Frits Kalshoven aptly puts it, while 'at the time the practice of shooting hostages was only too well known; yet not a single reference to it is found in the records of the Conference'.[32]

Publicists tended to deplore the practice. In her survey of the development of the law of occupation between 1863 and 1914, Doris Graber concluded that depending on the precise phase of the development of the law, majority opinion found the practice to be 'outmoded', legal with the reservation that hostages should be treated as prisoners of war, or positively illegal. She also observed that military manuals continued to support the practice. Even a French manual, while generally opposed to the practice, tolerated it in cases of absolute necessity.[33] The American manual of 1914 was not as clear as it might have been, failing to distinguish between hostages offered as surety for the observance of treaties and hostages seized by the enemy for various purposes. Nevertheless it listed examples of recent practice without objection.[34] The British manual of 1914 noted that placing hostages on trains could not be considered a 'commendable practice', but only because it left no way of distinguishing between illegitimate acts of 'train wrecking' and the legitimate acts of 'raiding parties of the armed forces of the belligerent'.[35] To be sure, German practice in the First World War increased the level of criticism, but leading international lawyers on both sides of the Atlantic continued to endorse the legality of the practice.[36] Even during the Second World War a contribution to the *American Journal of International Law* concluded that though 'hostage taking has assumed so illegal and inhuman a character through contemporary German abuse, this is insufficient to warrant its abandonment as a legal instrument of war'.[37]

It was consistent with this position that the American Military Tribunal in Nuremberg presiding over the so-called Hostages Trial recorded that hostage taking and the putting to death of hostages was sanctioned by the military manuals of the United States, Britain, and France, though it did add that 'the provisions do not appear to have been given effect'. Nevertheless it held by the existing state of law: 'International law is prohibitive law and no conventional prohibitions have been invoked to outlaw this barbarous practice'.[38] The Tribunal went on to condemn the accused, but not on the principle of seizing or even executing hostages. It condemned them on such grounds as failure to follow an adequate procedure and utter lack of proportionality.

The Tribunal delivered its judgement on 19 February 1948. The following November, in a foreword to the volume of the *Law Reports of Trials of War Criminals* reporting the case, Lord Wright broke with normal practice in order to enter a caveat on the grounds that he felt 'that a decision that one may slaughter innocent hostages so long as the number slaughtered is not excessive, even subject to the pre-conditions specified in the judgement, is retrograde, and is in my opinion contrary to the general course of humanitarian jurisprudence which has been developed up to the present'.[39] The next year, the Fourth Geneva Convention specified in Article 34: 'The taking of hostages is prohibited'. It was the shortest article dealing with the 'Status and Treatment of Protected Persons'. The Report of Committee III to the Plenary Assembly of the Conference noted, 'The simplicity of the prohibition to take hostages … ensured its passage undisputed through the crucibles of Stockholm and Geneva.'[40] It is clear, however, that if American fears about potential resistance in either Germany or Japan had turned out to be accurate and the occupiers had implemented the planned measures, including hostage taking, there could have been no such undisturbed passage. As it was though, two members of the American delegation could note the prohibition in *The American Journal of International Law* and describe it as 'long overdue'.[41]

Food

The key point on the question of whether an occupying army was entitled to live off the land or alternatively obliged to provide adequate supplies of food to sustain the civilian population was made in 1944 before the end of the war by H. A. Smith in the *British Yearbook of International Law*. Having noted that eleven out of the fifteen articles constituting the Hague Regulations' provisions for occupied territory related to property, he promptly observed that

> All these rules have little to do with the real problems which now face an occupying power. In Italy … the actual facts are often the exact opposite of those which were envisaged by the draftsmen of the rules. So far from living on the country, the first task of the occupying army is now to feed a starving population and to supply it with a hundred other necessities.[42]

Smith was quite right in assuming that the draftsmen of the Hague Regulations had set out from the proposition that the occupying force would in substantial measure live from the resources of the occupied territory. Discussion and disagreement centred around how to control the demands of the occupying force, what method, for example whether resort to requisitioning of goods or monetary contributions, was more just, and how at least to introduce some form of order in the practices and provide for the possibility of the recompense of ordinary citizens.

It was not the case that occupants had always been indifferent to the often precarious condition of the occupied in respect to basic provision of food or that they had never made some attempt to alleviate their plight. The Allies, for example, had arranged for the supply of foodstuffs, including surplus army stocks, in the areas of the Rhineland they had occupied at the end of the First World War.[43] There was, then, precedent for the provision of food for the occupied. It remained the case, though, that the requisitioning and contributions exacted by the Germans in both the First and Second World Wars were more representative of the normal practice of occupants and clearly conformed to expectations about an occupiers' behaviour as anticipated in the prevailing international law of the time. The seizure of food, sometimes leaving the occupied destitute, was a striking dimension of the nineteenth and early twentieth century experience of occupation in all countries; a practice which local populations hated only slightly less than the billeting of enemy soldiers with which it was in any event often associated.[44]

Requisitioning of food and forced contributions were indeed often matters of sheer necessity for an occupying army. It was only later in the nineteenth century that developments in transport, particularly in the railway system, as well as organizational improvements in the management and structure of armies enabled the Prussian General Helmuth von Moltke to boast that one of the developments to really lessen the barbarity of war was 'vigilance of administration which provides for subsistence of troops in the field', while still disparaging the efficacy of codes of international law.[45] Yet the troops over which von Moltke had presided only a few years earlier in the Franco-German war of 1870–1 had embarked upon requisitioning and imposition of contributions with great vigour if not always as much 'vigilance of administration' as the General liked to proclaim.

The occupations preceding the Western Allies' occupations of the European mainland were then marked mostly by the requisitioning of food that had typically accompanied military occupation. That the 'benign' occupations by Britain and the United States after the Second World War would not be so characterized and that there would be some requirement to provide food for occupied populations was recognized by the rhetoric of the Allied leaders and by the planning that took place during the war, including the creation of UNRRA.[46] Nevertheless, the Western Allies underestimated the scale of the problem both in Europe and the Far East, which especially in the British and US Zones of occupation, was compounded by exigencies such as a heavily populated area dependent on food imports. The issue of supplying food was further complicated by competition for food between groups within occupied territories and between occupied and liberated territories, as well as by the punitive intent of occupation policy. That the Allies could manage these problems, avoiding mass starvation if not necessarily feeding people adequately, was testimony not only to the sheer productive capacity especially of the United States, but also to their logistical capacity to deliver food both to occupied populations and, in even greater abundance, to their own forces. It was indeed logistics as much as any change of mood that made this possible.[47] Ironically, it was the hard-pressed British, rather than the affluent Americans, who provided a striking illustration of this change in attitudes. Responding to German criticism that they drew on German produce, the British denied the charge, conceding that they had consumed local fresh fruit and vegetables only in the immediate aftermath of the invasion and had otherwise drawn only on imported foodstuffs.[48]

This change from the practice of requisitioning food and levying contributions, to self-contained supply systems for the occupant and the provision of substantial aid for occupied populations, amounts to one of the most dramatic transformations of the practice and background normative expectation in military occupation.[49] Although rations in all three of the western zones were set at the relatively low level of around 1,500 calories a day, and even this low level could not be met at times, the obligation of the occupier to provide sufficient food to avoid starvation was accepted on both moral and pragmatic grounds. As Field Marshall Montgomery, the British Military Governor, wrote in a telegram to the government in London in February 1946:

> In my opinion we must immediately have substantial imports of wheat or equivalent for Germany: if we do not do so we shall produce death and misery to an extent which will disgrace our administration in history and completely stultify every effort we are making to produce a democratic Germany.[50]

Yet, while a ready consensus had been found at the Geneva negotiations of 1949 for the prohibition of the highly contentious issue of hostage taking, considerable disagreement among the negotiators arose over the provisions relating to the specific responsibility of an occupying power for the food supply of civilian populations, the broader desirability of which they were all agreed upon. The disagreement, of course, surrounded the extent of any such obligation. Here, the Stockholm draft that constituted the initial basis for the negotiations baldly asserted: 'The occupying power is bound to assure the food supply of the civilian population'.[51] This elicited a significant amendment by the United States changing the nature of the obligation, so that the occupant 'shall endeavour, within the means available to it, to assure the food supply' and thus restricting the obligation to import foodstuffs so that it was 'subject to its military necessities'.[52] The American delegate Albert Clattenburg accepted the existence of a moral duty but expressed reservations about accepting a legal obligation which might exceed the ability of his country. The United States had benefitted from 'an unprecedented series of record crops' which could not be guaranteed in the future, nor could the effects of submarine warfare be predicted. Moreover, he insisted the food supply of the occupant's troops had to take precedence.[53] Most of the other contributors to the debate had in mind their own recent experience of occupation by Germany, which particularly in the case of eastern Europe had been very brutal. The UK and the United States, by contrast, had no such experiences. It was therefore unsurprising that the British broadly supported the American position. Germans and Japanese were, of course, absent from the conference. The Soviet delegate in particular was vociferous and expressed surprise that there was not 'sharp criticism' of the proposed American amendment. If the latter were adopted, he asserted, 'it would not be an exaggeration to say that the very existence of the population of occupied territories would be endangered'.[54] Unable to resolve the disagreement, the Committee referred the matter to a Working Party, which came back with a text that 'took account' of American reservations. Again the Soviets protested.[55] After voting on and rejecting the Soviet and other amendments to the new draft, the final text was adopted by twenty-six votes, with eight abstentions. Most notably, this draft included a qualification, designed to meet American concerns, that the obligation of the Occupying Power to provide food should be subject to 'the means available to it'. That was not, however, the end of the matter. The new obligation still sounded like an onerous one, even with the new qualifications. That was in evidence when the negotiators agreed that the Civilians Convention should 'cease to apply not earlier than one year after the termination of hostilities', giving as a part of the justification the example of the Allied occupations of Germany and Japan which 'show that the responsibility of the Occupying Powers for the welfare of the local populations was far less at present than during the period immediately following hostilities'.[56] No objection was raised to this argument and the final text specified that the application of the Convention would thus cease after one year, save for specified articles which would continue to apply 'for the duration of the occupation'. Article 55 setting out the obligation to supply food was not included in the list of those to be continued.[57] Had the Convention been in force at the end of the war it would have meant that the obligation to supply food to Germany would have ceased as the Germans faced the hunger winter of 1946–7; save for the provision in Article 59 imposing an obligation to facilitate relief schemes by third parties.

The Americans clearly had no intention of allowing what was arguably one of the most striking changes in the pattern of military occupation to become a legal obligation other than for a quite limited period, and even then to hedge it with qualification, all the while reserving the right to resort to requisitions. Still, even the watered-down phrasing of the final draft caused some members of the American military to worry about the possible consequences.[58] In one respect, the Geneva provisions, as finally agreed, were in fact potentially more onerous for the occupied than the Hague Regulations. Following proposals submitted by the British, the Convention not only specifically approved the occupiers' right of requisitioning, but also extended it to explicitly allow requisitioning for 'use by the occupation forces and administration personnel'. Protest by Belgium, seconded by the Danes, was brushed aside by the British on the grounds that in 1907 'occupying forces were not organized as they are at present and did not include an appreciable number of civilian administration personnel'.[59] Thus, despite the US and British Military Governments in Germany accepting that they had an obligation to provide sufficient food for the civilian population, the practice of the 'benign' occupations after the Second World War was only incorporated into international law in the subsequent Geneva Conventions of 1949 with significant qualifications that shielded future occupiers from any extensive longer-term legal obligation to feed the occupied population.

Regime transformation

As the occupants of the western zones of Germany embarked upon their respective occupations they did so with guidance that blended a strong punitive dimension with measures for substantial transformation of the regimes they were occupying and an urgent need to repeal or amend laws enacted by the Nazi regime. Whether the emphasis is placed on the punitive or more benign dimension of regime transformation, it was clear that what they were intending to do was not compatible with the injunction in Article 43 of the Hague Regulations to 'restore and ensure, as far as possible, order and public life, while respecting, unless absolutely prevented, the laws in force in the country'.[60] It is worth noting here that the extent of the discrepancy was striking especially because the conservationist language of the Hague Regulations had not been forgotten or dismissed as a historic curiosity that was evidently irrelevant to the current age.[61] The battles within the American administration for control of the machinery of occupation provide striking evidence of the perceived relevance of the conservationist language of the Regulations. US Secretary of War, Stimson, for example, proclaimed that:

> [The] ideal type of military government is one that preserves to the fullest extent consistent with military necessity, the local institutions and customs of the occupied area. Military government with this objective in view, is thus one that is superimposed upon the pre-existing local organization and seeks to shape the latter to the military and political exigencies of the occupations.[62]

German lawyers and publicists naturally invoked the Hague Regulations in order to set limits to Allied activity in the late 1940s as well as using it more or less explicitly as an instrument to wrest some moral advantage from the occupation authorities, with one British official noting the 'German tendency to complain of the violation of their rights under international law'.[63] This sufficiently worried William Asbury, regional commissioner for North Rhine-Westphalia, for him to request permission to publish a statement justifying British policies and refuting the applicability of the Hague Regulations.[64] That the Hague Regulations had to be treated as inapplicable was more or less unavoidable, even though there was some disagreement among British lawyers about the implications of an alternative understanding of the status of Britain in respect of Germany.[65] A series of judgements by the courts of the occupiers confirmed that the Hague Regulations were not applicable to the occupation of Germany. The reasons given in support of this position varied. The assumption of supreme authority by the Allies in the absence of any other German government and any contending army opposing the Allies were important reasons with their own implications and problems. In its simplest form, this led to asserting the traditional doctrine of subjugation or *debellatio*, but this raised awkward questions about the continuity of the German state and citizenship. One obvious interpretation of the consequences of the traditional doctrine of subjugation was that the German state and with it German citizenship had ceased to exist and that both the territory and the inhabitants had passed into the sovereign possession of the conquerors. Neither the Americans nor the British, however, had any intention of accepting such consequences. Consequently, much equivocation was necessary.[66]

In addition to those arguments, courts based their refusal to apply the Hague Regulations on various grounds. In July 1947, the Control Commission Court of Criminal Appeal of the British Zone held that the 'Military Government of Germany is unprecedented in its nature and has ideological and preventive objects which, although they may never previously have been the objects of any occupier, are in full accord with the principles underlying international relations'.[67] The US Military Tribunal introduced a different consideration in its rejection of the application of the Hague Regulations, arguing that 'by reason of the complete breakdown of government, industry, agriculture and supply, they were under an imperative humanitarian duty of far wider scope to reorganise government and industry and to foster local democratic governmental agencies throughout the territory'.[68] Recalling its own judgement of July 1947 and the US Military Tribunal's judgement, the British Appeal Court confidently asserted: 'We are satisfied that Section III of the Hague Regulations does not apply and has never, since the Allies assumed supreme authority over the occupied territory, applied to the present occupation of Germany'.[69] The final step in such logic was taken by Eric Beckett, the British Foreign Office's First Legal Adviser: 'Rules of International Law for such a case do not exist and therefore cannot have been violated'.[70]

One consequence of these kinds of argument is that the Allied occupations of Germany should be considered a legal anomaly, an exception to the experience of military occupation, that leave in force and leave untouched the Hague Regulations; save, of course, where new exceptions might be argued to exist. Perversely, the very momentous nature of the Allies' measures, according to this argument, put them outside any legal framework of occupation.

Subsequent attempts to incorporate Allied experience and practice into international law have proved to be difficult and often controversial. It is clear that the argument to the effect that the Hague Regulations were simply inapplicable to the *sui generis* occupation of Germany did not prevent the representatives of the occupying powers from feeling it necessary to in some way amend the Hague Regulations to take account of their own actions in Germany. Indeed, their initial intent had been to draw up a new code of the law of occupation that would replace the Hague Regulations, but the delegates at the Geneva negotiations drew back from this in Article 154 whereby they agreed that the Fourth Geneva Convention shall be supplementary to Sections II and III of the Hague Regulations, and hence that the Hague Regulations remained in force.[71]

The argument that the post-1945 law of occupation did change in response to the occupations of the Second World War, including the 'benign' occupations of the western zones of Germany and Japan, has been put most forcefully by Eyal Benvenisti, though others have also provided some striking if rather clipped observations.[72] Benvenisti mobilizes the experience of the Second World War behind his interpretation of Article 64 of the Fourth Geneva Convention, the article that plays the key role in his expansive view of the powers ascribed to the occupant by the Convention. Noting that the 'ongoing occupations of Germany and Japan were explicitly mentioned by the drafters', he argues that the Fourth Geneva Convention 'was drafted with the aim of imposing on occupants a "heavy burden" *beyond* their duties under the Hague Regulations. It therefore cannot be the case that the drafters of Article 64 sought to minimise the occupant's authority under Hague 43'.[73]

The contrast with the Hague Regulations also forms a key part of Benvenisti's interpretation of the article. Here his view is that the law of occupation must be understood in the historical context in which it was formulated, leading him to argue that according to the Geneva Convention the occupying power 'must be a proactive regulator, no longer the disinterested watch guard envisioned in the Hague Regulations'.[74] In his view, the Second World War and the 'benign' occupations by the Allies demonstrate both the bankruptcy of the old rules and the need for a new approach exemplified by the new reading of Article 64; thus forming a key turning point in the understanding and legal regulation of military occupation.

In terms of the drafting and meaning of Article 64 Benvenisti conceded that his interpretation was not and is not widely shared. As other scholars have recognized, Article 64 was the product of a mixture of issues, debated against a wider backcloth of concern about expanding the authority of an occupant beyond the remit provided by Article 43 of the Hague Regulations. More widely, rather than the practice of the 'benign' occupations leading to the sanctioning of regime transformation in international law, there is evidence in the record of the negotiations of clear awareness, in the words of a British negotiator, 'of the obvious difficulties which would arise if the provisions of the present Convention were to be applied either to Germany or Japan at the present time in the absence of a peace treaty'.[75]

Debate on what was to become Article 64 focused on an American proposal intended to deal with the American experience in Germany, where the delegate stated that they had found it necessary to abrogate 'a whole series of laws and provisions based on the National Socialist ideology, including, in particular, racial discrimination' and to 'suppress the Courts set up in Germany for the purpose of administering those inhuman laws'.[76] Other delegates took alarm at what they perceived to be the expansive nature of the American amendment, which gave the 'impression that the Occupying Power could change the legislation of the occupied territory as it thought fit'.[77] In the course of the debate two other specific concerns were invoked. The British referred to the problem they had encountered in Africa where local courts had ceased to function and they had been obliged to establish substitute courts.[78] The representative of New Zealand referred to the articles 'which required the Occupying Power to share its food supplies with the population of the occupied territory', adding that: 'It was important that the latter should not be exempted from any war legislation enacted to promote production and to regulate the distribution of food supplies'.[79] In the comments of the Committee Report on the article it was precisely those concerns along with care of children and public health and hygiene that had become the focus in the Committee's mind of the contentious second paragraph of Article 64, which specified that according to this second paragraph, 'an Occupying Power may subject the population to provisions which are essential to fulfil its obligations under the Convention ... and to maintain an orderly government'.[80]

Article 64 did not enshrine a new understanding of the role of an occupant, still less did it codify the denazification programme of the Allies in Germany. Rather, it was the product of a patchwork of concerns arising from recent Allied occupations, in Africa as well as in Europe, that had been put together against a background fear of an expansive reading of any such article and a readiness to invoke Article 43 as the advanced position of international law. There is also evidence that delegates were aware that, while the Fourth Geneva Convention enhanced the scope of an occupant's legitimate activity in specific areas, the provisions of the Fourth Geneva Convention could not be reconciled with the extent of Allied practices in Germany and Japan.[81] That did not imply criticism of the activities of the Allies in those conditions. It is notable here that in the discussion of Article 64 the delegate from Monaco, who warned that the American amendment 'gave the Occupying Power the right to legislate in place of the authorities of the occupied territory', added that: 'The reasons given in support of that proposal were satisfactory in the particular case quoted, but would not hold good as a general rule'.[82] In other words the American rationale won his moral approval in this particular instance, but was not, in his eyes, a sound basis for international law. That was consistent with the British legal view that events in Germany had to be treated as *sui generis*.

Conclusion

While some aspects of the Allies' experience of occupation during the war and after were subsequently translated into international law, as in the cases of hostage taking and, with significant qualification, the provision of food, regime transformation proved intractable. Evaluating the tension and discordance between the practices of the 'benign' occupations of Germany and Japan by the Western Allies and the international law of occupation, in the light of the historical record and law of military occupation generally, has to be problematic for some simple reasons. They are the only cases of the complete occupation of major powers since the occupation of France in 1814 and again from 1815 to 1818. Germany was the only case of a great power whose occupation could plausibly be construed as amounting to subjugation (*debellatio*) to the extent that it could be argued that the Hague Rules did not apply, and consequently that it was not occupied territory at all, even if that conclusion could not be consistently maintained. The Allied occupations in the post-war period are remarkable for the absence of resistance on a scale the occupants had feared and had led the Americans in particular to prepare for the seizure of hostages and other measures that would have tarnished the subsequent image of 'benign' occupations. Finally, they stand out for the sheer scale of the effort made to feed the populations of occupied territory.

Integrating those experiences into the law of occupation proved, however, more uneven and difficult. Many of the countries participating in the negotiations that led to the Geneva Conventions had been the victims of hostage taking and none of them had resorted to it on a significant scale, so they found it easy to agree upon prohibiting a practice that was in principle perfectly legal according to their own military manuals. Transforming their readiness to feed occupied populations into an obligation invoked much more caution and produced obligations markedly less extensive than the actual practice of the occupants in the immediate post-war period. It was, however, in relation to the wider authorization of the occupant within an occupied territory that the discrepancy between the occupiers' practice and international law was most apparent. In relation to 'regime transformation' even the supposedly benign and successful occupations of the western zones of Germany and of Japan could not serve as guides in formulating laws that would be acceptable to all the participants at the Geneva Conference of 1949.

The paradox is that international law as it existed in 1945 arguably provided clear justification for Allied policy but only on the basis of the doctrine of the conquest or subjugation of Germany. That doctrine, however, brought with it politically unacceptable consequences such as the annexation of territory and the resulting incorporation of its inhabitants into the state of the conqueror.[83] Indeed, the regime transformation the Allies in fact engaged in could be seen as not only pragmatically but also morally superior to the logic of the doctrine of conquest. Yet, legally, it stood in blatant contradiction to the only other legal model available at the time, that of the law of occupation. Conquest has subsequently lost all vestige of legitimacy, while regime transformation has yet to gain the sanction of the international law of occupation.[84] That discordance between the practice of occupation and the international law of occupation was part of the experience of the 'benign' occupations. It found its most succinct expression in the claim that legally what had happened in Germany had to be *sui generis*, that is outside the frame of any existing law. The failure to close the gap between Allied practices and international law at Geneva was part of the legacy of the 'benign' occupations with which we still live.

Notes

1 See Peter M. R. Stirk, *A History of Military Occupation from 1791 to 1914* (Edinburgh: Edinburgh University Press, 2016), 224–53.
2 Ernst Feilchenfeld, *The International Economic Law of Belligerent Occupation* (Washington, DC: Carnegie, 1942), 22–9.
3 Gregory H. Fox, *Humanitarian Occupation* (Cambridge: Cambridge University Press, 2008), 242.
4 See the chapter by Susan Carruthers in this volume and Susan L. Carruthers, *The Good Occupation* (Cambridge: Harvard University Press, 2016).
5 Gaël Eismann, *Hôtel Majestic* (Paris: Tallandier, 2010), 34–6, 132–4. German legal arguments in defence of the practice were indeed self-serving.
6 Foreign Relations of the United States 1941, vol. 1, 446–7.
7 United Nations War Crimes Commission, *History of the United Nations War Crimes Commission and the Development of the Law of War* (London: HMSO, 1948), 90.
8 Paul Buttin, *Le Procès Pucheu* (Paris: Amiot, n.d.).
9 Lord Wright, 'The Killing of Hostages as a War Crime', *British Yearbook of International Law* 25 (1948): 296–310.
10 Wright, 'The Killing of Hostages', 303. See also the assertion that 'the practice had by any other standard save the German become outmoded': William Wiley, '"Onward to New Deeds": The German Field Army and War Crimes during the Second World War' (PhD diss., York University, Ontario, 1996), 220.
11 Wright, 'The Killing of Hostages', 304.
12 Melissa Willard-Foster, 'Planning the Peace and Enforcing the Surrender', *Journal of Interdisciplinary History* 40 (2009): 33–56.
13 Basic Outline Plan for 'Blacklist' Operations to Occupy Japan Proper and Korea after Surrender or Collapse, Appendix 4, 1.
14 Basic Outline Plan for 'Blacklist' Operations to Occupy Japan, Appendix 4, 3.
15 SHAEF, *Combatting the Guerrilla* (n.p., 1 May 1945), 36.
16 SHAEF, *Handbook for Unit Commanders (Germany)*, rev. edn (15 February 1945), 5, 53.
17 Ibid., 52.
18 Ibid., 53.
19 SHAEF, *Combating the Guerrilla*, 1945, 36.

20 *Manual of Military Government and Civil Affairs*, FM 27-5, 8.
21 SHAEF, *Handbook for Unit Commanders*, 58.
22 SHAEF, *Combating the Guerrilla*, 6.
23 Christa Horn, *Die Internierungs- and Arbeitslager in Bayern 1945–1952* (Frankfurt am Main: Peter Lang, 1992), 241.
24 Klaus-Dietmar Henke, *Die amerikanische Besatzung Deutschlands* (Munich: Oldenbourg, 1995), 951–2.
25 Christina von Hodenberg, 'Of German Fräuleins, Nazi Werewolves and Iraqi Insurgents', *Central European History* 41 (2008): 74.
26 Perry Biddiscombe, *Werwolf! The History of the National Socialist Guerrilla Movement, 1944–1946* (Cardiff: University of Wales Press, 1998), 200–1.
27 'Allies Reaffirm Ban on Killing Prisoners', *New York Times*, 1 December 1944, 3 and 'Gen. Leclerc's Threat a "Closed Incident"', *New York Times*, 3 December 1944, 4. See the comment in the former article that 'it is hoped that it will be speedily re-established that the practice of shooting civilian hostages, so common with the Gestapo and SS, is not going to be condoned by Allied commanders'.
28 'Hostage Slaying Denied', *New York Times*, 4 December 1947, 38. See also the report by the *Times* of the court's judgement that: 'It was not shown … that a single hostage or reprisal prisoner had been killed by allied forces throughout the late war'; 'Field Marshall List Sentenced', 20 February 1948, 3.
29 Wright, 'The Killing of Hostages', 299.
30 Systematic study of hostage-taking is rare, but see Webb Garrison, *Civil War Hostages: Hostage Taking in the Civil War* (Shippensburg: White Mane Books, 2000).
31 *Correspondence Respecting the Brussels Conference on the Rules of Military Warfare, Miscellaneous no. 1* (London: Harrison, 1875), 178.
32 Frits Kalshoven, *Belligerent Reprisals* (Leyden: Sijthoff, 1971), 61.
33 Doris Graber, *The Development of the Law of Belligerent Occupation 1863–1914. A Historical Survey* (New York: AMS Press, 1949), 201, 204, 211–2.
34 *Rules of Land Warfare* (Washington, DC: War Department, 1914), 134. The 'confusion' was also noted by Ellen Hammer and Marina Salvin, 'The Taking of Hostages in Theory and Practice', *American Journal of International Law*, 38 (1944): 25.
35 War Office, *Manual of Military Law* (London: HMSO, 1914), 306.
36 See Lassa Oppenheim, *International Law*, 3rd edn, vol. 2 (London: Longman, 1921), 350–3; Charles Hyde, *International Law*, vol. 2 (Boston: Little, Brown, 1922), 384–5.
37 Hammer and Salvin, 'The Taking of Hostages in Theory and Practice', 33. See also Joseph Robinson, 'Punishment of War Criminals', *Judge Advocate Journal* 3 (Fall–Winter 1945): 17–8.
38 *Law Reports of Trials of War Criminals*, 8 (London: HMSO, 1949), 63.
39 Ibid., viii.
40 *Final Record of the Diplomatic Conference of Geneva of 1949*, vol. 2, Section A (Berne: Federal Political Department, 1949), 823. See also Kalshoven, *Belligerent Reprisals*, 263–4.
41 Raymund Yingling and Robert Ginnane, 'The Geneva Convention of 1949', *American Journal of International Law* 46 (1952): 412.
42 H. A. Smith, 'The Government of Occupied Territory', *British Yearbook of International Law* 21 (1944): 131.
43 James Edmonds, *The Occupation of the Rhineland 1918–1929* (London: HMSO, 1987), 126–30. See also I. L. Hunt, *American Military Government of Occupied Germany 1918–1920* (Washington, DC: Government Printing Office, 1943), 155–68.

44 On the impact of the requisitioning of homes by the British in Westphalia after the Second World War, see Bettina Blum's chapter in this volume.
45 Percy Bordwell, *The Law of War between Belligerents* (Chicago: Callaghan, 1908), 114.
46 See Jessica Reinsich, 'Introduction: Relief in the Aftermath of War', *Journal of Contemporary History* 43 (2008): 371–404 and several other contributions to this special issue on the theme.
47 See Linda L. Kruger, 'Logistics Matter: The Growth of Little Americas in Occupied Germany' (PhD diss., University of Kansas, Lawrence, 2014).
48 Michael Wildt, *Der Traum vom Sattwerden* (Hamburg: VSA, 1986), 38.
49 The French continued a system of onerous requisitioning and contributions. On this, see Jochen Thies and Kurt von Daak, *Südwestdeutschland Stunde Null* (Düsseldorf: Droste, 1979), 75–8; Volker Koop, *Besetzt. Französische Besatzungspolitik in Deutschland* (Berlin: ne.bra, 2005), 115–43. Occupation costs were effectively paid in the US Zone: Seymour Wurfel, 'Military Government – The Supreme Court Speaks', *North Carolina Law Review*, 40 (1962): 748–9.
50 Cited in Christopher Knowles, *Winning the Peace: The British in Occupied Germany, 1945–1949* (London: Bloomsbury, 2016), 23.
51 *Final Record of the Diplomatic Conference of Geneva of 1949*, vol. 1 (Berne: Federal Political Department, 1949), 121.
52 Ibid., vol. 3, 134.
53 Ibid., vol. 2, Section A, 666.
54 Ibid., 668.
55 Ibid., 745–6.
56 Ibid., 623.
57 Fourth Geneva Convention, Article 6.
58 Gerhard von Glahn, *The Occupation of Enemy Territory* (Minneapolis: University of Minnesota Press, 1957), 169.
59 *Final Record*, vol. 2, Section A, 746. For the impact of this in the French Zone where requisitioning was still relied on, see Karl-Heinz Rothenberger, 'Ernährungs- und Landwirtschaft in der französischen Besatzungszone 1945–1950', in *Die Deutschlandpolitik Frankreichs und die französische Zone 1945–1949*, ed. G. Scharf and H.-J. Schroeder (Wiesbaden: Steiner, 1983), 192. It is notable that modern surveys of the law of occupation put little emphasis on Article 55. See Eyal Benvenisti, *The International Law of Occupation* (Oxford: Oxford University Press, 2012); Yoram Dinstein, *The International Law of Belligerent Occupation* (Cambridge: Cambridge University Press, 2009); Yutuka Arai-Takahashi, *The Law of Occupation* (Leiden: Martinus Nijhoff, 2009).
60 Hague Regulations, Article 43. The translation is not the one normally found in English editions but is more accurate.
61 Such an argument was put forward by Hermann Göring in his Nuremberg trial: *Trials of the Major War Criminals*, vol. 17, 522–6.
62 Walter Hudson, 'The American Way of Postwar: Post-World War II Occupation Planning and Implementation' (PhD diss., Kansas State University, Lawrence, 2010), 171. On attitudes to occupation among members of the US administration, see the chapter by Susan Carruthers in this volume.
63 G. R. Rubin, 'British Military and Government Lawyers on the Defeat of Nazi Germany', *Military Law and Law of War Review* 47 (2008): 127.
64 Ibid., 128.

65 Ibid. and passim. See also Patricia Meehan, *A Strange Enemy People* (London: Peter Owen, 2001). According to Charles Fahy, legal adviser to OMGUS, the applicability or not of the Hague Regulations was 'one of the problems then much discussed in legal circles', when he arrived in Germany in July 1945: 'Legal Problems of German Occupation', *Michigan Law Review* 47 (1948): 12.
66 For surveys of these arguments, see von Glahn, *The Occupation of Enemy Territory*, 274–85 and Josef Kunz, 'The Status of Germany under International Law', *Western Political Quarterly* 3 (1950): 538–65. I leave entirely aside the complications arising from German territory that came into the sovereign possession of Poland and the Soviet Union.
67 '*Graeme v. The Director of Prosecutions*', *Annual Digest* 14 (1947): 233.
68 In 'Trial of Josef Altstotter and others', *Law Reports of Trials of War Criminals*, 6 (London: HMSO, 1948), 29.
69 '*Dalldorf and others v. Director of Prosecutions*', *Annual Digest* 16 (1949): 438.
70 Rubin, 'British Military and Government Lawyers', 130.
71 *Final Record*, vol. 2, Section A, 675–6, 787.
72 Gregory H. Fox, for example, summarizes the 'reformist reading of occupation law' as holding that the 'Geneva drafters, meeting in the shadow of Nazi atrocities in occupied Europe, effectively codified the Allies recent denazification efforts'. See *Humanitarian Occupation* (Cambridge: Cambridge University Press, 2008), 242. Fox also noted (pp. 245–6) that 'Nazi-era laws are the only examples given in some military manuals of those that may appropriately be repealed'.
73 Benvenisti, *The International Law of Occupation*, 97.
74 Ibid., 74.
75 *Final Record*, vol. 2, Section A, 624.
76 Ibid., 670.
77 Ibid., 671.
78 The British did try to maintain the existing system, though it proved difficult. See Lord Rennel, *British Military Administration of Occupied Territories in Africa* (London: HMSO, 1947), 252–3, 336–8; Tracey Watts, 'The British Military Occupation of Cyrenaica, 1942–1949', *Transactions of the Grotius Society* 37 (1951): 75–8.
79 *Final Record*, vol. 2, Section A, 672.
80 Ibid., 833. The articles are those of the Stockholm draft.
81 Ibid., 624 for the observation by a member of the British delegation.
82 Ibid., 671.
83 The fact that the United States and Britain acquiesced in varying degrees in Soviet and Polish acquisition of German territory merely confirms that they saw no principled legal obstacle to annexation. Indeed, as Kunz noted, the Allies effectively asserted the *jus disponendi* (right of disposal) of the territorial sovereign in sanctioning the loss of German territory: 'The Status of Germany under International Law', 559. It was the obvious political impossibility of incorporating millions of Germans into their own populations that precluded American and British acquisition of German territory. The more equivocal French attitude cannot be followed up here.
84 That regime transformation, not annexation, had become the norm was argued by Carl Schmitt against the background of German experience: *Glossarium. Aufzeichnungen der Jahre 1947–1951* (Berlin: Duncker & Humblot, 1991), 269.

Part Two

The Past in the Present: Transitional Justice and Managing the Nazi Legacy

4

Transitional Justice? Denazification in the US Zone of Occupied Germany

Rebecca Boehling

At Potsdam in July and August 1945, the three victorious Allies – the United States, Britain and the Soviet Union – and then shortly after the conference, France,[1] agreed in principle to the so-called 'four Ds' as the general policies to be pursued during their military occupation of Germany. The more punitive policies of denazification, demilitarization and decartelization were to facilitate the more positive 'D' of democratization.[2] Each ally was to implement these policies as they saw fit in their own zones, as long as their implementation did not conflict with their general agreed-upon goals, or affect the other zones without quadripartite agreement. Of course, each ally understood each of these concepts differently and had diverse views on how such occupation policies might conform with their national and international interests. Plans and theories played out differently in practice, while the particular way in which interactions between occupiers and occupied unfolded in each zone also transformed the application of these policies.

The pursuit of each of these 'D's overlapped in various ways with the pursuit of the other 'D's. For example, re-education and reorientation did not merely include educational, media and cultural policies, but were all related to the goals of demilitarization and denazification, and were thus very much a part of a broader attempt to plant the seeds of democratization. To be sure, contradictions abound when Military Governments seek to impose democracy. Perhaps the best a foreign occupier can achieve in a country they have fought, invaded and defeated in war, is to set up legal and participatory political structures and regulate socioeconomic frameworks in ways to restrict anti-democratic tendencies and promote opportunities for the growth of democracy.

In the western zones of Germany, each of the three occupiers, France, the United States and Britain, had a different conception of what constituted democracy. This affected what form of democracy they thought Germans should have, and this in turn had to take into some account Germans' own democratic experiences and perceptions of democracy. Although the United States had the most to say about and spent the most time planning denazification,[3] the approaches of the French and the British varied from that of the Americans, both in theory and practice. This chapter places US denazification policy in Germany within the context of transitional justice, which the United Nations has defined as 'the full range of processes and mechanisms associated with a society's attempt to come to terms with a legacy of large-scale past abuses, in order to ensure accountability, serve justice and achieve reconciliation'.[4]

Transitional justice was a term that did not exist at the time of occupation planning or during the formal military occupation phase, and even now in occupation studies one is more likely to encounter references to 'regime change'. As legal scholar David Cohen reminds us about post-war Germany, 'at least until 1951 the reckoning with past injustice was for the most part imposed, guided, or supervised by outside conquering powers rather than by internal forces that had overthrown the previous regime'.[5] The Allied military occupation of Germany was intended to establish the groundwork for a new, more democratic regime, a goal associated with transitional justice that went far beyond the mere removal of Nazis from political influence. Conceptualizing denazification as transitional justice therefore makes it easier to understand why some anti-Nazi Germans and some of the Allied occupiers understood denazification as part of a reckoning with the recent past in pursuit of truth and justice, believing that individuals had to be held accountable for their complicity in the Nazi regime, before they could be reconciled with those who had actively opposed the Nazis, and ultimately work together to achieve the democratization of German society. Although few Germans at the time would have regarded denazification as related to reconciliation, the terms of the Potsdam Agreement formally considered it a prerequisite to Germany's re-entry into the international order. Those Germans least complicit with the Nazi regime usually had the most interest in denazification as a way of redressing past injustices and transforming the political and social structure of German society. Some may have hoped for some retribution and revenge, but few were in a position to exact it even if they wanted it. More broadly, however, the lens of transitional justice allows us to conceptualize denazification in a way that helps bring to light the variety of approaches and understandings of the purpose of denazification in both the planning and implementation phase. It should also better illuminate why some aspects of the programme were more successful than others.

In general histories of the occupation period and in popular memory, denazification is typically understood as the arrest and detention of particularly incriminated Nazis, and the removal from office of Nazi Party members and sympathizers. Those deemed incriminated on the basis of various Nazi Party and auxiliary organization membership were to be removed from public or influential positions, at least until those prosecuted and found guilty of war crimes could be appropriately punished, and then 'lesser offenders' and so-called 'followers' (*Mitläufer*) would eventually be rehabilitated. Non-specialists (or those not specializing in the occupation) often make little distinction, however, between what were in practice three separate processes: arrest and prosecution for war crimes following a defined legal process; extrajudicial arrest, detention and internment, mainly but not exclusively undertaken soon after the end of the war for security reasons; and, finally, measures considered suitable for those not deemed war criminals or security threats. This third process was what actually became denazification: the removal of leading Nazi Party members and active supporters from public office, restrictions on future employment, and the imposition of penalties, including fines and in a few cases imprisonment, depending on the extent of an individual's active membership in the Nazi Party or leadership roles in associated organizations (such as the Hitler Youth) and active support for the Nazi regime.[6]

The word 'denazification' itself originated in April 1945 among political advisors to General Eisenhower, supreme commander of the Allied Expeditionary Force and the first Military Governor for the US Zone. Political scientist Elmer Plischke, who served as the head of the denazification desk under the Office of the Political Advisor to General Eisenhower, later claimed that he was the first person to use the word 'denazification' as a parallel term to demilitarization. He told the historian Lutz Niethammer that he needed to come up with a header for a list of a series of planned US occupation directives. Based on the content of these directives he devised the rubric, and a set of criteria, for the concept that he called denazification. This included:

1 dissolution of the NSDAP,
2 eradication of Nazism from German laws and regulations,
3 elimination of Nazi symbols, street names, and monuments,
4 confiscation of property and records of the NSDAP,
5 ban on all privileges emanating from Nazi rule,
6 internment of Nazi elites,
7 exclusion of all Nazis above the level of nominal party membership from public positions,
8 suppression of Nazi indoctrination in every form, and
9 prohibition of parades and Nazi demonstrations.[7]

As the list makes clear, according to this understanding denazification was a much broader category than simply a purge of former Nazis from public positions and included the elimination of many elements of Nazi political, cultural and societal influences, as transmitted through education, media, culture, the legal system and the public sector.[8] Broadly speaking, both the theory and practice of denazification therefore depended on whether one defined denazification as merely a personnel purge of certain Nazis or as a more structural purification. It also depended on how narrowly one defined democratization, and whether this was conceived as simply holding free elections, or as removing authoritarian structures and practices together with encouraging broader democratic attitudes and behaviour.

Beginning in the 1990s with the end of apartheid in South Africa and following the political transitions in Central and Eastern Europe, scholarly attention has increasingly turned to the question of how countries and societies can come to terms with a history of violence and war, oppression and human rights violations.[9] A decade ago the transitional justice working group at the University of Ottawa's Centre for International Policy Studies, for example, maintained that the concept of transitional justice should play a prominent role in discussions surrounding democratization, nation-building and state reconstruction, with widespread support from international organizations:

> Judicial proceedings and prosecution of individuals suspected to have committed gross violations of human rights, truth commissions designed to establish a record

> of wrongdoing, reparations to the victims and vetting or dismissals of persons from certain positions [should be integral parts] … of reforms recommended by international organizations, donor agencies and outside experts for societies in transition from war or authoritarianism.[10]

True reconciliation remains difficult in any traumatized society. Circumstances in post-war Germany were, of course, very different from South Africa after apartheid. But when some of the victorious occupiers spouted accusations of collective guilt, while some among the occupied Germans felt they were as much victimized by the Allies as those who had been truly victimized by the Nazi regime, some semblance of coming to terms with truth and justice had to occur prior to reconciliation between former enemies. But exactly what form of justice should be applied in the immediate post-war period was an intricate problem, with considerable differences of opinion among both the Allies and Germans regarding the scope, application and purpose of any specific measures. Unconditional surrender and foreign military occupation automatically set up genuine constraints on how much Germans themselves could shape the transition or pursue justice for crimes committed during the Third Reich; nevertheless, the occupiers had to interact and negotiate with the expectations of the occupied. Exploring denazification in post-war Germany as a specific and historically significant attempt to achieve transitional justice may help to pinpoint the similarities and differences with more recent cases of regime change, or with other instances when truth and reconciliation approaches have been employed in an attempt to manage the transition from authoritarian rule to liberal democracy. In particular, it illustrates that, in cases where transitional justice is combined with military occupation of a defeated country, the occupying powers may well find themselves hard pressed to find truth or facilitate justice as outsiders in the community, and have to be prepared to work closely with diverse elements within the local population.

Prevalent national stereotypes and preconceptions as well as historical and geopolitical circumstances influenced Allied approaches to denazification.[11] American policy makers regarded denazification as integral to democratization and re-education. At the same time, they sought to familiarize Germans with, and in some cases convert them to, the American way of life.[12] In contrast, in both the British and French cases, a long-standing deep distrust of Germans and a negative perception of German mentalities and militarism were reinforced by their experiences during the war. For the British and French, denazification was primarily a ruling strategy applied for security reasons – following the impact of German aggression on their homelands in both world wars – and to enable a new German government to become established that would, they hoped, be willing to cooperate with the occupiers.[13] Yet although security was foremost for the British and French, they, or at least segments of their administrations, also hoped to 're-educate' Germans individually and collectively, and so influence and if possible transform German politics, society and culture.

Yet while the number of American occupation personnel was smaller given the size of the population in its zone than that of the other Western Allies, it was the Americans who started off with the most all-encompassing, ambitious and schematic program of denazification. Given the unmanageable scope of the program in the midst of their diminishing numbers, it is perhaps not surprising that they backed off the soonest, introducing amnesties and downgrading categories of incrimination so that they could bring the process to a close. Both the British, who had been the most hesitant to turn over any decisive role in the purge to the Germans, and the French, who in a few areas under their control briefly entrusted the process to Germans, retained their oversight over the process in their zones much longer than the Americans, in fact until after the Military Governors were succeeded by High Commissioners in September 1949.[14] In contrast, the Americans handed over responsibility for denazification to German authorities comparatively early, with the Law for Liberation in March 1946. The French did so with some modification of the Law in mid-1947 and the British with a major revamping of the law to retain more authority at the end of 1947.[15]

Despite differences between the Western Allies, many of the issues they faced were the same, in particular how to reconcile demands of justice and restitution for the victims of Nazi crimes and oppression, with the practical necessities of economic, social and political reconstruction. This chapter therefore examines denazification in the US Zone as a basis for future comparisons both within post-war Germany and more widely. After exploring the theory and practice of denazification in the US Zone, it will examine the reactions of various Germans to denazification, revealing their understanding of the process and what it was intended to accomplish. The chapter concludes with an overall assessment of denazification in the US Zone of Germany, as a case study in transitional justice.

Denazification planning and practice in the US Zone

The historian Walter Dorn, who worked as an analyst for the Office of Strategic Services (OSS) and denazification advisor to the Military Governor of the US Zone, noted in 'Unfinished Purge', his history of denazification that remained incomplete and unpublished when he died in 1961, that Allied approaches to how National Socialism was 'to be expunged effectively as an active force from the political, economic and cultural life of post-war Germany' varied according to the analysis of 'what the driving forces of National Socialism actually were and how completely it had fastened its stranglehold on German life'. Dorn argued that an outlaw theory of Nazism, which promoted a 'purge based on individual responsibility and the degree of complicity in the Nazi regime',[16] influenced American denazification policy most. Dorn felt that JCS 1067, the US occupation policy directive that was in effect from July 1945 until July 1947, combined this outlaw-based individualized program of punishment of political elites with a Morgenthau Plan–like program of punishment against an entire society.[17] Both strategies, however, avoided a deeper, structural transformation of the German social order.

JCS 1067 thus attempted to create a compromise between the 'outlaw' and more comprehensive 'Morgenthau' approaches to denazification, by promoting some social democratization via changed personnel in top leadership positions, while US occupation practice changed from initially accepting, but then gradually subduing and ultimately disavowing the more punitive aspects and the repressive consequences of denazification. This compromise was intended to create a less antagonistic occupation, requiring fewer Military Government personnel, and a more expeditious road to German economic recovery and reintegration into the capitalist system. Such an occupation would assist the War Department's desire to get US personnel back home and the State Department's concern for Germany's economic recovery, because of its strategic role as a bulwark against Communist expansion.

Before JCS 1067 came into effect in July 1945, there had also been plans in the United States for more thorough structural changes within Germany, which stemmed from a desire to prevent a Nazi revival, to deter German authoritarian tendencies and to nurture German democratic traditions. These structural initiatives, however, came from the least influential quarters of US occupation planning, namely from the Research and Analysis Branch of the OSS, in which Dorn, alongside many other prominent US social scientists and refugee scholars from the Frankfurt School, had worked as an analyst from 1942 until 1945 before he became an advisor to the Office of Military Government, US Zone in Germany (OMGUS). In late 1943, the War Department's Civil Affairs Division had the OSS prepare manuals to provide insights into the German social order and make suggestions for contending with denazification, local administration, unions and other groups and institutions in Germany. These manuals advocated not only the removal of the Nazi elite but also the eradication of the social basis of National Socialism. Indeed, the social elite theory favoured within the OSS[18] regarded Nazi incrimination and complicity as existing not only among the highest echelons of the party hierarchy and the government elite, but also among the intermediate levels of the Nazi party and within the broader structure of German society. This included leaders of the auxiliary organizations, such as the SS, SA, the Hitler Youth and a large number of Nazi professional organizations, as well as the economic elite of the private sector. At the same time, the OSS criteria for denazification proposed a qualitative measure, which was to keep the number of people to be investigated to a manageable minimum. As it turned out, however, the actual US Military Government practice of denazification stressed quantity. In the first post-war year, US Military Government processed the 131-item questionnaires (*Fragebogen*) of 1.5 million Germans to discover their level of incrimination during the Nazi regime.[19] The historian and former OSS analyst, Carl Schorske, later described US occupation policy as comprehensive in its initial scope, because it was:

> based on a conception of the nature of Nazism as a thing of the mind, an evil idea that would have to be rooted out through the elimination of the bearers of the idea and the re-education of the German people as a whole. This conception of Nazism involves the introduction of no change in the fundamental structure of society. Property relations are unchanged. Administration has been largely entrusted to putatively non-political, middle-class technicians. Thus the continuity of the social structure of Imperial, Weimar, and National Socialist Germany is maintained in the Western zones.[20]

Uniform denazification procedures for the US Zone were not provided until 7 July 1945.[21] They stipulated that:

> All members of the Nazi party who have been more than nominal participants in its activities, all active supporters of Nazism or militarism and all other persons hostile to Allied purposes will be removed and excluded from public office and from positions of importance in quasi-public and private enterprises … Persons are to be treated … as active supporters of Nazism or militarism when they have (1) held office or otherwise been active at any level from local to national in the party and its subordinate organizations, or in organizations which further militaristic doctrines, (2) authorized or participated affirmatively in any Nazi crimes, racial persecutions or discriminations, (3) been avowed believers in Nazism or racial and militaristic creeds, or (4) voluntarily given substantial moral or material support or political assistance of any kind to the Nazi Party or Nazi officials and leaders. No such persons shall be retained in any of the categories of employment listed above because of administrative necessity, convenience or expediency.[22]

By the end of September 1945, two new directives widened the scope of denazification in the US Zone to include a purge of doctors and lawyers, because they had held positions of wealth, prominence and influence in their respective communities, while also targeting economic elites from private businesses and industries. This widening of scope beyond public officials hinted at social transformation. It was the closest the OSS structuralist approach to denazification came to realization in directive form. Law No. 8, the directive dealing with business and industry,[23] was intended to prevent all former active party members from practising in professions such as law and medicine, or as managers in business and industry, and limit their employment to manual or routine work. It placed the burden of proof on the accused, and removed the administrative burden from Military Government, instead making use of German review boards that were to be appointed at the local level by town and city mayors or senior officials in rural districts (e.g. *Landrat*). German public opinion, except in business circles, seemed favourably inclined towards the policy, and the newly licensed trade unions, in particular, supported Law No. 8.[24]

Yet in practice, only when news of specific Nazis remaining in power or being appointed to top posts reached the American public was there a detectable intensification of denazification by Military Government, and even then usually only temporarily.[25] When placed formally in charge of a company, Military Government officials often felt they needed the knowledge and expertise of the Germans familiar with the factories. They often therefore kept the original owner or manager in the top post or, alternatively, formally replaced him while keeping him in a lower position. Numerous politically incriminated managers and executives often only had to bide their time a short while before they were restored to their former positions, whether secretly or by a change in the job classification.[26] Additionally, only those who were official members of the Nazi Party fell under the jurisdiction of Law No. 8,[27] a practice that ignored OSS warnings that some incriminated individuals had managed not to join the party while remaining in highly influential positions in business and industry, and that some individuals who had joined were at best nominal members.

US Military Government detachment officers therefore made what Dorn referred to as 'a concession of justice to utility' when they retained certain German officials liable for dismissal but whom they considered indispensable to the economy and to the administration of government.[28] They tended to rely on incumbent German government officials, industrial, utilities and business managers, technicians and workers whom they considered essential for the effective performance of their own Military Government responsibilities.[29] This practice did not meet with universal approval among US officials at the time. In the eyes of several critical observers of US denazification policy, anti-Nazi Germans, even inexperienced ones, could have been trained on the job to replace some of these technical and administrative experts.

One such critic of American policy who worked on General Eisenhower's staff, Donald B. Robinson, complained bitterly in May 1946 that the US Military Government gave unconvincing excuses of expediency for not purging Nazis from German governmental and industrial posts. He asserted that Nazi officeholders did all they could to reinforce the American Military Government's belief that only those who had such positions during the Third Reich could do the work, since no one else had been able to acquire experience during the previous twelve years.[30] According to Robinson, for Military Government officers in the field, 'it looked better to have the town in running order than to throw out a Nazi; and it seemed safer to have a hospital functioning perfectly than to give a Hitlerite superintendent the bum's rush'. He claimed further that most American Military Government officers did not recognize the political significance of their tasks.[31]

This tendency was exacerbated by the fact that the technical aspects of the implementation of denazification in the US Zone were handled initially by Military Government detachments, who took control of German municipalities and districts in the final phase of the war and during its immediate aftermath, and did not have any special denazification personnel among their ranks.[32] Many US Military Government staff were engineers and technocrats in their civilian lives back in the United States, a factor contributing further to pragmatic and expeditious approaches to getting the country running again rather than pursuing political vetting of those Germans whose work they often considered apolitical. They regarded denazification as burdensome and gave it lower priority than the more pressing tasks of reconstruction, such as securing housing, food, water and power supplies.[33]

Responsibility for vetting for the purges was given in July 1945 to a specially created Special Branch Section within the Public Safety Division of the Military Government. The USFET directive of 7 July 1945 required all Germans in the US Zone 'occupying "public office" and positions of importance in quasi-public and private enterprises' to submit a denazification questionnaire (*Fragebogen*) of some six pages with questions about their past employment, political affiliations and involvement in the Nazi party or its affiliate organizations.[34] These *Fragebogen* were sorted and categorized by Special Branch officers according to five levels of political incrimination described as Major Offenders, Offenders, Lesser Offenders, Followers, and lastly those Exonerated or not affected by the law. (Criminal incrimination, including the arrest and prosecution of those suspected of war crimes, was handled through a separate process). Then, depending on the suspected level of incrimination (above Follower, for example), individuals and the data they provided on the *Fragebogen* were to be investigated further. Depending on the findings, an appropriate punitive action was taken, varying from dismissal from a post, temporary confiscation of property, restrictions on future employment, temporary loss of passive and active voting rights, or simply a fine. In some serious cases they were to wait to be brought to trial, in which case they might be subject to arrest and depending on the final verdict, imprisonment.[35]

Some 28 per cent of all German adults in the US Zone had to have their *Fragebogen* vetted in order to be able to work in a position above a menial level. As the number of *Fragebogen* submitted increased and the need for US personnel to process them expanded, more and more capable military personnel were returning to the United States, while their replacements were fewer in number and less qualified, which further diminished the efficacy of the programme.[36] This discrepancy between the growing number of Germans who needed to be vetted and the shrinking number of US personnel sufficiently familiar with the different levels of suspected political incrimination in Nazi Germany created a backlog of cases, with often those suspected of the least incrimination being tried first in order to get them back to work. In the US Zone, Germans suspected of any incrimination were not supposed to be employed above the level of manual labour until after they had been through the denazification process. Depending on the results of their trial, if they were exonerated or found minimally culpable, they were assessed with fines or confiscation of property but allowed to return to work above the menial level. In order to continue to limit their influence, some could have restrictions imposed on the type of employment they could perform, in particular in the public sector or in positions of authority. Others could suffer temporary restrictions on their rights to vote or run for public office as a way of limiting their influence.[37]

Denazification proceedings against the least incriminated were undertaken in 1945 and early 1946, at a time when punishment was most stringent and when few extenuating circumstances were considered. On the other hand, by early 1946 US Military Government Denazification (Branch) officials had already become increasingly frustrated, as they received more and more complaints from German administrators, from businessmen in commerce and industry and from other branches of the Military Government, claiming that economic, governmental, and other professional services that were crucial to getting German administrations functioning smoothly again could not operate if there were too many dismissals due to Law No. 8. The size, difficulty and thankless nature of the denazification process ultimately led to a decision to transfer denazification proceedings to German tribunals under Military Government supervision, which came into effect in March 1946 with the promulgation of a new 'Law for Liberation from National Socialism and Militarism'.[38]

US Military Government did eventually revise denazification policies further from mid-1946 onwards, but in ways that gave rise to even more dissatisfaction among those Germans and Americans, who like the original OSS planners were committed to the concept of a fundamental purge and democratization of society. Following the passing in March 1946 of the 'Law for Liberation from National Socialism and

Militarism', which devolved responsibility to German tribunals, Military Government practice ceased to be consistent with the principles behind JCS 1067, issuing various amnesties, individual exceptions and downgrading categories of incrimination. The first US amnesty, the Youth Amnesty, came in July 1946 and absolved some 900,000 incriminated persons, born after 1 January 1919, from almost all responsibility and thus penalties. Subsequently, the 1946 Christmas amnesty absolved a further 1,000,000 relatively low-income and disabled persons, who had been charged as either Class II Offenders or Class III Lesser Offenders. Moreover, almost 80 per cent of the remaining 1,400,000 presumed offenders of all categories (i.e. all those except mere Followers) were eventually charged as the least incriminated Class III Lesser Offenders, and soon thereafter automatically demoted to the lowest category, Followers, because of a further amendment promulgated in October 1947.[39] As mere Followers, these Germans no longer had to fear being penalized at all. It was those Germans who had been categorized as more incriminated and whose cases were pushed back behind those of the least incriminated who benefitted most from the 1946 amnesties and received more lenient sentences, further discrediting the programme, both in the eyes of those who had been tried first, as well as in the eyes of those who had, whether they knew the term or not, understood denazification as a form of transitional justice.

The October 1947 amendment was promulgated after a large group of congressional representatives visiting Germany became convinced that denazification was impeding German recovery and its conclusion should be expedited. However, Congress remained dissatisfied, and in March 1948 the House Appropriations Committee refused to approve an Army appropriations bill unless denazification was halted. Under pressure from German denazification authorities not to close down the programme, the US Military Governor, General Lucius D. Clay, managed to retain some of the most highly incriminated of the remaining Class I and II Offenders for trial, but by now this represented only 10 per cent of the cases still pending. The remaining 90 per cent were simply reclassified downward at least two notches to the category of Followers. These amnesties and amendments worked to the benefit of those originally charged in the more incriminated categories: those presumed originally to be the least incriminated had been tried prior to these changes, during the period when more stringent and harsher punishments were imposed. Because of this sequence of prosecution, many of those who might or should have been removed from positions of authority in public administration as well as in private industry never even came to trial. Altogether, in 1949, in the US Zone, after denazification had been stopped, only 27,000 individuals were still ineligible to hold public office.[40]

The schematic nature of denazification measures, the Herculean bureaucratic task of sorting through so many questionnaires with few personnel with skills adequate to judge the German population's degree of incrimination, and the retreat into amnesties that the high number of people to be screened made inevitable, as well as the general trend to place administrative efficiency and economic recovery over denazification and democratization, all contributed to the shortcomings of the US denazification process and help to account for the repeated shifts in US policy. In total, denazification proceedings in the US Zone eventually resulted in 200,000 Germans having been categorized in the top three categories as 'Offenders'; the great majority of whom were ordered to pay fines or endure (temporary) employment or voting restrictions. This 200,000 was a number that, surprisingly perhaps, coincided with the total number of Nazi officials and supporters that the OSS had originally wanted to investigate in the first place, though it included many lesser offenders rather than, as the OSS had originally intended, those who were the most highly incriminated.[41]

German responses to denazification

Denazification involved a high degree of interaction between the US Military Government and German officials, all of whom initially were appointed by Military Government (or OMGUS) officials. Subsequently, after the first local elections in 1946, the Americans increasingly had to deal with elected German politicians and officials. As might be expected, denazification came to be supported less and less by Germans, even among those few who had been its most ardent supporters early on. Most German non-Nazi and anti-Nazi critiques of denazification at the time were based on its unfairness: those tried early on – the nominal members or Followers – received the toughest sentences, while more incriminated Nazi Party members and supporters often got much less severe punishments or never came to trial.[42] Support for denazification – albeit more the theory than its actual practice – came to be more and more limited to the Social Democrats and the Communists. Yet even these parties of the Left began to distance themselves from strict denazification by the time of the second post-war municipal elections in 1948, after seeing that their association with the policy was a political liability.[43]

According to William Griffith, the former denazification chief in Bavaria, some of the German officials assigned to the task of implementing denazification under the March 1946 Law for Liberation may have had too much in common on a socioeconomic level with the Nazis who would appear before them in the tribunals, and may have been too fearful of the type of 'social revolution that severe denazification would bring' to fully support the programme.[44] Yet there were also some Germans for whom denazification had implied 'penetrating behind Nazism to revolutionize the authoritarian society'.[45] For such Germans, including some who worked in the tribunals, the concept of denazification encompassed measures to achieve political change, including restitution for victims of Nazism, the removal of privileges granted earlier to Nazi Party members, such as access to specific housing and employment, together with rehiring opponents of the Nazis fired during the Third Reich, and awarding them the appropriate promotions they would have achieved during that period of dismissal.[46] Other Germans, like those described by Griffith, came to regard denazification as a temporary cleansing process, involving a brief respite from one's profession or pension, or the payment of fees, or a temporary formal but not actual step down from a leadership role in a business, or at most a brief prison sentence, that enabled former Nazis to return to public life. In fact, increasingly those few who were punished rarely suffered serious socioeconomic consequences, with private property rights quickly trumping the desire to prevent former Nazis from continuing to profit economically from their former party roles and privileges. As the political scientist, John Herz, wrote in 1948 in a provocative piece on the 'fiasco' of denazification:

> Nothing could be more revealing than the strange modification of meaning that the term "denazification" itself has undergone. While at first signifying the elimination of Nazis from public life, it has now in German everyday language come to mean the removal of the Nazi stigma from the individual concerned, that is, the procedure by which he gets rid of certain inhibitions or restrictions.[47]

This difference is crucial for understanding both US and German discussions and conflicts surrounding the practice of denazification. For Griffith, Herz, and many German critics of the failure to fully pursue denazification, long-term changes to the structure of German society were essential prerequisites to democratization, as well as a deeply rooted denazification. But neither occurred.

There are numerous examples of German city council debates in the US Zone on how far-reaching denazification should be. Council members discussed whether it should be more narrowly defined as a temporary removal of those politically incriminated from influential posts, or more broadly as an almost revolutionary democratization of society. The municipality, as the earliest form of restored German administration, operated under early Allied Control Council (ACC) guidelines reflecting a broader and stricter interpretation of denazification, including a regulation that revoked any economic or legal privileges of members of militaristic or paramilitary organizations and of their families.[48] However, when questions arose as early as 1947 about whether former Nazis should be reinstated in their previous positions in the town or city administration, after either having been through their denazification trials or while waiting to be tried, further guidelines were needed from the German state (*Land*) governments. Unlike the municipal councils by this time, the three state authorities in the US Zone still received instructions directly from the US Military Government. Municipalities needed to conform with the policies of the *Land* to have both consistent practices and the assurance that they would be backed up by higher authorities in the event of an appeal. German *Land* guidelines were long in coming and Military Government provided little guidance in the meantime.[49]

The increasingly hands-off Military Government position was formalized in Military Governor Lucius D. Clay's directive issued after the elections, and Secretary of State, James Byrnes' September 1946 Stuttgart speech on German reconstruction, in which he stated that the United States had now turned away from punitive measures. Clay's directive reflected the new policy of transition from direct control at the municipal or district level toward Military Government observation, inspection, reporting and advising, with veto powers exercised only at *Land* or increasingly, at zonal level, if social, economic or political measures were deemed in clear violation of Military Government objectives. This directive was scheduled to go into effect following the adoption of *Land* constitutions in late 1946.[50] This meant, however, that no German *Land*-level laws already existed that allowed former Nazis to be penalized by employment restrictions or even with the loss of private property. Without specific German legislation or overt intervention from Military Government, German courts, often staffed with personnel not known for their anti-Nazi stances, felt free to ignore regulations handed down earlier in the occupation, such as the ACC regulation discussed above, revoking former Nazis' economic and social privileges. The lack of effective legislation directed at the denazification of private property or of public sector positions, which increasingly as of 1947 was supposed to come from the German *Land* governments themselves, albeit in accord with Military Government directives, allowed for a dramatic level of reinstatements of those incriminated Germans previously dismissed from their public positions.[51]

This policy shift was visible at different levels. In the first months of the occupation, for example, the newly reinstated German municipal governments in Munich, Frankfurt and Stuttgart – all Military Government appointees – had forced various NSDAP activists and officeholders to perform manual labour. They were assigned to remove bombing debris, while other party members were forced to share or give up their housing either to generally non-incriminated individuals or to victims of the Nazi regime.[52] Local US Military Government officials, in the absence of any *Land* or zonal policy, had allowed this practice and had even required it in some cases. In Stuttgart, for example, the Military Government detachment commander held the city mayor personally responsible in late September 1945 for the procurement of Nazi labour for rubble removal, for overseeing the confiscation of Nazi Party members' housing and for its redistribution to non-incriminated Germans.[53] At least at this early stage, therefore, both German local government and local US Military Government detachments shared similar conceptions of denazification.

Following municipal elections in the US Zone in May 1946, however, the first elected city councils were forced to reconsider certain denazification practices after *Land* governments issued decrees such as one in Bavaria that housing should be returned to incriminated persons and that non-incriminated and persecuted persons would have to vacate the premises.[54] Not all Germans were willing to resign themselves to the abandonment of a broadly conceived denazification programme that was intended to revamp society, rather than only dismiss a relatively small number of incriminated 'outlaws'. The Munich Social Democratic Party (SPD) City Councillor, Rudolf Bössl, in May 1948, for example, reiterated his position that those without political incrimination, as well as victims of the Nazis, should receive priority in employment, housing and in other areas. Bössl's position, however, was already in the minority by that time. Thus, in Munich thereafter, any general preferential treatment of non-Nazis and anti-Nazis, as well as discriminatory treatment of former Nazis, ceased.[55] A similar development occurred in Stuttgart, where the city council tried in the spring of 1948 to take away from former members of the SS their continued right to own what during the Third Reich had been SS settlements in the city, paid for at the time largely with public subsidies. A German administrative court judged that the former SS members and their families had a right to retain their housing, or collect rent from others living there, because it recognized the legality of their purchases at the time they acquired their homes. Because the city council had no authority over the court, it was ultimately powerless, although it did pass an unenforceable motion appealing to the *Land* parliament to pass new legislation about such settlements and calling on the mayor's office to protect the politically non-incriminated from being evicted in favour of the incriminated.[56]

The lack of effective legislation as well as Military Government intervention therefore limited any more wide-ranging socioeconomic and bureaucratic denazification of society. The fact that this legislation needed to come from above, rather than from the local level, meant that grassroots attempts at fundamental changes in society could no longer succeed in systems that had once again become bureaucratic top-down structures, in both the German and the US occupation administrations.

Concluding thoughts

In summary, some people at the time, both Americans and Germans, did perceive denazification as more than a purge of individuals, as a broad policy that formed part of a programme to achieve structural change in German politics and society. But US policy, and perhaps even more so, the actual practice, changed over time for various reasons, some of which involved typical American pragmatism, or perhaps, at times, naiveté.

Framing denazification within the context of transitional justice highlights the duality between the demands of justice, restitution and morality required as part of the attempt to achieve fundamental political and social change, versus the necessities of reconstruction, stabilization, expediency and just getting things running again, in the midst of a military occupation. The wartime planners' ideal goals about the peace they believed they had fought for met head-on the post-war realities of the push to bring 'the boys' home and limit occupation costs, as well as the specifics of pushing for quick economic recovery and social stability in the midst of Cold War concerns about the potential appeal of Communism. Many of these general tensions were not unique to post-Nazi Germany and might be expected in other cases of regime change following a period of conflict or authoritarian rule. Thus a transitional justice framework lends itself well to developing a broader comparative perspective across time and place. It reveals some of the issues and the difficulties faced by US occupiers when they implemented denazification in post-war Germany, not only as a purge of individuals, in theory and practice, but also as an attempt at democratization that involved confronting the past in order to transform the present and future structure of society. In doing so it can contribute to a better understanding of regime change more widely, highlighting in particular its inherent problems and limitations.

Applying the concept of transitional justice to occupation studies in general may suggest that foreign powers cannot realistically hope to find truth, facilitate justice or hope for a deep, structural democratization of politics and society in the midst of military occupation. On the other hand, many contemporary debates over the development and nature of transitional justice seem to echo differences between the theory and practice of denazification and its many shortcomings. Denazification was, as conceived by the Allies, a prerequisite to reconciliation, but less a reconciliation between different groups of Germans – former Nazis, anti-Nazis and non-Nazis – than the idea of Germans reconciling themselves to their defeat, in order to achieve a rehabilitation that would make them worthy of re-entering the international community. Certainly, most Germans quickly became reconciled to membership in the western international community, especially in the midst of the Cold War, and the Western Allies became reconciled to the need for an economically strong West

Germany. But repression of the fact of complicity of so many Germans either directly in, or through indifference to, the persecution of Jews, Sinti and Roma, leftists, pacifists, gays, the disabled and so many 'others' forced to work in Germany and across Europe, surely delayed both the revelation of truth and the pursuit of justice. Those Germans least complicit with the Nazi regime usually had the most interest in denazification as transitional justice, but were the least likely, at least in their lifetimes, to find its realization.

In transitional justice theory, reconciliation is defined as a process 'through which a society moves from a divided past to a shared future'.[57] Although moving together toward economic reconstruction and re-establishing the rule of law did occur from the late 1940s onward in West Germany, recognition and acknowledgement of responsibility for the injustice and suffering caused by the Third Reich as a prerequisite to reconciliation in a divided society and a divided world, took much, much longer.

Notes

1 See Appendix B of the Foreign Relations of the United States for 1945 for the French reactions to and correspondence with the United States during and immediately following the conference. In particular, the French were troubled by insufficient reparations and by the prospect of the return of a centralized German government, but not by the 'four Ds' per se. See http://images.library.wisc.edu/FRUS/EFacs/1945Berlinv02/reference/frus.frus1945berlinv02.i0039.pdf (accessed 25 September 2017).

2 Although historians have used the 'four Ds' as a convenient shorthand to describe the decisions reached by the Allies at Potsdam, ever since Carl J. Friedrich first coined the phrase in 1948, they disagree as to exactly which four words to use (with German schools often teaching about five Ds), referring to 'disarmament', 'deindustrialization' or 'decentralization', in addition to 'demilitarization', 'denazification', 'decartelization' and 'democratization'. See http://howitreallywas.typepad.com/how_it_really_was/2009/11/the-4-ds-of-the-potsdam-agreement-1945.html (accessed 25 September 2017).

3 Elmer Plischke, 'Denazification Law and Procedure', *American Journal of International Law* 41, no. 4 (October 1947): 807. See also Clemens Vollnhals (ed.), *Entnazifizierung: Politische Säuberung und Rehabilitierung in den vier Besatzungszonen 1945–1949* (Munich: Deutscher Taschenbuch Verlag, 1991), 7–9.

4 See the Guidance Note of the Secretary General of the United Nations for the UN Approach to Transitional Justice, March 2010. Available online: www.un.org/ruleoflaw/files/TJ_Guidance_Note_March_2010FINAL.pdf (accessed 25 September 2017).

5 David Cohen, 'Transitional Justice in Divided Germany after 1945', in *Retribution and Reparation in the Transition to Democracy*, ed. Jon Elster (New York: Cambridge University Press, 2006), 59.

6 On the arrest and internment of Nazi Party members and sympathizers and how this related to denazification more generally, see the chapter by Andrew Beattie in this volume. On one of the consequences of war crime trials – the disposal of the bodies of those condemned to death – see the chapter by Caroline Sharples in this volume.

7 Lutz Niethammer, *Die Mitläuferfabrik: Die Entnazifizierung am Beispiel Bayerns* (Berlin and Bonn: J. H. W. Dietz Nachf., 1982), 12. Elmer Plischke, who had coordinated denazification policy in 1945, told Niethammer, decades later, that he had come up with the term, conceiving of it in this way.

8 British civil servants and political advisors responsible for post-war planning similarly believed that a broad range of measures would be necessary in order to 'stamp out a whole tradition' and achieve a 'change of heart' once Germany had been defeated, although, rather than using the term 'denazification', they referred to the need for 're-education' and 're-orientation'. See, for example, The National Archives, FO 371/39093, which includes a much-cited memo by the Foreign Office official John Troutbeck on 'The Regeneration of Germany', 3 December 1943. For a general overview of British thinking at the time, see Jill Jones, 'Eradicating Nazism from the British Zone of Germany: Early Policy and Practice', *German History* 8, no. 2 (1990): 145–62; Nicholas Pronay and Keith Wilson (eds), *The Political Re-education of Germany and Her Allies after World War II* (London and Sydney: Croom Helm, 1985).

9 Jon Elster, *Closing the Books: Transitional Justice in Historical Perspective* (Cambridge: Cambridge University Press, 2004), ix–xii.

10 Oskar N. T. Thoms, James Ron and Roland Paris, 'The Effects of Transitional Justice Mechanisms: A Summary of Empirical Research Findings and Implications for Analysts and Practitioners', University of Ottawa Centre for International Policy Studies Working Paper, 1008, 9. Available online: http://aix1.uottawa.ca/~rparis/CIPS_Transitional_Justice_April2008.pdf (accessed 9 June 2017).

11 On different Allied approaches to denazification, see Cornelia Rauh-Kühne, 'Die Entnazifizierung und die deutsche Gesellschaft', *Archiv für Sozialgeschichte* 35 (1995): 35–70.

12 See Rebecca Boehling, *A Question of Priorities: Democratic Reform and Economic Recovery in Postwar Germany* (Providence and Oxford: Berghahn Books, 1996), 209, 263. See also her essay, 'U.S. Cultural Policy and German Culture during the American Occupation', in *Germany and the United States in the Era of the Cold War, 1945–1990*, ed. Detlef Junker (New York: Cambridge University Press, 2004), 388–93.

13 Cohen, 'Transitional Justice in Divided Germany after 1945', 70.

14 Justus Fürstenau, *Entnazifizierung: Ein Kapitel deutscher Nachkriegspolitik* (Neuwied: Hermann Luchterhand Verlag, 1969), 103.

15 Vollnhals, *Entnazifizierung*, 16.

16 IfZ, Walter Dorn, *The Unfinished Purge*, unfinished manuscript, 12–3.

17 Ibid., 61.

18 Alfons Söllner (ed.), *Zur Archäologie der Demokratie in Deutschland: Analysen politischer Emigranten in amerikanischer Geheimdienst.* Bd. I: 1943–5, (Frankfurt am Main, 1982), 146–7.

19 William E. Griffith, 'Denazification in the United States Zone of Germany', *Annals of the American Academy of Political and Social Sciences* 267 (1950): 69–70. Griffith was a Special Branch officer in Bavaria during the first two years of the occupation and then chief of Special Branch in Bavaria in 1947/8.

20 Carl E. Schorske, 'The Dilemma in Germany', *Virginia Quarterly Review* 24, no. 1 (Winter 1948): 30.

21 Griffith, 'Denazification in the United States Zone', 69.

22 For the full text, see *Germany, 1947–1949: The Story in Documents* (Washington, DC: US State Department, 1950), 21–33.

23 Dorn, *Unfinished Purge*, 227.

24 John G. Kormann, *U.S. Denazification Policy in Germany 1944–1950* (Historical Division, Office of the US High Commissioner for Germany, 1952), 38–9.
25 Plischke, 'Denazifying the Reich', 168.
26 See Paul W. Gulgowski, *The American Military Government of United States Occupied Zones of Post World War II Germany in Relation to Policies Expressed by Its Civilian Government Authorities at Home during the Course of 1944/45 through 1949* (Frankfurt a, M: Haag + Herrchen, 1983), 341.2. See also Kormann, *U.S. Denazification Policy*, 39.
27 Dorn, *Unfinished Purge*, 230ff.
28 Ibid.
29 Plischke, 'Denazifying the Reich', 168.
30 Donald B. Robinson, 'Why Denazification Is Lagging', *American Mercury* 62 (May 1946): 565.
31 Ibid., 567–8.
32 Plischke, 'Denazifying the Reich', 159.
33 On the professional backgrounds, previous experience and training given to US Military Government staff, see the chapter by Susan Carruthers in this volume. On the pragmatic approach of many US officials once in Germany, see, for example, Drew Middleton, *The Struggle for Germany* (London and New York: Allan Wingate, 1949), 33. Middleton reported a US Military Government officer in Bavaria as saying in 1945: 'What's our policy in Germany? ... Brother, I don't know. Maybe the big wheels in Frankfort can tell you. They snow me under with all sorts of papers. How 'm I going to read them when I'm doing forty-eleven different things to get this burg running again?'
34 For the text of this directive, see http://images.library.wisc.edu/History/EFacs/GerRecon/Denazi/reference/history.denazi.i0006.pdf (accessed 25 September 2017) and for a summary of it from the Political Advisor to the Secretary of State, Robert Murphy, see https://history.state.gov/historicaldocuments/frus1945Berlinv01/d347 (accessed 27 September 2017).
35 Lutz Niethammer (ed.), Editor's commentary in Walter Dorn, *Inspektionsreise in der US-Zone* (Stuttgart, 1973), 88ff.
36 Harold Zink, The *United States in Germany, 1944–1955* (Princeton: D. Van Nostrand, 1957), 158–9.
37 Wolfgang Friedmann, *The Allied Military Government of Germany* (London: Stevens and Sons, 1947), 114. See also Joseph F. Napoli, 'Denazification from an American's Viewpoint', *Annals of the American Academy of Political and Social Sciences* 264 (1949): 120. See also Boehling, *A Question of Priorities*, 234–46.
38 Boehling, *A Question of Priorities*, 234.
39 Kormann, *U.S. Denazification Policy*, 127.
40 Griffith, 'Denazification in the United States Zone', 72–4.
41 Söllner, *Zur Archäologie der Demokratie in Deutschland*, 146–8.
42 Kormann, *U.S. Denazification Policy*, 140.
43 Ibid., 263.
44 Griffith, 'Denazification in the United States Zone', 74.
45 Artur Sträter, 'Denazification', *Annals of the American Academy of Political and Social Science* (1948): 51. In late 1948, this former Westphalian Minister of Justice published an article on denazification in the US Zone, in which he criticized 'the fact that nothing decisive has thus far been done in favor of indemnities for those persecuted by the Nazi regime, for the prisoners of the concentration camps, for the survivors of those murdered or deprived of their civil rights'.

46 Ibid.
47 John H. Herz, 'The Fiasco of Denazification in Germany', *Political Science Quarterly* 63, no. 4 (1948): 590.
48 Boehling, *A Question of Priorities*, 243–5.
49 Municipal-level Military Government detachments were withdrawn within thirty days of the 1946 elections, replaced by small security liaison units at the city (*Stadtkreis*) and district (*Landkreis*) levels. See 1 October 1945 USFET memorandum: 'Reorganization of Military Government Control Channels in Order to Develop German Responsibility for Self-Government', POLAD/730/ 20, 2 of 4, RG 84, Institut für Zeitgeschichte, Munich.
50 Seymour R. Bolten, 'Military Government and the German Political Parties', *Annals of the American Academy of Political and Social Sciences* 267 (1950): 56. Bolten was the executive officer of the Political Activities Branch of the Civil Affairs Division.
51 Boehling, *A Question of Priorities*, 245.
52 Stadtarchiv Frankfurt a. M., S1/25 Nachlass B. Müller.
53 Verfügung des amtierenden Bürgermeisters an das Wohnungsamt, 20 June 1945; Protokoll der Besprechung des OBs bei der Militärregierung, 25 September 1945, Hauptaktei 0052-2, Stadtarchiv Stuttgart. See also 'Arbeitskräfte für die Trümmerbeseitigung' and 'Tätigkeitsberichte der Stadtverwaltung an die Militärregierung', 10–16 November 1945 and 19–24 November 1945, Hauptaktei 6231-3, Stadtarchiv Stuttgart.
54 Decrees such as this had to have Military Government approval in this early phase and, more often than not, they were decrees for which Military Government wanted the Germans to take public responsibility. This occurred prior to the passage of the state (*Land*) constitutions and more state-level German self-government and before Clay's late 1946 directive on the transition to more of an advisory Military Government role.
55 Stadtratssitzung, 25 May 1948, RP 721/1, Stadtarchiv München.
56 Gemeinderatssitungsprotokoll, 26 May 1948, 423ff., Stadtarchiv Stuttgart.
57 David Bloomfield et al. (eds), *Reconciliation after Violent Conflict*, International IDEA Handbook Series (Stockholm: International Institute for Democracy and Electoral Assistance, 2003), 12. Available online: www.un.org/en/peacebuilding/pbso/pdf/Reconciliation-After-Violent-Conflict-A-Handbook-Full-English-PDF.pdf (accessed 25 September 2017).

5

The Allied Internment of German Civilians in Occupied Germany: Cooperation and Conflict in the Western Zones, 1945–9

Andrew H. Beattie

The extrajudicial internment of hundreds of thousands of civilians in occupied Germany has long been overshadowed by more spectacular Allied trials of Nazi criminals, by the broader denazification process and by the mass detention of German prisoners of war. Numerous accounts of the occupation mention the Allies' early arrests of German civilians, but do not go beyond noting that 'full internment camps and empty offices' were the results of initial denazification efforts.[1] Indeed, in the 1990s the most influential historian of denazification, Lutz Niethammer, described internment as a neglected 'stepchild' of scholarly research.[2] Since East Germany's collapse in 1989–90, much has been written about internment in the Soviet Zone of occupation, where about one third of internees died.[3] But much less has been written on the western zones.[4] There has also been very little comparative analysis across the zones. Discussion of the Soviet case often refers to what allegedly happened in the West, but draws on, and reproduces, idealized misunderstandings of western internment.[5] Among the western zones, the US Zone dominates, with scant attention paid to the other two.[6] Dissimilarities among the western zones are sometimes overlooked, not least because they seem to pale in comparison with those with the Soviet Zone. Yet intra-western differences are also occasionally exaggerated. As in other facets of the history of occupied Germany, there is thus considerable scope for a critical, comparative re-examination of the western zones.

This chapter examines internment in the three western zones, with occasional glances to the East. In what follows I want to do three things: first, to compare the three Western Allies' approaches to civilian internment; secondly, to discuss the diverse interactions between the occupiers and the occupied that internment produced; and finally to consider what all of this reveals about the occupation in general. Internment was more extensive in the western zones than is often recognized, and most extensive in the US Zone. Yet it was not a singularly American obsession to the extent that is sometimes claimed, but an important strategy of rule for all three western powers. It was a complex part of a complex occupation. In part, it supported the 'transitional justice' goals of truth, justice and democratization.[7] But it was also about security and power politics. It was inherently extrajudicial and was largely unregulated by international law in advance of the 1949 Geneva Convention Relative to the Protection of Civilian Persons in Time of War, which for the first time codified norms for the treatment of interned civilians, as opposed to Prisoners of War (POWs).[8] Internment was thus an illiberal measure applied in the name of liberalization. It was a temporary expedient, but one that lasted longer than is often recognized. Unsurprisingly, therefore, it prompted a range of responses from the German population. The interactions between Germans and the Allies in the everyday practice of internment demonstrate the diversity and dynamism of the relationship between the occupiers and the occupied. Ultimately, internment adds to the growing body of evidence that suggests that the occupation of western Germany was not the straightforwardly 'good occupation' it has widely come to be viewed as.[9]

The internment policies of the western powers

A comparative, transnational examination of the development of internment policy reveals that internment was not an American idea that the other powers begrudgingly adopted, as is often suggested. Following the creation of the tripartite European Advisory Committee in late 1943, it was the British who first proposed interning Germans, including Nazi Party functionaries and members of the SA (*Sturmabteilung*, the Nazi Stormtroopers), SS (*Schutzstaffel*, Himmler's elite guard) and the Gestapo (the secret state police).[10] Nevertheless, the Americans compensated for their belatedness with rigour. In July 1944, the German émigré social theorist Herbert Marcuse – who was serving in the US Army's Office of Strategic Services – proposed the internment of approximately 220,000 people.[11] Anglo-American military planners incorporated most of his proposal into a draft *Handbook of Military Government for Germany Prior to Defeat or Surrender* of 15 August 1944.[12] The date is important because it indicates that plans for mass internment cannot be attributed to the notorious intervention into US policy on Germany by US Treasury Secretary Henry Morgenthau in late August/early September. In the ensuing inter-departmental conflict, the War and State Departments objected to Morgenthau's proposals to summarily execute 'arch-criminals' and to pastoralize the German economy, but supported the detention of 'large groups of particularly objectionable elements, such as the SS and the Gestapo'.[13] In London, meanwhile, there were concerns about the feasibility of interning the huge numbers the Handbook envisaged, but leading Foreign Office advisors believed it 'better to aim pretty high and fall short of the aim if circumstances make this necessary, rather than to err on the side of leniency'. They suggested exempting certain groups, but adding others.[14] Mass internment was thus accepted as an element of occupation rule on both sides of the Atlantic and among the advocates of 'harder' and 'softer' approaches to Germany.

But what was its purpose? Internment is often misunderstood either as a preventative security measure to ensure the physical safety of Allied personnel against sabotage or as a form of pretrial custody for suspected war criminals, especially members of the organizations indicted before the International Military Tribunal (IMT) at Nuremberg.[15] It served both of these purposes. But it also performed broader, political functions. Various policy statements described it as promoting the 'eradication of Nazism', the 'dissolution and disbandment' of Nazi organizations and the 'disarmament' of paramilitary and security groups.[16] The common thread was the pacification and containment of the personnel of key organs of the Nazi state and the removal of obstacles to Allied rule. The wording of the Potsdam Agreement between Britain, the United States and the Soviet Union of August 1945 highlights that not only physical attacks were to be prevented: 'Nazi leaders, influential Nazi supporters and high officials of Nazi organizations and institutions and any other persons *dangerous to the occupation or its objectives* shall be arrested and interned'.[17] Internment was thus inherently political, a point overlooked in comparative discussions where the arrest of real or alleged 'obstacles' to Soviet objectives is seen as evidence of the Soviets' politicized misuse of internment. In mid-1946, Deputy Military Governor of the British Zone, Brian Robertson, reported that arrests 'as a result of subversive activities *committed since the Occupation*' continued to be made.[18] In 1947 the British and Americans interned numerous members of neo-Nazi networks, including 133 people following a raid in February.[19] Thus in every zone, internment was, above all, an attempt to exercise control over key representatives of the Nazi regime and to prevent and contain subversion, while it also helped clear the way for the installation of a new ruling elite that was more favourable to the occupiers' objectives.

While subversives were detained as security threats and war crime suspects were interned pending investigation and prosecution, the major mechanism for internment in the western zones was 'automatic arrest', which called for the detention of all occupants of certain ranks and positions within specified German organizations and professions. It is sometimes suggested that the French did not implement automatic arrest and that the Americans followed their own more punitive directive for the post-surrender period known as Joint Chiefs of Staff (JCS) 1067/6. In fact, all three western powers initially applied the arrest provisions of the final December 1944 version of the above-mentioned *Handbook* and, from April 1945, a new arrest order issued by Supreme Headquarters, Allied Expeditionary Forces (SHAEF). The latter called for the automatic arrest of a wide range of German intelligence, security, police and public officials, including all *Landräte* (district administrators), civil servants appointed to the *Höherer Dienst* (higher grade) since 1939, Nazi Party personnel down to *Amtsleiter* (departmental leaders) of the local branches (*Ortsgruppen*), and anyone occupying the rank of *Gemeinschaftsleiter* (held by cell leaders) or higher, equivalent ranks in the Hitler Youth, League of German Girls and other mass organizations, and officers and non-commissioned officers in the SS and the Waffen-SS (Armed SS) down to the rank of *Unterscharführer* (sergeant) and *Scharführer* (staff sergeant) respectively.[20] In late 1945 and early 1946, first the British, then the French and finally the Americans began to make modest reductions to the automatic arrest categories being used in their zones. There were two main reasons for this: on the one hand, the occupying powers were struggling to resource internment camps with burgeoning populations; on the other hand, in the words of an American official in March 1946, they had 're-estimated the security situation' and come to the conclusion that many internees did not pose a threat.[21]

The practice of internment in the western zones

The number of people interned by the Soviets is sometimes exaggerated. Estimates range as high as 260,000, but the number of people detained in the Soviet camps in occupied Germany was closer to 189,000, a figure that includes foreigners as well as Germans who were serving sentences handed down by Soviet military tribunals, leaving approximately 130,000 non-convicted German internees.[22] In contrast, the number of people interned by the western powers is frequently underestimated. The combined total for the western zones is often reported as having approximated 180,000 people.[23] But the actual figure was probably over 280,000. There were large differences in the numbers detained by the various western powers. The French interned only 21,500 people; the British at least 91,500 and possibly 100,000; while the Americans interned around 170,000.[24] Based on the 1946 zonal populations, Niethammer calculated that the Americans (and Soviets) interned approximately one in every 140 residents of their zones, while the French and British interned roughly one in every 260 or 280.[25] The differing internee numbers certainly reflected varying degrees of zeal among the western powers, but other factors also contributed to the high American numbers. It should be borne in mind that the German population was hardly sedentary in 1945 when most (but by no means all) arrests occurred. Many officials who feared capture or worse had fled into the interior of the Reich as the front approached. Additionally, many Waffen-SS and SS members were deployed far from home and fell into the hands of a different power from that which occupied their hometown. Such mobility helps to account for the fact that the Americans interned significant numbers of residents of the other western zones as well as of Germany's eastern territories that were now under Polish and Soviet control. In July 1946, only 54 per cent of the approximately 18,000 internees in the Darmstadt camp, the Americans' largest, were residents of the US Zone.[26]

There were further differences among the western zones in the practice of internment. The Americans displayed the greatest proclivity to physically abuse their prisoners, with beatings being common, particularly of new arrivals and especially in 1945.[27] Yet they also demonstrated the most generosity in allowing communication with the outside world and setting ration levels. No internees starved in their zone, unlike in the other western zones (and, to a much greater extent, the Soviet Zone).[28] The French made the most extensive use of internee labour for the purpose of reconstruction and the least effort to re-educate their internees.[29] Anglo-American re-education efforts should not be exaggerated, however: they were belated and variable. The limited attention to re-education reflected the belief that internees, as hardcore Nazis, were incapable of re-education, and that efforts had to focus on those Germans who were likely to be more responsive.[30]

Numerous similarities, but also important differences and changes over time were evident in the institutions that were responsible for implementing internment in the various zones. Arrests and a range of other functions were initially above all in the hands of the American and British Counter Intelligence Corps and the French *Direction Générale de la Sûreté*.[31] The British army ran the British camps until April 1946, when they became the responsibility of the Control Commission for Germany (British Element), specifically its Legal Division, Penal Branch, while Intelligence Division interrogated, categorized and released the detainees.[32] Until 1946 various US occupation armies and eventually only the Third Army ran internment camps in the US Zone, with its G-1 section (personnel) administering them and G-2 (military intelligence) responsible for detainees' interrogation and categorization. From late 1946, however, most camps in the zone were transferred to the administration of the new German state governments, specifically their ministries for 'political liberation' or 'special tasks', although the Office of Military Government (US Zone) and especially the Special Branch of its Public Safety Division maintained oversight and had to approve any releases.[33] A similar situation emerged later in some states in the decentralized French Zone, as camps were handed to the German state governments of Württemberg-Hohenzollern and the Saarland in 1947–8, but the *Sûreté* retained complete control of camps in Baden and Rhineland-Palatinate until they closed. Even where they remained under Allied control, German involvement in the provisioning or guarding of camps increased over time.

Allied practices of processing, assessing and releasing internees had much in common, but were also marked by important differences. All three western powers made extensive use of administrative reviews and reductions in automatic arrest categories, a fact that confirms that internment was not simply pretrial custody as is sometimes suggested. As an extrajudicial measure, it was only natural that nonjudicial methods determined most internees' fate. Only the British implemented what initially were American proposals to prosecute internees simply for being members of the organizations the IMT at Nuremberg had declared criminal (including the Nazi Party's leadership corps and the SS). But the German-staffed *Spruchgerichte* (summary courts) established for this purpose in 1947 judged less than one quarter of all internees in the British Zone. Apart from a much smaller number prosecuted by British military courts for individual war crimes (as opposed to membership of a criminal organization), the remainder, and thus the vast majority of British Zone internees, was handled nonjudicially.[34] In addition to the prosecution of members of the criminal organizations by the *Spruchgerichte*, another anomaly was the British introduction in 1947–8 of new purely administrative procedures for detaining 'dangerous' Nazis and militarists, mainly for senior personnel from groups not declared criminal by the Nuremberg tribunal, such as the SA, the Hitler Youth and the Wehrmacht, who could not be prosecuted by the *Spruchgerichte*. Most internees, however, were neither subjected to such procedures nor charged by German-staffed summary courts, but released without charge following nonjudicial British assessments of their Nazi-era incrimination and present-day risk. The assumption that tens if not hundreds of thousands of Germans were 'too dangerous to be at large' had underpinned 'automatic arrest' and internment from the beginning, but by January 1948 Robertson thought that of the approximately 400 people still held solely on that basis all but twenty to forty could be safely released.[35] The available evidence suggests that the key drivers of such British reassessments were a sense of procedural fairness, a commitment to the temporariness of and controls over extrajudicial detention, and a desire to alleviate strained resources.

Procedures in the US and French Zones did not distinguish so carefully between the punishment of members of criminal Nazi organizations and broader considerations, nor did the Americans or French seek to develop mechanisms for ongoing preventative detention of 'dangerous' Germans. Indeed, after abandoning plans to prosecute members of the criminal organizations, the Americans subjected internees to the same denazification processes that applied to the entire population of the US Zone under the March 1946 Law for the Liberation from National Socialism and Militarism (unlike in the British Zone, where denazification reviews were compulsory only for people seeking employment in particular fields). US Zone internees' cases thus came before *Spruchkammern* (denazification panels), which should not be confused with the *Spruchgerichte* in the British Zone.[36] Some less incriminated internees were released in advance of their hearing and were dealt with by panels in their hometowns. Yet many others were processed by dedicated *Spruchkammern* established at the internment camps and were kept interned until their verdict was finalized. Similar procedures were followed somewhat belatedly in the French Zone. In both cases, internees were judged not (or not primarily) on the basis of criminal offences or membership of the criminal organizations, but according to broader political-moral assessments of the behaviour, character and attitudes they had displayed during the Nazi years.

Irrespective of these and other differences, internment in all three western zones was marked by continuing arrests into 1946 and even 1947 (not least of personnel released from POW status), but also, and increasingly, by releases. In winter 1947–8, significant numbers were still interned: 13,766 in the British Zone in December 1947, 6,403 in the French Zone in January 1948 and 23,801 in the US Zone the same month. By the end of 1948, the number of internees in each zone had fallen to three figures, with just over one hundred left in the British Zone, a couple of hundred in the French Zone and several hundred in the US Zone, the majority of whom were now serving labour camp sentences imposed by *Spruchkammern*. The final internees in the proper sense, as opposed to such labour camp convicts, were released at the very latest by the end of 1949.[37] Extrajudicial internment was thus an extensive phenomenon that lasted throughout the occupation period preceding the establishment of the Federal Republic.

Interactions between the occupiers and the occupied

Internment produced diverse interactions between the occupiers and the occupied, which have not been systematically researched. Historians of Soviet internment often assume that western internment provoked little conflict or criticism. Meanwhile, studies of western internment highlight various criticisms but, drawing largely on Allied records, often do not go beyond generalizing about what 'the German side' thought.[38] In contrast, this chapter draws on German sources and highlights the diversity of

German responses and of German–Allied interactions. Here, too, there were basic similarities across the three western zones, but also some important differences.

The most obvious relationship produced by internment was that between the interning forces and the internees. It was inevitably dominated by conflict and criticism. Internees wanted to be released and generally believed they were unjustly detained.[39] This belief was due not least to the fact that the Allies had repeatedly announced their intention to punish war criminals, but said nothing publicly about extrajudicial internment until the Potsdam Agreement, and even thereafter the details remained sketchy. Moreover, it took months for internees to be interrogated and they often remained in the dark about the reasons for their arrest.[40] Mistreatment and tough conditions, including overcrowded and inadequate accommodation, insufficient rations and lack of communication with the outside world, heightened internees' antagonism towards their captors.[41] Yet diverse forms of cooperation developed. Individual internees were appointed to perform administrative and other duties within the camps, and these functionaries became a crucial interface between internees and the occupation forces. Some used their positions to undermine the Allies, for instance, by helping prisoners wanted for prosecution to escape. Others took on tasks that the Allies were reluctant or inadequately resourced to perform, becoming missionaries for democratization in the camps. For instance, future West German chancellor Kurt Georg Kiesinger, who had been a Nazi party member since February 1933 and had occupied an important position in the German Foreign Office after 1940, became a cultural officer in the American camp at Ludwigsburg-Oßweil, overseeing a 'camp university' and running a study group for youthful internees.[42] Still others were recruited by Allied intelligence services.[43] Trust levels increased over time, as demonstrated by the granting of furlough to large numbers of detainees in 1947–8.[44] While many internees continued to harbour resentment over their incarceration, a minority subsequently expressed gratitude for the opportunities (for reflection, retraining or refamiliarization with Christianity) that internment afforded. Kiesinger, for instance, spoke of having things 'that otherwise are almost always lacking: time and leisure to talk, listen, think through and discuss'.[45]

Internment created numerous further interactions between the occupiers and various other Germans. On the one hand, internees' families, friends, neighbours, colleagues and other sympathizers objected to their detention as much as internees themselves did. Such sympathizers petitioned Allied and German authorities, seeking information, contact, or internees' release. Some wives, however, were arrested or even shot for approaching camps from the outside.[46] On the other hand, many Germans welcomed the arrest of 'Nazis'. Indeed, some were actively involved. Émigrés who returned to Germany in Allied uniform were responsible for making arrests and interrogating detainees. Local antifascists reported Nazis' whereabouts or identity or arrested them and handed them over to the Allies.[47] Such activism reflected the fact that most German anti-Nazi resistance groups had envisaged the use of extrajudicial detention, albeit on varying scales. On the radical Left there was a degree of excitement in spring 1945 about the prospect of a 'changing of the guard in the concentration camps', and subsequent disappointment that more Nazis were not detained and that German antifascists were not more involved.[48]

Internment also entailed several forms of cooperation between the Allies and local and regional German authorities. In all three western zones, German authorities were called upon to contribute human and material resources. For varying reasons, they often did so reluctantly. According to the Red Cross, in autumn 1945 French Zone mayors were displaying insufficient 'good will' to provide the internment camps with food of adequate quantity and quality.[49] This reflected a sense that internees were the least deserving of the many groups needing to be fed. On the other hand, in later years city and regional governments were often unwilling to provide police or other personnel to guard internees. This reflected shortages of manpower (which internment exacerbated) as well as a disinclination to be associated with a legally problematic and increasingly unpopular policy.[50] In 1947–8, German authorities were also called upon to support internees' re-education and retraining. Both the occupying powers and the German authorities belatedly recognized the need to integrate internees into the labour market, civilian life and Germany's nascent democracy. They cooperated on this front, while also keeping a watchful eye over former internees after their release.[51]

The simultaneity of cooperation and conflict is perhaps best demonstrated by the responses of the major Christian churches to internment. Church opposition to denazification and war crimes trials is well known, and church leaders were among the fiercest critics of internment. To cite just one of many examples: at Easter 1946, a controversy erupted over American opposition to the reading of a pastoral message from the Catholic bishops of the Cologne and Paderborn church provinces (which covered much of the British Zone but also reached into the US and French Zones). The message claimed to express Germans' deep disappointment at the continuation of legal insecurity since the end of the war. In particular, it criticized the arrest

> of thousands of people without judicial verdict, their deprivation of liberty without the possibility of defence, without the possibility of contacting their closest relatives ... If an internal recovery (*innere Gesundung*) of the people (*Volk*) is to be initiated, then everything that reminds us of Gestapo, concentration camps and similar things must be banished from public life.[52]

In this vein, the Catholic and Protestant churches styled themselves as the only entities willing and able to stand up for helpless Germans in Allied hands and they competed with one another for the allegiance of internees and their families. Internment thus gave the churches a welcome opportunity to enhance their public profile. For all their criticism, however, the churches were also among the Allies' closest German collaborators, working with them to meet internees' spiritual, psychological and physical needs to an extent not widely recognized.[53]

The most extensive secular German cooperation occurred in the US Zone. As early as autumn 1945, the Americans displayed a unique preparedness to involve Germans. Their first formalized procedures for assessing internees' suitability for release, by Security Review Boards, incorporated German Review Boards in an advisory capacity. The German Boards supported internees' release in most cases they handled, indicating a general dislike of internment and a preparedness to give internees the benefit of the doubt.[54] Later, as already mentioned, only the Americans systematically transferred the camps' administration to regional German governments. The British considered, but rejected, such a move, due to security concerns as well as a sense of responsibility for what was an occupation measure. In the decentralized French Zone, the situation varied across the states: the camps passed into German hands in Württemberg-Hohenzollern and the Saarland, but in Baden and Rhineland-Palatinate they remained in French hands until the end, prompting calls from various quarters to bring the camps there under German control.[55] The Americans' transfer – beginning in autumn 1946 – was part of their broader delegation of responsibility for denazification to the Germans. It reflected the expectation that large numbers of people, especially internees, would be deemed Offenders or Major Offenders under the 1946 Law for the Liberation from National Socialism and Militarism. The internment camps were thus to become labour camps where such convicted offenders would serve sentences imposed by the *Spruchkammern*. Responsibility for administering most camps thus passed to the 'ministries for political liberation' that were executing the Liberation Law. The Americans held on to war crime suspects and hostile witnesses (mainly at Dachau). They also retained the authority to authorize releases, and 'automatic arrest' continued.[56] The state governments were thus in a delicate situation: on the one hand, they were acting as the extended arm of Military Government, which kept a close eye on their performance; on the other hand, they came under increasing pressure to release internees and struggled with the fact that they did not enjoy full authority and could be seen as responsible for implementing the occupiers' policies. While supporting tough sanctions against serious Nazis, they had reservations about continuing extrajudicial internment, and the camps' closure was in their financial and political interest.[57] The conflict generated by this asymmetrical cooperation was exemplified by the Americans' refusal to grant the International Committee of the Red Cross access to German-administered camps, against German wishes, a position that set the Americans apart from the more accommodating British and French.[58]

Conclusion

What does all of this tell us about the occupation more broadly? First, it suggests that occupied Germany was not so different from other instances of foreign rule at the time or more broadly in modernity. Encampment was and is a widely used tool of control, and the mid-twentieth century was its high point. Each occupying power had experience of interning unwanted and 'dangerous' people whether in the context of war or in their colonies.[59] Meanwhile collaborators and fascists were being interned across Europe.[60] The difference in the German context was that it was done to a defeated enemy by foreign occupying powers, which was perhaps convenient for those Germans who supported detention but were exempted from taking on responsibility for its implementation.

Second, internment shows that accounts of the western powers as benevolent, 'friendly enemies' downplay the coercive elements of their occupation. Niethammer's notion of a 'liberal occupation dictatorship' and contemporary British references to 'imposing liberalism by authority' better capture the complex reality.[61] Internment was a key coercive strategy of rule employed by every occupier, if to differing extents. Moreover, understanding, rather than glossing over internment relativizes perceived differences among the western powers: in particular, while the British lagged well behind the Americans in dismissing Germans from their positions, they were not quite so far behind in detaining key representatives of Nazism and German militarism, and while the French may have set less store in denazification and interned fewer Germans, they held on to proportionally more of those they had detained for longer than the Americans.

Third, internment sheds light on the continuing debate about whether the Allies accused the Germans of 'collective guilt'. It suggests that they eschewed undifferentiated charges against the entire nation, but did regard large groups (such as the SS or Nazi party leaders) as collectively suspect. Yet even the members of these groups were, eventually, individually assessed.

Fourth, internment suggests that the relationship between occupiers and occupied changed less radically over time than is often suggested. On the one hand, internment was never intended to be permanent, and the western powers began reducing arrest categories and releasing internees in the first post-war winter. It is thus misleading to suggest that the Cold War introduced a sudden, total abandonment of punitive policies in favour of integration. The Allies already felt firmly in control and were keen both to divest themselves of the administrative and material burden of maintaining the camps and to neutralize a growing source of public criticism. On the other hand, Allied security concerns lingered longer than is often recognized, as did internment in general.

Finally, like the overall occupation, internment met with diverse, if reasonably predictable, responses from various German social, political and religious groups, highlighting that German society was riven by divisions and hardly presented a united front vis-à-vis the occupiers. Like the occupation in general, internment produced cooperation, but also considerable friction and conflict, especially as it continued into 1947–8. This, too, was not just a function of Cold War politics, but reflected a growing sense that the state of exception that legitimated extrajudicial detention, like occupational rule generally, could not continue indefinitely. If Germans became increasingly forthright in criticizing the Allies, that is ultimately, perhaps, precisely what the Allies wanted.

Notes

1 Lutz Niethammer, *Die Mitläuferfabrik: Die Entnazifizierung am Beispiel Bayerns* (Berlin: J. W. H. Dietz, 1982), 12. On denazification and the punishment of war criminals, respectively, see the contributions of Rebecca Boehling and Caroline Sharples in this volume.

2 Lutz Niethammer, 'Alliierte Internierungslager in Deutschland nach 1945: Vergleich und offene Fragen', in *Von der Aufgabe der Freiheit: Politische Verantwortung und bürgerliche Gesellschaft im 19. und 20. Jahrhundert: Festschrift für Hans Mommsen*

zum 5. November 1995, ed. Christian Jansen, Lutz Niethammer and Bernd Weisbrod (Berlin: Oldenbourg Akademieverlag, 1995), 469.

3 For a recent overview, see Enrico Heitzer, 'Speziallagerforschung und Gedenkstättenarbeit seit 1990', in *Moskaus Spuren in Ostdeutschland 1945 bis 1949: Aktenerschließung und Forschungspläne*, ed. Detlef Brunner and Elke Scherstjanoi (Berlin: De Gruyter Oldenbourg, 2015), 109–19. On the politics of commemorating the Soviet camps, see Andrew H. Beattie, 'Gedenkstätten als Katalysatoren geschichtspolitischer Konflikte: Umstrittene Erinnerung und Konkurrenz der Opfer', in *Von Mahnstätten über zeithistorische Museen zu Orten des Massentourismus? Gedenkstätten an Orten von NS-Verbrechen in Polen und Deutschland*, ed. Enrico Heitzer, Günter Morsch, Robert Traba and Katarzyna Woniak (Berlin: Metropol Verlag, 2016), 84–94.

4 Monograph-length studies dedicated to western internment can be counted on one hand: Heiner Wember, *Umerziehung im Lager: Internierung und Bestrafung von Nationalsozialisten in der britischen Besatzungszone Deutschlands* (Essen: Klartext, 1991); Christa Horn, *Die Internierungs- und Arbeitslager in Bayern 1945–1952* (Frankfurt/Main: Peter Lang, 1992); Karl Hüser, *'Unschuldig' in britischer Lagerhaft? Das Internierungslager No. 5 Staumühle 1945–1948* (Cologne: SH-Verlag, 1999); Kathrin Meyer, *Entnazifizierung von Frauen: Die Internierungslager der US-Zone Deutschlands 1945–1952* (Berlin: Metropol, 2004); Kristen J. Dolan, 'Isolating Nazism: Civilian Internment in American Occupied Germany, 1944–1950' (PhD diss., University of North Carolina, Chapel Hill, 2013).

5 See, for instance, Bettina Greiner, *Suppressed Terror: History and Perception of Soviet Special Camps in Germany* (Lanham, MD: Lexington Books, 2014).

6 For an example of a comparative discussion dominated by the US Zone, see Niethammer, 'Alliierte Internierungslager'.

7 On transitional justice, see also the contribution by Rebecca Boehling in this volume.

8 Convention (IV) Relative to the Protection of Civilian Persons in Time of War, Geneva, 12 August 1949. Available online: https://ihl-databases.icrc.org/applic/ihl/ihl.nsf/vwTreaties1949.xsp (accessed 18 January 2017). See Jordan J. Paust, 'Judicial Power to Determine the Status and Rights of Persons Detained Without Trial', *Harvard International Law Journal* 44, no. 2 (2003): 505–14; Mark Lewis, *The Birth of the New Justice: The Internationalization of Crime and Punishment, 1919–1950* (Oxford: Oxford University Press, 2014), ch. 8; and Peter Stirk's chapter in this volume.

9 See Susan L. Carruthers, *The Good Occupation: American Soldiers and the Hazards of Peace* (Cambridge, MA: Harvard University Press, 2016), and Carruthers's chapter in this volume.

10 'Terms of Surrender for Germany – Memorandum by the United Kingdom Representative, 15 January 1944, Annex 2: "Draft German Armistice"', in *Dokumente zur Deutschlandpolitik*, Series I, vol. 5: *Europäische Beratende Kommission, 15. Dezember 1943 bis 31. August 1945*, ed. Herbert Elzer (Munich: R. Oldenbourg, 2003), 741.

11 Herbert Marcuse, 'Dissolution of the Nazi Party and Its Affiliated Organizations', 22 July 1944, in Franz Neumann, Herbert Marcuse and Otto Kirchheimer, *Secret Reports on Nazi Germany: The Frankfurt School Contribution to the War Effort*, ed. Raffaele Laudani (Princeton, NJ: Princeton University Press, 2013), 256–9.

12 (Draft) Handbook of Military Government for Germany, 15 August 1944, The National Archives of the United Kingdom (TNA), FO 371/39166. See Tables D, E and F, as well as ch. II, paragraphs 22 and 23, for the positions subject to detention.

13 'Secretary of Treasury (Morgenthau) to the President: Suggested Post-Surrender Program for Germany', 5 September 1944, and 'Riddleberger to Secretary of State', 4 September 1944, both in *Foreign Relations of the United States: The Conference at Quebec 1944* (Washington, DC: Government Printing Office, 1972), 105–7, 94.

14 J. M. Troutbeck to Charles Peak, SHAEF, with Detailed Criticisms of 'Handbook of Military Government for Germany', 29 August 1944, TNA, FO 371/39166.

15 For an example of the former view, see Horn, *Die Internierungs- und Arbeitslager*, esp. 19, 241; for an example of the latter, see Bertram Resmini, 'Lager der Besatzungsmächte in Rheinland-Pfalz: Kriegsgefangene, Internierte und Verschleppte im Rheinland nach dem Zweiten Weltkrieg', *Jahrbuch für westdeutsche Landesgeschichte* 19 (1993): 602.

16 See, for example, 'Directive No. 7: Dissolution and Disbandment of Nazi Organisations, etc.', October 1944, in Elzer (ed.), *Dokumente zur Deutschlandpolitik*, 877; SHAEF Office of the Chief of Staff, *Handbook for Military Government in Germany Prior to Defeat or Surrender*, December 1944, Part III, ch. 2. Available online: http://cgsc.cdmhost.com/cdm/ref/collection/p4013coll9/id/11 (accessed 13 January 2017).

17 'Extracts from the Report on the Tripartite Conference of Berlin (Potsdam)', 2 August 1945, in *Documents on Germany under Occupation, 1945–1954*, ed. Beate Ruhm von Oppen (London: Oxford University Press, 1955), 43 (emphasis added).

18 Report on Persons Held in Internment Camps, sent by Robertson to Sir Arthur Street, Control Office for Germany and Austria, London, 2 July 1946, 3, TNA, FO 938/345 (emphasis added).

19 Perry Biddiscombe, 'Operation Selection Board: The Growth and Suppression of the Neo-Nazi "Deutsche Revolution" 1945–47', *Intelligence and National Security* 11, no. 1 (1996): 72, 74.

20 SHAEF Office of the Chief of Staff, *Handbook for Military Government in Germany Prior to Defeat or Surrender*, December 1944; SHAEF directive, 'Arrest and Detention – Germany', 13 April 1945, reprinted in Meyer, *Entnazifizierung von Frauen*, 262–4.

21 Wember, *Umerziehung im Lager*, 47–9; Rainer Möhler, 'Internierung im Rahmen der Entnazifizierungspolitik in der französischen Besatzungszone', in *Internierungspraxis in Ost- und Westdeutschland nach 1945*, ed. Renate Knigge-Tesche, Peter Reif-Spirek and Bodo Ritscher (Erfurt: Gedenkstätte Buchenwald, 1993), 63–4; Meyer, *Entnazifizierung von Frauen*, 66–8. See also discussions about such modifications in the context of the Allied Control Authority's (ACA) failed attempt to develop a quadripartite arrest policy, as documented in the 1945–6 Minutes of the ACA's Nazi Arrest and Denazification Subcommittee, TNA, FO 1005/635 and 636. Quotation from Minutes of the 21st Meeting, 13 March 1946, 1, TNA, FO 1005/636.

22 Klaus-Dieter Müller, 'Verbrechensahndung und Besatzungspolitik: Zur Rolle und Bedeutung der Todesurteile durch Sowjetische Militärtribunale', in *Todesurteile sowjetischer Militärtribunale gegen Deutsche (1944–1947): Eine historisch-biographische Studie*, ed. Andreas Weigelt, Klaus-Dieter Müller, Thomas Schaarschmidt and Mike Schmeitzner (Göttingen: Vandenhoeck & Ruprecht, 2015), 36.

23 Wolfgang Friedmann, *The Allied Military Government of Germany* (London: Stevens & Sons, 1947), 332; Donald M. McKale, *Nazis after Hitler: How Perpetrators of the Holocaust Cheated Justice and Truth* (Lanham, MD: Rowman & Littlefield, 2012), 99.

24 Möhler, 'Internierung', 64; Wember, *Umerziehung im Lager*, 7; Meyer, *Entnazifizierung von Frauen*, 98.

25 Niethammer, 'Alliierte Internierungslager', 474.
26 Falko Heinl, '"Das schlimme Lager, in dem man gut leben konnte": Das Internierungslager in Darmstadt von 1946 bis 1949' (MA diss., Technische Universität Darmstadt, 2005), 34.
27 See Entwurf für eine Denkschrift über Vorgänge im Interniertenlager 74 (in Ludwigsburg), September 1946, Hauptstaatsarchiv Stuttgart (HStAS), Nachlaß Gottlob Kamm, Q1/16, no. 5; Horn, *Die Internierungs- und Arbeitslager*, 161–3, 165, 173–5; Meyer, *Entnazifizierung von Frauen* 122–5; Wember, *Umerziehung im Lager*, 92–6; Alyn Beßmann, '"Der sozusagen für Euch alle im KZ sitzt": Britische Internierungspraxis im ehemaligen KZ Neuengamme und deutsche Deutungsmuster', and Andreas Ehresmann, 'Die frühe Nachkriegsnutzung des Kriegsgefangenen- und KZ-Auffanglagers Sandbostel unter besonderer Betrachtung des britischen No. 2 Civil Internment Camp Sandbostel', both in *Beiträge zur Geschichte der nationalsozialistischen Verfolgung in Norddeutschland*, vol. 12: *Zwischenräume: Displaced Persons, Internierte und Flüchtlinge in ehemaligen Konzentrationslagern*, ed. KZ-Gedenkstätte Neuengamme (Bremen: Edition Temmen, 2010), 40, 26. Cf. Andrew H. Beattie, 'L'internamento dei civili tedeschi dopo la seconda guerra mondiale e la questione della violenza', trans. Camilla Poesio, in *Oltre il 1945: Violenza, conflitto sociale, ordine pubblico nel dopoguerra europea*, ed. Enrico Acciai, Guido Panvini, Camilla Poesio and Toni Rovatti (Rome: Viella, 2017), 105–20.
28 On communication, see Horn, *Die Internierungs- und Arbeitslager*, 220–7; Meyer, *Entnazifizierung von Frauen*, 139–40; Wember, *Umerziehung im Lager*, 136–40; Rainer Möhler, *Entnazifizierung in Rheinland-Pfalz und im Saarland unter französischer Besatzung von 1945 bis 1952* (Mainz: v. Hase & Koehler, 1992), 369, 384. Cf. Andrew H. Beattie, 'Die alliierte Internierung im besetzen Deutschland und die deutsche Gesellschaft: Vergleich der amerikanischen und der sowjetischen Zone', *Zeitschrift für Geschichtswissenschaft* 62, no. 3 (2014): 243–4; Andrew H. Beattie, '"Lobby for the Nazi Elite"? The Protestant Churches and Civilian Internment in the British Zone of Occupied Germany, 1945–1948', *German History* 35, no. 1 (2017): 54–7. On rations and starvation, see Horn, *Die Internierungs- und Arbeitslager*, 217–20; Meyer, *Entnazifizierung von Frauen*, 112–20; Wember, *Umerziehung im Lager*, 112–6; Beßmann, 'Der sozusagen für Euch alle im KZ sitzt', 38–41; Ehresmann, 'Die frühe Nachkriegsnutzung des Kriegsgefangenen- und KZ-Auffanglagers Sandbostel', 26; Camps d'internés civils, politiques et administratifs, 6 October 1945, 2–4, Archives of the International Committee of the Red Cross, Geneva (ACICR), B G 44 02-058.01; Rainer Möhler, 'Die Internierungslager in der französischen Besatzungszone', in *Speziallager – Internierungslager: Internierungspolitik im besetzten Nachkriegsdeutschland*, ed. Gedenkstätte Berlin-Hohenschönhausen (Berlin: Gedenkstätte Berlin-Hohenschönhausen 1996), 58; Möhler, *Entnazifizierung in Rheinland-Pfalz und im Saarland*, 384.
29 On internee labour, see Horn, *Die Internierungs- und Arbeitslager*, 209–17; Ulrich Müller, 'Die Internierungslager in und um Ludwigsburg 1945–1949', *Ludwigsburger Geschichtsblätter* 45 (1991): 185–7; Meyer, *Entnazifizierung von Frauen*, 140–1; Wember, *Umerziehung im Lager*, 133–6; Camps d'internés civils, politiques et administratifs, 6 October 1945, ACICR, B G 44 02-058.01; Möhler, *Entnazifizierung in Rheinland-Pfalz und im Saarland*, 41 (fn. 49), 372; Resmini, 'Lager der Besatzungsmächte in Rheinland-Pfalz', 616.
30 On re-education and democratization in the camps, see Horn, *Die Internierungs- und Arbeitslager*, 204–6; Meyer, *Entnazifizierung von Frauen*, 141–2, 171–202; Wember,

Umerziehung im Lager, 167–77; Beßmann, 'Der sozusagen für Euch alle im KZ sitzt', 43–6; Ehresmann, 'Die frühe Nachkriegsnutzung des Kriegsgefangenen- und KZ-Auffanglagers Sandbostel', 27–30.

31 Horn, *Die Internierungs- und Arbeitslager*, 34–43.

32 Wember, *Umerziehung im Lager*, 120–3.

33 Meyer, *Entnazifizierung von Frauen*, 70–1.

34 The summary courts delivered ca. 19,000 judgements, overwhelmingly against internees. See Wember, *Umerziehung im Lager*, 276–357; Sebastian Römer, *Mitglieder verbrecherischer Organisationen nach 1945: Die Ahndung des Organisationsverbrechens in der britischen Zone durch die Spruchgerichte* (Frankfurt/Main: Peter Lang, 1995).

35 See Wember, *Umerziehung im Lager*, 85–6; Robertson to Permanent Under-Secretary of State, Foreign Office (German Section), Re: Policy in the British Zone of Germany with Regard to Detention Without Trial and Extradition', 12 January 1948, TNA, FO 1032/2230.

36 In fact, the *Spruchgerichte* were initially called *Spruchkammer*, but the former designation quickly superseded the latter. Compare 'Ordinance 69: Trial of members of Criminal Organizations/Verordnung Nr. 69: Prozeß gegen Angehörige verbrecherischer Organisationen', 1 November 1946, *Military Government Gazette Germany, British Zone of Control* 16 (1947): 405; and 'Verordnung über die Errichtung der Dienststelle eines Generalinspekteurs in der britischen Zone für die Spruchgerichte zur Aburteilung der Mitglieder der in Nürnberg für verbrecherisch erklärten Organisationen vom 17. Februar 1947', *Verordnungsblatt für die Britische Zone* 2 (30 April 1947): 22. Both available online: http://deposit.d-nb.de/online/vdr/rechtsq.htm (accessed 27 July 2017).

37 Wember, *Umerziehung im Lager*, 371–2; Möhler, *Entnazifizierung in Rheinland-Pfalz und im Saarland*, 386; Möhler, 'Die Internierungslager in der französischen Besatzungszone', 57; Meyer, *Entnazifizierung von Frauen*, 102.

38 Karl Wilhelm Fricke, '"Konzentrationslager, Internierungslager, Speziallager": Zur öffentlichen Wahrnehmung der NKWD/MWD-Lager in Deutschland', in *Instrumentalisierung, Verdrängung, Aufarbeitung: Die sowjetischen Speziallager in der gesellschaftlichen Wahrnehmung, 1945 bis heute*, ed. Petra Haustein, Annette Kaminsky, Volkhard Knigge and Bodo Ritscher (Göttingen: Wallstein, 2006), 52; Kathrin Meyer, 'Die Internierung von NS-Funktionären in der US-Zone Deutschlands', *Dachauer Hefte* 19 (2003): 47.

39 See Horn, *Die Internierungs- und Arbeitslager*, 240; Wember, *Umerziehung im Lager*, 52–3; Beßmann, 'Der sozusagen für Euch alle im KZ sitzt', 47–9; Beattie, 'Die alliierte Internierung', 245.

40 Wember, *Umerziehung im Lager*, 102, 182.

41 See the stinging, resentment-laden criticism in Ernst von Salomon, *Der Fragebogen* (Reinbek bei Hamburg: Rowohlt, 2011; 1st edn. 1951), 518–668.

42 Wember, *Umerziehung im Lager*, 106–7; Beßmann, 'Der sozusagen für Euch alle im KZ sitzt', 42–3; Meyer, *Entnazifizierung von Frauen*, 190–1; Philipp Gassert, *Kurt Georg Kiesinger 1904–1988: Kanzler zwischen den Zeiten* (Munich: Deutsche Verlags-Anstalt, 2006), 166–75.

43 Thomas Boghardt, 'Dirty Work? The Use of Nazi Informants by U.S. Army Intelligence in Postwar Europe', *Journal of Military History* 79, no. 2 (2015): 401, 404, 410. On Allied recruitment of more or less compromised German personnel, see the chapters of Dominik Rigoll and Michael Wala in this volume.

44 Ordinariat des Erzbistums München und Freising to Seelsorgeklerus der Erzdiözese München, 15 March 1948, Archiv des Erzbistums München und Freising, Nachlaß Faulhaber, no. 8533/2; Der Lagerältester, Internierungs- und Arbeitslager Dachau, to Bishop Hans Meiser, 24 March 1948, Landeskirchliches Archiv Nuremberg, Landeskirchenamt, no. 167; Möhler, *Entnazifizierung in Rheinland-Pfalz und im Saarland*, 369.
45 Wember, *Umerziehung im Lager*, 184–93, 229–34; Gassert, *Kurt Georg Kiesinger*, 170.
46 Beattie, 'Die alliierte Internierung', 246–7; Wember, *Umerziehung im Lager*, 52; Meyer, *Entnazifizierung von Frauen*, 125, 139; Hüser, *'Unschuldig' in britischer Lagerhaft?*, 43–4.
47 Müller, 'Die Internierungslager in und um Ludwigsburg', 172; Horn, *Die Internierungs- und Arbeitslager*, 37–8; Meyer, *Entnazifizierung von Frauen*, 54–6.
48 Werner Hansen (Cologne) to Willi Eichler, 25 May 1945, in *Deutschland im ersten Nachkriegsjahr: Berichte von Mitgliedern des Internationalen Sozialistischen Kampfbundes (ISK) aus dem besetzten Deutschland 1945/46*, ed. Martin Rüther, Uwe Schütz and Otto Dann (Munich: K. G. Saur, 1998), 174.
49 Camps d'internés civils, politiques et administratifs, 6 October 1945, 2–4, ACICR, B G 44 02-058.01.
50 See, for instance, Oberbürgermeister der Stadt Ulm to Innenministerium Württemberg-Baden, re. Abordnung von Polizeikräften des Vollzugsdienstes, 6 September 1946; and Landespolizei Württemberg, Direktion, to Innenministerium Württemberg-Baden, re. Bewachung der Interniertenlager, 22 July 1946, both in HStAS, EA 2/301, no. 41.
51 For instance, the Minister for the Interior of North Rhine-Westphalia instructed district administrators (Kreisräte and Landräte) and lord mayors (Oberbürgermeister) on 1 March 1948 to keep an eye on internees released from the US Zone. Wember, *Umerziehung im Lager*, 243–4.
52 Bischöfe der Kölner und Paderborner Kirchenprovinzen, Hirtenbrief über die politischen und wirtschaftlichen Verhältnisse, 27 March 1946, in *Hirtenbriefe und Ansprachen zu Gesellschaft und Politik 1945–1949*, ed. Wolfgang Löhr (Würzburg: Echter Verlag, 1985), 97. For church criticism of French Zone internment, see Möhler, *Entnazifizierung in Rheinland-Pfalz und im Saarland*, 367–8. For initial responses of Catholic clergy, see Johannes Kuber's chapter in this volume.
53 See Beattie, 'Die alliierte Internierung', 253–4; Beattie, 'Lobby for the Nazi elite?'
54 Horn, *Die Internierungs- und Arbeitslager*, 56–69.
55 Wember, *Umerziehung im Lager*, 123–7; Möhler, 'Die Internierungslager in der französischen Besatzungszone', 53; Peter Fäßler, 'Lahr unter französischer Besatzung 1945–1952', in *Geschichte der Stadt Lahr*, vol. 3: *Im 20. Jahrhundert*, ed. Gabriele Bohnert and Dieter Geuenich (Lahr: Kaufmann, 1993), 200.
56 Horn, *Die Internierungs- und Arbeitslager*, 74–102; Meyer, *Entnazifizierung von Frauen*, 109.
57 See the statement by the Minister for Political Liberation in Württemberg-Baden, Gottlob Kamm, in the state parliament on 25 April 1947, *Verhandlungen des Württemberg-Badischen Landtags, Wahlperiode 1946–1950: Protokoll-Band I, 1.–25. Sitzung* (Stuttgart: Ernst Klett, 1948), 355. Cf. Beattie, 'Die alliierte Internierung', 252.
58 See ICRC Special Delegation Berlin, Memorandum Concerning Visits of Civilian Internment Enclosures Located in the US Zone of Germany by Delegates of the International Committee of the Red Cross, 4 June 1947, ACICR, B G 44 02-054.04; Meyer to ICRC Central Agency for POWs, 26 June 1947, ACICR, B G 44 02-054.06;

Gallopin to Gower, 17 October 1947 and 4 May 1948; Gower to Gallopin, 2 April 1948, ACICR, B G 44 02-055. Cf. Burkhard Schoebener, 'Dokumentation einer Kontroverse: Die Bemühungen des Internationalen Roten Kreuzes 1946/47 um den völkerrechtlichen Schutz deutscher Zivilinternierter in der US-Zone', *Die Friedenswarte: Journal of International Peace and Organization* 68 (1990): 140–51.

59 See, for instance, Aidan Forth, 'Britain's Archipelago of Camps: Labor and Detention in a Liberal Empire, 1871–1903', *Kritika: Explorations in Russian and Eurasian History* 16, no. 3 (2015): 651–80.

60 See, for instance, Helen Grevers and Lawrence Van Haecke, 'The Use of Administrative Internment after WWII: The Different Policies of the Belgian and Dutch Governments', in *Justice in Wartime and Revolutions: Europe, 1795–1950*, ed. Margo de Koster, Hervé Leuwer, Dirk Luyten and Xavier Rousseaux (Brussels: Algemeen Rijskarchief, 2012), 277–94; Joël Kotek and Pierre Rigoulot, *Das Jahrhundert der Lager: Gefangenschaft, Zwangsarbeit, Vernichtung* (Berlin: Propyläen, 2000), 468–71. On the broader context, see István Deák, Jan T. Gross and Tony Judt (eds), *The Politics of Retribution in Europe: World War II and Its Aftermath* (Princeton, NJ: Princeton University Press, 2000).

61 Niethammer, *Die Mitläuferfabrik*, 653; Control Commission for Germany (British Element) Intelligence Review No. 1, 12 December 1945, in *Documents on British Policy Overseas*, Series I, vol. 5: *Germany and Western Europe, 11 August–31 December 1945* (London: Her Majesty's Stationery Office, 1990), 440.

6

What Do You Do with a Dead Nazi? Allied Policy on the Execution and Disposal of War Criminals, 1945–55

Caroline Sharples

In the aftermath of the Second World War, thousands of former Nazis were prosecuted for crimes against peace, conspiracy, war crimes and crimes against humanity. The high profile quadripartite International Military Tribunal (IMT) at Nuremberg, held between November 1945 and October 1946, focused on the remnants of the Nazi leadership (Hermann Göring et al.), while a plethora of trials against concentration camp staff, doctors, industrialists and other compromised individuals were conducted by each of the Allies within their respective zones. Many of these defendants received the death penalty for their crimes.

In western Germany, three key centres emerged for dispatching condemned prisoners: Hameln in the British Zone, Rastatt in the French Zone and Landsberg in the US Zone. Collectively, these sites accounted for the execution of nearly 500 Nazi war criminals.[1] Most were hanged, but some were shot or guillotined depending on the available manpower, resources and sensibilities of the relevant Allied power. The method of execution, however, was just one of many points of variation between the zones in how Nazi bodies were disposed. The policies adopted by the three Western Allies affected how the National Socialist legacy was remembered long into the future, both in private by the families of those executed as well as in public by Nazi sympathizers, the popular press and West Germans more generally.

The impact of these war crimes proceedings, and the sense of German victimhood generated by the wider denazification process, is well documented.[2] Norbert Frei and Ronald Webster, meanwhile, have provided detailed analyses of the levels of public support shown toward condemned prisoners, and the general amnesty campaign that had emerged in West Germany by the early 1950s.[3] Yet the results of these trials reveal more than just public criticism of war crimes proceedings, or reluctance to countenance the existence of a wider circle of perpetrators beyond the immediate Nazi leadership. Tracing the implementation of trial sentences provides important insights into the limits of Allied planning, the impact of growing ideological tensions over occupation policy and the difficult relationship between the occupiers and the occupied. The physical enactment of the death sentence is typically taken as a neat end point to the perpetrators' story; little attention has been paid to how the Allies implemented these procedures, or how they coped with the aftermath. One exception to this trend is Richard Evans, who discusses Allied attitudes towards capital punishment, the drafting of clemency procedures and public reactions to executions for crimes against the occupation itself, such as the post-war possession of firearms. However, while he acknowledges zonal variations in execution methods, he does not consider the disposal of the resultant corpses.[4] Elsewhere, Norman Goda offers a detailed exploration of conditions in Spandau Prison and exposes the gaps in Allied preparations for holding (living) war criminals. Goda argues, convincingly, that the Allies were so preoccupied with the idea of executing the leading IMT defendants that they paid no serious attention to how, or where, the remainder of these men might serve their prison sentences.[5] Goda's argument, however, can be pushed further: while capital punishment was certainly anticipated for the majority of the Nuremberg defendants, even this form of sentencing was poorly conceived and subject to protracted quadripartite discussions.

Considering the fate of executed Nazis underscores the challenges of 'doing occupation', especially the difficulty of balancing an ethical treatment of the dead with the realities of a post-conflict environment. Drawing upon policy documents, memoranda and reports from the UK National Archives, this chapter explores the fate of the IMT defendants and the results of the western zonal trials to illustrate the variations in Allied policy. Consequently, the diversity of the occupation experience demonstrates that it is highly misleading to couch this period in simplistic terms of East versus West. Moreover, examining the zonal trials helps to reframe the conventional post-war chronology, reminding us that the IMT was not the first war crimes trial to take place, and providing an opportunity to consider the impact of individual Allied practices on the formation of quadripartite policy and the longer-term legacy of Nazi rule.

Anticipating death sentences for major war criminals

The Allied Declaration of December 1942, published amid growing reports of the brutal persecution of Jews in occupied Poland, pledged to bring all those guilty of atrocities to account after the war. The Moscow Declaration of October 1943 reaffirmed this.[6] However, it was only at the 1945 London Conference that the Allies agreed upon an international tribunal to dispense this justice.[7] The intervening period saw Churchill, Stalin and Roosevelt all contemplating the summary execution of leading Nazis to the extent that, in September 1944, the Allies issued draft instructions for the disposal of their remains.[8] These arrangements would release bodies to next-of-kin for burial, a procedure that complied with existing German law. The main points of concern at this time were ensuring that the condemned individual had access to a chaplain, and that a minimum interval was set between sentencing and actual execution to avoid seeming too 'hasty'.[9] There was an underlying sense that bodies should be handled with dignity and that German customs should not be trampled upon. While there is no direct evidence of the motives behind this approach, we might well assume that the Allies were hoping to avoid anything that might arouse local resentment and destabilize the occupation.

Given that all four Allied nations (and Germany itself) retained the death penalty at the start of this period, there was ample collective experience and legislation available for overseeing the execution and disposal of convicted criminals.[10] Yet the treatment of Nazi personnel did not run smoothly. What model should they follow for disposing of the criminal corpse? Did the particularly horrific nature of Nazi crimes demand special measures? By the start of the first war crimes cases (Belsen, Dachau and the IMT) in autumn 1945, the disposal instructions of the year before had been revisited. The Allies now had a better sense of the sort of perpetrators with whom they were dealing and realized that releasing remains to relatives would no longer suffice. The liberation of concentration camps in spring 1945 had generated revulsion across the world and led to increasing calls for harsh measures against the Germans, seen most evidently through media denouncements of Nazi perpetrators as 'beasts', 'devils' and 'monsters'.[11] There was also mounting concern about the potential for burial sites to be transformed into Nazi shrines, exemplified by an Allied campaign to eradicate all vestiges of National Socialism from the German landscape.[12] However, rejecting familial burials was one thing. It would take another year before the Allies were able to determine an alternative method of disposal.

The IMT Charter, signed in London on 8 August 1945, empowered the Tribunal to impose the death penalty but said nothing about implementing such sentences.[13] Richard Overy suggests that the Allies turned their attention to this problem shortly after the opening of the IMT on 19 November 1945. He notes that the Allied Control Commission recommended the suspension of conventional German law vis-à-vis the disposal of executed criminals (restoring remains to relatives) in favour of secret burial within prison grounds, and that a common policy to this effect was drawn up before the end of the year.[14] However, the principal directive he cites to support this argument is actually a British document referring to practices within the British Zone. As will be shown later in this chapter, this in itself came about amid British frustration at a lack of Four-Power consensus on the matter. Likewise, while Overy accepts that the disposal issue was revived in March 1946, thanks to an American suggestion to transfer prisoners from Nuremberg to Berlin for execution, he conveys the impression that the Allies' compromise solution of cremating remains in Munich emerged swiftly thereafter. In reality, Allied policy regarding the Nuremberg defendants moved at a much slower pace.[15]

Once the IMT began, the Control Council in Berlin, in which Allied policy was coordinated among the four occupying powers, debated arrangements for potential clemency appeals and the wisdom of allowing the press to observe executions, but paid no serious attention to the execution process itself.[16] Some guidance finally emerged in September 1946, just as the IMT was drawing to a close, with the issuing of Control Council Directive No. 35. This confirmed that death sentences handed down by the IMT would be carried out on the fifteenth day after sentencing, an interval deemed sufficient for hearing appeals.[17] The Directive added that 'unless otherwise ordered by the Tribunal, the death sentence shall be carried out without publicity by means of hanging or by guillotine, within the prison enclosure where the defendants concerned were confined at the time of the sentence, and the bodies of the said defendants shall be disposed of according to the instructions of the … [quadripartite] commission'.[18] This was a significant advance, but, as the source indicates, there remained unanswered questions about precise disposal procedures.

In September 1946, one month before the verdicts were delivered, a Quadripartite Commission was finally established, charged specifically with overseeing the execution of the IMT sentences. Naturally, the Allies had other pressing matters to attend to during the first year of the occupation, yet the belated formation of this unit suggests that the practicalities of upholding the IMT's decisions were something of an afterthought; it left little time for detailed discussion.

The Quadripartite Commission comprised of military commanders Brigadier Edmund Paton-Walsh (UK), Brigadier General Paul Morel (France), Major General Paul Molkov (USSR) and Brigadier General Roy Rickard (the United States), who convened in Nuremberg six times between 27 September and the eventual execution of IMT defendants on 16 October 1946.[19] The first meeting was chaired by Paton-Walsh, who quickly noted the IMT Charter's failure to prescribe a method of execution for condemned war criminals. The commission took the pragmatic view that they ought to prepare a decision in case the IMT failed to specify a killing method during sentencing, but they failed to reach agreement. The British and French called for the use of the guillotine, with Paton-Walsh arguing that this was the conventional form of death for a 'common felon' in Germany. The Americans preferred hanging, while the Soviets advocated firing squads. Molkov, however, conceded that since Control Council Directive No. 35 only permitted hanging or beheading, he would back the Americans. In the end, it was decided that if the IMT failed to specify the mode of execution, the default option adopted by the Commission would be hanging, with the Americans taking charge of the process as Executive Agents of the Commission. If, however, the IMT ruled that the war criminals should be dispatched by guillotine, the British and the French would share execution duties with the former providing the equipment and the latter supplying the personnel to wield it.[20]

The disposal of Nazi remains generated further debate. Paton-Walsh called for the burial of prisoners, again basing his decision on existing precedent but this time drawing upon domestic British practices for his frame of reference. Molkov, Rickard and Morel, however, were united in their preference for cremation and, with three against one, it was agreed this would become policy with the resultant ashes scattered in a secret location. This initial meeting of the Commission then adjourned so that the American representative could determine 'what facilities, if any, existed in the locality for the cremation of the bodies'.[21]

It is unclear exactly why the French, Soviets and Americans favoured cremation over burial. We might surmise it was considered easier logistically, and the best means of preventing shrines. Subsequent meetings of the Quadripartite Commissioners certainly stressed the need to avoid 'manifestations and pilgrimages at the places of burial'. The potential for mythmaking around dead Nazis had actually been raised by the most high-profile IMT defendant Hermann Göring, who had asserted that death was preferable to a prison sentence 'because those who are sentenced to life imprisonment never become martyrs'.[22] Some of the Allied leadership cautioned, however, against too much concealment. A memorandum from the forty-third meeting of the Control Council, held on 10 October 1946, thus recorded that 'General McNarney [Military Governor of the US Zone] was opposed to an excess of secrecy about the executions as he felt that it would lend itself to rumours and to the building up of legends'.[23] As it transpired, McNarney's fears were not entirely groundless.

The arrangements drawn up by the Quadripartite Commission, though, remained the basis for handling the Nuremberg executions. Further meetings, all chaired by Morel, were devoted to refining their implementation. The IMT eventually specified hanging for the condemned men when sentencing them on 1 October 1946 and, as agreed, the Americans duly took the lead on this, with Rickard immediately employing technicians from the Third US Army to prepare the execution site. The Commission, meanwhile, developed its action plan for handling the remains, noting that bodies would be taken to a nearby crematorium 'during the hours of darkness', and the ashes would then be transported to Nuremberg airport and 'dispersed from an airplane'.[24] By the fifth Commission meeting, held on 14 October 1946, the Americans were still looking for a suitable place to strew the ashes.[25]

In all, ten IMT defendants were hanged at Nuremberg on 16 October 1946; Göring cheated the executioner by taking cyanide but was cremated alongside his former comrades. Despite its last-minute formation, the Commission initially appeared to have succeeded in its key objective: maintaining secrecy around the disposal arrangements. A report sent to the Control Council in Berlin three days later proudly proclaimed that 'no person other than the four members of your commission are aware of the time, place or method of dispersal'.[26] Subsequently, it has become commonly accepted that the ashes were scattered in the River Isar, a tale that has made its way into tourist literature, despite there being no documentary evidence for this.[27] Furthermore, the absence of human remains did not prevent physical markers to the Nazi dead from springing up. Relatives of Joachim von Ribbentrop, Alfred Jodl and Wilhelm Keitel erected memorial stones to their loved one within their family cemetery plots. Their personal grief and desire to mourn is understandable, but, over the years, these sites have attracted others anxious to recall the Nazi past. The website *findagrave.com*, for example, displays a photograph of Jodl's memorial but notes that the facility to leave 'virtual flowers' on the webpage is switched off 'because it was being continually misused'.[28] Thus, despite the Allies' best efforts to conceal the final disposal location of the executed IMT defendants, the *imagined* resting place of these most notorious Nazi war criminals continues to excite fascination and acts of commemoration.

Zonal trials and variations

The IMT, however, was just one element of the Allied war crimes programme. Thousands of other Nazis were prosecuted before single-power military tribunals across occupied Germany. Control Council Law No. 10, drawn up on 20 December 1945, stipulated that these zonal trials could also impose the death penalty for serious offenders.[29] There was no mention, though, as to the means of execution or disposal of prisoners' remains. Once again, the Allies moved slowly: by the time this crucial law was published, the fifty-four-day 'Belsen trial' was over, verdicts delivered and appeals heard, Josef Kramer and ten others had, in fact, been executed seven days earlier. Rather than pre-emptively determining policy, Control Council Law No. 10 appears a belated, reactive response to repeated British requests for guidance on how to proceed with the first set of major war criminals.

Moreover, Control Council Law No. 10 stated that 'the tribunal by which persons charged with offences hereunder shall be tried and the rules and procedure thereof shall be determined or designated by each Zone Commander for his respective Zone'.[30] The Allies thus had the freedom to approach the execution and disposal of war criminals however they felt fit. A uniform policy across all four occupation zones was considered desirable but untenable. Variations were to be expected, given the diverse local conditions in each zone, disparities in the number of bodies being processed, different domestic traditions, different levels of resources and, of course, changing political circumstances as the wartime alliance unravelled towards the end of the decade. Nonetheless, the failure to standardize disposal policy significantly impacted on German–Allied relations and prompted different approaches to commemorative culture and managing the Nazi past across occupied Germany.

The British Zone

The first set of executions to occur as a result of a zonal trial came at the end of the 'Belsen trial' on 13 December 1945. Throughout the autumn, British legal, military and Foreign Office staff wrestled with the disposal question. A Special Legal Research Unit (SLRU) was charged with investigating whether existing German law prohibited the burial of executed remains within prison grounds, the standard UK procedure.[31] While the SLRU confirmed there was no specific provision in German law to prevent this, it stressed that 'pursuant to section 454 of the German Criminal Code of criminal procedure, the body of the executed prisoner <u>must</u> be handed over to the next-of-kin at their request for a simple burial without ceremony'.[32] Unclaimed bodies would be handed over for medical research at the nearest university, and, if this facility renounced its claim, local police would bury the remains; 'presumably', noted the SLRU, this could then take place within the prison precincts.[33]

The reminder of these existing directives prompted some members of British Military Government to press for a policy akin to the original 1944 instructions, arguing that 'bodies of war criminals executed in British zone should be disposed of according to normal German procedure. There seems no reason for introducing British procedure and to do so would surely give rise to criticism'.[34] Such sentiment again suggests a concern about maintaining good relations between occupiers and occupied, yet the logic was flawed. The decrees cited by researchers were formulated during the Third Reich. Adhering to them after 1945 contradicted wider Allied efforts to discredit the Nazi system, and enabled an unfortunate equation between Nazi war criminals and the remains of those executed by the Nazis themselves. The British were also seemingly ignorant of the irony that the Minister of the Interior ultimately responsible for instituting the existing measures was one of the men now on trial in Nuremberg.[35]

Two days before the scheduled Belsen executions, the British were still mooting different disposal options including cremation and burial at sea.[36] Given the lack of guidelines from the Allied Control Council, there was a growing realization that Britain needed to adopt its own solution. Consequently, on 11 December 1945, General Brian Robertson, Deputy Military Governor for the British Zone, decreed that 'bodies of executed war criminals shall be buried without publicity or ceremony and without any signs to indicate positions of their graves, in unconsecrated ground in the prison precincts'.[37] There is no archival evidence as to why Robertson seemingly ignored the advice proffered by both the Foreign Office's SLRU in London and Military Government staff in Germany, but for all of the initial concern about upholding German law, the British ultimately chose the disposal method most familiar to them, and one which avoided protracted discussions with relatives, medical institutions or local police. The decision enabled British penal staff to simply get on with the job soon after execution.

In all, a total of 155 war criminals were hanged in Hameln by the British between 1945 and 1950, ninety of whom were interred in prison grounds as directed, away from the public gaze.[38] These were rough-and-ready affairs: simple coffins stacked three deep without grave markers. By the end of 1946, though, the prison was running out of space so subsequent corpses were transported at night, in covered trucks by plainclothes military police officers, to the nearby public cemetery, *Friedhof am Wehl*.

Secrecy was the central feature of British disposal policy but this was to have a negative impact on the German population. Throughout the occupation, the British received numerous petitions from friends, relatives and former comrades of the deceased, anxious to determine their loved one's final resting place and learn more about the burial procedure itself. A Herr Schmidt from Kiel, for example, enquired whether his son had been buried in a coffin, whether a parson had performed a burial service and if the grave was tended.[39] Likewise, a Frau Schneider from Munich sought more information about her 'good husband', asking if she might buy and 'care for' his grave.[40] The wife of Hermann Lommes proved especially tenacious, sending several letters requesting the return of her husband's remains, and subsequently enlisting her lawyer and local curate to lobby on her behalf. She insisted:

> Both my children and myself have an innate desire for their father to be buried in Neuendorf and for him to have a Christian burial. This was, moreover, the last wish of my husband. Therefore, I most humbly beseech the Military Government for the body to be handed over and transported home. I hope confidently that you will grant this, the last request of a sorrowing widow.[41]

The mother of Wilhelm Scharschmidt likewise sought the repatriation of remains, writing, 'I beg [you] … Let me … bring my son home and … bury him here'.[42]

The pleading language used throughout these sources seemingly points to a universal code for the proper handling of the dead, one that the Allies were expected to recognize and uphold. The obvious emphasis on familial ties (husband, father, son) presented the war criminals as 'ordinary', lovable men, a theme summed up by the fiancé of Karl Amberger, who repeatedly declared him to have been 'the best and dearest person in all the world'.[43] For the most part, these letters steered clear of making any comment on the trials or their verdicts. However, it is striking that three of those referenced here (Amberger, Lommes and Scharschmidt) had been stationed together during the war and prosecuted amid British investigations into the murder of Allied prisoners of war at Dreierwald Aerodrome. This raises the question as to whether the relatives were writing independently of one another, or whether they were trying to galvanize an organized campaign against the perceived injustices of the occupying Military Government. The British, however, refused to divulge information or acquiesce to any of these appeals.

Alongside these emotive, written protests, Hameln witnessed attempts to enact physical memorials to the dead, including a 1948 proposal to erect individual wooden crosses for the war criminals interred in the cemetery, a site to which the local population had ready access. This was quickly quashed by the British.[44] Yet the fate of the executed Nazis was not so easily suppressed, and when the prison was restored to the Germans in 1953, the issue erupted into an international scandal. Descriptions of clandestine executions and burials appeared across the West German press, with leading tabloid *Bild-Zeitung* depicting the prison grounds as a 'Yard of Horror'.[45] The *Illustrierte Post*, meanwhile, offered a vivid account of how flowers, delicately placed in the vicinity by grieving relatives, had been cruelly thrown away by British prison staff.[46]

While such articles repeatedly implied that the British had behaved in a callous or inhumane manner, the Nazi perpetrators were treated sympathetically. The press routinely inserted inverted commas around the term 'war criminal', implicitly casting doubt on their involvement in Nazi atrocities. The *Illustrierte Post* referred to the dead as 'political detainees', while both *Bild-Zeitung* and the *Hannoversche Allgemeine Zeitung* used the term 'survivors' to refer to those who had been transferred from Hameln to another prison.[47] The corpses, then, were portrayed as victims of occupation and victors' justice.

In 1954, the government of Lower Saxony announced that remains previously buried in Hameln prison would be exhumed and reinterred in the cemetery. *Bild-Zeitung* was one of several newspapers to express its hope that 'the dead will find . . . that peace which has so long been denied them'.[48] In fact, the burial site continued to attract publicity as the setting for Nazi and anti-Nazi political demonstrations and Waffen-SS veterans' reunions until the site was finally levelled in 1986, showing that occupation policy could cast very long shadows.[49]

The US and French Zones

The Americans conducted more war crimes prosecutions than either of their Western Allies, with the result that Landsberg Prison saw 284 executions compared with Hameln's 155. The death procedure within the US Zone was also a more protracted affair thanks to a lengthy appeals process. The first Dachau trial, for example, imposed death sentences against former camp commandant Martin Gottfried Weiss and thirty-five others on 13 December 1945, yet the hangings themselves did not take place until 28–29 May 1946.[50] Traces of the dead also lingered longer in the public consciousness given the US propensity, unlike the British or French, for photographing the condemned prisoner mounting the scaffold or lying in a coffin after the fact. Such images were supposed to show justice had been served, reducing unnecessary speculation about the fate of former Nazis.

American disposal policy also differed from that practiced in the British Zone, giving next-of-kin the chance to reclaim bodies after execution. This immediately avoided the stress of not knowing about a relative's final resting place and, in turn, helped to reduce conflict between occupiers and occupied. Just over half of those executed in Landsberg remained unclaimed and were buried by US prison staff in the attached cemetery at Spöttinger. These were neat, individual graves with markers identifying the dead permitted later on, a notable contrast to the anonymous burials in Hameln. 44 per cent of those hanged in Landsberg, however, were claimed and repatriated to towns all over Germany, including many within the British Zone.[51] Consequently, it could be argued that American practices regarding the Nazi dead fuelled the clamour for information regarding the Hameln executions. An awareness of divergent practices between occupation zones would only encourage Germans to view the whole matter as unfair.

Yet the American approach was not without controversy. In June 1951, the return of Otto Ohlendorf's body to Hildesheim (in the British Zone) attracted crowds of mourners and Hitler salutes.[52] The US Vice Counsel Ernest Ramsaur reported back to Washington, DC the presence of 'right-wing' political groups and funeral wreathes bearing inscriptions such as 'no more beautiful death in this world than to be struck down before the enemy'.[53] This reception owed much to Ohlendorf's notoriety as the chief defendant in the 1947–8 *Einsatzgruppen* case and position as one of the so-called Landsberg Seven, the last batch of war criminals to be executed by the Americans. Ohlendorf had been the focal point for a well-publicized amnesty campaign and his funeral thus became an opportunity for venting political protest against the occupation and the continuing imprisonment of other war criminals. Two other Nazis, Paul Blobel and Georg Schallermair, who were executed on the same day, likewise became the object of public mourning when interred in Spöttinger. Some fifty people had to be turned away from the scene by US military police, and several floral wreathes were left outside the cemetery.[54] The case of the 'Landsberg Seven' was especially emotive since the Basic Law of the newly formed Federal Republic had abolished capital punishment.[55] Ohlendorf and his comrades were caught in the awkward interregnum between the proclamation of the new West German state in 1949 and the awarding of full sovereignty in 1955, enabling Allied-imposed death sentences to still be performed.

War crimes policy in the French Zone is less well documented in the existing historiography and primary research of tripartite materials has, so far, failed to reveal any clear rationale for French actions.[56] Rastatt, however, held several notable cases between 1945 and 1951 including the prosecution of Heinrich Schwartz *et al* as part of the Natzweiler concentration camp trial, held between December 1946 and February 1947, and the 1946 trial of Fritz Schmoll and other staff from Neue Bremm camp. Further trials of German personnel were performed in France itself. Within the zone, some sixty people were executed, the method of which differed sharply from the general practice in the US and British Zones. Fifty-one of these war criminals were dispatched by firing squad in the early hours of the morning within the woods at Baden-Oos; the remaining nine were guillotined in Rastatt Prison. The former method quickly generated headlines about war criminals being 'shot at dawn' in the UK press.[57] The connotations of this phrase – commonly associated with deserters – implied that the dead were purely military figures. Similarly, the French tended to bury their executed war criminals within nearby cemeteries alongside other war dead, a juxtaposition that would inevitably help to blur the identities of the deceased and present them as 'normal' victims of conflict.[58] Indeed, some sense of this persists today online with websites such as *kriegstote.org*, which includes the final resting places of five of those shot by the French within a longer compilation of notable graves from the First and Second World Wars.[59] In reality, the majority of cases appearing before the French military tribunals involved SS and Gestapo personnel from various concentration camps.

There is at least one recorded case, though, of the French permitting a relative to reclaim a body. In July 1951, the remains of former Ravensbrück commandant Fritz Suhren were released to his sister for reburial in their hometown of Varel. The move was made on the proviso she did not 'misuse the occasion by staging any provocative demonstrations'.[60]

In search of a four-power agreement

The Western Allies thus proceeded to adopt their own course within their individual zones. Very often, their practices reflected typical domestic procedures for handling the criminal corpse. However, while there was never any second, international trial of Nazi personnel, the four powers continued to work together on the issue of the *potential* Nazi corpse, which in itself is revealing of broader ruling strategies and policies pursued by the different occupiers. Spandau Prison held the seven men imprisoned by the IMT and, although technically located within the British sector of West Berlin, it operated under quadripartite control in keeping with the constitution of the original trial. It was overseen by the Allied Kommandatura, the governing body for occupied Berlin and chairmanship of the prison governors rotated monthly between the four powers. With two prisoners, Konstantin von Neurath and Erich Raeder, already suffering poor health and old age, and three serving life sentences, there was an obvious need for the Allies to develop a contingency plan for deaths in custody.

In October 1947, the Kommandatura accepted a proposal drawn up by the prison directors recommending cremation and secret scattering of ashes.[61] Despite echoing the measures applied to the executed IMT defendants, the policy did not find universal approval. The British Kommandatura representative recommended that anyone who died in Spandau be treated like an 'ordinary prisoner' with their body returned to relatives.[62] Given that the Kommandatura would have no say over the disposal of former prisoners who died as free men, he felt there was 'no reason' to treat those who died in custody any differently.[63] The Americans rejected this argument, reminding their allies that 'if the bodies were released, the prisoners might come to be regarded as martyrs'.[64] The Soviets agreed, adding that releasing the bodies would contravene procedures established by the IMT. The French remained neutral on the matter and the British were forced to concede the point.

Interestingly, the arguments advanced here by the British and Americans reveal a fundamental disconnect from their own zonal practices. The Americans, of course, were willing to release other remains, and the British, as we have seen, took the opposite line in Hameln. In part, this discrepancy may be viewed as the natural outcome of different personnel operating at different levels of the occupation bureaucracy. It is also the case that the Allies quickly came to distinguish between 'major offenders' who had been condemned to death, and those who received a prison sentence; posthumous control over the latter was regarded as an unnecessary aggravation of their sentence.[65] In British eyes, therefore, these figures merited alternative disposal arrangements.

The matter was revived at the start of the 1950s amid a changing international political climate. Two separate German states had been established in 1949 and, as the Korean War marked the globalization of the Cold War, the Federal Republic was increasingly recognized as an important ally in the fight against Communism. This, together with greater temporal distance from the Second World War, helped soften attitudes towards the Germans and earlier fears about potential shrines to Nazism also appear to have diminished. In 1952, for example, a British Information Report concluded that 'no undue demonstrations should be expected' if deceased Spandau prisoners were handed over to relatives for burial.[66] Amid campaigns for a general amnesty for war criminals, members of the fledgling West German government were also taking an interest in the prison conditions at Spandau. An enquiry from Chancellor Adenauer about disposal procedures could be interpreted as a subtle form of pressure on the Allies.[67] The main impetus for policy revision, however, was the deteriorating health of von Neurath in 1951. Suddenly, the death of a prisoner went from an abstract possibility to an impending reality. As the Allies were forced to make logistical decisions about hospital transport and family visits, the British, never entirely happy with the 1947 ruling, seized their opportunity to call for a change in disposal policy. They initiated a new round of discussions by recirculating the text of their original dissent regarding cremation. Calls for prisoners to be released for familial burial were couched in terms of the changed political situation and the 'humanity' that had to be shown towards prisoners' relatives, the latter theme no doubt amplified by the increased dialogue then underway between prison governors and von Neurath's concerned relatives. Certainly, the family endeavoured to arouse compassion for their cause, with Von Neurath's wife appealing to another famous spouse, Clementine Churchill, to exert influence on the matter. Frau Neurath pleaded, 'we have not been together on our golden wedding day but we hope to be together in death'.[68]

Accordingly, the three western powers met in July 1951 to discuss the possibility of releasing bodies for burial. While the aim was to present a united front to the USSR, tripartite approval on the matter was hardly guaranteed. The French High Commissioner, André Francois-Poncet, initially opposed the move, warning that 'the return of bodies to families would give rise to further nationalistic demonstrations as … occurred recently in the case of certain of the Landsberg war criminals'.[69] He was undoubtedly referring to the unfortunate scenes surrounding Ohlendorf's burial the previous month. Unsurprisingly, US High Commissioner John McCloy took issue with Francois-Poncet's statement, pointing out that such demonstrations had, technically, taken place in the British Zone rather than Landsberg, and arguing that determined nationalists 'could equally make capital out of a cremated body'.[70] McCloy's words seem to have swayed the French representative: Francois-Poncet removed his objection and a new, western proposal based upon 'reasons of humanity' was consequently presented to the Soviets, calling for the body of a dead prisoner to be released to relatives for burial.[71] The Soviets, however, were unmoved and merely reiterated the text of the 1947 agreement.[72]

Undeterred, US, British and French representatives on the Allied High Commission spent the next three years plotting alternative courses of action to persuade the Soviets to reconsider. These included verbal approaches to key Russian personnel, the preparing of legal reports outlining precedents for releasing bodies and the drafting of preparatory press releases that, in the event of the sudden demise of a prisoner, would make it abundantly clear to the public that Soviet intransigence was to blame for next-of-kin being unable to bury their relative.[73] By 1952, frustration was mounting to such an extent that the American representative proposed that, should the United States be serving as Prison Chair at the time of an inmate's death, they would simply seize the body so it could 'be removed as expeditiously as possible to the zone and handed over for burial to the family'.[74] Unsurprisingly, the British and French representatives immediately raised several objections: efforts to 'override' the Soviet Prison Governor could 'jeopardize' the West's ability to moderate prison conditions for inmates, and there was a danger that the Soviets 'might resort to force to prevent the removal of the dead body'. There was also confusion as to what would happen if a death occurred under British or French chairmanship of the prison.[75]

Collectively, these concerns prevented the adoption of such a radical measure and for the remainder of 1952, the Western Allies focused firmly on presenting a démarche to the Soviets. On 1 September, all three western High Commissioners sent identically worded letters to General Vasily Chuikov, Soviet Commandant of Berlin, requesting a change to disposal policy, alongside other general improvements to the prison regime. However, it took until April 1954 (and a personal request to Molotov himself) before the Four Powers were able to sit down together to discuss these proposals. Finally, on 29 April 1954, a new quadripartite agreement was drawn up, stipulating that 'in the case of the death of one of the major German war criminals, the body of the deceased must be buried in the territory of the Spandau Prison'.[76] While the original policy of cremation was dropped, the Soviets could not bring themselves to accede to western requests to release the body to next-of-kin, despite the British confessing that similar practices in Hameln had resulted in a lot of 'agitation'.[77] Agreement, however, was reached regarding the performance of a religious service and the presence of the deceased's immediate family at the funeral.

Reflections

The disposal of the Nazi corpse remained an enormous challenge for the Allies throughout the occupation era and a continual talking point between all four powers. Indeed, this is one area where the general periodization of the 'occupation era' merits reconsideration. Although West Germany formally became a sovereign state under the Bonn-Paris Conventions of May 1955, Spandau Prison constituted an isolated remnant of Allied rule and the fate of its inmates remained an Allied concern. This situation persisted until the demise of the final prisoner, Rudolf Hess, in 1987.

Furthermore, policies on the criminal corpse were not static but continually revisited, revised and reversed. By 1970, even the Spandau issue was being reconsidered. Practical considerations played a role here as the prison chapel, previously identified as a suitable burial space for prisoners, fell into disrepair. Political considerations, however, were even more important amid the growing realization that a physical grave for a Spandau prisoner might require the same quadripartite governance as the prison itself. The Western Allies thus concluded cremation might be the better policy after all, as the demise of the final prisoner would ensure the removal of Soviet influence from West Berlin.[78] The Nazi corpse had become a powerful political tool.

The case of the executed war criminals underscores the myriad issues facing the Allies when they arrived in Germany in spring 1945 and, as shown through the Hameln episode, offers a clear example of the emotive dialogues that sprang up between the Allies and the 'ordinary' German population. An ongoing tension persisted between the bureaucratic face of the occupation and the basic human desire to mourn lost relatives, even those who had been tried and condemned to death as war criminals. The failure to agree a common disposal policy across the whole of Germany generated unrest among the German people, having the reverse effect of what the Allies had intended. Rather than simply disappearing from the public consciousness, continual speculation about the whereabouts of Nazi graves and contested efforts at memorialization, coupled with reburial campaigns, ensured that the names of the dead continued to be remembered.

Notes

1 One hundred and fifty-five war criminals were executed in Hameln (The National Archives Kew, hereafter TNA, FO1060/4122); 284 in Landsberg (Landsberg Citizens' Association; see www.buergervereinigung-landsberg.org/english/historicalfacts/warcriminals.htm, accessed 21 September 2017); and, according to sources uncovered so far on this project, 60 in the area around Rastatt (author's correspondence with Stadtarchiv Rastatt).

2 See Donald Bloxham, *Genocide on Trial: War Crimes Trials and the Formation of Holocaust History and Memory* (Oxford: Oxford University Press, 2001); Martin Broszat, 'Siegerjustiz oder Strafrechtliche "Selbstreinigung": Aspekte der Vergangeheitsbewältigung der deutschen Justiz während der Besatzungszeit, 1945–1947', *Vierteljahreshefte für Zeitgeschichte* 4 (1981): 477–544; Christoph Burchard, 'The Nuremberg Trial and Its Impact on Germany', *Journal of International Criminal Justice* 4 (2006): 800–29; Caroline Sharples, *West Germans and the Nazi Legacy* (New York: Routledge, 2012), 9–29.

3 Norbert Frei, *Adenauer's Germany and the Nazi Past: The Politics of Amnesty and Integration* (New York: Columbia University Press, 2002); Ronald Webster, 'Opposing "Victors' Justice": German Protestant Churchmen and Convicted War Criminals in Western Europe after 1945', *Holocaust and Genocide Studies* 15, no. 1 (2001): 47–69.

4 Richard Evans, *Rituals of Retribution: Capital Punishment in Germany, 1600–1987* (Oxford: Oxford University Press, 1996).

5 Norman Goda, *Tales from Spandau: Nazi Criminals and the Cold War* (Cambridge: Cambridge University Press, 2007), 20.
6 TNA FO371/57610: Inter-Allied Declarations on the Punishment of War Crimes (1942); Joint Four Nation Declaration, Moscow Conference (October 1943), Yale Law School, The Avalon Project: Documents in Law, History and Diplomacy. Available online: http://avalon.law.yale.edu/wwii/moscow.asp (accessed 21 September 2017).
7 International Conference on Military Trials: Agreement and Charter (8 August 1945). Available online: http://avalon.law.yale.edu/imt/jack60.asp (accessed 21 September 2017).
8 TNA FO1060/930: Instructions for the Imposition and Execution of Death Sentences, September 1944. On summary executions, see Shlomo Aronson, 'Preparations for the Nuremberg Trial: The OSS, Charles Dwork and the Holocaust', *Holocaust and Genocide Studies* 12, no. 2 (1998): 259–61.
9 TNA FO1060/930: Ministry of Justice Control Branch to Legal Division (23 September 1944).
10 The USSR abolished the death penalty on 26 May 1947 but reintroduced it on 12 January 1950. A renewed abolition campaign in 1940s Britain was ultimately defeated and capital punishment remained in place until 1965 – see TNA FO937/156: Death Penalty. On capital punishment in Germany, see Evans, *Rituals of Retribution*.
11 See, for example, 'The Guilt', *The Observer*, 22 April 1945, which declared 'whatever punishment international law imposes on these monsters will be trivial compared with the enormity of their misdeeds'.
12 Control Council Directive No. 30 for the Liquidation of German Military and Nazi Memorials and Museums (May 1946).
13 Article 27, Charter of the International Military Tribunal (8 August 1945). Available online: http://avalon.law.yale.edu/imt/jack60.asp (accessed 21 September 2017).
14 Overy, *Interrogations*, 204, bases his argument on the ruling of the Deputy Military Governor, British Zone (11 December 1945) in TNA FO1049/286.
15 Overy's summary of the final fate of the executed prisoners is based on a second-hand reading of defence lawyer Gustav Steinbauer's memoir (see n. 8, p. 589).
16 TNA FO1060/1385: Quadripartite Commission for the Detention of Major War Criminals (hereafter QC).
17 TNA FO371/57552: Control Council Directive No. 35: Sentences of the IMT (7 September 1946). If the fifteenth day fell upon a Sunday, the execution would be delayed until the Monday.
18 Control Council Directive No. 35.
19 Records of QC meetings can be found in TNA FO1060/1384 and FO1060/1385.
20 TNA FO1060/1384: First QC Meeting, Nuremberg (27 September 1946).
21 First QC Meeting.
22 Recorded in Gustave M. Gilbert, *Nuremberg Diary* (London: Eyre and Spottiswoode, 1948), 274.
23 TNA FO371/57552: 43rd meeting of the Control Council, Berlin (10 October 1946).
24 TNA FO1060/1384: Third QC Meeting, Nuremberg (2 October 1946). By the fourth meeting, the plan had been adjusted slightly with 'one or several aeroplanes' now taking off from a Munich airfield, rather than Nuremberg – see minutes of 3 October 1946, TNA FO1060/1384.
25 TNA FO1060/1384: Fifth QC Meeting, Nuremberg (14 October 1946).
26 TNA FO1060/1385: First Report on the Work of the QC (19 October 1946).

27 There is no further documentary evidence on the fate of the IMT defendants after the minutes of the sixth QC meeting on 15 October 1946, suggesting that the military commanders did not trust details of the dispersal point to paper. How, or when, stories about the River Isar emerged is unclear, but it is now a standard reference. See, for example, Overy, *Interrogations*, 205; Lawrence Raful, Herbert R. Reginbogin and Christoph J. M. Safferling (eds), *The Nuremberg Trials: International Criminal Law since 1945* (Munich: K. G. Saur, 2006) 109; Whitney R. Harris, 'Tyranny on Trial', *International Lawyer* 40, no. 1 (2006): 13.

28 Alfred Jodl is named on a cenotaph in his family's burial plot at Fraueninsel Cemetery in Chiemsee. Wilhelm Keitel has memorial stones in Bad Gandersheim and Hamburg. Joachim Ribbentrop is memorialized in his wife's family's plot near Wiesbaden. See, for example, 'Alfred Jodl', www.findagrave.com/cgi-bin/fg.cgi?page=pv&GRid=7010&PIpi=2255578 (accessed 10 August 2013).

29 Control Council Law No. 10: Punishment of Persons Guilty of War Crimes, Crimes Against Peace and Against Humanity, Berlin (20 December 1945). Available online: http://avalon.law.yale.edu/imt/imt10.asp (accessed 21 September 2017).

30 Article 3.2, Control Council Law No. 10.

31 TNA FO1060/90: Burial of Executed Prisoners.

32 TNA FO1060/90, Report by the SLRU, London (19 October 1945). Author's emphasis.

33 Report by the SLRU.

34 TNA WO309/1645: Bercomb to Concomb, Confidential Message No. TD301 (8 December 1945).

35 This was Wilhelm Frick who was among those executed in October 1946.

36 TNA FO1060/239: Executions Policy Vol. 1.

37 TNA FO1060/4122: Executed War Criminals – Burial Policy.

38 Figure cited in TNA FO1060/4122: Bonn Telegram No. 133 (6 March 1954). See also Peter Krone (ed.), *'Hingerichtetengräber' auf dem Friedhof Wehl, Hameln: Historische Dokumentation* (Hameln, 1987).

39 TNA FO1060/4122: Letter from Ernst Schmidt, Kiel (26 November 1950).

40 TNA FO1024/101: Letter from Therese Schneider, Munich (10 May 1948).

41 TNA FO1060/240: Letters regarding Hermann Lommes (1947–8).

42 TNA FO1060/239: Letter from Emma Scharschmidt (17 August 1948).

43 TNA FO1060/239: Letters from Henny Dufen (30 May and 6 June 1946).

44 TNA FO1024/101: F. H. Rogers, British Governor Hameln Prison (2 February 1948).

45 *Bild-Zeitung*, 'German Mass Grave in Hameln Penitentiary', 26 November 1953.

46 *Illustrierte Post*, 'Secret 202: Though the Grass Grew Above', 8 August 1953.

47 *Bild-Zeitung*, 'German Mass Grave in Hameln Penitentiary', 26 November 1953; *Hannoversche Allgemeine Zeitung*, 'Menschlicher Abschluss der Zuchthaustragoedie in Hameln: sämtliche Namen trotz Allierter Geheimhaltung ausfindig gemacht', 3 March 1954.

48 *Bild-Zeitung*, 'German Mass Grave in Hameln Penitentiary', 26 November 1953.

49 For more details, see Caroline Sharples, 'Burying the Past? The Post-Execution History of Nazi War Criminals', in *A Global History of Execution and the Criminal Corpse*, ed. Richard Ward (Basingstoke: Palgrave Macmillan, 2015), 249–71.

50 Eight of these death sentences were commuted to periods of imprisonment. Harold Marcuse, *Legacies of Dachau: The Uses and Abuses of a Concentration Camp, 1933–2001* (Cambridge: Cambridge University Press, 2001), 71.

51 Thomas Raithel, *Die Strafanstalt Landsberg am Lech und der Spottinger Friedhof (1944–1958)* (Munich: Oldenbourg, 2009), appendix.

52 The scene was captured by ACME staff photographers, Yad Vashem, Digital Collections, 1458/110.
53 Cited in Peter Maguire, *Law and War: International Law and American History* (New York: Columbia University Press, 2010), 178.
54 *Daily Telegraph*, 'Mourners for Hanged Nazis', 8 June 1951.
55 Article 102 of the Basic Law of the Federal Republic of Germany (1949), German History in Documents and Images. Available online: http://germanhistorydocs.ghi-dc.org/sub_document.cfm?document_id=2858 (accessed 21 September 2017).
56 A rare example is Yveline Pendaries, *Les procès de Rastatt: le jugement des crimes de guerre en zone française d'occupation en Allemagne de 1946 à 1954* (Berne: Lang, 1995).
57 See, for example, 'Shot at Dawn', *Hartlepool Northern Daily Mail*, 20 March 1947.
58 Author's correspondence with Dr Oliver Fieg, Stadtarchiv Rastatt (15 September 2015).
59 The five war criminals are Heinrich Arnold, Friedrich Buchs, Jakob Quinten, Fritz Schmoll and Peter Weiss, all members of Neue-Bremm Gestapo camp. See www.kriegstote.org/cgi-bin/baseportal.pl?htx=/Kriegsopfer/kriegsopferfriedhof_bilder&friedhof=Rheinm%FCnster-S%F6llingen (accessed 21 September 2017).
60 TNA FO1060/4122: Intelligence Division, Baden-Baden to Office of the Legal Advisor, Wahnerheide (9 July 1951).
61 TNA FO1060/545: Allied Kommandatura Meeting: Spandau Prisoners (17 October 1947).
62 Allied Kommandatura Meeting: Spandau Prisoners.
63 Ibid.
64 Ibid.
65 TNA FO1060/546: Law Committee Report (7 April 1952).
66 TNA FO1060/545: Informative Report on Modification of Regulation Disposing of Remains of Prisoners Detained in the Allied Prison, Spandau (11 February 1952).
67 TNA FO1060/546: Konrad Adenauer to Ambassador Walter J. Donnelly (11 November 1952).
68 TNA FO1060/545: Baronin von Neurath to Mrs Churchill (undated).
69 TNA FO1060/545: Telegram No. 725 Wahnerheide to FO (20 July 1951).
70 Telegram No. 725: Wahnerheide to FO.
71 TNA FO1060/545: Minutes of the 13th Meeting of the Berlin Commandants (31 July 1951).
72 TNA FO1060/545: Spandau.
73 Ibid. See also TNA FO1060/546; FO371/109330–4.
74 TNA FO1060/546: Allied High Commission Meeting of the Council (April 1952).
75 Allied High Commission Meeting of the Council.
76 TNA FO371/109333: Report on the Fourth Quadripartite Meeting (29 April 1954).
77 TNA FO371/109333: Eighth Tripartitely Agreed Report on Spandau Talks (27 April 1954).
78 On this next round of debates, see TNA FCO90/28 and FCO90/31–3: Hess Death Procedures; FCO33/5882–4: Disposal of Hess's Remains; US National Archives RG 59 Entry (A1) 5667; ZZ1004: Hess Remains.

Part Three

Doing Occupation: Image and Reality

7

'My Home, Your Castle': British Requisitioning of German Homes in Westphalia

Bettina Blum

The requisitioning of private houses by the occupiers was one of the most important factors influencing Anglo-German relations from the end of the war until the mid-1950s, lasting for ten years and leading to thousands of people losing their homes. In July 1947 there were still 33,034 requisitioned properties in the British Zone (after giving 44,024 back by the end of June 1947).[1] At the end of 1951 requisitions still numbered 15,565 flats in 8,427 buildings in the *Land* North Rhine-Westphalia.[2] The importance of this subject at a personal level was clearly visible when, as part of a recent research and exhibition project on the 'History of the British in Westphalia',[3] nearly 200 people – British and Germans – were interviewed or provided stories and photographs. Everybody who had experienced the occupation period still remembered the problem of requisitioning. Several Germans contacted the project leaders explicitly with the intention of telling the story of how they or their parents had lost their homes, demonstrating that more than sixty years after the houses have been given back, requisitioning continues to be a highly emotional issue.

Although the occupying power also requisitioned bicycles, barracks, land, administrative buildings, stockrooms, cinemas as well as telephone lines and exchanges,[4] the requisitioning of private family homes was the most controversial aspect of the policy and caused the greatest social tensions between the occupiers and the occupied. Losing their home and their very private space to the occupation forces made people feel that they personally and unfairly had to bear the brunt of the hardships of losing the war. The legal and moral basis for the policy was questioned with increasing intensity after the founding of the Federal Republic of Germany (FRG) in 1949. Exploring requisitioning in the British Zone can therefore reveal how occupiers and occupied assessed and perceived the situation, and how they negotiated and interacted with each other to try to protect and enforce their interests.

The following chapter is based on archival material, newspaper articles,[5] private material and twelve interviews with Germans and Britons, conducted in 2015 and 2016 as part of the project on the history of the British in Westphalia. The Germans who were interviewed for this project had experienced losing their home at a young age and most remembered vividly the fear and anguish they felt at the time. Their personal memories complement and help understand the general picture provided by contemporary newspaper accounts and in German and British official documents. The following chapter examines how British policy on requisitioning was implemented and how and why it was subsequently modified by the Military Government. In doing so, it also explores how requisitioning was perceived both by Germans and Britons, and how it affected encounters between the occupiers and the occupied. The chapter concentrates on conditions in Westphalia, which was the region that housed the headquarters of the British Army and Control Commission for Germany (British Element) (CCG) and where, as a result, a relatively high number of properties were requisitioned.[6]

Westphalia as British headquarters

At the end of March 1945, the British chose the towns of Bad Oeynhausen, Herford and Bad Salzuflen in the eastern part of Westphalia as their zonal headquarters and requested the Royal Air Force to leave the area 'free from air attack unless operationally essential'.[7] This region of eastern Westphalia is mainly a rural area with several spa towns. Unlike the cities of Hamburg, Cologne or the Ruhr, most towns in this area were relatively undamaged by the war. Reconnaissance groups checked out several municipalities in the region for their suitability and calculated that approximately 20 to 40 per cent of each would have to be requisitioned.[8] A pamphlet produced by the Military Government explained the advantages of the renowned spa town Bad Oeynhausen: 'It is nearly in the centre of the British zone, is well served by roads and railways and contains many buildings in good condition suitable to house the numerous and varied branches of an army'.[9] British troops occupied Bad Oeynhausen on 17 April, which had previously surrendered to the Americans on 3 April.[10] The Military Government subsequently requisitioned the entire town centre incorporating nearly 1,000 houses. On 4 May 1945, the residents were informed that everyone living within this area had to leave their homes by noon on 12 May. In total, the Military Government evicted 70 per cent of the population of Bad Oeynhausen, comprising between 6,500 and 9,000 individuals. Furniture had to be left in the houses.[11] In addition, since the new army compound also included the existing spa facilities and because Germans were no longer allowed access to this area, the town lost its function as a health resort, leading to a severe shortage of revenue for the town's administration.[12]

Similar requisitioning procedures took place in other towns nearby such as in Lübbecke, Minden, Bünde and Herford, where the occupiers set up the divisional headquarters of the civil administration, the CCG. In Herford, the British occupied a large area known as the *Stiftberg* and evicted nearly 6,500 people.[13] In these towns, the British established areas where entry was generally prohibited for the local population. These areas were cordoned off with barbed wire and Germans needed a special permit to pass through the barriers.[14] The barbed wire was removed from most of the towns during the late 1940s,[15] but remained in place in Bad Oeynhausen until 1 July 1951. Even after that date, however, a small part of the town remained a prohibited area.[16] Only after the British took the decision to move the British Army of the Rhine (BAOR) headquarters to Rheindahlen, in the western part of the zone near Mönchengladbach, did they derequisition the town centre, including the spa buildings and gardens, step by step between autumn 1954 and spring 1955.[17]

The procedure of requisitioning

The first requisitions in Westphalia were carried out by American and British combat units. Overall, these requisitions were irregular and often only lasted a few days or weeks. By autumn 1945, however, with the consolidation of the Military Government bureaucracy in the zone, the British increasingly formalized the requisitioning process.[18] They issued regulations, drew up official forms for requisitioning and derequisitioning, and fixed compensation rates for houses and furniture. This process created a range of technical problems for the occupiers. A British interpreter wrote to her family:

> I am very busy with a number of translations at present with a lot of difficult and untranslatable words in them; the technical difference between 'Vergütung' [pay] and 'Entschädigung' [compensation/reparation] for requisitioned property – 'In Anspruch genommene Räume' [claimed rooms] and what must be paid to the 'Leistungspflichtiger' i.e. person subject to the requisitioning order which brings in words like 'Mietzins' [rent] and 'Zinssatz' [interest rate] until one is perfectly dizzy.[19]

The requisitions were carried out by the Barrack and Quartering Service of BAOR, who had to make sure that the houses were suitable for their intended purposes and inform local Military Government officials giving fourteen days' notice. Responsibility for the evacuation and for finding accommodation for the evicted lay, however, with the local German administration.[20] This was often extremely difficult, as bombed-out families, displaced persons and a rising number of refugees also all needed a place to live. All these various groups and individuals therefore competed with each other for official recognition and help.[21]

In general, the housing problem was worse in the British Zone than in other parts of Germany, because northwestern Germany, a heavily industrialised area, had faced the most severe wartime damage in comparison to other areas.[22] The average floor space per person (children under 14 counting as half) in the British Zone was 6.2 square metres – compared with 7.6 in the US and 9.4 in the French Zones. Furthermore, many of the remaining dwellings lacked effective sanitation, heating and cooking facilities.[23] The housing situation in the rural parts of Westphalia was not as severe as in the big cities in the zone, such as Hamburg or Cologne, but many families had to endure very difficult living conditions for many years. Lieselotte H., for example, had to live together with her husband and parents for eight years in inadequately insulated rooms with only a provisional kitchen and without a bathroom, toilet or sewerage system so that they had to carry the dirty water downstairs in buckets.[24]

The British generally occupied whole houses, rather than sharing them with their previous owners, and were often reluctant to let Germans move into army/CCG compounds when a house was no longer needed.[25] These official rules, however, could sometimes be circumvented. The family of Eckehart S., for instance, was allowed to live in the former coach house of their requisitioned property despite the fact that it was situated within the prohibited area in Detmold.[26] Some Germans negotiated with the occupiers and reached an agreement that allowed them to use the garden, kitchen or spare rooms in the house. The (British) parents of Sarah G., for example, allowed a member of the German family to stay in the upper floor of the requisitioned house. Sarah G. remembered her as a 'kind old lady' with whom they spent pleasant hours.[27] Ultimately, however, these concessions always depended on the goodwill of the British family occupying the property – if they moved out and the next British tenants wished to use the house or garden exclusively for themselves, the Germans inevitably had to leave.[28]

The arrival of British families in the zone

The situation became more complicated with the arrival in the British Zone of the families of British servicemen and Military Government personnel, as this meant further requisitioning and demonstrated that the British had come to stay. The House of Commons approved the dispatch of families to Germany in June 1946.[29] The first families arrived on 1 September 1946,[30] and by 1949 approximately 12,000 wives and over 12,000 children were living in the British Zone.[31] The size of the house allocated depended on rank. Civilian personnel in the CCG had an 'honorary military rank' according to which accommodation and other entitlements were allocated.[32]

The arrival of families in the British Zone caused conflicts not only within the German community, but also among the British. Some Army or CCG staff members were concerned that their own accommodation would suffer as more space was made available for families. One British civilian employee wrote that she feared 'for the worst, especially as there are rumours that I may have to move out to make room for "married families". I am going to be extremely wary about that though and I am not going to be put off with an inferior room just anywhere in order to fit into an already crowded billet'.[33] Similarly, Edna Wearmouth, a young women who had been recruited to work in Germany as a CCG employee in 1946, had expected to be sent to the British Zone directly after her introductory course about Germany, but her departure was delayed after she was informed about the shortage of accommodation caused by 'the BAOR wives taking our quarters' and a planned reduction of CCG personnel.[34] When she eventually arrived in the British Zone a few weeks later, she admired the 'beautiful house' in Minden where she lived, but she was also fully aware what requisitioning meant to the Germans and empathized with their situation, explaining in a letter back home that 'everything within me objects to the fact that we, meaning British authorities, turned out Frau Thol & she has to live in the basement. It just doesn't seem fair & I can't help feeling for them.'[35]

Germans responded to the presence of the British occupiers in different ways. For some, knowing that at least a few of the British occupiers felt sorry for them and wished to help them, made it possible to reconcile themselves to the situation. Helga K., for instance, lived with her family in provisional rooms above the stables when their house was used as a sergeants' mess until 1953. She remembered her anger when she saw that other girls had better living conditions and could invite friends to their home, while this was impossible for her. But as the British officers behaved in a polite and friendly manner, the family managed to cope with the situation and establish friendly relations. She remembered that they chatted when they met and the officers sometimes brought food or took her to the British cinema.[36] The situation might have been easiest for children who often accepted the situation as it was, and played with their neighbours irrespective of nationality. Peter F., whose family moved to Germany in 1946, learned his first German sentence while he was playing 'hide and seek' with a group of German children: 'Eins, zwei, drei, vier Eckstein – alles muss versteckt sein!'[37]

Most Germans reacted to eviction and the loss of their homes and neighbours with feelings ranging from sorrow and sadness to indignation and fury, complaining repeatedly about the British presence. As a result, some British families had to face constant anger and resentment. British children were insulted as '*Tommybrut*' (Tommy brat) and German wives of British men as '*Tommyhure*' (Tommy whore). Some families were ignored by their German neighbours or subjected to symbolic displays of antipathy, such as rubbish being dumped in their doorways. In one case, a British family in Detmold allowed the German house owner to use the woodshed of the requisitioned house, yet instead of feeling thankful, the German lady chopped wood there when she knew that the British children were in bed and would be woken by the noise.[38]

In many towns, including for example Bad Oeynhausen, Detmold, Hamm, Münster, Minden, Dortmund and Bielefeld, the evacuees established societies for those affected by the hardships of the occupation, the *Notgemeinschaft der Besatzungsgeschädigten*. The group in Bad Oeynhausen was founded in early 1948.[39] These communities were organized at a local level, but worked closely together and had representatives on district, state and later also on a federal level.[40] They acted as pressure groups, organized demonstrations and discussions with politicians and submitted information to local newspapers about the plight of those suffering under requisitioning. In the early 1950s, the organization had its own newspaper based in Bad Oeynhausen that informed readers about political discussions and new laws relating to requisitioned property, and circulated information about local activities and administrative proceedings.[41]

Difficult relationships

German criticism of British requisitioning practices revolved around a number of key issues that had a major impact on Anglo-German relationships in Westphalia, including accommodation standards, the problem of requisitioned houses remaining unoccupied, the use of gardens and the level of compensation. These issues contributed to broader discourses on the legitimacy of the occupation and German victimhood.

One of the most frequently discussed aspects throughout the occupation was the size of requisitioned accommodation in relation to the number of people living there. The space allocated to an officer depended on his rank rather than the size of his family.

This created situations that the population perceived as unjust, such as when a large German family would be evicted from their home in order to allow one British officer and his wife to occupy it.[42] Another key problem was that requisitioned houses often remained unoccupied for long periods. In most cases, the houses were held for the arrival of new regiments or families.[43] This often created situations that the population regarded as unfair and unwarranted. In Minden, for example, the British evicted a house owner in 1945 and did not return his house until 1948, even though it had not been occupied at any time during the previous two and a half years.[44] The British Military Government, however, became increasingly aware of the resentment that unoccupied properties created among the local population and tried to make sure that vacated and no longer needed accommodation was derequisitioned within one month.[45]

The requisitioning of gardens as well as of houses caused further difficulties, as food was scarce in the immediate post-war years and many Germans tried to supplement their diet by growing fruit and vegetables. Requisitioning deprived them of that possibility.[46] On the other hand, as food was also rationed in Britain, and because British rations in Germany sometimes lacked fresh vegetables since these had to be imported,[47] several British families made use of the gardens themselves.[48] The Military Government tried to find a compromise and decided in January 1947 that 'where gardens, or parts of gardens, of requisitioned properties can NOT be fully cultivated, the former German occupant is allowed to use them'.[49] Apparently this ruling was not always implemented, and officials in several cities complained that only few of those evicted from their houses were granted access to their gardens.[50]

Those evicted received financial compensation for their requisitioned houses, but they often considered the level to be inadequate. This compensation was part of the occupation costs that were eventually repaid by the German tax payer.[51] The evicted usually received a monthly payment for the use of their house and furniture, but that sometimes did not even cover the cost of maintaining the house or was lower than the rent for the house or flat they were evacuated to. The evicted still had to pay insurance and tax on requisitioned properties, despite not living there – not to mention retaining responsibility for street cleaning and waste collection.[52] When the properties were released, the owners received compensation for damage, but only if this had occurred after 1 August 1945.[53] Most Germans were not aware that the British authorities issued detailed guidance to those occupying requisitioned houses, demanding respectful and responsible behaviour, and even, for example, discussing whether or not the occupiers were allowed to use a piano.[54] Nevertheless, some rooms were damaged and furniture was frequently moved from one place to another, subsequently becoming lost.[55] Furthermore, houses could be re-requisitioned after they had been returned to their previous owners, if new troops arrived and more accommodation was needed. In Iserlohn, for instance, considerable social tension arose after private houses, which had been returned in summer 1947 and were subsequently refurbished by the owners, were to be confiscated again at the beginning of 1948 – while other requisitioned houses were left unoccupied.[56] Situations such as this created a feeling of uncertainty and powerlessness among the local German population, which could easily turn into anger.

This sense of injustice was exacerbated by the fact that the British deliberately chose spa areas, grand hotels and villas as headquarters and living space for high-ranking officers. Through such actions, the British demonstrated their status as the new rulers of Germany, displaying their power not only through issuing orders and instructions, but also symbolically through the occupation of high profile and conspicuous spaces. At the entrance of the spa gardens of Bad Oeynhausen – the heart of the town – stood a sign with the words 'Eintritt für Deutsche nicht gestattet' (access denied for Germans).[57] The notion that the British had taken over German public spaces and were now fully in charge was also communicated through other symbolic practices. In late 1945, for example, BAOR issued Christmas greetings cards displaying a picture of the central spa building of Bad Oeynhausen, which was now being used as the British headquarters.[58] Individual soldiers were also very aware of their status as members of an occupying force. When four houses in a street in Bielefeld were requisitioned for individual soldiers in 1946 – in the middle of a German neighbourhood – the soldiers raised the Union Jack as a symbol of victory and power.[59]

This caused a feeling among many Germans affected by requisitioning of being subjected to victors' justice. This remained the main discourse among German evacuees up to the 1950s and reflected the views of the majority of Germans who had not been persecuted by the Nazi regime during the Third Reich.[60] Many of the evicted claimed that requisitioning was an 'unsagbares Unrecht' (unspeakable injustice), as one speaker proclaimed at a public demonstration in Detmold in 1952, and an illegitimate and 'undemocratic' measure.[61] In fact, the term 'democracy' was repeatedly used by the *Notgemeinschaft Detmold* in order to accuse the British as well as the German authorities of dealing with the problem of requisitioning in an undemocratic, almost 'dictatorial' way.[62] Some of their posters displayed strong words taken from the Bible or from common sayings, which would be familiar to both the British and Germans, such as 'Du sollst nicht begehren deines Nächsten Gut' (Thou shalt not covet thy neighbour's property)[63] or '<u>My</u> home, <u>your</u> castle',[64] implying that those evicted from their homes still had moral, if not legal rights and deserved to be treated with respect and consideration. By referring to a shared religious and cultural heritage, the evicted were claiming that they deserved equal treatment as a Christian and 'civilized' nation. Furthermore, by demonstrating that in this case it was the British who were contravening moral principles generally accepted in both countries, they implied that they were as entitled to discuss moral aspects as the British, while disregarding the question of German guilt that the British frequently raised. The evicted regarded themselves only as victims of war, and accused the Allies of treating them as 'minderwertig, schuldhaft belastet und entrechtet' (inferior, burdened by guilt and deprived of their rights) in a way that they considered wholly inappropriate and unacceptable for a civilized people ('Kulturvolk').[65]

With the British returning responsibility to the Germans step by step, those increasingly insisted on equality. Requisitioning was also criticized as a colonial technique that, in the view of many Germans, was inappropriate in a 'civilized' country. They argued that they had a right to expect higher standards of living than those accepted by the 'natives' in British colonies. 'Sind wir ein Kolonialvolk?' asked, for example, the *Westfälische Zeitung* in February 1952.[66] Similarly, the *Notgemeinschaft*

Detmold proclaimed in 1953 that: 'as [Germany is now] a partner with equal rights in treaties agreed with the Allies, we are not willing to be treated any longer as a colonial people ["Kolonialvolk"]'.[67] The presence of British families was also criticized on similar grounds, as the evicted felt overrun (as they understood the natives in British colonies had been) by a foreign people who installed an entire infrastructure of their own within the German neighbourhoods.[68] With the advent of the Cold War and the gradual integration of western Germany within the Western Bloc in the 1950s, they necessarily accepted the soldiers as protectors, but only in their professional role, not as people with families, wishing to live together and lead a normal family life.[69] While criticisms of the British for adopting colonial practices in Germany may have been as much rhetoric as substance, and a successful strategy for Germans to highlight the contrast with British claims to be promoting democracy in Germany, British officers in Germany with colonial experience did indeed sometimes adopt certain techniques, attitudes and prejudices they had previously used in the Empire.[70]

Disputes over requisitioning did not end with the creation of the (semi-sovereign) FRG. As the future relationship of the FRG with the Western Allies was high on the public agenda in the early 1950s, the chairmen of the *Notgemeinschaften* lobbied the German authorities, unsuccessfully, to try to ensure that the Allied Forces would lose the right to retain requisitioned houses.[71] Protest culminated in the early to mid-1950s. The *Notgemeinschaften* organized demonstrations with several hundred participants, published their demands in the press, wrote a letter to Adenauer, but discovered that they were not able to influence international politics. They were bitterly disappointed and began not only to accuse the British, but also increasingly the German government of neglecting their needs.[72]

Interactions: Fighting, talking, compromise

In spring 1947, the severe shortage of houses and accommodation in the British Zone led to a significant deterioration in Anglo–German relationships and in some cases to open conflict with the Military Government. One such incident revealing significant tensions between the occupiers and the occupied occurred in Hamm, where the British identified six houses to be requisitioned for married families in March 1947 and the city council was unable to find alternative accommodation for the sixty-two occupants. At this time, 1,400 locals were still living in bunkers. Consequently, the German house owners refused to sign the requisition forms, and Hamm City Council threatened to resign if the Military Government insisted on requisitioning.[73] A similar case occurred around the same time in Essen, when the city administration passed a resolution refusing to implement a requisitioning demand.[74] The British authorities took these cases very seriously and perceived them as a direct threat to their authority. As they were afraid of losing control of the situation, they decided to react strongly, insisting that the German authorities had a duty to cooperate and telling them that a refusal would be regarded as resistance, maybe even as sabotage.[75]

Despite taking a hard line in public, British officials acknowledged in internal discussions that the housing situation was a severe problem that had to be alleviated by all means. The Chief Manpower Officer warned: 'I cannot emphasise too strongly that, in my opinion, the indefinite continuance of requisitioning in very badly blitzed areas is leading rapidly to a crisis, when the German Housing Administration will most probably break down'.[76] In order to avoid a serious crisis, a conference on requisitioning in North Rhine-Westphalia was held at the Regional Governmental Office in Düsseldorf on 31 March 1947 at which it was recommended to ensure full use of already occupied houses, to set a limit to further requisitioning, and to waive requisitioning demands in severely affected, so-called black spot areas.[77] To accompany efforts to reduce requisitioning as much as possible, the British authorities set up inspection teams to regularly check if houses could be derequisitioned.[78] Subsequently, Anglo-German groups were established, such as in Bad Oeynhausen, where the British military commander of the district and the Kreis Resident Officer (KRO) would meet the German Mayor and the *Stadtdirektor* (the senior administrative official in the town) and discuss local problems. The British officers could only make very small concessions, but as these meetings provided an opportunity for the German authorities to present the cases brought to their attention by the local population, they were considered useful.[79] More important than such meetings, however, was the launch of building programmes for the German as well as the British population from the late 1940s. By 1955 about 17,000 new flats had been built in North Rhine-Westphalia, while about 5,600 flats remained requisitioned at the end of the year, most of them in the district of Detmold.[80]

Despite these alleviating measures, the situation remained critical. Even if towns were exempt from further requisitioning, the British still sometimes needed additional accommodation. As military units were often moved, it was difficult for the Military Government to foresee how many officers and married families had to be accommodated at any one time. Consequently, the British sometimes broke their promises to local officials and the German administration had to suddenly cope with new requisitions, without being able to shield the population from these measures.[81] As the German administration had to try and meet the demands of the British on the one hand but also take into consideration the interests of the evicted, in several cities they tried to establish working committees with representatives from both sides.

The cases of Herford and Detmold can help us understand how the various actors dealt with conflicts around requisitioning. When the Control Commission left Herford and handed over around 250 houses to the BAOR in 1951, British and German authorities decided to set an example of how to deal successfully with the problem of accommodation in what became known as the 'Herford Plan'. The German administration guaranteed to satisfy British accommodation requirements and in return suggested the idea of partial derequisitioning. If a house was big enough for two or more separate flats and not fully occupied by British families, one flat should be formally derequisitioned and given back to the German owners. This was the first time that Germans and British would officially live together in one building, which represented a significant shift from earlier policy.[82] The development of the Herford Plan was also of high symbolic significance as it signalled a change in the relations between the British and the Germans. Thus, when representatives of the Federal and Land governments, the British Army, the town council, and the *Notgemeinschaft* all agreed to the proposal in summer 1951, newspaper articles praised the experiment for having removed the 'iron curtain' between the occupiers and the occupied and as such it was hailed as an example for the whole zone.[83]

But success was not easy to achieve. A committee formed by members of the British and German administrations as well as the local *Notgemeinschaft* visited every house that was likely to meet the stipulated requirements and decided which buildings would be suitable. That took a lot of time: the committee inspected 215 houses in nine months and discussed every single case. In February 1952, twenty-four complete houses, thirty-nine flats and thirty-six attics were derequisitioned,[84] and by mid-June the British had returned a total of thirty-six houses and seventy-two flats.[85] Nevertheless, many of the evicted considered this as insufficient and the procedure too slow, as the *Notgemeinschaft* stated that Herford had about 600 requisitioned flats at the beginning of 1952.[86] In January 1952, *Notgemeinschaft* Herford complained to the Land Commissioner, criticizing that only very few single family houses had been derequisitioned.[87] Subsequently, in a letter to BAOR, the British Land Commissioner, Brigadier Lingham, suggested that some of the grievances raised by the *Notgemeinschaft* should be examined. He explained that even if the Germans were simply trying to manipulate their British counterparts, communication would at least help to reduce a tense situation:

> Herford has acquired some notoriety as a testing ground for the Germans to see how far they can get us to relax our standards of accommodation. That is tough on the local staff but it has, I think, done on the whole a deal more good than harm. Certainly, last spring I was beginning to fear trouble and disorder in that area whereas now I feel reasonably happy that the present calm conditions will continue.[88]

Colonel Darley, who as the representative of the Army had to negotiate with the German side, felt less comfortable. He explained that the Army could not accept a policy of derequisitioning primarily single-family houses, since they were difficult to share and were needed for officers, as accommodation had to meet Army standards. He complained that

> The trouble with these Germans is that they never give any credit for concessions we have made. The word 'compromise' does not exist in the German language. They expect that we should give way to every request they make on compassionate grounds quite regardless of our own needs and, whenever we do settle any compassionate cases, a couple more come out of the bag as a matter of routine.[89]

Nevertheless, meetings continued and in September 1952 about 170 houses were (partly) given back to the owners.[90] In spring 1953, approximately 150 German families were living together with British occupants.[91]

For the most part, cohabitation of British and German families worked well and sometimes led to friendships. The house of the Meyer family, for example, on the *Stiftberg* – the prohibited area – had been requisitioned in 1945 and one flat was derequisitioned in December 1951.[92] The family moved back and met very friendly and German-speaking British occupants with whom they chatted, ate and exchanged recipes. When a year later a new family moved in, the two families established a close relationship once they discovered that three of the female inhabitants – the British wife, her baby daughter and the German daughter – were all called Ellen. This relationship turned into a lifelong friendship spanning two generations. From a child's perspective, there were no conflicts between the nations on the *Stiftberg*. Hans-Dieter M. remembered that all the children went sledging together and afterwards enjoyed tea and biscuits with a British family.[93]

Several Westphalian cities tried to replicate the Herford project, but often with less favourable results. Success in Herford owed much to the fact that the CCG had left; other towns, by contrast, did not have a surplus of vacated houses.[94] In Detmold, for example, after lengthy discussions and inspections, the British derequisitioned only six attics.[95] The evicted were bitterly disappointed, and felt neglected and left alone with their problems. They declared that they refused to believe further promises and announced that they would fight for their rights if nothing happened in the immediate future.[96] This was the emotional backdrop to the decision of the Detmold *Notgemeinschaft* to take action following a report by an evicted woman, Frau Rumbke, to the effect that her house had been vacated and left unoccupied for some time. The *Notgemeinschaft* decided to use her situation to showcase their anger and set an example. Supported by the *Notgemeinschaft*, the Rumbke family illegally reoccupied their house at night. This action was well organized and heavily publicized to attract public attention: Bielefeld *Notgemeinschaft* printed posters, the local press reported daily on the case, a private company provided a loudspeaker van which informed the local population about the events, and several hundred evacuees from different towns came to support the family when the British threatened to evict them by force.[97] When Frau Rumbke refused to let the British KRO into her house for negotiations and he left the property, the crowd began to sing the German national anthem,[98] suggesting that resistance against requisitioning was not only a question of regaining individual living space, but rather of resisting what many saw as a 'colonial' occupation force, claiming the moral high ground and reasserting German sovereignty.

Although the British authorities made it clear that they would insist on regaining possession of the house, they decided to avoid violence and negotiated with Frau Rumbke, with members of the *Notgemeinschaft*, and with the city council for several days. After two weeks, Frau Rumbke gave up. She felt unable to resist the pressure from British as well as German authorities that she might be evicted by force. The *Notgemeinschaft* was disappointed – even more so when Frau Rumbke left the community having been evacuated to a nice flat elsewhere.[99]

While the *Notgemeinschaft* had gained support from the media, relations between the population and the British Army in Detmold deteriorated. In order to prevent similar occurrences, the Army started to guard unoccupied houses.[100] Meetings between the KRO and members of the *Notgemeinschaft* and the town council to discuss compassionate cases were becoming increasingly difficult, and the KRO was regularly accused of alleged colonial methods.[101] Relations worsened even further on New Year's Eve, when letters were posted through the letterboxes of requisitioned houses, addressed to 'the British occupants of our houses':

> We should like to call your attention to the fact <u>that it is not right for you</u> to live in our property … As we do not wish you to stay any longer in our property, we ask you to leave our houses as quickly as possible. Germany is not a Colony of the Allied Forces, and the German will know how to resist Colonial measures … The Evacuees.[102]

This letter caused considerable disquiet among British families, and the KRO made clear that the British Army did not intend to accept such methods. In June 1953, he stated that his efforts to achieve further derequisitioning by working together with the City Council and *Notgemeinschaft* were failing because the BAOR refused to cooperate after the aggressive activities by the evicted.[103] Only several months later were any further properties derequisitioned by the BAOR in Detmold.[104]

The situation remained tense in many Westphalian towns and disputes over requisitioning were eventually resolved only after new residential areas were built in the 1950s. Most private requisitioned houses in Westphalia were given back to their owners by 1955, but the last house in Paderborn, requisitioned in 1946, was not returned to its German owners until March 1958.[105]

Conclusion

Housing and finding suitable accommodation was one of the most important issues determining relations between occupiers and occupied in the British Zone. Requisitioning implied more than the technical problem of giving everyone a roof over their head. It was also an emotional question, as it deprived people of their home as the centre of family life, and a political issue as this deprivation was caused by the occupation forces. Although the fate of having lost their homes was shared by millions of people in post-war Germany and elsewhere due to other reasons, such as forced labour, imprisonment, bombing or expulsion, many of the Germans considered in this chapter, evicted due to requisitioning by the British in Westphalia, felt that they had to carry the burden of the lost war to an exceptional degree, through no fault of their own. They rarely placed their circumstances in a broader context, or compared it with the plight of other people in Europe in countries occupied by Germany during the war, let alone contrasted it to the suffering of those persecuted by the Nazi regime, or saw their present difficulties as a consequence of a war of aggression launched by their own country.

Even if living conditions in the rural areas of Westphalia were not as harsh as in the big cities, the evicted still lost what they considered was their right to have a private space where no one was allowed to intrude, and many objected to being squeezed together with strangers without sufficient privacy. They felt they were being treated in an unfair and 'uncivilized' way, like 'natives' in the British colonies, which was humiliating for those who had been taught to think of themselves as *Herrenmenschen* only a few years earlier. As political interest in the FRG in the early 1950s shifted to other victim groups such as returning German prisoners of war or the German expellees, the anger of those evicted from their homes due to requisitioning rose, as they felt that their own needs and concerns were not being properly addressed.

The evicted founded pressure groups and tried on the one hand to create publicity by placing their demands in the press and organizing demonstrations. They also tried to negotiate with both German and British officials and, after the formation of the FRG, lobby German politicians when future relations with the Western Allies were discussed. The British authorities, for their part, tried to involve Germans to some degree. Anglo-German committees were established in the late 1940s, comprising German and British officials, who discussed housing problems as well as the use of confiscated swimming pools or cinemas. Even if concessions were small at the beginning, it was a feasible way for the British to let the Germans have their say, and for the German authorities to demonstrate that they did their best to negotiate on behalf of the general public with the occupiers. In the 1950s working groups were established in several cities which included the *Notgemeinschaften* as partner. While the British made clear that they would resist direct protests as a challenge to their authority in the early years of the occupation, they tolerated and attempted to respond to discontent and criticism in the 1950s, as shown in the Herford case. Being prepared to talk and discuss issues of concern to the occupied was an important technique which often helped to pacify a tense situation. Talking and getting to know each other as individuals was crucial also on a personal level. Those evacuees who came to know the British occupiers through personal encounters sometimes accepted even a difficult housing situation. To some extent therefore, the presence of British families created conflict, but it also helped to establish relationships between individuals.

The building of new residential areas eventually solved the housing crisis, though it also created new challenges. Some residential areas for British occupying troops were built close to German neighbourhoods, but most were not integrated with the existing urban infrastructure. In the 1960s, for example, a large housing development for British married couples was constructed in Detmold near the Army barracks but quite far from the town centre, so that the British and Germans lived segregated lives.[106] The British were largely self-sufficient, with a NAAFI shop, schools, sports as well as leisure and medical facilities all nearby. No one had to leave the Army compound to go about their daily lives and some people hardly ever went to the town centre.[107] Consequently, these 'married quarters' became known as 'Klein London' (Little London).[108] This marked a new stage in Anglo–German relationships, as British and German lives no longer intersected daily as they had in the early years of the occupation.

Notes

1 Calculation by the Housing Branch of Manpower Division, CCG. Control Commission for Germany (BE), Public Relations Branch: Press Release PR/concomb33, 11 July 1947; The National Archives, London, FO 1013/1724.

2 Calculation by the Federal Statistical Office of the FRG; published in *Die Notgemeinschaft. Mitteilungsblatt der Besatzungsverdrängten*, November 1951.

3 'The British in Westphalia 1945–2017', a collaborative project of the city of Paderborn together with Paderborn University, archives, museums and other institutions in the eastern part of Westphalia. Research began in 2015.
4 Christopher Knowles, *Winning the Peace: The British in Occupied Germany, 1945–1948* (PhD thesis, Kings College London, 2014), 222; Peter Speiser, *The British Army of the Rhine and the Germans (1948–1957): From Enemies to Partners* (PhD thesis, University of Westminster, 2012), 112; StA Lübbecke, D 26 Bd. 2; 'Hoffnung für Fernsprech-Anwärter', *Westfälische Zeitung. Anzeiger für Stadt und Kreis Herford*, 17 July 1951.
5 I would like to thank Sandra Holtrup for her thorough research of newspaper articles.
6 Speiser, *British Army of the Rhine*, 128.
7 Exfor to SHAEF, 28 March 1945, TNA, WO 205/349.
8 Report on M. G. Recce Bad Oeynhausen, 8–10 April 1945, TNA, WO 205/349.
9 Photocopy of the pamphlet 'Bad Oeynhausen', StA Bad Oeynhausen.
10 Nina Gehring, Rico Quaschny and Ursula Tewes, 'Zeittafel. Ausgewählte Daten zur Geschichte von Deutschland und Bad Oeynhausen 1945–55', in *Bad Oeynhausen zwischen Krieg und Frieden. Kriegsende und Besatzungszeit in Zeitzeugnissen und Erinnerungen*, ed. Rico Quaschny (3rd edn., Bielefeld: Verlag für Regionalgeschichte 2015), 367–87.
11 Klaus Peter Schumann, 'Vorwort zur 3. Auflage 2015', in Quaschny, *Bad Oeynhausen*, 8–13; Town mayor to the inhabitants of Bad Oeynhausen, 4 May 1945, StA Bad Oeynhausen: Bildband der Stadt Bad Oeynhausen Bd. 3; Fred Kaspar, 'Die Besatzungsstreitkräfte und ihr Wohnraumbedarf nach 1945. Grundlagen zur denkmalkundlichen Bewertung der baulichen Zeugnisse eines politischen, administrativen und militärischen Bestandteils der Bundesrepublik Deutschland', *Westfalen. Hefte für Geschichte, Kunst und Volkskunde* 81 (2003): 217–34.
12 Bad Oeynhausen. Eine leidende Stadt, 1952, StA Bad Oeynhausen, NGB 8–13.
13 Kaspar, *Besatzungsstreitkräfte*, 230–1. Wolfgang Günther, 'Zwischen Kirche und Kasernen: Der Stiftberg', in *1200 Jahre Herford. Spuren der Geschichte*, ed. Theodor Helmert-Corvey and Thomas Schuler (Herford: Maximilian-Verlag Herford 1989), 157–72.
14 CCG(BE), Office of the Chief of Staff to the Mayor of Lübbecke, 3 August 1945, StA Lübbecke, D 54 Bd. 1.
15 Verwaltung des Staatsbades Bad Oeynhausen to Regierungspräsident Detmold, 13 December 1949, Landesarchiv NRW, Abt. Ostwestfalen-Lippe (LAV NRW OWL), D1/11977.
16 'Bad Oeynhausen nach dem 1. Juli', *Notgemeinschaft*, July 1951.
17 Gehring, Quaschny and Tewes, *Zeittafel*, 384–6.
18 Bezirks-Feststellungsbehörde Minden to finance minister NRW, 29 May 1948, LAV NRW OWL, M1/I/R/211.
19 Mary Bouman to her family, 1 April 1946, Imperial War Museum (IWM), documents 16779.
20 Requisitioning Policy in Germany of Accommodation and Furniture, 17 January 1947 (and Appendix A: Accommodation, 14 October 1946), TNA, FO 1013/1724.
21 Bürgermeister Schwerte to Kreis-Militärregierung Iserlohn, 10 December 1947, LAV NRW W, Amt für Verteidigungslasten Soest no. 23.
22 Speiser, *British Army of the Rhine*, 113.

23 This was discussed in the training centre for CCG staff: COD & TC (Training Wing): 'Germany Today, Part I'. Precis No. MC.51, TNA, FO 1032/992B. I would like to thank Diana Goldsworthy for drawing my attention to this document.
24 Interview with Lieselotte H., Detmold, 1 December 2015.
25 70 HQ CCG, HQ Int. Division, to 60 HQ CCG, Chief Admin. Officer Maintenance III, 10 October 1946, TNA, FO 1013/1727.
26 Interview with Eckehart S., Detmold, 1 December 2015.
27 Sarah G., 'Germany 1947–51. Göttingen, Dortmund, Mönchengladbach, Düsseldorf', 2016 (unpublished manuscript in the author's possession).
28 TNA, FO 938/320; Kreisverwaltung Halle/Westfalen to Bezirksfeststellungsbehörde Minden, 20 May 1948, LAV NRW OWL, M1/I/R/211.
29 Sarah Paterson, 'Operation "Union": British Families in Germany', 1946, *Imperial War Museum Review* 10 (1995): 7483.
30 Michael Ahrens, *Die Briten in Hamburg. Besatzerleben 1945–1958* (Munich and Hamburg, 2011), 146.
31 British Army of the Rhine, *A Guide for Families in BAOR* (September 1949), introduction.
32 Speiser, *British Army of the Rhine*, 33.
33 Mary Bouman to her family, 6 August 1947, IWM, documents 16679.
34 Edna Wearmouth to her father, 11 February 1947, IWM, documents 5413.
35 Edna Wearmouth to her father, 15 March 1947, IWM, documents 5413. For a more detailed discussion of Edna Wearmouth's experiences in Germany, see the chapter by Daniel Cowling in this volume.
36 Interview with Helga K., Bielefeld, 2 November 2015.
37 German children say this while playing hide-and-seek to announce when they are ready to start looking for others. Interview with Peter F., 12 September 2016.
38 Interview with Edeltraud S., Detmold, 7 December 2015.
39 Vereinsregister, Aktenzeichen V R 91 Amtsgericht Bad Oeynhausen, StA Bad Oeynhausen, NGB 1.
40 Arbeitsgemeinschaft der Landesverbände der Besatzungsgeschädigten im Bundesgebiet to Notgemeinschaft der Besatzungsgeschädigten Detmold, 13 April 1953, LAV NRW OWL, D 107/3; Landesverband NRW der Besatzungsgeschädigten, minutes, 14 May 1955, LAV NRW OWL, D 107/4.
41 *Die Notgemeinschaft. Mitteilungsblatt der Besatzungsverdrängten*. The newspaper was published in Bad Oeynhausen from January 1951 onwards, at least until May 1952.
42 Regional Commissioner Land NRW to Ministerpräsident NRW, 30 July 1947, TNA, FO 1013/1726.
43 British Resident Münster-Rural to Oberkreisdirektor Landkreis Münster, 23 November 1949, StA Münster, Kreis C/182.
44 Bezirks-Feststellungsbehörde Minden to the finance minister NRW, 29 May 1948, LAV NRW OWL, M1/I/R/211.
45 HQ BAOR, 18 March 1947, TNA, FO 1013/1724.
46 Bezirks-Feststellungsbehörde Minden to the finance minister NRW, 29 May 1948; LAV NRW OWL, M1/I/R/211.
47 British Army of the Rhine, *A Guide for Families in BAOR* (September 1949), 17–9.
48 Sarah G., 'Germany 1947–51', unpublished manuscript.
49 BAOR/5301/14/Q(Maint)2: Requisitioning Policy in Germany of Accommodation and Furniture, 17 January 1947, TNA, FO 1013/1724.

50 Bezirks-Feststellungsbehörde Minden to the finance minister NRW, 29 May 1948, LAV NRW OWL, M1/I/R/211.
51 Finanzminister NRW to Bezirksfeststellungsbehörde Regierungspräsident Detmold: Fragebogen zur Ausarbeitung eines Besatzungsstatuts, 3.5.1948, LAV NRW OWL, M1/I/R/211.
52 Die Notgemeinschaft, February 1951; Abt. Für Besatzungsangelegenheiten to Stadtdirektor Detmold, 2 December 1952; StA Detmold: D 106/1647; Interview with Lieselotte H., 1 December 2015.
53 CCG, Public Expenditure Branch, HQ Finance Division: Finanztechnische Anweisung No 94, 12 February 1947 (copy); CCG, Finance Division: Technische Anweisung No 99, StA Münster, Kreis C/215.
54 *A Guide for Families in BAOR*, 3–10.
55 *Die Notgemeinschaft* (December 1951).
56 Bürgermeister Iserlohn to Military Government, 1 January 1948, LAV NRW W, Amt für Verteidigungslasten Soest no. 23.
57 Photo, around 1950; StA Bad Oeynhausen, Bildarchiv C1/6/6.
58 Christmas card, 1945; StA Bad Oeynhausen.
59 Unpublished photograph, 1946, private property.
60 Robert G. Moeller, 'Deutsche Opfer, Opfer der Deutschen. Kriegsgefangene, Vertriebene, NS-Verfolgte: Opferausgleich als Identitätspolitik', in *Nachkrieg in Deutschland*, ed. Klaus Naumann (Hamburg, 2011), 29–58.
61 Script for a speech by Liselotte Heldmann on a demonstration in Detmold, 9 February 1952, LAV NRW OWL, D 107/T/2.
62 Ibid.; Jugend der Besatzungsgeschädigten von Ostwestfalen-Lippe to Bundeskanzler Adenauer, 15 April 1953, LAV NRW OWL, D 107/T/3.
63 *Freie Presse, Lippisches Volksblatt*, 22 September 1952.
64 LAV NRW OWL, D 81 Nr. 3857.
65 'Zeichen der Zeit', *Die Notgemeinschaft*, February 1951.
66 'Frauen fordern ihr Eigentum zurück', *Westfälische Zeitung*, 11 February 1952.
67 Notgemeinschaft Detmold to the Mayor of Detmold, 4.2.1953, LAV NRW OWL, D 107/T/3. The original German was 'dass wir als gleichberechtigte Partner der deutsch-alliierten Verträge nicht gewillt sind, uns noch länger als Kolonialvolk behandeln zu lassen' (editors' translation).
68 Notgemeinschaft der Besatzungsgeschädigten Detmold to Dr. Neubronner, 20 February 1952, LAV NRW OWL, D 107/T/2.
69 'Der Herforder Plan, eine Aktion des guten Willens', *Die Notgemeinschaft*, October 1951; 'Beratung mit höchsten Stellen gefordert', *Freie Presse*, 13 September 1952.
70 Norman B., *Recollections of a Young British Army Officer BAOR August 1950 to March 1952*, written in 2016 (document in author's possession); interview with Norman B., 2 October 2016. Mary Bouman repeatedly used the term 'natives' referring to Germans, such as 'Now that I have been here some time it is easier to sum up the attitude of the natives' (letter of 20 January 1946), IWM, private documents 16779.
71 'Besatzungsverdrängte und Generalvertrag', *Westfälische Zeitung*, 6 February 1952; 'Enttäuschende Bestimmungen der Verträge', *Freie Presse Bad Oeynhausen*, 11 July 1952; 'Wohnraumbedarf der Truppe unverändert', *Mindener Tageblatt*, 29 October 1956; 'Deutsches Eigentum bleibt beschlagnahmt', *Mindener Tageblatt*, 15 December 1956.

72 'Enttäuschende Bestimmungen der Verträge', *Freie Presse Bad Oeynhausen*, 11 July 1952.
73 HQ Mil Gov RB Arnsberg to the Regional Commissioner Land NRW, 24 March 1947, TNA, FO 1013/1726.
74 Resolution, 21 March 1947, TNA, FO 1051/150.
75 Minutes of the meeting on requisitioning in Essen, 22 March 1947, TNA, FO 1051/150.
76 Chief Manpower Officer, HQ Mil Gov. Düsseldorf, to Deputy Chief Berlin and Manpower Housing Lemgo, 24 March 1947, TNA, FO 1051/150.
77 Minutes of the conference on requisitioning held by the Regional Commissioner 31 March 1947, TNA, FO 1013/40.
78 Regional Commissioner Land NRW to Ministerpräsident NRW, 30 July 1947, TNA, FO 1013/1726.
79 Meetings of the Garrison Commander, Bad Oeynhausen, with the German Municipal Authorities, 23 July 1949, TNA, FO 1013/2240.
80 Thomas Tippach, 'Wohnungsbau für die Besatzungs- und Stationierungsstreitkräfte in Westfalen', *Westfalen. Hefte für Geschichte, Kunst und Volkskunde* 81 (2003): 235–89.
81 Several examples in LAV NRW W, Amt für Verteidigungslasten Soest no. 23.
82 Stadtverwaltung Herford: Herforder Plan, 12 June 1951, TNA, FO 1013/2427.
83 'Zwei Nationen unter einem Dach', *Die Welt*, 29 February 1952; 'Eiserner Vorhang zwischen Besatzung und Deutschen gefallen! Herforder Experiment gelungen/ Eine historische Stunde der deutsch-englischen Beziehungen', *Mindener Tageblatt*, 13 August 1951; 'Die 'Aktion des guten Willens' jetzt auch in Minden', *Mindener Tageblatt*, 6 September 1951.
84 General comments by Col Darly on the Herford Plan, February 1952, TNA, FO 1013/ 2427.
85 Stadtdirektor Wöhrmann: Herforder Plan: Stand vom 15 June 1952, Kreisarchiv Herford, 20/372.
86 Notgemeinschaft Detmold to Regierungspräsident Drake, 23 February 1952, LAV NRW OWL, D 107/T/2.
87 Notgemeinschaft Herford to the Land Commissioner NRW, 24 January 1952, TNA, FO 1013/2427.
88 Brigadier Lingham to HQ BAOR, Major General G. S. Hatton, 7 February 1952, TNA, FO 1013/2427.
89 'General comments' on the situation in Herford by Col. Darley, February 1952, TNA, FO 1013/2427.
90 'Kein Wehrdienst vor Herstellung des Rechts', *Freie Presse*, 29 September 1952.
91 'Englisches Ja für Herforder Bautyp', *Freie Presse*, 29 April 1953.
92 Stadtverwaltung Herford: file note, 7 December 1951, KAH 20/298.
93 Conversation with Hans-Dieter M., 15 September 2016.
94 British resident Detmold to the members of the advisory Anglo-German committee, September 1951, StA Detmold, D 106/1678.
95 Notgemeinschaft der Besatzungsgeschädigten Detmold to Regierungspräsident Detmold, 23 February 1952; LAV NRW OWL, D 107/T/2; and StA Detmold, D 106/ 1678.
96 Speech of Liselotte Heldmann at a demonstration in Detmold, 9 February 1952, LAV NRW OWL, D 107/T/2.
97 Interview with Lieselotte H., 1 December 2015.
98 'Beratung mit höchsten Stellen gefordert', *Freie Presse*, 13 September 1952.

99 Lieselotte Heldmann to Karl Heller, Gießen, 7 April 1953, LAV NRW OWL: D 107/T/2; 'Frau Rumbke verlässt ihr Haus freiwillig', *Freie Presse*, 23 September 1952.
100 British resident Paderborn to Stadtdirektor Detmold, 19 June 1953, StA Detmold, D 106/1653.
101 File note on a meeting between Herford officials, Notgemeinschaft and the KRO, 9 March 1953, StA Detmold, D 106/1669; interview with Lieselotte H., 1 December 2015.
102 Letter dated 31 December 1952, StA Detmold, D 106/1653.
103 British resident Paderborn to Stadtdirektor Detmold, 19 June 1953, StA Detmold, D 106/1653.
104 Stadtdirektor Detmold to British resident Paderborn, 22 March 1954, StA Detmold, D 106/1653.
105 Ordnungsamt Paderborn to Maria Becker, 20 March 1958, Stadt- und Kreisarchiv Paderborn, B 368/362; interview with Hildegard B., 27 January 2016.
106 Maria Junker, Malte Leimbach and Jan Schmelter, 'Konflikt und Entspannung zwischen Kontakt und Segregation. Die Nachbarschaft von Briten und Deutschen in Detmold nach dem Zweiten Weltkrieg', *Lippische Mitteilungen* (2015): 129–31.
107 Interview with Michael and Susanne H., 25 February 2016.
108 '20 neue Wohnungen für Besatzung. Freigabe beschlagnahmter Häuser. 1953 Baubeginn in, Klein London', *Freie Presse*, 28 April 1953.

8

Game Plan for Democracy: Sport and Youth in Occupied West Germany

Heather L. Dichter

In the aftermath of the Second World War, the Allies realized they needed to provide new opportunities for German youth to participate in physical activity, to replace the state-controlled monopoly of sports programmes during the Third Reich. Following the Allied victory, German youth were left with no organized activity groups. As a British report noted, the collapse of the Third Reich and forced closure of all Nazi organizations 'brought nothing to replace them but a spiritual vacuum and political confusion'.[1] In a country facing severe destruction as a result of the war, these problems compounded the difficulties already faced by Germans to obtain basic necessities such as food, coal and shelter for survival.

One of the earliest pieces of occupation policy passed by the quadripartite Allied Control Authority was Directive 23 on the 'Limitation and Demilitarization of Sport in Germany'. Passed in December 1945, Directive 23 applied the punitive functions of the occupation as defined at the Potsdam Conference to the field of sport, setting out how organizations should be denazified, demilitarized and decentralized.[2] However, the Allies realized that sport could also be used to introduce democratic ideas to the German population more broadly. All three of the western occupation powers therefore assigned Military Government officials in their zones of occupation to oversee youth and sport programmes, many of which began as a combined initiative involving both the Military Governments and Germans. Much has been written about the German Youth Activities programme, sponsored by the US Army, and on re-education activities more generally, such as the courses held for Germans at Wilton Park in Britain.[3] Less well known are the sports programmes organized by the three Military Governments, in conjunction with specialist civilian sport administrators and other youth leaders recruited from home, designed to help develop and foster democratic ideas within Germany.

Although Allied Control Directive 23 was issued by the four occupiers jointly, each Military Government independently developed specific policies and programmes to implement within its zone. The policies of the Americans, British and French shared many features, but they were also distinctive. By using sport to further their objectives in Germany, the Western Allies were quite visibly 'doing occupation', attempting to shape ordinary Germans' daily life outside on sport grounds or inside sport halls. Just as the rationale why someone participates in sport today can vary greatly – simply enjoying the activity, socializing with friends, challenging oneself or improving one's health – the image, reality and rhetoric surrounding the use of sport during the occupation helps to reveal the variation and complexity of the different occupiers' aims and the German responses. The high participation rates in sport clubs and activities allowed the Western Allies to present a successful image of smiling athletes playing games to people at home, and so claim that their programmes were achieving occupation goals. Comments from German participants which reinforced the occupiers' stated aims were repeated and promoted, whereas any comments from people who just wanted to play sport and did not care about how a club was led – which very probably existed – were absent from occupation records. Nonetheless, the broad popularity of sport among Germans, young and old, enabled the US, British and French Military Governments to work closely with 'ordinary' Germans at local level, rather than deal exclusively with a political or social elite of party politicians, officials or administrators.

The occupation powers wanted Germans to learn and adopt democratic practices, but the experience of the Third Reich prevented the use of blatant propaganda, as the occupiers wished to avoid being accused of using similar methods to the Nazis. Sport instead allowed for more subtle promotion of occupation goals to Germans. As the Western Allies began shifting their focus from the more punitive policies of denazification and demilitarization pursued in the first months of the occupation to an emphasis on democratization by late 1946, the three western powers implemented programmes focused on teaching democracy.[4] With sport activities having the highest participation rates among young people compared to religious or cultural activities, while also being popular among adults, the occupiers saw sport as an important component of their efforts to impart ideas about democracy and teamwork to a broad portion of the population. The Allies considered that what the German youth did in their time outside the four walls of the classroom was important for providing a democratic foundational basis. All three of the Allies believed that the future of Germany depended on young people, rather than an older generation whom they feared would remain committed to Nazi ideas, and sport could be an effective means of 'teaching democracy', as it was more subtle than blatant propaganda, offered high participation rates, and complemented classroom education and other activities designed to promote democratic ideals among German youth.

Sport for democracy

During the Third Reich, the National Socialists placed sport organizations under their firm control and emphasized the militaristic characteristics of sport. One year into the regime the National Youth Leader, Baldur von Schirach 'wrested control over basic physical exercises for young teenagers from the previously non-party-political National Association for Physical Exercise'.[5] The National Sport Leader (*Reichssportführer*), Hans von Tschammer und Osten, became von Schirach's deputy and was given responsibility for the integration of sport within the Hitler Youth (*Hitlerjugend*). Sport organizations now had to comply with the policy of coordination (*Gleichschaltung*) and adopt Nazi policies, or else they were closed. German youth could therefore only participate in sport through the Hitler Youth, with activities designed to further Nazi aims. The Hitler Youth in particular favoured boxing, a sport which Hitler had mentioned as an important component of pre-military training in *Mein Kampf*, as well as team sports which promoted a sense of national community (*Volksgemeinschaft*). For girls, the focus was not so much on sports which required physical strength but rather on group rhythmic gymnastics, which promoted collective movement and grace. In keeping with official Nazi views of the role of women in society, the 'flow of gymnastic movements was closely related to the feminine anatomy' and the 'future role of women as childbearers'.[6] Under the Nazis' leadership, the National Sport Competition, a national sport tournament for school pupils first established in 1920, grew from 1.5 million teenage participants in 1933 to seven million in 1939, nearly 80 per cent of all German teenagers.[7] The Nazis used sport specifically to strengthen the nation and prepare for war, and Germans who wanted to participate in athletics accepted the presence of National Socialist ideology, some willingly and some reluctantly for the sake of competing. The complete control of sport by the Nazis and its coupling with militaristic goals prompted the Allies to create Allied Control Directive 23, designed to prevent sport activities and institutions from being used as a vehicle through which Nazi ideas might persist and eventually revive. The directive, however, left the question of how specifically to establish alternative structures and encourage activities that would promote democracy rather than National Socialism to the discretion of each occupation power within their zone.

In designing sport policies for Germany, the western occupiers drew on attitudes towards sport current in their own societies. In Great Britain, there was a long-standing custom of emphasizing the societal benefits of sport structured around key principles such as fair play, amateurism and health. These principles were also fundamental for the development of sport and physical education in North America, where the large number and size of secondary schools and universities contributed to the adoption and regulation of sport within education.[8] There were, of course, differences in emphasis. Thus, headmasters at British public schools used sport to control rowdy and undisciplined pupils while simultaneously instilling the ideals of what constituted a well-rounded man of the British Empire.[9] But there were also numerous similarities. On both sides of the Atlantic and the Channel, for example, factories beset with strikes established sports teams with employees as the players seeking to reinforce the workers' identification with their employer through the provision of company teams.[10] Similarly, the playground movement, arising in both Britain and the United States in concert with the concept of the settlement house as responses to the ills of urban slums at the end of the nineteenth century, used sport as a method of social control and moral improvement for urban youth. The construction of playgrounds and supervised playtime for children was intended to alleviate social problems.[11] The decision by the Allies to employ sport for political ends in Germany was therefore not a great departure from the occupiers' experiences at home, where sport had long been used both as a method of domestic social control and as a way to prepare the upper classes for their role as future leaders and rulers.

Drawing on such domestic experiences with how sport could be used to promote social change at home, the Western Allies incorporated sport within their programmes to help develop a democratic understanding among Germans. A September 1945 American directive on youth activities stated that 'a positive program should be allowed to develop which will give German youth opportunities to prepare for the eventual reconstruction of German life on a democratic and peaceful basis', and that 'these groups should aim to make possible the successful development of democratic ideas and the cultivation of ideals of fair play, tolerance and honesty'.[12] Similarly, a British Military Government Physical Education Officer reported in 1946: '[our] attitude to physical education and sport is one of positive encouragement:– (a) in order to obtain a healthy and balanced development of the child's personality. (b) in order to loosen up the narrowly academic tradition in German education'. While the first objective should be the 'balanced development of the body', physical education should also seek the 'promotion of the psychological characteristics summed up in the word "sportsmanship"'.[13]

Youth and sport activities fell under the broader purview of education divisions within the Military Governments, and both the British and French designated specific officials to direct the occupiers' sport policies on the ground. John G. Dixon, the Chief Sports Officer for the British Zone, had been the Senior Physical Education Master at Dover Grammar School and the Area Adviser on Physical Education to the Kent Education Committee, while Guy Du Mesnil, *Chef du Bureau des Sports* in the French Zone, had previously served as *Inspecteur de l'Éducation Physique et Sports*, a mid-level bureaucratic position primarily entailing visiting educational institutions and sporting associations to ensure that they met the expectations and obligations put forward by the French state.[14] The Americans did not create a similar position, but their officers at the *Land* level who dealt with sport matters often had youth or recreation experience prior to the war. These men implemented policies within their areas of jurisdiction and met together throughout the occupation to coordinate actions and share information across the zones. While Allied occupation goals, on the surface, were to prevent Germany from instigating yet another world war, the aim underlying US, British and French actions in the field of sports policy progressed from denazification and demilitarization to teaching Germans how to be democratic and run democratic organizations, and eventually to promoting friendship with the occupying powers to overcome the animosity encouraged by the Nazis.

In addition to coordinating sport policies within their education divisions, which demonstrated the Western Allies' commitment to influencing German youth through schools, the Allies also developed broader youth programmes. Extra-curricular activities for young people were extremely popular in the immediate post-war period. The Americans, for instance, noted that one-fourth of the two million boys and girls between the ages of ten and eighteen in their zone participated in such activities in 1946, and the British found comparable numbers for their zone.[15] It was therefore unsurprising that the US Military Government manual made a direct connection between what the local population did in their spare time and the goal of democratization, stating that they wanted Germans to have a 'constructive use of leisure time and the successful development of democracy in terms of ideas, initiative, responsibility and the practice of democratic procedures'.[16]

An early report compiled by the United States Education Mission to Germany, commonly referred to as the Zook Report, reinforced the importance of youth activities, both within the education system and outside of it.[17] Participating in the Mission was Paul M. Limbert, a Young Men's Christian Association (YMCA) official who, just before he left for Germany, had become President of Springfield College in Massachusetts.[18] Limbert wrote that even with the difficulties of living in post-war Germany, youth work should provide hope that Germans could be re-educated democratically.[19]

For youth programmes to contribute to the occupiers' aims effectively, the Zook Report recommended initiatives designed to develop new youth organization group leaders. The report anticipated that these groups would then 'make a significant contribution to the training of young people in democratic ways of thinking and living' and provide 'experiences that will develop understanding and cooperation among the various groups'. Contact with other German youth groups in cultural and recreational activities, instead of only mingling with similarly minded individuals, the report argued, could soften traditional divisions in German society.[20] However, the report also acknowledged that many of the problems which confronted education officials in general also affected the development of youth activities: the shortage of facilities and a lack of denazified German instructors with democratic leadership experience. The Zook Report recommended an increase in American personnel to assist youth programmes and optimistically believed that the necessary resources to support such activities could be obtained. The report stated that 'because of the deep interest of Americans in sports and recreation, it is easier to secure popular support among American soldiers and civilians for the reconstruction of youth activities in Germany than for any other phase of re-education'.[21]

Although the French, like the British, had created specific positions within their Military Government to address sport and physical education, their approach to sport was more cautious and restrictive than that of their Allies. The French passed two pieces of legislation on 4 February 1946 to implement Directive 23 in their zone of occupation. *Ordonnance 33* authorized the constitution of sport associations in the French Zone, stipulating that clubs practising sport or physical education must pursue only those ends and no others within their organizations.[23] *Arrêté 40* provided additional clarification for the creation of sport associations, detailing that they had to be omni-sport clubs, associations where people could participate in several different sports. The *Arrêté* even specified the sports permitted in these clubs, which included football, handball, basketball, and any two other authorized, individual sports.[24] The only exceptions to the omni-sport club policy were for sports which required specific locations or equipment that could not readily be accommodated with other sports, 'such as winter sports, cycling, equestrian sports, tennis, golf, polo and cricket'.[25] This highly vigilant approach was in many respects a result of French security concerns. Thus, the French Military Government wanted Germans to form multi-sport clubs 'in order to avoid the proliferation of these clubs, thereby reducing the number of sites required for their existence and especially to facilitate their control'.[26] As the French

Figure 8.1 German youth being instructed by US soldiers in badminton, January 1947[22] (photo courtesy: US National Archives and Records Administration).

turned from a formerly occupied people to being the occupiers themselves, specific lessons from their previous experiences under German occupation were carried over into their new role. As one notable report explained, the French introduced their cautious sport policy in Germany because 'in France the small sports groups were the best cover for the Resistance Movement, while a large group can be more easily supervised and the members do not get to know each other well enough to organise underground activities'.[27]

Each occupation power therefore drew on its own domestic experiences and pre-existing practices when shaping zonal policies regarding sport. While this led to some differences in practice, in general all three western powers believed that sport was a valuable tool through which Germans – like their own populations – could learn how to participate in democratic society. Wanting to broaden these efforts within Germany and complementing these initiatives, the Americans, British, and French implemented exchange programmes for sport and youth leaders. These programs, the Western Allies hoped, would help encourage post-war international reconciliation, particularly at the individual level, while simultaneously teaching Germans the tenets of democracy, as they understood it.

Sport exchanges

Just as they had done after the Great War, international sport organizations expelled Germany after the Second World War ended, this time using the justification that no sovereign state existed as a result of the occupation, and so prevented member states from playing games against German teams.[28] Although influential sport leaders such as Football Association President Stanley Rous sought to prevent members of the British military from playing matches with Germans, the western Military Governments instead promoted this type of competition and developed sport exchanges with Germans because of the perceived benefits of democratization and international reconciliation. Following an experimental contact between German and French youth in 1946 and its 'fruitful' results, all four Allied representatives on the quadripartite Allied Education Commission resolved 'as a positive contribution to the re-education of Germany to democratic ideals, [that] active steps be taken to bring the youth of Germany into contact with the youth of the United Nations'.[29] The initial French proposal stated: 'The purpose of these contacts is to widen the horizon of German youth and to show them the democratic way of life of which they had no knowledge during the Hitler period'.[30] In one of the rare instances of inter-Allied agreement in late 1946, even the Soviet delegate 'fully shared the point of view of the French delegate and that the democratic youth of allied countries should influence the re-education of German youth in the democratic spirit'.[31] The Allies viewed the transfer of ideas as a cross-cultural benefit, and therefore agreed to promote more exchanges with Germans and report back on their efforts in six months. Although the initial French proposal did not specifically mention sport, the youth programmes implemented by the Western Allies generally included sport and physical education.

Exchange programmes worked in both directions, with experts coming to Germany and Germans going abroad. The Western Allies brought athletes, coaches and recreation professionals to occupied Germany to share practical knowledge regarding sport, physical education, recreation and organizational methods and so instil democratic practices within the running of clubs. Even before the US Education Mission completed its report, the Americans began sending sport experts to Germany for the purpose of re-education. For two weeks in May 1946, at the request of General Lucius Clay, then Deputy Military Governor of the US Zone, civilian athletic consultants from the United States provided demonstrations and instruction in a variety of sports for German children and their parents in Stuttgart. Organizing weekday evening courses in softball, swimming, volleyball, tennis, track and golf, the instructors included Mercer Beasley, the former Tulane and Princeton tennis coach, and Matt Mann, the swimming and diving coach at the University of Michigan who later coached the American Olympic men's swimming team. One of the civilian athletic consultants told Clay 'that through the field of athletics it is possible to instil into the German people the true meaning of sportsmanship for the boys and girls who will be the future citizens of Germany'.[32]

The interest aroused among the Germans for such courses, as well as the support from occupation officials and encouragement from the invited instructors, led to requests for an expansion of the programme. Upon his return to the United States, for example, Mann wrote to Clay about his experiences leading these classes for German youth. Convinced of the benefit of his work, he informed Clay that sport instruction 'is going to be the place where we can really teach democracy to the German people. As you know, democracy is not in books. It can't be taught. It must be really lived. Our system of athletics is such that we teach fair play, the obeying of rules and the individual effort at all times'.[33]

Similarly, youth leadership schools established by the Western Allies in conjunction with trusted German partners, such as with Klaus von Bismarck in May 1946 at Vlotho in the British Zone and the Wuerttemberg Youth Committee at Ruit in May 1948 in the US Zone, employed British and US instructors to help the Germans in teaching their various courses. The Military Governments were also, however, aware of some of the potential problems inherent in establishing such schools and sport organizations across occupied Germany. In 1947, the US Military Government, for example, was especially troubled by 'the danger of nationalistic elements again exerting too much control in large sports organizations. The tendency for a few at the top to set the policy and pass it down the line is contrary to the democratic objectives of our reorientation program.'[34]

The following year, George E. Little and Harry G. Carlson, the athletic directors at Rutgers University and the University of Colorado, visited the *Land* of Hesse in the US Zone to observe physical education and sport activities, and to consult with the leaders of German sport organizations. Little and Carlson urged the US Military Government to send more experts to Germany to help teach Germans activities 'through which social values can be learned by actual practice'. They believed that the extra-curricular 'German sports leaders are too "performance-minded"'. Instead, in their view, sport and physical education had to be built upon the foundation of character and had to stress 'honesty, fairness, and a respect for essential human worth'.[35] The two athletic directors also recommended the creation of a large-scale exchange scheme to enable German physical education teachers and students to visit the United States and so learn about 'healthy trends' in the field. At the same time, they emphasized the importance of establishing teacher training and youth leadership schools to increase the number of qualified physical education instructors in Germany. These programmes should be designed to help teachers and sport instructors move away from 'mass demonstrations of machine-like manoeuvres' and instead allow them to formulate programmes incorporating individual exercises as well as competitive team sports. Such programmes, they continued, should 'afford a priceless opportunity for the formation of good habits and attitudes. The competitive playing field is an excellent laboratory for the practice of self control, individual initiative, respect for the other fellow and all that is implied by the word sportsmanship.'[36]

Following Little and Carlson's visit and recommendations, the US Military Government brought experts to Germany to assist with short courses designed to train sport organizers and administrators and support democratization efforts. Each regional Military Government at *Land* level in the US Zone proposed specific youth programmes, many of which focused on sport, and suggested possible international experts that should come and visit their *Land* to give guidance to German groups and institutions.[37] One such *Land*-level programme, for example, brought David Davison, a British football coach, to the Ruit Youth and Sport Leadership School for three months. Davison's duties were 'to give expert guidance among sports organizations in matters of organization programs, coaching, Youth Leadership Training methods and standards'.[38] The Americans asked Davison to teach football techniques as well as more general courses on the purpose of sport and physical education, the place of sport within general education, and fair play in order to develop a higher standard of soccer competition.

More generally, however, Davison's short courses were designed to foster democratic attitudes among Germans through sport, and internal American reports suggested that his work was well received.[39] The curriculum for his four week-long courses at Ruit, which had approximately thirty athletes each, consisted of five key elements: British methods of training, practice in the fundamentals of football, lectures on the duties of referees and players, lectures on the rules of football and their proper interpretation as well as emphasizing good sportsmanship and fair play.[40] However, in practice matches, Davison was dismayed that German players put too much effort into winning the game, which, 'if it is overemphasized ... is detrimental to the highest standards and traditions of sportsmanship and fair play'. To try to instil the principles of sportsmanship, which was often tacitly or explicitly linked to democratization, among Germans Davison also organized a three-day session for forty-three referees which primarily consisted of discussions on the rules and 'methods of refereeing and cooperation with the linesmen'. At the end of his stay, he appeared to have been pleased with the results, reporting that sport in general but football in particular 'is a great contributary [*sic*] factor to the future of good relationship [*sic*] between nations'.[41]

The British developed similar programmes to bring physical educators and athletes to their zone. The head of the Physical Education Department at Birmingham University, for example, visited the new German sport university (*Deutsche Sporthochschule*) in Cologne for two weeks in 1948, setting up a long-running faculty and student exchange.[42] By 1948, the emphasis on sports policy – in line with broader occupation policy – had emphatically shifted towards establishing good relations between the British and the German population. Thus, after competing in 1948 against the British Army of the Rhine, the University of Oxford's track and field team – including an 18-year-old Roger Bannister, who later became the first man to run a sub-four-minute mile – participated in a meet against German university students.[43] The British also sent football teams to Germany; a British select football team, for instance, played in Berlin against BSV 92 in the spring of 1949. The game, according to the British Military Government monthly report, 'was, if not a triumph for British sport, a move in the right direction in Anglo-German relations'.[44]

Figure 8.2 Group shot of the British (white shirt and black shorts) and German teams at the Brentano sports field in Frankfurt, 26 April 1950[45] (photo courtesy: *New York Times*).

Whereas both the British and Americans participated in athletic competition with Germans relatively early in the occupation, the French initially remained adamant in their policy of non-fraternization in sport. However, in March 1948, the French Military Governor, General Pierre Koenig, declared that exemptions to the non-fraternization policy could be granted.[46] With this policy change and a novel approach towards the amelioration of Franco–German relations, the French began to organize sport exchanges, and these programmes eventually became broader than similar American or British efforts. One French exchange sent skiers to Germany in the winter of 1949–50 for the Germans and French 'to become acquainted with each other and live together in a friendly manner'.[47] The following winter, the French sent 124 skiers to Germany and began planning for a summer 1951 exchange for mountaineering and water sports. While attitudes within the French occupation administration varied, as these programmes became established, at least some French officials came to believe that 'sport is an excellent base of bringing people together, particularly for young people of different nationalities'.[48]

In addition to sending their own citizens to Germany, the three powers also promoted exchanges which sent Germans abroad. With the assistance of private organizations within the western Allied home countries, the Military Governments developed and funded extensive programmes for specially selected Germans to visit the United States, Great Britain and France, which they justified on the basis that it enabled them to study democracy and its practices through first-hand experience. German youth and sport leaders who participated in these programmes, chosen because of their activities during the occupation and lack of anti-western sentiments, had the opportunity to return home and impart this new knowledge to other Germans through their leadership positions as *Kreisjugendpfleger* at the local level or within institutions such as the Young Women's Christian Association (YWCA). All three Western Allies brought German athletes from their zones to Great Britain, France, or elsewhere in western Europe to participate in athletic competition. In conjunction with the programme to send French skiers to Germany, the French also brought several Germans to France for ski instruction, mountaineering and water sports.[49] Similarly, England's Football Association invited a representative from the Bavarian Football Association to London 'to confer on [the] latest methods of training' and receive 'instruction and aid in modern British training procedures'.[50] The BSV 92 football team, having first hosted the British select team, then travelled to Denmark and Sweden in 1950 to play a series of friendly matches.[51] American programmes meanwhile sent Germans to Great Britain, France, Sweden, Denmark, Finland, Switzerland and the Netherlands.[52] These visits were not intended to confront Germans with a specific model or a defined catalogue of attributes that made up democracy in the view of the different occupiers. Rather, as one French memorandum stated, the contacts made during such trips 'could not but have the best effects towards the task of re-educating German youth. The purpose of these contacts is to widen the horizon of German youth and to show them the democratic way of life of which they had no knowledge during the Hitler period.'[53]

The Americans in particular found it beneficial to bring young Germans who demonstrated an openness and receptiveness to learning new ideas to the United States for both short-term and extended visits. One such programme organized together with the US National Social Welfare Assembly (NSWA) in 1948 brought seven German youth leaders (four women and three men, aged 21–35) to the United States for a period of six to ten months. Funded by the Rockefeller Foundation, the seven Germans studied at universities, often in schools of social work. The participants knew that upon their return to Germany, some of them would be selected as staff for youth leadership schools in the US Zone.[54] Melitta Dressel, the youngest of the group, had already worked as a sport and folk dancing instructor at Ruit. She returned to the school following two terms at Springfield College in Massachusetts. While at Springfield, Dressel enrolled in classes on 'group work, youth serving agencies, gymnastics, dancing, music, and American History, the last because she felt that she could better understand the American people if she were to have insight into their past'.[55] Dressel's advisor at Springfield College was David DeMarche, who had previously visited Bavaria as an expert to study youth issues.[56]

The NSWA, State Department and the US Military Government no doubt were pleased with Dressel's final report on her exchange experience, in which she described positively the democratic practices she observed in the United States. She began her eight-page report by stating that:

> I was so glad that I have had the opportunity as one of the very few to leave behind [my] needs, ruins, and narrowness of Germany, and to look forward to learn to know people of another country, their customs and different ways of life; to take to heart and to learn as much as possible without any prejudice, and to put into action these experiences after my return to Germany. Thus I can contribute so that the German youth may find a better way of life.[57]

Dressel noticed differences between Germany and the United States in higher education as well as in extra-curricular activities. Although she did not believe that every aspect of American life was better than German traditions, she nonetheless reported that 'I am anxious to put into action these ideas'.[58]

In a similar fashion, the British Military Government, through its Chief Sports Officer J. G. Dixon, arranged for German youth and sport leaders to visit Great Britain to observe and learn democratic practices. Prior to the war Dixon had developed an appreciation for Germany over several visits to the country,[59] and with this knowledge of both Germany and physical education, he was perfectly suited for his position. Dixon coordinated with private British organizations, in particular with the Friends' Educational Council, to fund German youth visits, especially after Military Government funding ceased in 1947. From his many visits to German schools across the British Zone, Dixon reported in October 1948 that they were not providing sufficient time for physical education. Material difficulties were 'not an adequate excuse', he argued, and a once-a-week class was 'particularly unsuitable for young or debilitated children, and highly unsatisfactory at any stage'. More significantly, articulating a line of criticism common among foreign observers of German education, he complained that German physical education classes primarily consisted of 'over-directed, mechanically and meekly performed techniques'. By going to the UK, German physical education teachers would therefore learn educational techniques and methods which 'encourage independence and initiative and allow for exploratory and creative activity. Games, creative forms of dance, and activities with apparatus other than the stereotyped German forms should be included.'[60] At the same time, the British also had broader concerns about activities within sport clubs in Germany, which thus required careful watching. At one meeting of British Youth Control Officers, it was argued that 'the sports organisations undoubtedly constituted a potential political force in Germany; their members must not be forgotten or overlooked in our efforts to widen the German horizon through closer contacts abroad'.[61]

Many British exchanges were specifically for physical education instructors. With the assistance of the Central Council for Physical Recreation in London, Dixon arranged for six men and six women, two each from North Rhine-Westphalia and Lower Saxony and one each from Hamburg and Schleswig-Holstein, to visit Great Britain for a few weeks in 1948.[62] In February 1949 sixteen German physical education teachers visited Great Britain for two weeks. Eight men visited London schools and teacher training colleges while eight women spent the duration in residency at teacher training colleges. The aim of these visits, noted the Education Advisor of the British Zone, was 'to give the German lecturers some idea of the organization of the English Colleges and, in particular, the place of Physical Education in their curricula'.[63] The British Education Branch also developed separate plans to send female physical education instructors to England for professional development, and in autumn 1949, the British eventually sent German physical education lecturers to participate in courses in Yorkshire.[64]

While the Americans established more exchange programmes than the British and French for German youth, all three of the Western Allies understood the importance of international contacts for shaping German attitudes and supported such visits as much as was feasible. The financial position of the United States after the war enabled the

Figure 8.3 John G. Dixon, Chief Sports Officer for the British Zone, at the Deutsche Sporthochschule (image courtesy: Dixon family).

occupation power geographically farthest from Germany to develop and implement the greatest number of exchange programmes. While interacting with citizens of other democratic western countries, the Western Allies hoped that German sport and youth instructors and administrators could learn about different structures and democratic decision-making processes which they could then implement in their own clubs and associations to ensure that they differed from the centralized and authoritarian structures which had previously dominated organized sport in Germany.

Conclusion

Attempting to introduce democratic ideas through youth and sport organizations and selective exchange programmes formed an integral part of Allied plans to influence the future development of German society. All three Western Allies established sport organizations in their zones of occupation after abolishing the national Nazi bodies, promoted sport activities as part of school curricula and in youth groups, trained sport leaders and organizers as part of their youth leadership programmes, and arranged numerous exchanges involving sport and coaching. Henry Kellermann, a member of the US State Department who coordinated many of these projects, wrote many years later that 'the exchange experience, after all, was no more than a means to an end; its purpose was to help assist Germans in creating a new society modelled on western democratic concepts'.[65] In the field of sport, this practice meant an emphasis on fair play, sportsmanship, teamwork and opportunities for everyone.

With a new generation of German sport coaches and administrators running sport clubs, many of whom had been trained by the Allies, Germans could successfully claim that they had adopted democratic ideals, and push for the creation of new national German sport organizations, once the occupation officially ended and the three western powers rescinded Allied Control Directive 23. Many pre-war German sport leaders who had been members of international sport federations and the International Olympic Committee resumed their places representing Germany internationally, but they did so only after long negotiations with the Western Allies.[66] In reality, the continuation of these individuals' careers in conjunction with the re-founding of national governing bodies, which the international sport federations duly recognized, showed that the international sport community cared more about pre-war connections and the sport itself rather than about politics and democratic attitudes. Yet the image presented by German officials and personalities from the field of sport to the Western Allies and the world was that German sport had fundamentally changed. Formally at least, German sport organizations now had democratic structures and decision-making practices enshrined in their (Allied-approved) constitutions, statutes and by-laws. At the more practical level, German sport no longer focused on service to the state but instead emphasized personal development and contributing positively to society as a citizen, ideas which the exchange programmes had helped solidify.

Of course, determining the ultimate success of these programmes is difficult. Is success measured in terms of short-term goals, such as physical education teachers incorporating ideas they had learned in Britain into their classes? Or can success only be considered after a number of years, after the initial group of Germans who had learned coaching skills from Allied instructors such as David Davison had trained more Germans who had, in turn, imparted this knowledge to an even larger number of pupils? At the time, the Americans attempted to gauge the success of their sport programmes through public opinion surveys conducted by the US Military Government Reactions Analysis Branch. A March 1950 report stated that almost eight out of every ten Germans in the US Zone believed that individual students and experts as well as Germany as a whole benefitted from exchange visits to the United States, although how specifically they did so remains a vexed question.[67] Similarly, reflecting on his work with the German expert program, Henry Kellermann stated that 'in time the German leader-specialist exchange became not only the largest but, as regards impact on the German populace, the most significant and effective programme. The secret of its success lay in the careful and calculated selection of the best participants, but, perhaps even more so, in its project-oriented nature'.[68] Dixon also attributed the success of his programmes to the careful selection of Germans for the visits to Britain.[69] By selecting individuals – the experts who visited Germany as well as the Germans who went abroad – who could have broad influence on a large number of Germans over time, the western occupiers hoped to achieve a large-scale change in sporting culture inside Germany. While one might expect Kellermann and Dixon to frame their work in Germany in such a self-congratulatory manner, and while the specific sports which appealed to individuals varied greatly and were often influenced by class, education, gender and geography, taken together, it seems fair to conclude that the three western occupiers' sport activities influenced large numbers of Germans directly and indirectly, and contributed at least to some degree to the achievement of Allied aims.

All three Western Allies believed that reforming the attitudes and behaviour of young people in Germany was crucial for the future of the country as well as Europe and the world at large. The early policies of introducing democracy to the youth of Germany focused on training youth leaders, primarily through the establishment of zonal leadership schools. Through these learning-by-doing experiences, the western occupation powers hoped to avoid the danger which Little and Carlson had identified in their 1947 report:

> There is a general agreement among those who know Germany that her chances of developing along democratic lines depends upon the education of her youth … We recognize that we cannot teach democracy to others by using autocratic methods and we do not so propose. We do, however, see a grave danger in being too hasty in turning the educational leadership back to German leaders who are unqualified or unwilling to introduce democratic practices.[70]

The Western Allies could not interact with every single German directly, but they recognized the wide appeal of sport in Germany and how this had been exploited and abused by the Nazis. They therefore increased their programmes designed to foster democratic ideals in Germany through sport activities, exchange visits and promoting teamwork, fair play and sportsmanship, even as they decreased the number of Military Government personnel. Through encouraging 'democratic' sport and youth activities, as practiced at home in the United States, Britain and France, the Western Allies hoped to influence relatively large numbers of 'ordinary' Germans, prevent a revival of Nazi ideas and promote democratization and eventual international reconciliation. The Allied attempt to reform German sport was therefore a significant part of 'doing occupation', as they sought to translate their geopolitical aims for a new Germany into practical activities that could directly reach individual Germans, in addition to establishing new institutions and working indirectly through social, political and business elites.

Notes

The author would like to thank Caroline Sharples and Keith Rathbone for their feedback and suggestions for this chapter.

1 Memo, German Political Branch, 28 March 1946, FO 1050/82, National Archives, London (TNA).
2 CORC/P(45)180(Revise), 10 December 1945, FO 1005/391, TNA.
3 Petra Goedde, *GIs and Germans: Culture, Gender and Foreign Relations, 1945–1949* (New Haven: Yale University Press, 2003); David Welch, 'Citizenship and

Politics: Legacy of Wilton Park for Post-War Reconstruction', *Contemporary European History* 6, no. 2 (1997): 209–14; Richard Mayne, *In Victory, Magnanimity in Peace, Goodwill: A History of Wilton Park* (London: Frank Cass, 2003), 62–4.

4 Alexandra F. Levy, 'Promoting Democracy and Denazification: American Policymaking and German Public Opinion', *Diplomacy & Statecraft* 26, no. 4 (2015): 614–35; F. Roy Willis, *The French in Germany, 1945–1949* (Stanford: Stanford University Press, 1962), 147–79; James Tent, *Mission on the Rhine: Reeducation and Denazification in American-Occupied Germany* (Chicago: University of Chicago Press, 1982); Ian D. Turner (ed.), *Reconstruction in Post-War Germany: British Occupation Policy and the Western Zones, 1945–55* (Oxford: Berg, 1989); Brian M. Puaca, *Learning Democracy: Education Reform in West Germany, 1945–1965* (New York: Berghahn Books, 2009).

5 Gerhard Rempel, *Hitler's Children: The Hitler Youth and the SS* (Chapel Hill: University of North Carolina Press, 1989), 178.

6 Michael H. Kater, *Hitler Youth* (Cambridge, MA: Harvard University Press, 2004), 82.

7 Ibid., 30, 82; Rempel, *Hitler's Children*, 178–8.

8 Andrei S. Markovits and Steven L. Hellerman, *Offside: Soccer & American Exceptionalism* (Princeton: Princeton University Press, 2001), 42–3.

9 J. A. Mangan, *Athleticism in the Victorian and Edwardian Public School: The Emergence and Consolidation of an Educational Ideology*, 3rd edn (London: Frank Cass, 1981; reprint 2000), 34.

10 Markovits and Hellerman, *Offside*, 80–1; Ted Vincent, *The Rise & Fall of American Sport: Mudville's Revenge* (Lincoln: University of Nebraska Press, 1981), 8–10; Marion Fontaine, *Le RC Lens et les 'Gueules Noires'* (Paris: Les Indes savantes, 2010).

11 Steven A. Riess, *City Games: The Evolution of American Urban Society and the Rise of Sports* (Champaign: University of Illinois Press, 1991).

12 M. C. Stayer to Chief of Staff, 26 September 1945, Record Group (RG) 260, Entry 1, Box 20, National Archives, College Park, Maryland (NACP).

13 Report, Visit of Physical Education Officer to Munster and Buer, December 1946, FO 1050/1094, TNA.

14 John G. Dixon, 'The Founding of the Cologne Sporthochschule', *Sports International* 6 (1982): 14; Stefanie Woite-Wehle, *Zwischen Kontrolle und Demokratisierung: Die Sportpolitik der französischen Besatzungsmacht in Südwestdeutschland 1945–1950* (Schorndorf: Hofmann, 2001), 44.

15 Paul M. Limbert, 'Youth Activities in Germany, Prepared for Educational Record', n.d., RG 260, Entry 612, Box 138, NACP. This appears to be a more detailed version of Limbert's section on youth activities contained in the Zook report. *Report on a Survey of Youth Activities in the British Zone*, 25 February 1946, FO 1050/13, TNA.

16 Military Government Regulation, Title 8, Change 3, 14 March 1947, RG 260, Entry 33, Box 649, NACP.

17 Fred W. Buddy, 'George Frederick Zook: An Analysis of Selected Contributions of an American Educator' (PhD diss., University of Akron, 1990), 41–6.

18 Paul M. Limbert, *Reliving a Century* (Asheville: Biltmore Press, 1997), 140–1.

19 Paul M. Limbert, 'Youth Activities in Germany, Prepared for Educational Record', n.d., RG 260, Entry 612, Box 138, NACP.

20 Report of the United States Education Mission to Germany, 20 September 1946, RG 59, Entry 5323, Box 7, NACP.

21 Ibid.

22 RG 260, Entry 26, Box 273, NACP.

23 General Koenig, Ordonnance No. 33, 4 February 1946, AC 78/2, Direction Generales des Affaires Culturelles, Bureau des archives de l'Occupation française en Allemagne et en Autriche, Ministère des Affaires Étrangères, Colmar, France (hereafter AOFAA). This archive has since been relocated to La Courneuve.
24 E. Laffon to Messieurs les Délégués Supérieurs, 26 February 1946, AC 78/2, AOFAA.
25 E. Laffon, Arrêté No 40, 4 February 1946, AC 78/2, AOFAA.
26 E. Laffon to Messieurs les Délégués Supérieurs, 26 February 1946, AC 78/2, AOFAA.
27 Visit of Representatives of Youth and Sport Section, 25 October 1945, FO 1050/1293, TNA.
28 Heather L. Dichter, 'Sporting Relations: Diplomacy, Small States, and Germany's Postwar Return to International Sport', *Diplomacy & Statecraft* 27, no. 2 (2016): 340–59.
29 DIAC/AEC/P(46)30, 13 November 1946, RG 260, Entry 1807, Box 232, NACP; DIAC/AEC/M(46)14, 18 December 1946, FO 1005/620, TNA.
30 DIAC/AEC/P(46)30, 13 November 1946, RG 260, Entry 1807, Box 232, NACP.
31 DIAC/AEC/M(46)14, 18 December 1946, FO 1005/620, TNA.
32 A. R. Bolling to Lucius Clay, 14 May 1946, RG 260, Entry 26, Box 87, NACP.
33 Matt Mann to Lucius D. Clay, 14 June 1946, RG 260, Entry 26, Box 87, NACP.
34 Community Recreation and Sports, 20 April 1947, RG 260, Entry 612, Box 137, NACP.
35 Weekly Report, Hesse, May 27, 1947, RG 260, Entry 612, Box 143, NACP; Harry G. Carlson and George E. Little to Chief, Education and Religious Affairs Branch, n.d. [1947], Box 178, Folder 6, Series I, Central Administration President's Office, University of Colorado at Boulder Archives, Boulder, Colorado (hereafter UCBA).
36 Ibid.
37 'Request for Recreation and Sports Experts', 25 October 1948, RG 260, Entry 610, Box 125, NACP; 'Physical Education and Sports', 'Recreation Planning in Cities and Counties' and 'Recreation and Sport Activities for Girls and Women', n.d., RG 260, Entry 1452, Box 724, NACP.
38 L. E. Norrie to Miss May, 18 February 1949, RG 260, Entry 610, Box 114, NACP.
39 Aksel G. Nielsen to Lester Davison, 21 March 1949, RG 260, Entry 1693, Box 970, NACP; Youth Activities Monthly Report, August 1949, RG 260, Entry 1692, Box 959, NACP.
40 Report on the Activities of Mr. David D. Davison, Physical Education and Sports Consultant from 4 April to 31 July 1949, 12 August 1949, RG 260, Entry 1692, Box 961, NACP.
41 Ibid.
42 Report by Mr. Munrow, 1–14 August 1948, FO 1023/2213, TNA; Dixon, 'The Founding', 19.
43 Dixon, 'The Founding', 20; Minutes, 95th Conference, 19 July 1947, FO1050/1254, TNA; Minutes, 96th Conference, 26 July 1947, FO1050/1254, TNA.
44 Monthly Report, 1 June 1949, FO 1050/1089, TNA.
45 RG 306-NT, Box 800, NACP. Another photograph in the file from this game noted 'London team was in very good shape and easily defeated the German boys 8–0'.
46 The prohibition of sporting events between French and Germans, however, remained. Le Général d'Armée Koenig to MM. Le Délégué Supérieur pour le G. M. de Bade, du Wurtemberg, le Land Rhéno-Palatin, 31 March 1948, AC 421/2, AOFAA.
47 H. Schmelzer, 5 October 1950, AC 423/1, AOFAA.
48 Echanges UNCM – Institut für Internationale Begegnungen, n.d. [1950], AC 423/1, AOFAA.

49 Ibid.
50 OMG-Bavaria Monthly Report for Period Ending 31 August 1948, RG 260, Entry 612, Box 143, NACP.
51 Monthly Report, 28 January 1950, FO 1050/1090, TNA.
52 Henry J. Kellermann, *Cultural Relations as an Instrument of U.S. Foreign Policy: The Educational Exchange Program between the United States and Germany, 1945–1954* (Washington, DC: Government Printing Office, 1978), 163.
53 DIAC/AEC/P(46)30 Addendum, 12 December 1946, RG 260, Entry 1807, Box 232, NACP.
54 Youth Division, National Social Welfare Assembly, 13 September 1948, RG 260, Entry 610, Box 129, NACP; Aksel Nielsen, Daily Report, 24 March 1949, RG 260, Entry 1692, Box 960, NACP.
55 Minutes, National Social Welfare Assembly Youth Division Advisory Committee German Leadership Training Project, 11 March 1949, RG 59, Box 5323, Box 28, NACP.
56 Final Report of Melitta Dressel, March 1949, RG 260, Entry 610, Box 129, NACP; Charles D. Winning to L. E. Norrie, 27 October 1948, RG 260, Entry 610, Box 126, NACP.
57 Final Report of Melitta Dressel, March 1949, RG 260, Entry 610, Box 129, NACP.
58 Ibid.
59 Dixon, 'The Founding', 14.
60 Report, J. G. Dixon, October 1948, FO 1050/1255, TNA.
61 Minutes, Fifth Conference, Youth Control Officers, 18 November 1947, FO 1050/1174, TNA.
62 Minutes, Conference, 2 February 1948, FO 1050/1087, TNA.
63 Monthly Report, Office of the Educational Adviser, February 1949, FO 1050/1103, TNA.
64 Minutes, 148th Conference, 1 November 1948, FO 1050/1110, TNA; J. G. Dixon, H. M. I's Report on Physical Education, October 1948, FO 1050/1255, TNA; Minutes, 170th Conference, 4 November 1949, FO 1050/1110, TNA.
65 Kellermann, *Cultural Relations*, 163.
66 Dichter, 'Sporting Relations'; Heather L. Dichter, 'Sport Is Not so Separate from Politics: Diplomatic Manipulation of Germany's Postwar Return to the Olympic Movement', in *Defending the American Way of Life*, ed. Kevin Witherspoon and Toby Rider (Little Rock: University of Arkansas Press, forthcoming).
67 Germans View the US Reorientation Program, III. Opinions on the Cultural Exchange Program, Report No. 12, Series No. 2, 30 March 1950, NARA, RG 306, Research Reports on German Public Opinion, Box 1.
68 Kellermann, *Cultural Relations*, 40.
69 Report, J. G. Dixon for Oct 28–29, 1948 meeting, October 1948, FO 1050/1255, TNA.
70 Harry G. Carlson and George E. Little to Chief, Education and Religious Affairs Branch, n.d. [1947], Box 178, Folder 6, Series I, Central Administration President's Office, UCBA.

9

Occupying the Environment: German Hunters and the American Occupation

Douglas Bell

On 18 December 1948, members of the *Bayerischer Jagdschutz & Jägerverband* (BJV – Bavarian Hunting Organization) assembled in Nuremberg for the first time in fifteen years. Although the gathering was celebratory, the speech given by President Oskar Kellner focused on two significant challenges. The first problem, Kellner told BJV members, was that American Military Government laws that forbade Germans from hunting and prevented them from properly monitoring wildlife were leading to the destruction of animal populations by 'illegal hunting, poachers, and trappers'. The second problem, linked to the first, was the American attempt to replace the Nazi era Reich Hunting Law (*Reichsjagdgesetz*) with supposedly more democratic hunting laws, following an American model. Kellner urged BJV members to protest the plans to rewrite the *Reichsjagdgesetz* and argued that if implemented in Germany, the American laws would increase the number of hunters, destroy wildlife populations and neglect the *Waidgerechtigkeit*, a concept embodying German hunting rituals and ethics.[1] Kellner's opposition to the proposed American reforms indicates that hunting rights and wildlife management were not only a regular point of contention between the occupiers and the occupied, but also provided a space for Germans to contest Military Government policy and articulate an alternative political vision that owed much to older German customs and traditions that pre-dated the Nazi period.[2]

This chapter argues that the conflict and debates around hunting and other environmental issues contributed to the re-emergence of local politics and civil society in post-war Germany. Debates about nature, wildlife and hunting have deep cultural roots in German society, and differing American ideas and approaches towards the environment elicited strong responses. Hunting became an especially contentious subject, as American occupation personnel hunted in German forests and fields with little regard for either German hunting laws or American Military Government regulations. This damaging behaviour later provided German hunters, politicians and the press with compelling arguments for opposing the implementation of an American influenced hunting law in Bavaria following the repeal of the *Reichsjagdgesetz* in 1948. While the debates over the new hunting law emphasized the legal and cultural differences between American and German hunting, these discussions also provide insights into questions relating to the environment, the nature of democracy and the exercise of power and sovereignty in occupied Germany.

Discussions between the American Military Government and the Bavarian government on the issue of hunting focused on the different conceptions of private property in the German *Revierjagdsystem* (district hunting system) and the American *Lizenzsystem* (license system). The German *Revierjagdsystem* permitted landowners or members of *Jagdgenossenschaften* (hunting cooperatives) to hunt on individual properties and *Jagdreviere* (hunting districts), and they defined game animals as private property belonging to the landowner or *Jagdgenossenschaft*, regardless of who shot the animal. In the American *Lizenzsystem*, by contrast, individuals purchased hunting permits from the state or federal government for specific species, allowing hunters to shoot a certain number of game animals on private and public property. The US Military Government advocated altering German game laws to align them more closely with American 'democratic' game laws because, in their view, this would open hunting to those who were not landowners or members of cooperatives. On the other hand, the Bavarians contended that the American *Lizenzsystem* would destroy wildlife populations and violate private property rights. This fear led the press, hunting associations and the Bavarian government to invoke German legal and cultural traditions during the discussions over the future Bavarian hunting law and finally persuade the Americans that although the *Reichsjagdgesetz* was promulgated by the Nazi government, it encompassed a much longer German tradition that was untainted by Hitler's regime.

Witnessing the hunting practices of American occupiers, the Bavarian hunters feared that American designed hunting laws would lead to overhunting throughout occupied Germany, significantly lowering and even leading to the destruction of wildlife populations. This prospect represented an existential threat to all German hunters. Rather than developing feeding grounds, culling herds and practicing their cultural traditions, German hunters, like American hunters in the United States, would be buying permits from the government that would allow them to participate in the annual hunting season. Although on the surface, the discussions focused on legal differences, the debates over hunting illustrate the different views of nature held by the occupiers and occupied, and help us understand that German opposition to any alteration to their hunting laws was based on the fear that this would fundamentally change how they engaged with the environment more generally.

In contending and discussing these legal and cultural differences, German hunters were participating in what Konrad Jarausch has described as a 'collective learning process' that aided Germany's long road to re-civilization.[3] This learning process started during the occupation when the Western Allies sought to break Germany's negative political traditions and reorient German society towards the model of liberal democracy practiced in their own countries. In terms of hunting, the American occupiers sought to eradicate German hunting laws and traditions that they considered 'undemocratic' and influenced by the Nazi regime; though this was challenged by German hunters, politicians and the press who emphasized the legal, practical and cultural values of German hunting. These negotiations, along with the formation of the semi-sovereign Federal Republic of Germany (FRG) in 1949, eventually led the

American occupiers to withdraw their demands and allow the Bavarians to draft a hunting law that reflected German legal and cultural traditions.

American hunting

In the United States, hunting laws and practices developed from the colonial experience. Initially, colonists and settlers hunted for subsistence purposes in isolated locations and used whatever means they could, including 'guns, traps, snares, deadfalls, pits, and poison baits' as well as 'small cannon that fired half a pound of nails and shot'.[4] By the 1830s, eastern upper-class hunters started questioning these behaviours along with 'pot hunting' for meat and commercial 'market hunting'. New Englanders and recent British immigrants advocated a more recreational style of hunting that mimicked the practices of the British upper class, and they soon adopted the concept of sportsmanship.[5] The concept was subsequently popularized by Henry William Herbert, a British noblemen writing under the pseudonym Frank Forester, who argued that hunting was not an activity to supply food, but rather a recreational pursuit for gentlemen.[6]

These ideas caught on among the upper classes in New England, who formed some of the first sportsmen's clubs in the 1840s, which soon proliferated across the United States with more than 300 sporting magazines established by the 1870s.[7] These magazines and clubs sought the transformation of American hunting culture from one based on subsistence and market hunting to one based on a sportsman's conservation program that advocated following state laws, leaving game for the next season and hunting only in season. Market hunters, according to sportsmen, hunted for profit and destroyed wildlife populations, and by the 1880s, it was clear that market hunters' actions were killing off game across the country, a trend that had become especially evident with the sudden decline in the American buffalo.[8]

To prevent the excessive destruction of wildlife, sportsmen focused their attention on the enforcement of game laws. Although game laws had existed in some form since the colonial period, by the 1880s, state game laws 'had proliferated into a tangled mass of confusing and often contradictory statutes'.[9] Additionally, many farmers and western ranchers claimed the sportsmen's program was only for the elite, hindered their ability to protect property, and encroached on their hunting rights. To counter these arguments, men like George Bird Grinnell, a zoologist and confidant of Theodore Roosevelt, contended that the enactment and enforcement of game laws benefited the 'poor man' because bag limits would increase the overall game populations.[10] Throughout the latter part of the nineteenth century and into the early twentieth century, individual states and the federal government started adopting Grinnell's game management principles. By placing wildlife under federal management, game animals became 'public property managed by the state, even on private land', creating conflicts between federal authorities and local hunters, especially in the west.[11] Moreover, the establishment of nature reserves, bird sanctuaries and game reserves created new laws and new crimes that local hunters in both the east and west believed favoured wealthy eastern hunters, whereas government officials considered local hunters to be no more than poachers who disregarded the law.[12] Contrasting perceptions of the role and purpose of hunting at home in America were later reflected in widely varying views among the US occupiers on hunting in Germany.

By the 1920s, the sportsmen's conservation program dominated upper and middle-class hunting in the United States and was adopted by local and federal governments.[13] However, only in the 1930s did game management and early ecological ideas begin to coalesce under the direction of Aldo Leopold, a former federal forest assistant in Arizona and New Mexico who became the first professor of game management in the United States. By the 1930s, Leopold came to view wildlife management as a natural system rather than one that produced game animals for sport.[14] Many of his ideas were solidified by a 1936 trip to Germany where he criticized an over managed system that privileged elite hunters.[15] Yet, on the eve of the Second World War, ecological game management concepts remained in their infancy, and class differences remained within American hunting culture.

German hunting

By the end of the Middle Ages, the German Electors and other princes in central Europe claimed hunting as an exclusive right while the lower nobility, clergy and urban elites maintained minor hunting rights.[16] Increasingly, princes and nobles sought to control resources and limit peasant access to forests, and they introduced legal instruments to 'protect' the forests that gave them exclusive rights to natural resources, including, wood, minerals and wildlife.[17] Within these forests, the foresters and hunt masters who managed the nobles' forests practiced the *Hege* (care/protection), a collection of informal rituals and practices that sought the continued regeneration of wildlife populations by protecting pregnant females, preventing overhunting, culling predators, providing food in winter and following long-established customs such as honouring the dead animals through horn music and the last bite, whereby a sprig of oak, pine or alder is placed in the dead animal's mouth.[18] However, the protection and care of wildlife often came at the expense of peasants who were unable to defend their fields and forests from the larger numbers of game animals, were required to assist in noble hunts and received no compensation for damage to their property.[19]

By the eighteenth century, extravagant princely hunts reached their culmination with the establishment of fenced hunting parks and the transportation of live animals to 'aristocratic playgrounds'.[20] During this era, hunting rights were a princely favour granted only to aristocratic landowners and nobles while some town founders and patricians were permitted to hunt 'smaller game' such as hares and foxes.[21] Aristocratic hunting privileges continued until the 1848 revolutions when the Frankfurt Parliament abrogated noble hunting rights, permitted hunting by all landowners and made hunting subject to territorial laws in each of the German states (*Länder*).[22] The liberalization of hunting, especially where states were slow to enact new laws, created an uncertain situation that allowed peasants to hunt without restriction, often characterized by opponents to liberal hunting laws as '*Jagdexcessen*' (hunting excesses).[23] These new territorial hunting laws, however, also ensured that hunting rights and landownership remained linked. In Prussia, the 1850 hunting law permitted hunting only by individuals who owned a cohesive plot of more than 300 acres (75 hectares), 4 per cent of all landowners. In Bavaria, one needed to own a unified plot of 300 *Tagewerke* (day's work) in the plains and 600 in the mountains. Additionally, most *Länder* banned Sunday hunting to limit bourgeois landowners' hunting activities.[24]

While many hunters owned large estates, most *Länder* laws allowed for the formation of *Jagdgenossenschaft* that permitted individuals to pool their land and create *Jagdreviere* (hunting districts) on which the members of the *Jagdgenossenschaft* hunted and practiced the *Hege*. Besides individuals, the *Länder* also rented out the hunting rights on public land. Individuals with hunting licenses could also be invited to hunt on *Jagdreviere*. As a result, there was a significant increase in *Jagdvereine* (hunting associations) after 1848. These organizations sought to advocate for hunting interests, pressurize the bureaucracy and influence politics using member donations.[25] The upheavals caused by the 1848 Revolutions not only resulted in new laws, but also in a stronger emphasis on practices that allowed aristocratic hunters to distinguish themselves from the emerging bourgeoisie. This resulted in a stress on following the *Hege* and the *Waidgerechtigkeit*, a term traced to the eighteenth century.[26] The *Waidgerechtigkeit* encompassed the *Hege* and involved upholding hunting laws, maintaining and preserving hunting culture, feeding game in winter, protecting animals from poachers and following hunting ethics.[27] Throughout the nineteenth century, the *Waidgerechtigkeit* became central to aristocratic and bourgeois hunters, who frowned upon any hunting actions that violated these laws and customs. Thus, by the end of the 1930s, hunting in Germany was an activity mostly reserved for the aristocracy and wealthy bourgeois who could afford hunting rents, and socialization among hunters was based around an ethos devoted to the concepts and ideals embedded in the *Waidgerechtigkeit*.

When the Nazis came to power in 1933, as part of their general drive to eliminate any independent groups or institutions, the regime forced independent *Jagdvereine* to disband and formed the national *Deutsche Jägerschaft* (German Hunting Association). Many German hunters celebrated the passage of a new national hunting law in 1934, the *Reichsjagdgesetz*, which transformed the 'confusing jumble of hunting decrees' of the *Länder* into a unified national hunting law that incorporated the *Hege* and the *Waidgerechtigkeit* and maintained land ownership requirements.[28] Yet the law was also highly racialized and saw the protection and management of wildlife as crucial for the health of the German people, linking it to the *Blut und Boden* (blood and soil) ideology of Nazi conservationists. Visiting Nazi Germany on the eve of the Second World War, Leopold contended that the new law produced an 'abnormal density of deer' through 'artificial winter feeding and predator control' leading to damage of forest and agricultural vegetation. This process, he concluded, occurred because hunters 'are unwilling to curtail their private pleasure for the public good'.[29]

Although they developed along different lines, German hunting and the American sportsmen's program shared many similarities on the eve of the Second World War. Hunters in both nations sought to maintain animal populations through predator control and hunting seasons, mandated hunting licenses to ensure hunters were properly trained and developed regulations to prevent poaching and to prosecute those who hunted illegally. Conversely, German and American ideas about property and game ownership contrasted sharply. In the United States, sport hunters paid a fee to the state or federal government for hunting stamps or permits for individual species, allowing hunters to shoot a certain number of game animals on private and public property. The American hunter, after shooting the animal, retained possession of the game. In Germany, by contrast, each state developed an *Abschussplan* determining the species and amount of game hunted on each property and *Jagdreviere*; moreover, once shot, the game remained the property of the landowner or cooperatives, though invited hunters might pay a fee to take possession of the hunted animal. These legal and cultural distinctions would create significant controversy when drafting new hunting laws after the Second World War.

Hunting in occupied Germany, 1945–7

After the end of the war, Ordinance No. 1, concerning Crimes and Offenses, issued by the American and British Supreme Headquarters Allied Expeditionary Force (SHAEF), specified that unauthorized firearm possession was a capital offense.[30] The quadripartite Allied Control Council, subsequently issued Order No. 2, in January 1946, prohibiting the 'carrying, possession or ownership of arms or ammunition by any person' and stating that all arms and ammunition were to be turned over to the nearest Allied commander within ten days.[31] While the banning of firearms was clearly for security purposes, it also prevented German hunters from using firearms, and hindered their ability to participate in wildlife management during the occupation.

This disarmament of German society, combined with the neglect of game management during the war, enabled wildlife populations to grow unchecked. The main culprit was the large numbers of wild boar digging up crops and threatening agricultural production. Captain H. B. Miller, stationed in *Landkreis* Alsfeld, north of Frankfurt, for example, described the destruction of almost 20,000 pounds of potatoes by wild boar in the first six months of the year.[32] In neighbouring *Landkreis* Alzenau, the local US army detachment unit reported a 'boar plague' that uprooted several fields of potatoes that required replanting and concluded that the 'pigs increase faster than they can be killed'.[33] Already in August 1945, the Bavarian State Forestry Administration asked for the rearmament of their personnel, writing that unarmed forestry personnel were helpless and unable to adequately perform their duties.[34] Although peasants and farmers had previously dealt with wildlife rooting up their fields, the severe shortage of food in the first three years after the war was the dominant issue in occupied Germany.[35] With millions of refugees in need of food, calories came to not only represent the Allied commitment to human welfare, but also became 'an instrument of power'.[36] With their caloric intake limited by the occupiers, Germans relied heavily on home gardens and their own agricultural production to supplement their diets.[37] Protecting fields and crops from wild boar and other game animals was essential to maintain supplies from domestic production. However, as the possession of firearms was now illegal, German farmers lacked the ability to defend their crops from destruction and had to rely on the actions of the occupiers.

Although many American soldiers started shooting wildlife during the war to supplement their rations,[38] Military Government started organizing American soldiers to help decrease the wild boar population and 'alleviate the food situation' in September 1945.[39] This problem was reemphasized in May 1946 when the headquarters of US Forces in Europe (USFET) directed all *Kreis* (district) Military Government detachments to assist army tactical units 'in their efforts to reduce damage to crops by wild animals' by securing 'lists of farms and communities where damage to crops is reported'.[40] While these organized hunts aimed to prevent crop reduction, most American personnel in Germany hunted individually or small groups to obtain food supplies for themselves, leading USFET to publish hunting regulations in October 1945. The 'Hunting and Fishing Policy' allowed Americans to use the German forests for sport hunting as long as they accepted German game seasons, obtained a hunting license from their commander and did not use automatic weapons.[41] These individual and group hunts often proved the most troublesome. In *The American Riflemen*, R. J. Ackert, described befriending the German owner of a brewery whose gamekeeper took him on several hunting outings. Ackert characterized the German practice of waiting for deer to be driven out of the woods as 'absurdly easy' and never questioned why his host, whom he called 'Mr. Beer', still possessed firearms.[42] Another soldier, writing about his free time Germany, detailed his frequent hunting trips to test out the numerous rifles he collected in occupied Germany. Based on this one article alone, he shot approximately eighteen deer between 1944 and 1946 which he provided to his fellow soldiers for dinner.[43] The most egregious recorded example was that of Sergeant Glen A. Davison of the Third US Army, who described hunting 128 deer and ten elk while in Germany between 1944 and 1947.[44]

While American soldiers continued to hunt without knowledge of the US regulations, or else simply disregarded them, German civilians and government officials considered the American actions to be dangerous and illegal. Sebastian Dürnreuther, a former politician of the *Bayerischen Volkspartei*, for example, wrote that American soldiers in groups of 60–100 men shot anything with hair and hunted with little regard for safety, in one instance firing thirty shots for one animal and coming dangerously close to hitting local farmers.[45] Similarly, a Bavarian forester wrote that American soldiers regularly shot animals out of season and, in one case, he described how after shooting an animal, the Americans poured gasoline 'on the rest of the animal and then set [it] on fire'.[46] American soldiers even hunted roe deer and pheasants in the city of Munich, in the *Englische Garten*, Munich's centrally located public park. While perhaps not expressly forbidden, such actions were certainly dangerous and, as the park's forester complained, represented a 'threat to public safety'.[47]

The questionable behaviour of American hunters came to the attention of American officials as well. Food and Agricultural Officer Willis P. Duruz acknowledged the 'uncontrolled hunting by U.S. military personnel' in 1945 and noted that soldiers disregarded instructions, endangered persons and damaged property.[48] An ensign in the US Navy complained that US officers and enlisted men hunted without licenses, used machine guns, left wounded animals in the forest and used jeep spotlights at night.[49] In addition, in direct response to Davison's exploits, a Military Government forestry official, W. F. Bond, commented that he would do 'everything in my power to see to it that this record never again is equalled' while Master Sergeant Rudolph asked the US army newspaper, the *Stars and Stripes*, to 'take some time out and tell some of these trigger-happy officers and men what became of the millions of buffalo, sea otter, antelope, passenger pigeon and dozens of other birds and animals we once had with us in the States'.[50]

Although American hunting angered Germans and some Americans, few mechanisms existed to enforce hunting regulations or to discipline violators. The most important organization in charge of policing American behaviour was the US Constabulary forces. Formed in October 1945, the Constabulary was a military police force responsible for maintaining security, controlling the borders of the US Zone and working with the nascent German police forces to stop black marketeers, locate former Nazi leaders and conduct general law enforcement practices. Although formally allocated 32,000 men, the Constabulary was consistently under manned due to redeployment and experienced 100 per cent turnover in 1946 and 1947.[51] In working with the Bavarian forestry administration, General Hobard Gay, commander of the Constabulary forces, informed Bavarian *Landesforstmeister* Alfred Hoepffner that to aid Bavarian forestry officials, the forest offices should contact passing Constabulary patrols, inform them of poaching locations and report license plate numbers and any other characteristics of the illegal hunters.[52] But while General Gay declared his willingness to aid the Bavarian Forestry Administration, one American official later commented that rather than preventing illegal hunting, the 'Constabulary accounted for the largest part of hunting and fishing violations'.[53]

The event that finally engendered a change to American hunting policies came from within the American military. In December 1946, Colonel Frank Chamberlin, a twenty-year veteran of the Medical Corps, commander of the 279th Station Hospital in Berlin and a consultant to the game conservation office in his home state, wrote a thirteen-page letter concerning hunting conditions in the US Zone to General Joseph T. McNarney, commander of all American forces in Europe, in which he stated that the 'unsportsmanlike practices conducted by our officers in the forests of Germany are on a par with the V.D. rate'.[54] Through this letter, Chamberlin asserted that the American 'hunting license is a joke' because licenses were simply handed out by commanding officers to any soldier who requested one. He also claimed that hunting seasons had no meaning as no authority enforced them or checked the game shot by American hunters and declared that most banned practices, such as hunting at night and using automatic weapons, were common practices for American soldiers. As for the hunting regulations, Chamberlin wrote that organized hunts usually involved soldiers surrounding a section of woods and shooting 'anything that can crawl' with all types of weapons.[55]

The actions and behaviours of American servicemen meticulously described in Chamberlin's letter directly resulted in the development and implementation of new regulations by the higher levels of Military Government. Issued in February 1947, USFET Circular No. 11 (later adopted as Circular 58 by EUCOM, the United States European Command, and referred to by this number) did make the process of obtaining a hunting license more stringent and required that all hunting of deer and wild boar be done in hunting parties rather than individually.[56] Nevertheless,

Chamberlin found this new policy wanting and continued his criticisms. Eventually his remarks reached the desk of American Military Governor General Lucius Clay who responded to Chamberlin's reproaches. Clay thanked Chamberlin for his concerns and his interest 'in the preservation of wildlife in Germany' but also defended the behaviour of American soldiers, stating 'I do not believe that the wanton killing of wildlife has been malicious but rather has resulted from thoughtlessness and from our failure to have adequate regulations really enforced'.[57]

As the comments over the new regulations indicate, there were strong differences of opinion within the American Military Government. Critics of American hunting behaviour, like Chamberlin and those who criticized Davison, tended to be professional foresters or have strong ties to sport hunting, and they regarded American hunting practices in Germany as dangerous, illegal and unsportsmanlike. Therefore, they recognized the importance of German hunting practices and wanted American personnel to respect them. Other American officials simply suggested that American's destructive hunting actions were a policy failure that could be resolved quickly through education and better enforcement of the regulations. Once educated, these rule breakers would follow the new regulations, bringing an end to the worst excesses of American hunting. These individuals, however, were proved wrong as the destructive behaviour continued.

From Reichsjagdgesetz to Bayerisches Jagdgesetz, 1947–9

The most important debate between occupiers and occupied over hunting in the US Zone started in April 1948 when the American civilian overseeing Bavaria, Murray Van Wagoner, wrote a note strongly critical of US army hunting practices in Germany: 'for thousands of years Germany has followed a policy of conservation and game management' but 'this good hunting is threatened. Here in Bavaria much of the fault lies squarely with the occupation forces'. The occupiers, according to him, were guilty of numerous violations, including 'dynamiting of fish, the slaughter of pregnant does, illegal hunting at feeding grounds stations and on restricted grounds and mass drives with automatic weapons at a terrible risk to human lives'. Van Wagoner contended that these prohibited behaviours carried obvious dangers: the 'game supply is threatened, good sportsmanship suffers and our prestige in the performance of the occupation mission is lowered. We are not behaving like good Americans or good sportsmen'. Due to these violations, Van Wagoner asked all commanders to vigorously prosecute any individual who violated his order and stated that hunting would remain prohibited until new regulations were developed.[58]

Van Wagoner's memorandum not only highlights the continued troubles with American hunting behaviour, but also reveals that he believed the hunting issue was undermining American credibility. As occupiers attempting to demonstrate democratic values, American soldiers' actions towards wildlife undermined these efforts. Additionally, Van Wagoner emphasized that these destructive actions further eroded the concept of sportsmanship and also indicated to Germans that American sportsmanship could be violent and brutal. These factors led Van Wagoner to revoke all American hunting privileges until new regulations had been issued, in an effort to halt the violence and start rebuilding trust between Germans and Americans. A month later, at the end of May 1948, he issued new guidelines for hunting and fishing in Bavaria. Although they simply reiterated that American personnel must strictly adhere to Circular 58, they also closed over a dozen *Landkreis* to all hunting of any kind. The closure was perhaps the most drastic action taken by Van Wagoner to prevent wildlife destruction and occurred in regions such as Berchtesgaden, Freising, Landsberg, Garmisch-Partenkirchen and Munich where large numbers of American personnel were located.[59]

Van Wagoner's actions opened a debate within Bavaria over the future of hunting and fishing. In early August 1948, Bavarian *Ministerpräsident* Hans Ehard (Christian Social Union) submitted a comprehensive memorandum drafted by the Bavarian Ministry for Agriculture, Food and Forestry concerning the future of hunting and fishing policy. This ten-page memorandum detailed many of the German complaints against American hunters. Highlighting the differences between US and German conceptions of game ownership, the memo implied that with the suspension of German hunting in 1945, 'the introduction of the American law have [*sic*] created conditions which urgently require revision, unless hunting and sport fishing shall be fully exposed to ruin'.[60] Moreover, the memorandum asserted that the imposition of American game laws 'in a small country like Bavaria', where the population was much denser than in the United States, would 'lead to the game certainly becoming extinct within few years [*sic*]'.[61]

Within the US Military Government, Birger Berg, Chief of the Forestry Branch in Bavaria, reviewed the Bavarian memorandum and sent a detailed point-by-point response to Kenneth W. Ingwalson, the director of the Bavarian Food, Agriculture and Forestry Division. Throughout this document, Berg rejected the Bavarian complaints and defended American policy, falling back on Circular 58 to argue that the majority of American hunters abided by the established rules. Regarding German fears that wildlife would become extinct, he conceded that 'possibly one-third to two-thirds of the game was killed' in the early months of 1945, but asserted that 'since 1947 at the beginning of the season the killing of game has been carried out according to a shooting plan prepared by the Bavarian Ministry'.[62]

After defending American personnel, Berg continued by arguing that German hunting was a privileged, elite practice undertaken by only a small number of individuals. While Ehard emphasized hunting's environmental and cultural value, Berg stressed the political and social aspects. He conceded that hunting held 'cultural and ethical value', but for only 'a small group of privileged people'. For Bavaria, he estimated this to be '22,000 privileged characters' in a total pre-war population of 6.5 million. Moreover, he accused these individuals of undermining the American wildlife control programs, claiming that 'from the very start the ugly head of the old German hunting aristocracy was popping up. The gentlemen with the "Gemsbart" [chamois hat decoration] wanted to run this show'. Finally, in response to Ehard's claim that 'hunting and fishing mean so much to this country', Berg claimed this should instead read 'mean so much to that privileged small group which can afford to lease hunting grounds'. In conclusion, Berg remarked that Bavarian hunting, by limiting the number of hunters, was undemocratic and elitist, and was prone to encourage authoritarian leaders, stating that 'according to the American democratic principles anyone should be allowed to go hunting'.[63]

The Bavarian memorandum was only the beginning of what Ingwalson described as a 'definite campaign' by the Germans 'to regain control over hunting'.[64] During the first years of the occupation, hunting organizations like the BJV remained banned because they were considered paramilitary organizations with links to Goering and the Nazi regime. They were only permitted to reorganize in the US Zone in September 1947.[65] According to a US Military Government investigation into the BJV, the organization was founded by Kellner, a 'financially well off' individual from Augsburg, who appointed himself president and started organizing the association unofficially as early as November 1946.[66] Relations between Kellner and the Americans were often tense. One Military Government report claimed the BJV 'disseminated hostile political propaganda' and saw 'democratization [as] something by which only the stupid shall be affected'.[67] Kellner publically denied all of these charges on numerous occasions, suggesting that Military Government and some Munich hunters sought to suppress his organization.[68] He also argued that the American 'free hunting' system was both dangerous and illegal, basing this argument on a comparison between population size and landmass in the United States and Germany, and stated that the population density in Bavaria was 130 people per square kilometre in contrast to the United States' 17 individuals per square kilometre. To Kellner, the United States' 'immense vastness' protected game animals, in a way that was impossible in Bavaria due to its size and population. Instead, Bavarians required stricter hunting laws and adherence to game seasons and shooting plans to protect wildlife from over hunting.[69] Similar critiques appeared in the German press. The *Süddeutsche Zeitung*, for example, asked 'how would this system of free hunting affect the over populated areas of the western zones'? Answering its own question, the newspaper claimed that, with American hunting laws and practices, German 'nature is destined for destruction'.[70]

Ingwalson claimed that the growing press campaign against American hunting practices sought the restoration of German sovereignty over hunting laws. His claim that the debate was as much about sovereignty as a detailed critique of American hunting practices would appear to have been correct, as the BJV and their supporters in the German press were responding to high-level Military Government discussions in both Munich and Frankfurt over a future Bavarian hunting law. Towards the end of 1948, the occupiers and the German authorities had started discussing a new constitution which would allow Germans to take over administrative, legislative and judicial control of the FRG; however, the Allies would retain the right to take direct action in certain areas, including security and disarmament.[71] Due to its connection with the use and possession of firearms, together with its reputation as an activity for a privileged elite and the fact that the *Reichsjagdgesetz* had been passed in 1934, hunting remained a contentious issue. While they still had the authority to do so and before the transfer of power to German civilians, the American Military Government recommended a review of 'all National Socialist Laws to see if any remain that should be repealed'.[72]

In Munich, Van Wagoner formed a committee under the direction of Civil Administration Division head Albert Schweizer to review the *Reichsjagdgesetz*. Meeting in October 1948, the committee apparently ignored Van Wagoner's earlier criticisms of US hunting practices and reemphasized the arguments developed by Berg, condemning Germany's 'feudalistic system' that reserved hunting for the privileged few.[73] Similarly, at a second meeting, Schweizer's committee made several policy recommendations designed to fundamentally reform German hunting practices, declaring that Bavarian hunting should be 'democratized' and open to all qualified and licensed hunters regardless of land ownership, and that wild game should be considered as public, not private property. The committee acknowledged, however, that the implementation of these proposals required the repeal of the *Reichsjagdgesetz*, and that this would result in 'resistance by the German *Jagdwirtschaft* [hunting community] and the German administration'.[74]

At the same time that Schweizer's committee was meeting in Bavaria, Clay's staff at the Office of the Military Governor (OMGUS) was also discussing the future of hunting. They considered the *Reichsjagdgesetz* 'strongly Nazi and militaristic' and 'unsalvageable because of the Nazi phraseology'.[75] They particularly honed in on three aspects of the law. First, they argued that thc law was based on the 'Fuehrer principle' whereby state hunting officials could interfere on private property to manage wildlife. Second, they contended that the law extended 'the Nazi concept of the corporate state' and forced all hunters to join the *Deutsche Jägerschaft*, the sole hunting association permitted under the Nazi regime. Third, they asserted that the *Reichsjagdgesetz* safeguarded hunters' actions through 'Hunter Honor Courts' that could cancel or suspend hunting licenses and created an 'exaggerated pride and solidarity similar to that which existed in German military units'. Finally, they maintained that the law was 'built around the Nazi catchword "blood and soil"', making it the 'embodiment and vehicle of Nazi ideology'.[76] Based on these features, Clay's staff recommended repealing the law and returning control of hunting 'to the individual state[s]'.[77] Clay agreed and issued the 'Repeal of the Reich Hunting Act' on 15 November 1948, reverting all German hunting legislation back to those laws that were in power before 1934. Clay's repeal entered into effect on 1 February 1949, giving the German *Länder* in the US Zone two months to draft and develop new hunting laws.

As Schweizer's committee had predicted, the repeal of the *Reichsjagdgesetz* brought immediate protest from the BJV. Kellner rejected the American efforts at federalizing the hunting laws, advocating instead a national law over a series of confusing *Länder* laws. The *Reichsjagdgesetz*, he claimed, was something Germans could still take pride in, and he confidently asserted that 'there are undoubtedly areas where we Germans lead'. Kellner argued that hunting did not privilege the former aristocracy as 'most Bavarian hunters are farmers, small craftsmen and businessmen and only a small part of hunting is controlled by the former nobility'.[78] A similar defence of the *Reichsjagdgesetz* was also voiced in the *Süddeutsche Zeitung*. The newspaper acknowledged that the law was repealed because of National Socialist language, but claimed that Military Government should not throw out the good with the bad, arguing that the principals of the law were developed much earlier than 1933 and the Nazi state had simply 'garnished' the law with their ideology. Additionally, the paper asserted that there remained a set of 'good principles' that German hunters developed over centuries to protect and care for German wildlife.[79]

Although the *Reichsjagdgesetz* was repealed in November 1948, the American and Bavarian officials did not meet until early January 1949 to discuss a new law. By this time, West Germany was on the brink of regaining most of its sovereignty as the Basic Law entered into effect in May 1949. As this date approached, American occupiers became more willing to defer to Germans in questions over future laws. This flexibility was particularly evident as the occupiers relented in their harsh critiques of German hunting practices and allowed the Bavarians to draft a new hunting law, the *Bayerische Jagdgesetz*, without significant American interference. While seemingly a dramatic turn for an occupying force, after US officials Berg, Ingwalson and Schweizer's committee had all previously strongly criticized the 'undemocratic' nature of German hunting, this change in American policy was also a consequence of a deliberate decision by the US Military Government at the highest levels not to interfere in what they now considered to be domestic German politics.

Nonetheless, during the first meeting between Military Government and the Bavarians in 1949, the Americans still followed through on their meetings from the previous October and demanded an end to the *Reviersystem*. The Bavarians, however, refused to agree, stating that no further discussions were possible if the principles outlined in the recommendations of Schweizer's committee were incorporated in new hunting legislation.[80] Ingwalson and the Bavarian Minister for Food, Agriculture and Forestry, Alois Schlögl, met at the end of March and attempted to reach a compromise. However, the draft of the law submitted by the Bavarians to the US Military Government at the end of April 1949 was again critiqued for lacking 'the principles of a good democratic law'. Nevertheless, by June, a month after the Basic Law entered into effect, Ingwalson had to admit that he could no longer express the 'approval or disapproval' of Military Government over the new hunting law, only act in an advisory capacity.[81] The Bavarians had therefore successfully managed to block an American attempt to reform the existing German law, through buying time and waiting for the passing of the German constitution, by which time the issue no longer appeared central to the achievement of US goals in Germany. The American unwillingness to intervene, as they could still have done, for example by claiming that hunting and the possession of firearms had to be controlled for security reasons, allowed for the passage of Bavarian Hunting Law through the *Landtag* Committee for Food and Agriculture in July 1949 and five months later, it became law.[82]

By stepping aside, the US Military Government allowed the Bavarians to promulgate their own hunting law and so participate in the democratic process, even if the law as eventually passed retained features the Americans found inherently undemocratic. The German hunters, press and government officials all acknowledged that the *Reichsjagdgesetz* was tainted by Nazism, but they also saw many benefits to the law. Thus, when drafting the new Bavarian hunting law, they openly rejected those portions of the *Reichsjagdgesetz* that contained racialized language and *Blut und Boden* ideology, while seeking to preserve those features that they believed retained fundamental German traditions, especially concerning private property. This process did not radically transform German hunting culture, but ensured that the *Blut und Boden* ideology was publicly rejected, resulting in a subtle reorientation of German hunting culture. The hunters therefore gained a political victory. Through seeing their environmental and cultural concerns and interests represented in the making of the new law they also acquired a stake in the new government and a reason to support the new democratic processes emerging from the ashes of the Third Reich.

Conclusion

As the negotiations over hunting in occupied Germany demonstrate, issues related to nature and the environment contributed to the re-emergence of civil society in post-war Germany. Prior to the Second World War, Americans and Germans had different legal and cultural traditions concerning the practice of hunting. During the occupation, these ideas came into contact and interacted with one another. As the victorious occupier, the US Military Government established policies to regulate the actions of American personnel, but initially only engaged with German hunters on matters relating to security and the ban on firearms, and then subsequently in relation to the post-war food crisis. Yet while addressing these problems, Military Government disregarded both German and American complaints about destructive American behaviours. According to these complaints, the US authorities were not doing enough to regulate American hunting activities that often proved dangerous and encroached on German conceptions of private property. German hunters, the press and politicians believed that the Americans, with their focus on meat and trophies, disrespected nature and wildlife and hunted in a manner that would rapidly lead to the violent devastation of animal species, as had already occurred in parts of North America. Most importantly, they believed that the introduction of American style hunting laws would increase the number of hunters, bring about the destruction of German wildlife and eliminate German traditions that should be preserved.

Although voiced throughout the occupation, these issues culminated in 1949, following the repeal of the *Reichsjagdgesetz* and the need for new hunting legislation to be passed by each of the three *Länder* in the US Zone. During the early discussions in Bavaria, the American occupiers appeared adamant in their demands that American designed hunting laws be implemented in Bavaria, but as the formation of the Federal Republic neared, the debates over the different hunting systems soon became entangled with the transfer of sovereignty. The American officials most closely involved sincerely wanted to reform German hunting laws, as is evident in the numerous critiques offered by Berg and Schweizer, but the staunch position of the Bavarians and the transfer of sovereignty to German politicians prevented them from succeeding in their aim.

The inability of the American Military Government to introduce American fashioned and supposedly more democratic hunting laws into West Germany could be considered a political failure, but the debate around hunting still played a role in the reorientation of German society. In effect, their opposition to American designed hunting laws led Germans to participate in processes of negotiation and discussion with the American Military Government, eventually reaching a compromise in which both the Americans and Germans achieved part of their respective goals: the Americans abolished the *Reichsjagdgesetz* and its Nazi language against the desire of most German hunters, while the Germans were able to prevent the implementation of the American *Lizenzsystem* and ensure the passage of a new German hunting law that contained many features of the *Reichsjagdgesetz* but no longer included language and concepts derived from Nazi ideology.

Thus, in defending their legal and cultural traditions and enshrining them into a new hunting law, initially in Bavaria and then in 1952 for the FRG as a whole, German hunters played an active, vocal and highly symbolic role in the transfer of sovereignty, and in the process of decision-making in the immediate post-war period. Starting as external critics of the US occupation regime, by 1949, as power and sovereignty was progressively returned to German politicians and to newly established democratic institutions such as the Bavarian *Landtag*, German hunters were given the space to articulate their concerns and so gained a well-founded belief that their interests were being taken into consideration. In this way, their long-standing concerns over environmental issues contributed to the re-emergence of a civil society in Germany, in which decisions were made after extensive public discussion and debate, rather than imposed from above by an autocratic government.

Notes

1 'Die Jagdverhältnisse in Bayern', *Sonderdruck Mitteilungen / Bayerischer Jagdschutz- und Jägerverband* 1 (January–February 1949): 2.
2 The German Academic Exchange Service (DAAD) provided support for this research.
3 Konrad Jarausch, *After Hitler: Recivilizing Germans, 1945–1995* (New York: Oxford University Press, 2006), vii.
4 Thomas R. Dunlap, 'Sport Hunting and Conservation, 1880–1920', *Environmental Review* 12, no. 1 (Spring 1988): 52.
5 John Reiger, *American Sportsmen and the Origins of Conservation*, 3rd edn (Corvallis: Oregon State University Press, 2001), 7–13.
6 Ibid., 32–6.
7 Dunlap, 'Sport Hunting and Conservation, 1880–1920', 53.
8 Reiger, *American Sportsmen and the Origins of Conservation*, 95–6.
9 Ibid., 91.
10 Ibid., 92–3.
11 Louis S. Warren, *The Hunter's Game: Poachers and Conservationists in Twentieth-Century America* (New Haven: Yale University Press, 1997), 12.
12 Karl Jacoby, *Crimes against Nature: Squatters, Poachers, Thieves and the Hidden History of American Conservation* (Berkeley: University of California Press, 2001).
13 Thomas R. Dunlap, 'Values for Varmints: Predator Control and Environmental Ideas, 1920–1939', *Pacific Historical Review* 53, no. 2 (May 1984): 143–6.
14 Aldo Leopold, *Game Management* (New York: Scribner's, 1933).
15 Aldo Leopold, 'Notes on Game Administration in Germany: Old World Methods Vary Greatly from Those in the New World', *American Wildlife* 25, no. 6 (1936): 85, 92–3.
16 Hans-Wilhelm Eckardt, *Herrschaftliche Jagd, bäuerlich Not und bürgerliche Kritik* (Göttingen, 1976), 17; Werner Rösener, *Die Geschichte der Jagd. Kultur, Gesellschaft und Jagdwesen im Wandel der Zeit* (Düsseldorf: Artemis & Winkler, 2004), 87.
17 Joachim Radkau, *Wood: A History* (Cambridge: Polity Press, 2012), 56–92.

18 Hubertus Hiller, *Jäger und Jagd: Zur Entwicklung des Jagdwesens in Deutschland zwischen 1848 und 1914* (Münster: Waxmann Verlag, 2003), 132–9.
19 Eckardt, *Herrschaftliche Jagd*, 17.
20 Martin Knoll, 'Hunting in the Eighteenth Century: An Environmental History Perspective', *Historische Sozialforschung* 29, no. 3 (2004): 9–36.
21 Regina Schulte, *The Village in Court: Arson, Infanticide, and Poaching in the Court Records of Upper Bavaria, 1848–1910* (New York: Cambridge University Press, 1994), 121.
22 Hiller, *Jäger und Jagd*, 30–7; Rösener, *Die Geschichte der Jagd*, 367.
23 Hiller, *Jäger und Jagd*, 34–5.
24 Rösener, *Die Geschichte der Jagd*, 366–70; Alois Schlögl, *Bayerische Agrargeschichte: Die Entwicklung der Land- und Forstwirtschaft seit Beginn des 19. Jahrhunderts* (München: Bayerischer Landwirtschaftsverlag, 1954), 694. A *Tagewerk* is roughly 3,400 square metres.
25 Wolfram Theilemann, *Adel im Grünen Rock: Adliges Jägertum, Großprivatwaldbesitz und die preußische Forstbeamtenschaft 1866–1914* (Berlin: Akademie Verlag, 2004), 114–9.
26 Hiller, *Jäger und Jagd*, 132–3.
27 Ibid., 122–3.
28 Charles Closemann, 'Legalizing a Volksgemeinschaft', in *How Green Were the Nazis? Nature, Environment and Nation in the Third Reich*, ed. Franz-Josef Brüggemeier, Mark Cioc and Thomas Zeller (Athens: Ohio University Press, 2005), 31.
29 Aldo Leopold, 'Deer and Dauerwald in Germany II. Ecology and Policy', *Journal of Forestry History* 34, no. 5 (May 1936): 461–3.
30 See *Military Government Gazette Germany, Twelfth Army Group Area of Control* 1 (18 September 1944): 2–3. Available online: http://deposit.d-nb.de/online/vdr/rechtsq.htm (accessed 7 September 2017).
31 'Confiscation and Surrender of Arms and Ammunition', *Allied Control Authority Germany* 2 (January–February 1946), 1. Available online: https://www.loc.gov/rr/frd/Military_Law/Enactments/Volume-II.pdf (accessed 7 September 2017).
32 Weekly Intelligence Report Liaison & Security Office Landkreis Alsfeld, 7 June 1946, National Archives College Park, Maryland (hereafter NACP), RG 466/250/84/26/06/1.
33 Landkreis Alzenau Monthly Historical Report, May 1946, NACP, RG 260/390/47/19/4/193.
34 Bavarian State Forestry Administration to Military Government Bavaria, 3 August 1945, Bayerisches Hauptstaatsarchiv, Munich (hereafter BayHStA), Ministerium für Ernährung Landwirtschaft und Forsten (MELF), 4471.
35 For Allied food policy, see John Farquharson, *The Western Allies and the Politics of Food* (Dover: Berg, 1985); Günter J. Trittel, *Hunger und Politik: Die Ernährungskrise in der Bizone (1945–1949)* (New York: Campus Verlag, 1990).
36 Nick Cullather, 'The Foreign Policy of the Calorie', *American Historical Review* 112, no. 2 (April 2007): 339.
37 Adam Seipp, *Strangers in the Wild Place: Refugees, Americans, and a German Town, 1945–1952* (Bloomington: Indiana University Press, 2013), 64–5.
38 See R. J. Ackert, 'European Deer Hunt: Yankee Style', *American Riflemen*, 19 May 1946, 14–6, 30; Bill Boni, 'Davison Files His Defense of Record Bag', *Stars and Stripes*, 22 March 1947, 9.
39 'GI Rifles Point at Wild Boars for Food Crop', *Stars and Stripes*, 5 September 1945, 3.

40 Crop Damage by Wild Animals, 29 May 1946, Institut für Zeitgeschichte (hereafter IfZ), OMGUS 45–46/110/8.
41 Hunting and Fishing Policy, 4 October 1945, IfZ, OMGUS 45–46/110/8.
42 Ackert, 'European Deer Hunt', 14–6, 30.
43 F. W. Beckert, Jr., 'Roebuck for Sport . . . and GI Good', *American Riflemen*, 19 March 1947, 10–2.
44 Dexter Freeman, 'ET Happy Hunting Ground Sgt. Gets 128 Deer, 10 Elk', *Stars and Stripes*, 8 February 1947, 7.
45 Sebastian Dürnreuther to B. Landesforstverwaltung, 11 August, 1945, BayHStA, MELF 4479.
46 Wildabschuss, 5 June, 1945, BayHStA, MELF 4479.
47 Jagdfrevel im Englischen Garten, 8 March 1947, BayHStA, MELF 4471.
48 Weekly Detachment Report Unit E1 F3, 8 August 1945, NACP, RG 260/390/4/33–34/07-1/ 3.
49 Violations of Hunting Restrictions by US Troops, 24 October 1945, IfZ, OMGUS FA/132/5.
50 Bill Boni, 'Readers Fire Both Barels at Game Hogs', *Stars and Stripes*, 21 February 1947, 9.
51 Kendall D. Gott, *Mobility, Vigilance, and Justice: The US Army Constabulary in Germany, 1946–1953* (Fort Leavenworth, KN: Combat Studies Institute Press, 2012), 9–18. Available online: www.arcic.army.mil/App_Documents/LPD/Gott-Mobility-Vigilance-and-Justice-The-US-Constabulary-in-Germany.pdf (accessed 7 September 2017).
52 Vollzug der Jagdvorschriften durch die Zonenpolizei, 29 August 1947, Staatsarchiv München, FA 18661.
53 Recommended Policies and Procedures for Sport-Hunting and Fishing in Bavaria, 8 March 1948, NACP, RG 260/390/47/22/07/168.
54 Col. Frank Chamberlin to Gen. Joseph McNarney, 7 December 1946, IfZ, OMGUS 47/191/6.
55 Ibid.
56 USFET Circular 11: Hunting and Fishing Policy, 15 February 1947, IfZ, OMGUS 47/191/6.
57 Gen. Lucius D. Clay to Col. Frank T. Chamberlin, 6 March 1947, IfZ, OMGUS 47/191/6.
58 Restricted Game Season in Bavaria, 22 April 1948, NACP, RG 260/390/47/22/07/168.
59 New Hunting Regulations, Bavaria, 2 June 1948, NACP, RG 260/390/47/22/07/168.
60 Petition Concerning Hunting and Sport Fishing in Bavaria, 30 July 1948, NACP, RG 260/390/47/22/07/168.
61 Ibid.
62 Petition Concerning Hunting and Sportfishing in Bavaria, Submitted by the Bavarian Minister President, 10 August 1948, NACP, RG 260/390/47/22/07/168.
63 Ibid.
64 Return of Hunting and Fishing Privileges, 21 September 1948, NACP, RG 260/390/47/22/07/168.
65 Kellner to Military Government, 15 February 1948, NACP, RG 260/390/47/22/07/169.
66 Reorganization of the Bavarian Hunters' Association, 10 October 1948, NACP, RG 260/390/47/22/07/169.
67 Biweekly report No. 4 for Regierungsbezirk Oberbayern-Oberpflaz, 16 October 1948, NACP, RG 260/390/48/02/04/165.

68 'Was geht in der bayerischen Jägerschaft vor'?, *Süddeutsche Zeitung*, 31 March 1949, 3.

69 Oskar Kellner, 'Amerikanisches Jagdrecht in Bayern?', *Sonderdruck Mitteilungen / Bayerischer Jagdschutz- und Jägerverband* 2 (March 1949): 3, NACP, RG 260/390/47/22/07/168.

70 'Die Jägerei war nie das Privileg einer Kaste', *Süddeutsche Zeitung*, 17 March 1949, 3.

71 US Department of State, Office of the Historian, 'Occupation Statute Defining the Powers to be Retained by the Occupation Authorities, Signed by the Three Western Foreign Ministers, 8 April 1949', *Documents on Germany, 1944–1985* (Washington, DC: Office of the Historian, Bureau of Public Affairs, 1985), 212.

72 Repeal of Reich Hunting Act, 8 October 1948, IfZ, OMGUS 1948/186/7.

73 Meeting on Hunting Regulations, 19 October 1948, NACP, RG 260/390/47/22/07/168.

74 Staff study on Proposals for the New German Hunting and Fishing Laws, 8 November 1948, NACP, RG 260/390/47/22/07/168.

75 Repeal of Reich Hunting Act, 7 October 1948, IfZ, OMGUS 1948/186/7.

76 Repeal of Reich Hunting Act, 10 August 1948, IfZ, OMGUS 1948/186/7.

77 Repeal of Reich Hunting Act, 7 October 1948, IfZ, OMGUS 1948/186/7.

78 'Die Jagdverhältnisse in Bayern', *Sonderdruck Mitteilungen / Bayerischer Jagdschutz- und Jägerverband* 1 (January–February 1949): 5, NACP, RG 260/390/47/22/07/168.

79 'Platonische Jagdgesetze', *Süddeutsche Zeitung*, 20 November 1948, 3,

80 Stenographischer Bericht über die Verhandlungen des Bayerischen Landtags, 15 September 1949, Anlage: Rede des Staatsministers Dr. Schlögl zum Bayerischen Jagdgesetz, Veröffentlicht im 'Bayerischen Staatsanzeiger' Nr. 29 vom 22 Juli 1949.

81 Ibid.

82 Ibid.

Part Four

Experiencing Occupation: Daily Life and Personal Relationships

10

The Sexualized Landscape of Post-War Germany and the Politics of Cross-Racial Intimacy in the US Zone

Nadja Klopprogge

In 1947 Friedrich Seidenstücker, one of the most prominent visual chroniclers of post-war Germany, captured a scene on film that was unimaginable only two years earlier. The black and white picture taken at Wannsee beach, a popular bathing place on a lake in the western outskirts of Berlin, depicts the flirtatious interaction between three presumably German women and two African American soldiers.[1]

A few months earlier the *Afro-American*, an African American newspaper based in Baltimore, ran its own stories on the friendly encounters between occupiers and occupied at Berlin's probably most famous beach. In an idiosyncratic collage of images – all broadly addressing the issue of the colour line – the editors of the *Afro-American* placed three photographs of the Wannsee beach in a prominent position and assured their readers 'NO NAZIS HERE: An American GI and German fraulein relax at Wansee [*sic*] lake'.[2] For both Seidenstücker and the editors of the *Afro-American*, place and plot corresponded. Undeniably, Seidenstücker, famous for documenting the curiosities and vicissitudes of everyday life among the post-war urban landscape of ruins, deemed the scene at Wannsee noteworthy enough to capture with his camera; but the coverage of cross-racial bathing in Berlin by the black press adds yet another layer, turning the scene into a place with historical meaning and political weight.

The Wannsee was not the only place in Germany that gained a new subtext in the immediate post-war years due to intimate encounters between black GIs and German women. By tracing how three different places were represented and interpreted by African American writers – the economic space of the black market, the recreational space of the Wannsee and what Neil Gregor has designated the 'haunted' space of the city of Nuremberg – this chapter explores the intimate landscape of post-war Germany. These three places appeared regularly in black American visual and textual reflections on occupied Germany and its recent past. Rather than focusing on occupation policy or on German and US military reactions to cross-racial encounters in the US Zone, this chapter draws attention to the African American perspective, and aims to tease out some of the main concerns of individual GIs and African American writers.

It thus strives to go beyond an analysis of the meaning of race and the tenacity of racist attitudes in post-war Germany. In doing so, however, it builds on research that has carved out the changing meaning of race in Germany in the aftermath of the Holocaust, alongside the persistence of certain tropes dating back to German colonialism and what was referred to as the 'Schwarze Schmach' (the 'black shame'), when French colonial troops occupied the Rhineland.[3] Similarly, instead of following research that has described the US Zone as 'a microcosm of the racial and civil rights struggle that would dominate America in the 1950s and 1960s',[4] this chapter considers the occupation years as a distinct historical moment in the African American struggle for racial justice. It illustrates how the presence of African American troops in the immediate post-war years reshaped and redefined iconic spaces connected with Nazi rule, racialized sexual paranoia and post-war concerns over a 'moral collapse' in Germany. While also associating them with questions of intimacy and sexuality, African Americans, instead, linked the memory enshrined in those places with the struggle for racial emancipation in the United States.[5]

Shifting the focus of the impact of everyday encounters in the US Zone away from the occupied, this chapter tries to historicize the repercussions of these experiences on the occupier.[6] More precisely, it investigates how the African American press, black writers and individual GIs made sense of the presence of black occupation soldiers in the specific historical circumstances of post-war Germany, at a time that was in many respects a liminal moment both for the history of Germany and for African Americans in the United States. The years following the defeat of the Third Reich marked a period of transition from Nazi rule to liberal democracy in Germany, but they were also a time of considerable hope for change among African Americans. The black press and African American leaders translated their service to the nation during the Second World War, the occupation objectives of denazification and democratization and the expanding human rights discourse of the early post-war period into a moment of (betrayed) opportunities.[7] The black market, the Wannsee and Nuremberg provided three distinct settings for the black press to address issues of great significance for their struggle, such as the continued segregation of US military facilities units and positions, the historical trajectories of violated sexuality, and the Nazi past, as well as the economic, social and political discrimination of African Americans.

A racially segregated occupation

Following US troop reductions in Germany in the months immediately following the unconditional surrender of the Wehrmacht, approximately 614,000 servicemen and women remained as occupying forces in the US Zone. Just under 10 per cent of the troops were African American – an official quota imposed by the War Department that was supposed to represent the demographics of the United States. Yet, in practice the actual number of black military troops based in Germany never reached the 10 per cent mark. Black GIs mostly served in support units and were excluded from prestigious positions in the headquarters of the Military Governor in Frankfurt, in the Allied Control Council in Berlin, or in the later established Constabulary Forces that protected the borders between the American and the Soviet Zones. But more than the positions held, it was the comprehensive racial segregation of black and white US troops, including separate mess halls, recreational facilities and even blood banks, that outraged the African American community.[8]

Ever since the Nazis took over power in Germany, African American intellectuals, the black press and civil rights organizations, such as the National Association for the Advancement of Colored People (NAACP), cast a glance across to the other side of the Atlantic and sought to use the moral outcry over the persecution of European Jews to draw attention to their own legal and de facto discrimination in the United States and in the racially segregated armed forces in particular.[9] The US government, however, proved deaf to these pleas and sent racially segregated troops to Europe, just as they had done during the First World War, arguing that the war was not the time to deal with race relations. When the war was won and the American military installed occupation troops in Germany, they came with proclamations that they would denazify and democratize the country, but also with the firm intention to keep their own troops racially segregated. A number of military officials, including the Deputy Chief of Staff for Personnel at the Supreme Headquarters of the Allied Forces in Europe, Willard Stewart Paul, even considered it a poor decision to send African American troops to Germany in the first place, believing that the German people might feel insulted by the authority black soldiers wielded over them, thus potentially leading to conflicts between the occupiers and the occupied.[10] Despite such concerns, the War Department allowed African American troops to be stationed in Europe as part of the occupying forces, fearing pressure from civil rights groups in the United States, but at the same time imposed restrictions regarding their number and the positions they could hold.[11]

An old anxiety of segregationists, and even of more moderate white Americans, ran like a common thread through discussions on the opportunities provided for African Americans in the military throughout the Second World War and the subsequent occupation: the fear of what they called the 'amalgamation of the black and white races'.[12] Determined segregationists such as Mississippi senator Theodor Bilbo and also Secretary of War, Henry Stimson, were afraid that the new opportunities provided and social transformations catalyzed by the war might motivate African American men to push the boundaries of interracial intimacy.[13] Segregationists feared that the existing system that kept the races apart, at least romantically and sexually, would start to be eroded.[14]

The black market

The foreigner has coffee and sugar.
And if he comes by, offering chocolate
His skin color won't matter – you'll jump at it!
(*German street poster*)[15]
Black Market
Laces for the missis
Chewing gum for kisses! …

To you for your 'K' ration: my passion and maybe
An inkling, a twinkling or real sympathy
I'm selling out – take all I've got!
Ambitions! Convictions! The works!
Why not? Enjoy my goods, for boy my goods
Are hot!

(Black market lyric, sung by Marlene Dietrich in the film *A Foreign Affair*)[16]

In the immediate aftermath of the Second World War many observers, both American and German, drew a direct link between the black market and acts of intimacy. In their imagery the black market was not only an illegal economic space but also an immoral space promoting acts of sexual transgression.[17] As historians have noted many times before, intimate encounters between US occupation troops and German women were frequent after the US army entered Germany in 1944, despite the strict ban on fraternization.[18] Although the ban was relaxed in September 1945, seemingly 'harmless' gestures of intimacy, such as holding hands in the streets and dancing in nightclubs, roused the suspicion and anger of many observers, both among occupiers and occupied. Most significantly, the perceived frequency and visibility of sexual acts in public spaces became the focal point of moral anxiety. The black market, not only as a physical but also as a symbolic space, came to epitomize public sexual indecency in the imagination of US military authorities, the US government, authors and journalists, and a variety of different observers in Germany.[19]

For many Germans after the war, the sight of women eating chocolate, smoking a cigarette or wearing nylon stockings transformed the black market into a place of deviance and prostitution, and a symbol for the betrayal of the nation.[20] Such women supposedly sold sexual favours to American soldiers for luxury goods in pure self-interest, thus disgracing the honour of German women and returning Wehrmacht soldiers alike.[21] Contemporary derogative neologisms, such as *Schokoladenhure* (chocolate whore) linked the economic and sexual activities of women, while also denouncing the transgression of racial boundaries.

US military officials such as Lieutenant Woodburn Williams, a regional Military Government official in Middle Franconia, likewise related what he framed as the greed of 'notorious female characters' and the 'generosity' of black soldiers to the crossing of sexual and racial lines, which not only transferred 'Allied property such as rations and clothing [to] German homes' but which he feared would also weaken the strength of the troops due to the spread of venereal disease.[22] Thus, for both German civilians and US military observers, the black market came to signify more than an unlawful, alternative economic system at a time of material crisis. As it became associated with (cross-racial) intimacy and sexuality, the black market evolved into a space representing moral decay and sexual deviance – for the Germans a symbol for national defeat and disgrace; for the American occupiers a danger to the occupation effort and more generally a threat to social, personal and sexual norms based on racial segregation.[23]

Correspondents of the American black press based in Germany also took notice of how cigarettes and other goods in short supply had become the unofficial currency in the US Zone. Yet, the sight of black soldiers providing German civilians with rare goods, such as chocolate, nylon stockings and cigarettes, produced different narratives among these correspondents. Early accounts in African American newspapers described the black market as a space which facilitated the first contacts between black GIs and German civilians. More importantly, they also portrayed it as a space where bartering enabled social interactions, which would help to prove racial prejudices wrong. Often ignoring longer trajectories of anti-black racism in Germany they assumed that, at a time when food and other essential items were in short supply, the generosity of African American servicemen would erode German racial anxieties and hate based on fascist propaganda. As one newspaper expressed it:

> Their Hunger has made [Germans] very objective on such matters as racial attitude. It didn't take long for them to see that there is no difference between food, chocolate, cigarettes and soap in the hands of white Americans and similar items possessed by Negro Americans … I think we have shown them the falseness of Hitler's racial propaganda.[24]

Furthermore, economic relationships in the black market could develop into intimate cross-racial relationships that the black press found symbolically significant. As another newspaper reported: 'Most of them [German women] become friendly with soldiers out of self-interest to get cigarettes, coffee, soap and other rare items. But before long, many find their colored GI friends good companions and sometimes fall in love.'[25] In this way, instead of undermining the occupation effort, African American journalists framed the social relations facilitated within the fluid boundaries of the black market as vehicles for German re-education – a notion of re-education based on the experience of African Americans in their own country.

Thousands of miles away from their homes on the other side of the Atlantic, black American GIs, mostly from poor backgrounds, gained visibility and agency through the black market. They temporally escaped the precarious economic conditions they faced at home. Instead of being confined to the worn down parts of the cities, easy access to rare goods opened up economic and social possibilities they had never known in the United States.[26] Since many black GIs held positions in army support groups responsible for transport and supply, they often had better access to products in high demand than troops in white army units. Cigarettes and other rare goods functioned as gifts for their female friends, as tips in restaurants and paid for food and entertainment on date nights. They could even be used to pay Germans for domestic household services, a form of labour that black men and women commonly performed themselves, rather than paid others to do for them, on the other side of the Atlantic.[27] One black journalist, for example, wrote that through their possession of cigarettes, which were 'a better medium of exchange in Germany than the mark … American soldiers can support a German girl well. Thus you see the German girls wearing nylon stockings and most of the other things that the American wives of our American soldiers wear in Germany'.[28] In this account, the black market is not a space of moral decay, and nylons and cigarettes do not figure as manifestations of sexual transgression. Rather, cigarettes, the currency of the black market, symbolize the economic standing of black soldiers in Germany and their successful fulfilment of the role of the provider.

In contrast to white narratives labelling German women as prostitutes seeking black market goods, the nylons on their legs transformed them in the eyes of this African American author into respectable women and possible soldiers' wives. Black market goods, when purchased by a man and provided as a gift, turned into evidence of his ability to support his girlfriend, and a family.[29] At the same time, the black press included intimate cross-racial friendships and family groups, economically facilitated and sustained through the black market, into their descriptions of a post-war desire for 'normality'.[30] Contrary, though, to hegemonic white American and German post-war ideas of 'normality' that sought a return to a supposedly better past, 'normality' in the lines of the black press offered the promise of a better future of social and economic equality that had never previously existed for African Americans.[31]

Wannsee: The politics of cross-racial bathing

The second half of the 1940s has been described as a 'liminal moment' – a time of transition, new possibilities, and as Dagmar Herzog has argued, of 'considerable sexual liberality'.[32] The Wannsee beach, a prominent recreational and eroticized space on the outskirts of Berlin where couples met to chat, flirt, swim and sometimes explore the possibility of a sexual relationship, epitomized precisely this liminal moment in the aftermath of the Second World War. Journalists and writers in the black press depicted the undisturbed, intimate and comfortable interaction between black GIs and German women, both in their writing and with photographic images. Furthermore, they contrasted this iconic public beach in Berlin with conditions in the United States and in the armed forces. In doing so, they articulated an implicit critique of segregation and sometimes violent discrimination against African Americans in the United States. In particular, they protested against the treatment of black soldiers within the US military, and attempted to demonstrate to their readers that if change was possible even in Germany, 'the land of hate', it should be achievable in the United States.

Strandbad Wannsee (the Wannsee bathing beach) had in fact changed its face earlier, during the Third Reich when it was shaped by Nazi ideology and anti-Semitic policies. In 1935, a sign was erected at the entrance which declared that 'Jews are denied bathing and entrance',[33] while two large flags parading swastikas towered above it. In 1938, a general ban on Jews bathing in public places made the sign obsolete. The prime objective of this prohibition was to deter and if possible prevent intimate contacts between Jews and non-Jews. As Alexandra Przyrembel has argued, convinced followers of Nazi ideology transcribed their own sexual anxieties to places such as public bathing pools and beaches, which were seen as having the potential for racial transgression and disgrace.[34] One of these anxieties was the fear of 'racial mixing', which according to Nazi racial thinking would lead to the 'irrevocable mental and bodily damage' of the woman involved. The enduring circulation of rumours and stereotypes, reinforced by Nazi anti-Semitic propaganda, that portrayed Jewish men as 'sexual threats', was exploited as another reason to ban Jews from public bathing facilities.[35]

While the racial segregation of public bathing facilities in Germany was brought to an end after the defeat of the Nazis in 1945, public pools in the United States were still segregated in the same period to prevent intimate contacts between black and white Americans. Indeed, sexual and racial anxieties associated with bathing had a longer history in the United States than in Germany – not only in the former Confederate states, where almost all public spaces were racially segregated, but also north of the Mason Dixon line, where although racial segregation was not legally sanctioned, as it was in many southern states, municipal authorities and swimming enthusiasts found ways to keep black citizens out of recreational facilities,[36] in some cases using force and outright violence to prevent them entering pools unofficially reserved for whites only.[37]

In keeping with official War Department policy, the US Military Government continued to implement the practice of strict racial segregation of recreational facilities at their army bases in Germany. For example, the swimming pool at the former *SS Panzer-Division Leibstandarte Adolf Hitler* barracks in Berlin, renamed *Andrew Barracks* after it had been taken over by US forces, was racially segregated. As a report by Reverend William J. Walls, who visited the US Zone as part of a delegation of fourteen clergymen, explained to Army Secretary Kenneth Royall in 1947, 'white and colored troops must use the swimming pool at Andrew Barracks in Berlin on separate days. The pool is drained after colored use before the white soldiers swim.'[38] Only a few miles away at the public beach on the Wannsee, however, black soldiers who were not allowed to swim in the same water as their American comrades shared a beach and went swimming with white German women.

Against this backdrop, it is not surprising that the Wannsee beach, with no restrictions on cross-racial mingling, was given full symbolic effect in African American accounts of their experiences in occupied Germany. The collage published in the *Afro-American* and cited above devoted three out of eleven pictures to cross-racial bathing and relaxing on the beach. All three photographs portrayed either a black and white couple standing next to each other in the water, relaxing on a blanket at the beach, or a group of young men and women having fun on a floating platform in the lake. All the pictures and accompanying text portrayed moments of intimacy, friendship and fun rather than following conservative narratives linking intimate relationships between men and women to marriage, reproduction and the domestic sphere. Conversely, the photographs and texts told the story of intimate togetherness and playful exuberance within a public recreational space. Similarly, three photographs portraying the 'close friendship' of black GIs and German women at the Wannsee, printed in the African American magazine *Ebony*, also blurred the lines between juvenile friendship, romantic partnership, flirtatious adventure and seduction.[39]

Not yet following the morally and sexually conservative debates and norms associated with the 1950s, calling for stability and invoking the home and family,[40] these accounts in *Ebony* and the *Afro-American* described relationships that implied change and the pleasure of uncertainty, reflecting the sound of jazz which readers might imagine as background music to the photos. Indeed, Jazz and its contemporary bodily expression, the jitterbug, could be heard and seen in enlisted men's clubs throughout the American occupation zone. In the Wannsee photographs, post-war cross-racial intimacy was presented as spontaneous and open, resembling the sound of improvised jazz in that it could lead anywhere.[41] Amidst the ruins of the Third Reich, the intimate friendships that crossed the colour line represented the liminal

Figure 10.1 *Ebony* magazine reporting on black GIs in Germany (Getty Images).

character of the moment, aptly described in *Ebony*: 'Strangely enough, here where once Aryanism ruled supreme, Negros are finding more friendship, more respect and more equality than they would back at home – either in Dixie or on Broadway.'[42] In the view of the African American press, at Wannsee, African American soldiers could escape the racialized politics of sexuality as well as social norms locating 'proper' sexual and romantic intimacy only within the realm of marriage and for the purpose of reproduction.[43]

The *Afro-American*'s editorial and the six-page article published in *Ebony* added even more layers of meaning to Wannsee beach. In addition to portraying the happy interaction of young adults, black and white, male and female, the reports from Germany reminded the readers of the very recent history of the setting. As the caption to one of the pictures stated explicitly: 'AFTER HITLER: view of Wansee [*sic*] Lake where Hitler and Nazi big shots once lolled. German frauleins and tan GI's [*sic*] now use is [*sic*] as a recreation spot.'[44] Similar to the 'NO NAZIS HERE'[45] quote discussed earlier, this caption, in combination with the picture that served as visual proof, sought to emphasize that the Wannsee beach and its visitors had changed. Within only a few months racial hatred seemed to have vanished, at least from this particular place in Germany. Cross-racial couples had replaced 'Nazi big shots', and the young men and women in the photo as well as the Wannsee itself now stood as symbols of change. The message conveyed to the readers seemed clear: change was possible, even in the former 'land of hate'.[46]

The protocol by Adolf Eichmann on the Wannsee Conference, which discussed the so-called Final Solution of the Jewish Question, had not yet been made public when these black writers discovered the Wannsee.[47] Yet the *Afro-American* and *Ebony* journalists seemed to display a sensitive attitude towards the history of the area. The surrounding neighbourhoods were, indeed, tainted by the past. Only a few years earlier, as part of the *Arisierung*, the forced confiscation of Jewish owned property, 'Nazi big shots' such as Goebbels, Speer, and Hitler's personal physician Theodor Morell had moved to the shores of the Wannsee. Meanwhile, the *Strandbad* itself had been a recreational hotspot for Nazi body cult and leisure programs.[48] Instead of uniform groups of Hitler Youths performing synchronized choreographs, groups of young men and women, black and white, now found their own pace and individual forms of interaction. In other words, while alluding to the Nazi past of the lake and its surroundings, the accounts of black writers did not seek to provide an explanation of the past or how the horrors of Nazism were possible. Rather, their narrative was dedicated to accounting for rupture and change. The black press, thus, spoke to their own readers encouraging them that now was the moment for change also in the United States.

Drawing on his own experiences as a clerk typist in the US occupation forces in Berlin, together with military documents and newspaper articles, the African American writer William Gardner Smith archived the situation of black troops in post-war Germany in his bestselling semi-autobiographical novel, *Last of the Conquerors,* first published in 1948.[49] The plot revolves around the love story between Hayes Dawkins, a black GI from Philadelphia, and his white German girlfriend Ilse. A prominent scene is set at the Wannsee.[50] While lying at the beach thoughts rush through the protagonist's head:

> I had lain at the beach many times, but never before with a white girl. A white girl. Here, away from the thought of difference for a while, it was odd how quickly I forgot it. It had lost importance ... No one stared as we lay on the beach together, our skins contrasting but our hearts beating identically ... Odd it seemed that here in the land of hate, I should find this one all-important phase of democracy.[51]

His own past as well as the demise of National Socialism formed the backdrop to Dawkin's reflections. Gardner Smith's protagonist was not only far away from home in terms of space, but he had also gained temporal distance from a history of oppression, entering a new age, 'this all-important phase of democracy'. The moment of lying at the Wannsee beach with his white German girlfriend served as an indication of change and a symbolic, yet fleeting, realization of democracy, defined by the 'logic of equality'.[52] Aware of the temporal limits of his experience Dawkins 'felt bitter'. He was only 'away from the thought of difference *for a while*'. His pending departure from Germany, and from Berlin in particular, set the limits to his sojourn in democracy and expressed the fragility of his hopes that Germany, and maybe also the United States, would eventually be reconstructed as a democracy based on true equality.

The black press, Gardner Smith and individual soldiers agreed that both the denazification effort and their struggle for racial justice were endangered by white servicemen, officers and commanders.[53] Juxtaposing the joyful interaction of black GIs and German women at the Wannsee with continued verbal and physical attacks on cross-racial intimacy on the part of their fellow soldiers, they sought to highlight the hypocrisy immanent in the US re-education effort. According to the *Afro-American*, it was white Americans, rather than Germans, who spread 'propaganda ... against their fellow soldiers'.[54] Other contemporary commentators in the black press would be more forthright in their criticism of US hypocrisy in Germany, and the attempt by the military authorities to promote democracy while continuing to discriminate against their own soldiers. For example, in an article in the *Chicago Defender*, drawing on his own experience, First Sergeant Washington Davis noted:

> German girls are eager to talk and walk with ... Bronze Joes ... The whites have sought to find ways to tear these things down ... The supposed democracy that America is trying to enforce in Germany is a lost cause ... we have been discriminated against in army mess halls, Red Cross clubs, and army swimming pools.[55]

The symbolic meaning the African American press and William Gardner Smith assigned to the Wannsee beach, and cross-racial bathing in particular, offered the promise of a better life, but had its limits, both spatially and temporally. The social freedom they experienced on the shores of the lake ended within US military facilities in Germany, or when the troops returned to the United States. Black and white couples also had to fear the arbitrariness of US military and German police who would specifically target cross-racial couples on street patrols and in vice raids.[56] As, for instance, Cliff MacKay, correspondent of the *Afro-American* noted in 1948, white US army officers transported the system of racial segregation to the occupation zone 'to make another Georgia out of Germany'.[57] Indeed, starting in the late 1940s, German business owners and their employees gradually implemented segregationist principles in their establishments. The spatial arrangements of garrison towns in the US Zone and the Federal Republic increasingly formed a mirror image of the racially segregated patterns of the Southern United States, and many parts of the North too for that matter.[58]

Nuremberg: Of all places

In 1952, the manager and two employees of a Nuremberg public swimming pool faced a hearing in front of a US court. Six years after the *Afro-American*, *Ebony* and the *Chicago Defender* had run their articles and editorials celebrating cross-racial bathing in the Wannsee, the attempt by three men working at a public pool in Nuremberg to keep the facility 'white only' caught the attention of the *Defender*. The place where the incident occurred was of particular importance to the editors, as shown by the headline: '3 Face U.S. Court For Race Bigotry – But Guess Where!'[59] Tainted by party rallies, racial laws, and the publication of anti-Semitic and anti-black propaganda by Adolf Hitler and Julius Streicher,[60] British historian Neil Gregor has described Nuremberg as a 'haunted city'.[61] Nuremberg's history, however, not only affected and 'haunted' the Nurembergers themselves, but also played a significant role in the African American narrative of their

Figure 10.2 Nuremberg in Allied hands, 1945. An American solider stands in the Zeppelin stadium and looks towards a Nazi swastika (Getty Images).

own experiences in post-war Germany.[62] The Allied trials against Nazi war criminals, the infamous Nuremberg laws of 1935, the discriminatory practices of the US military against African American personnel, the commitment of African American activists after victory abroad to also overthrow racial hate at home, and the (initial) lack of racial segregation in occupied Germany all merged in the image the black press created of this historic city.

In the 1930s, following the implementation of the Nuremberg Laws 'for the Preservation of German Blood and Honour' prohibiting sexual relations between white Germans and 'Jews, Blacks, Gypsies and their bastards',[63] African American newspapers and black intellectuals related them to their own history of legal and violent repression and to the persecution of cross-racial sexuality, with its most brutal manifestation in the lynch mob.[64] The Nuremberg laws thus provided a compelling example for African Americans to compare their own situation in the United States to the conditions of Jewish people in Nazi Germany. Consequently, with the entrance of the United States into the war, the black press construed the participation of African Americans in the war effort as a transnational struggle against racial discrimination and violence.[65] As one journalist wrote: 'Now, America must remember that the lynching of Negroes, their brutalization and denial of civil rights are as one with ... the persecution of Jews ... The question is whether the past of racism is stamped out.'[66] Furthermore, as anti-miscegenation laws in over thirty states seemed to prove to African American activist intellectuals and journalists, white supremacists in the United States and Nazis shared an abhorrence of interracial sex.[67] In pointing at the similarity between the Nuremberg laws and anti-miscegenation laws in the United States, African American writers construed black Americans and European Jews as common victims of a global evil: the myth of racial superiority. During the Second World War black Americans thus followed the battle call to fight a war on two fronts: against racial discrimination both abroad and at home.[68]

With the unconditional surrender of Germany and the subsequent occupation by the Allies, victory in Europe had been won, but for African Americans, victory at home was still pending. Although the war was over, the call to win a double victory still rang in the ears of African American civil rights activists, and they were anything but willing to give up their demands. As one journalist wrote: 'V-E Day! To the Negro soldier, it means that half of ONE war is won … Germany [is] not the only country in need of de-Nazification'.[69] Nuremberg, which already held the potential for African Americans to connect their own history of racial discrimination with Nazi racial laws, evolved into a place charged with the hopes of African Americans that the proceedings of the International Military Tribunal would be reflected on the other side of the Atlantic.

Their hopes, however, were to be disappointed, as the black press complained that the verdicts of the trials had no repercussions in the United States. Already disappointed that no African American lawyers would be actively involved in the trials, the unfulfilled promise of universalization of the trial's verdict frustrated African American observers: 'RACIAL PERSECUTION [*sic*] has been registered as a cause of war, a factor in aggression, and a crime against humanity. That, for us, is one of the positive results of the Nuremberg Trials', were the words with which John Robert Badger started an article on the trials in September 1946. Praising 'the universal truth contained in the Nuremberg indictment', the question that logically followed for him was 'what about … the present oppression of Negro Americans?'[70] The contradiction between the 'universal truth' presumed at the Nuremberg trials and the adoption of US segregationist patterns and the harassment of black and white couples by white US military police and German authorities in Nuremberg appeared especially significant to the black press. Preston Amos, correspondent of the *Atlanta Daily World*, reported that 'White military policemen patrolling the streets of Nuremberg, scene of the famous war criminals trial, virtually have a picnic checking the credentials of Negro GIs in the presence of their escorts … Many German civilian policemen threaten girls seen with colored troops with stiff jail sentences'.[71] While all the world was concerned with the proceedings inside the courthouse, white US occupation troops and commanders acted upon their sexual anxieties and racial beliefs and 'cripple[ed] the entire purpose of the occupation of Germany'.[72]

Given its history in African American imagery, a black and white wedding in the chapel of the former *SS Casern* (barracks) in Nuremberg, could take on a symbolic meaning of defying both the Nuremberg laws and US anti-miscegenation laws, and restoring a feeling of hope that was lost when the verdicts of the Nuremberg trials appeared to have had no impact on the struggle for civil rights in the United States. Cross-racial weddings in Germany had attracted the attention of the black press since the War Department had permitted occupation troops to marry the former enemy in 1946, subject to certain conditions including the approval of their commanding officer.[73] Yet Ollie Stewart's coverage of the wedding between Erna Deinzer and John D. Rowland, a black occupation soldier from Waterbury, Connecticut, in 1948 gave a specific significance to its taking place in the city of Nuremberg. 'The South Casern, where formerly some of Hitler's most efficient SS men were trained, was … buzzing with excitement … A marriage was about to take place in the Casern chapel'.[74] Within the broader symbolism of a city shaped by its recent history, now devastated by ruins and preoccupied by the trials 'where Nazi war lords found death by the noose',[75] the wedding between an African American soldier and his German bride represented the ultimate interruption of the recent German past and, thus, an important step in interrupting a transnational order based on white supremacy.

Yet instead of portraying intimate friendships within a moment of multiple possibilities, as in the reports of cross-racial intimacy on the Wannsee beach, the wedding in Nuremberg, according to Stewart, represented the idea of social progress through the acceptance and performance of post-war 'American values': domesticity, hard work and being a 'good American citizen', including service for the nation.[76] Stewart did not mention the difficulties many black soldiers faced when they applied for marriage in Germany nor did he discuss the continuing discrimination of cross-racial couples in the streets of Nuremberg and other garrison towns.[77] Marriage and adherence to middle class (white) values now appeared as a means to circumvent discrimination and second class citizenship.[78]

Conclusion

Ever since the Nazis took over power in Germany, African American intellectuals, civil rights organizations in the United States and the black press compared and entangled their own history of racial oppression with the Third Reich's persecution of the Jews. When the United States sent occupation troops to Germany in the aftermath of the Second World War, both histories, the Nazi past and the history of racial discrimination in the United States including its armed forces, became intimately intertwined in African American accounts of the situation of black GIs in Germany. The friendly, romantic and sexual interaction of black troops and German women provided a common thread in a transnational interpretation of the relevance of these past histories to the discrimination faced by African Americans as occupation troops in Germany and on their return home to the United States.

Examining different places that provided prominent backdrops in African American accounts enables their meaning and significance to be critically investigated, while preserving the integrity of the historical moment. The black market provided an alternative economic space that allowed black Americans from marginalized economic backgrounds to gain material and economic agency and escape for a while from a life that had previously been defined by economic precariousness. As part of the social space created through the unofficial economy, black troops established (intimate) contacts with German civilians and were able to take over the role of the provider. According to the black press, and in contrast with (white) US and German accounts of the black market as a place of moral degeneracy, this combination of possibilities promoted social relations between occupiers and occupied. These relations demonstrated the falsity of Nazi racist, anti-black propaganda, thus also transforming the black market into a space for German re-education, contributing to the achievement of US goals in Germany. Meanwhile, the recreational space of the Wannsee and its joyful and carefree visitors were contrasted with national socialist and white supremacist sexual anxieties over 'racial mixing'. The Wannsee also served as a forceful reminder of the spatial and temporal limits of this recreational environment and also of the historical moment. The lake, thus symbolized the pending demobilization and redeployment of US troops as well as segregated army camps in Germany. It also alluded to unfulfilled African American hopes for social change in the United States, and their pessimistic foreshadowing of a failed thorough re-education of Germans based on the principle of racial equality. Finally, Nuremberg epitomized the common history of institutionalized legal prosecution of cross-racial intimacy on both sides of the Atlantic. Yet it also provided an example of individuals who had defied the ban, celebrating a cross-racial wedding in the city, and so held out the promise of a better future. In the accounts of the black press, Nuremberg, the scene of the Nazi war criminal trials, came to represent the hypocrisy of the American occupation.

As the Cold War gradually materialized in the late 1940s, Nuremberg, the Wannsee and the black market slowly faded from the African American press's coverage of black troops in Germany. The anti-communist paranoia and witch-hunts, which white supremacists infused and associated with their fear of 'social equality',[79] led to a conscious reframing of cross-racial intimacy by the black press.[80] Black soldiers and German women would continue to intimately meet, have sex and sometimes get married. As foreshadowed in the example of the wedding in Nuremberg, however, from the late 1940s onwards, the black press increasingly started to present these encounters, and the discrimination African Americans faced both in Germany and in the United States, within the context of the Cold War and conservative ideals of domesticity current in the 1950s. Instead of adopting a distinctive position, asking why, if change was possible in Germany, it could not also occur in the United States, the black press now followed their white colleagues in portraying German 'war brides' and their black husbands as embodiments of American values linked to liberal democracy, individual freedom, and consumerism.[81] For African American journalists and civil rights activists, cross-racial intimacy in the exceptional, transitory and spatially limited conditions of post-war Germany – especially when located in the iconic and historically charged spaces of the black market, the Wannsee beach and the city of Nuremberg – was to remain a moment of hope but unfulfilled possibilities.

Notes

1 Friedrich Seidenstücker, 'Flirting at the Wannsee (1947)', in *German History in Documents and Images*. Available online: http://germanhistorydocs.ghi-dc.org/sub_image.cfm?image_id=1056&language=german (accessed 5 January 2017).

2 No title, *Baltimore Afro-American*, 9 November 1946, 20.

3 See, for instance, Heide Fehrenbach, *Race after Hitler: Black Occupation Children in Postwar Germany and America* (Princeton: Princeton University Press, 2007); Timothy Schroer, *Recasting Race after World War II: Germans and African Americans in American-Occupied Germany* (Boulder: University of Colorado Press, 2007).

4 David Brion Davis, 'The Americanized Mannheim of 1945–1946', in *American Places: Encounters with History*, cited in: Maria Höhn and Martin Klimke, *A Breath of Freedom: The Civil Rights Struggle, African American GIs, and Germany* (New York: Palgrave Macmillan, 2010), 2.

5 I am using the term 'intimacy' as a broader notion incorporating sexual relations as well as friendly interaction.

6 Susan L. Carruthers, *The Good Occupation: American Soldiers and the Hazards of Peace* (Cambridge, MA: Harvard University Press, 2016); *Donna Alvah, American Ambassadors: American Military Families Overseas and the Cold War, 1946–1965* (New York: New York University Press, 2007); Höhn and Klimke, *A Breath of Freedom*. For another account of the impact of everyday encounters on the occupiers, as revealed through the experiences of two women in the British Zone, see the chapter by Daniel Cowling in this volume.

7 Jonathan Rosenberg, *How Far the Promised Land? World Affairs and the American Civil Rights Movement from the First World War to Vietnam* (Princeton: Princeton University Press, 2005), chs 5 and 6.

8 Morris J. MacGregor, *Integration of the Armed Forces, 1940–1965* (Washington, DC: Center of Military History, United States Army, 2001; first edition 1981), 3–16.

9 Höhn and Klimke, *A Breath of Freedom*, 21–38.

10 Ibid., 214.

11 Magaret Geis, 'Negro Personnel in European Command, 1 January 1946–30 June 1950' (Office of the Chief Historian of Military History, European Command, Historical Division, 1952), 52–8.

12 Renee Romano, *Race Mixing: Black-White Marriage in Postwar America* (Cambridge, MA: Harvard University Press, 2003), Kindle edition, position 229–53; Höhn and Klimke, *Breath of Freedom*, 75–6.

13 Theodor Bilbo in front of the Mississippi Legislature, House of Representatives, 1944, 603; on Henry Lewis Stimson's private opinion on the deployment, see, for instance, Henry Lewis Stimson diary entry quoted in Richard Dalfiume, 'The "Forgotten Years" of the Negro Revolution', *Journal of American History* 55 (January 1968): 106.

14 Howard W. Odum, *Race and Rumors of Race: The American South in the Early Forties* (Baltimore: The Johns Hopkins University Press, 1997), 58.

15 Street poster cited in Fehrenbach, *Race after Hitler*, 46.

16 Marlene Dietrich, Black Market Lyrics, *A Foreign Affair*, directed by Billy Wilder (Los Angeles: Paramount Pictures, 1948).

17 See, for instance, Petra Goedde, *GIs and Germans: Culture, Gender, and Foreign Relations, 1945–1949* (New Haven and London: Yale University Press, 2003) ch. 3; see also Meader Report, Special Senate Committee Investigating the National Defense Program George Meader, chief counsel, 22 November 1946.

18 John Willoughby, 'The Sexual Behavior of American GIs during the Early Years of the Occupation of Germany', *Journal of Military History* 62, no. 1 (1998): 155–74.

19 Goedde, *GIs and Germans*, ch. 3; Meader Report.

20 Perry Biddiscombe, 'Dangerous Liaisons: The Anti-Fraternization Movement in the U.S. Occupation Zones of Germany and Austria, 1945–1948', *Journal of Social History* 4 (Spring 2001): 611–47. Biddiscombe also mentions the nobler voices, such as the

US Military Government newspaper, *Die Neue Zeitung*, which argued that not all relations between occupier and occupied were based on greed and self-interest: ibid., 617; Elizabeth Heinemann, *What Difference Does a Husband Make? Women and Marital Status in Nazi and Postwar Germany* (Berkeley and London: University of California Press, 1999), 75–90.

21 Ibid., 616–7; Louise Herz, 'Mitten in der Zeitenwende: Tagebuch von der Flucht aus Breslau bis zum Neuanfang in Hersfeld', Deutsches Tagebuch Archiv (DTA), 548 I+II, 22.

22 Letter by Lieutenant Woodburn Williams to the public safety officer for Bavarian Military Government, cited in Schroer, *Recasting Race*, 106, 107.

23 On the efforts to re-establish 'normality' in the realm of sexual politics, see Willoughby, 'Behavior of American GIs in Germany'. For the German perspective, see Dagmar Herzog, *Sex after Fascism: Memory and Morality in Twentieth-Century Germany* (Princeton and London: Princeton University Press, 2005).

24 'The Negro GI in Germany: Biased Americans Influence Natives', *New Journal and Guide*, 1 September 1945, 15.

25 'Germany Meets the Negro Soldier', *Ebony*, October 1946, 5; Roi Ottley, 'Tan Yanks', *Pittsburgh Courier*, 8 December 1945, 13.

26 Ollie Stewart, 'GI Who Wed Man Faces 10-Year Term: Germans no Longer Dazed', *Afro-American*, 20 April 1946, 1; Thomas W. Young, '"Scrounge Bags" Tell Story of Illicit Trade', *New Journal and Guide*, 5 June 1948, 11; Stewart, 'It's Getting Tougher: GI's in Germany Feel Effect of New Economy', *Afro-American*, 10 July 1948, 1.

27 Doug Hall, 'Christmas Finds These Americans in GERMANY', *Afro-American*, 27 December 1947, M12.

28 Carter Wesley, 'Carter Wesley Notes Poverty in Germany', *Atlanta Daily World*, 8 May 1948, 1.

29 Ollie Stewart, 'New Problem: Ollie Stewart Estimates There Are 3,000 Brown Babies in Germany and 1,000 More Will Be Born Each Year', *Afro-American*, 3 July 1948, B6; Chaplain Douglas Hall, 'Berlin's "Wild Oats" Babies: I Ran a Nursery for Little Fellows Who Touched My Heart Strings…', *Afro-American*, 25 October 1947, M1.

30 Wesley, 'Carter Wesley Notes Poverty'; Doug Hall, 'Christmas Finds These Americans in GERMANY', *Afro-American*, 27 December 1947, M12.

31 William Gardner Smith, *Last of the Conquerors* (New York: New American Library, 1949), 238–9.

32 Herzog, *Sex after Fascism*, 6.

33 Gedenk- und Bildungsstätte Haus der Wannsee-Konferenz, Strandbad Wannsee: Sonderausstellung der Gedenk- und Bildungsstätte Haus der Wannsee-Konferenz, Berlin, 2000–6. Available online: www.ghwk.de/ghwk/sonderausstellung/villenkolonie/strandbad_wannsee.htm (accessed 26 January 2017).

34 Alexandra Przyrembel, *'Rassenschande': Reinheitsmythos und Vernichtungslegitimation im Nationanalsozialismus* (Göttingen: Vandenhoeck & Ruprecht, 2003), 76; Herzog, *Sex after Fascism*, ch. 1.

35 Przyrembel, *Rassenschande*, 77.

36 Jeff Wiltse argues that 'gender integration and the eroticization of swimming pools … were the most direct and crucial causes of racial exclusion and segregation at municipal pools in the North': *Contested Waters: A Social History of Swimming Pools in America* (Chapel Hill: University of North Carolina Press, 2007), Kindle version, ch. 5, position 123.

37 See, for example, Ernest McKinney, *Pittsburgh Courier*, 1932, cited in Wiltse, *Contested Waters*, 121.
38 'African Zion Bishop Hit GI Segregation: Alleges Jim Crowism on Rise in Germany', *Washington Post*, 22 October 1947, 7.
39 'Germany Meets the Negro Soldier: GIs Find More Friendship and Equality in Berlin Than in Birmingham or Broadway', *Ebony*, October 1946, 5–11.
40 On the increasingly conservative rhetoric and norms throughout the political spectrum, see, for instance, Herzog, *Sex after Fascism*, ch. 3.
41 On Jazz and African American GIs in Germany, see Schroer, *Recasting Race*, ch. 5; see also Uta G. Poiger, *Jazz, Rock, and Rebels: Cold War Politics and American Culture in a Divided Germany* (Berkeley, Los Angeles and London: University of California Press, 2000).
42 'Germany Meets the Negro Soldier', *Ebony*, 5.
43 On the liminality of the post-war moment and its repercussions upon sexual liberality, see Herzog, *Sex after Fascism*, 15 and ch. 2.
44 No title, *Baltimore Afro-American*, 9 November 1946, 20.
45 Ibid.
46 Smith, *Last of the Conquerors*, 27. See also 'In Berlin … One Time Citadel of Race Hatred … Negro GIs are Living in New World of Social Equality … Hitler Called Them "Semi-apes, but German Frauleins Find Negro GIs Likable and Human"', *Chicago Defender*, 14 September 1946, 7; 'Racial: Mädchen and Negro', *Newsweek*, 16 September 1946, 29.
47 On the discovery of the protocol in March 1947, see Robert M. W. Kempner, 'Entdeckung des Wannsee-Protokolls', Gedenk- und Bildungsstätte Haus der Wannsee Konferenz, 19 January 1992. Available online: www.ghwk.de/fileadmin/user_upload/pdf-wannsee/dokumente/kempner-1992.pdf (accessed 26 January 2017).
48 On the history of the Wannsee and surrounding area, see Gedenk- und Bildungsstätte Haus der Wannsee-Konferenz, Villenkolonien in Wannsee 1875–1945: Sonderausstellung der Gedenk- und Bildungsstätte Haus der Wannsee-Konferenz, Berlin, 2000–6. Available online: www.ghwk.de/fileadmin/user_upload/pdf-wannsee/sonderausstellungen/strandbad-wannsee.pdf (accessed 26 January 2017).
49 Smith, *Last of the Conquerors,* passim.
50 The scene has, for instance, been cited by: Fehrenbach, *Race after Hitler*, 38; Werner Sollors, *The Temptation of Despair: Tales of the 1940s* (Cambridge, MA: The Belknap Press of Harvard University Press, 2014), 191; Paul Gilroy, *Against Race: Imagining Political Culture beyond the Color Line* (Cambridge, MA: The Belknap Press of Harvard University Press, 2000), 311–2.
51 Smith, *Last of the Conquerors*, 27.
52 The terminology is taken from Jacques Rancière. In his definition, the 'logic of equality' is construed as an interruption of the 'logic of inequality' – a definition which highlights a spatial as well as temporal interruption of an order based on inequality: Samuel A. Chambers, *The Lessons of Rancière* (Oxford and New York: Oxford University Press, 2013), 10.
53 See the multiple letters of complaint written by black soldiers stationed in Germany: Library of Congress, NAACP Papers II, Veterans Affairs, Soldiers Complaints, multiple files, Box G 15; Smith, *Last of the Conquerors*, especially 130–43; Ashton Williams, '"For White Only" Signs Raised by Army Again', *Afro-American*, 28 February 1948, 1; Washington Davis, 'What the People Say: Finds Americans, Not Germans His Enemy', *Chicago Defender*, 1 September 1945, 12.

54 No title, *Baltimore Afro-American*, 9 November 1946, 20.
55 Davis, 'Finds Americans, Not Germans His Enemy', *Chicago Defender*, 1 September 1945, 12.
56 Cliff MacKay, 'Hard War Being Waged on European Love Front: Dixie-Born Officers Use All Kinds of Strategy to Keep Tan Yanks, Willing Frauleins Apart', *Afro-American*, 1 May 1948, 13; 'White Troops in Germany Stirring Up Prejudices', *Afro-American*, 3 April 1948, 14.
57 Mac Kay, 'Hard War Being Waged on European Love Front'.
58 Maria Höhn, *GIs and Fräuleins: The German-American Encounter in 1950s West Germany* (Chapel Hill: University of North Carolina Press, 2002), especially ch. 3.
59 '3 Face U.S. Court for Race Bigotry But Guess Where!', *Chicago Defender*, 9 August 1952, 1.
60 *Der Stürmer*, the infamous weekly propaganda newspaper founded by Julius Streicher in 1923, while predominantly committed to anti-Semitic propaganda, also repeatedly printed articles spreading hateful anti-black racism. See, for instance, *Der Stürmer*, 53/1925 and *Der Stürmer*, 24/1933, both cited in Daniel Roos, *Julius Streicher und 'Der Stürmer' 1923–1945* (Schöningh: Paderborn, 2014), 140 & 247.
61 Neil Gregor, *Haunted City: Nuremberg and the Nazi Past* (New Haven: Yale University Press, 2008).
62 Ollie Stewart, 'Ollie Stewart Gives First-Hand Report on GIs in Germany: Interesting People, Places Make Nuernberg, Triple Threat Section', *Afro-American*, 3 July 1946, A2.
63 Saul Friedländer, *Das Dritte Reich und die Juden: Die Jahre der Verfolgung 1933–1939* (Munich: dtv, 2000), 170. For a detailed account of the application of the Nuremberg laws in the case of Afro-Germans, see Tina M. Campt, *Other Germans: Black Germans and the Politics of Race, and Memory in the Third Reich* (Ann Arbor: University of Michigan Press, 2005), 143–8.
64 Roy Wilkins, 'Editorial: Negroes, Nazis, and Jews', *The Crisis*, December 1938, 393.
65 'Now Is Not the Time to Be Silent', *The Crisis*, January 1942, 7.
66 'Lessons Written in Blood', *New York Amsterdam News*, 12 May 1945, A10.
67 Joel A. Rogers, *Sex and Race: Negro-Caucasian Mixing in All Ages and Lands*, Vol. 1: The Old World (St. Petersberg, FL: Helgs M. Rogers, 1967 [1941]), 2; 'Hitler or Roosevelt – Which Do You Prefer, Dr. Gandy Asks', *New Journal and Guide*, 26 April 1941, 11; Wesley Curiwright, 'Two Big Problems', *New York Amsterdam News*, 12 November 1938, 10; 'FEPC Hearings Hailed by Permanent Council', *New Journal and Guide*, 10 June 1944, 4; Joel A. Rogers, 'Rogers Says: New York's FEPC Provisions Would Be Illegal in 13 American States', *Pittsburgh Courier*, 17 March 1945, 7; Earl Conrad, 'Yesterday and Today: Turning Back the Hate Tide', *Chicago Defender*, 10 March 1945, 11.
68 Ibid.; James G. Thompson, 'Letter to the Editor: These Men Developed the "Double V" Idea', *Pittsburgh Courier*, originally printed 31 January 1942; reprinted 11 April 1942, 5.
69 James Apperson, 'Negro GIs Fought War on Two Fronts', *Chicago Defender*, 12 May 1945, 2.
70 John Robert Badger, 'World View: The Nuremberg Trials', *Chicago Defender*, 7 September 1946, 15; John Robert Badger, 'World View: The De-Nazifying Process', *Chicago Defender*, 28 September 1946; Lucius C. Harper, 'Dustin of the News: We Should Have Had a Nuernberg after Civil War', *Chicago Defender*, 9 November 1946, 1.

71 Preston E. Amos, 'Writer Reports on Racial Conditions in Germany Today', *Atlanta Daily World*, 25 March 1947, 3.
72 Ibid.; see also Cliff McKay, 'Hard War Being Waged on European Love Front', *Baltimore Afro-American*, 1 May 1948, 13; 'The Negro GI in Germany: Biased Americans Influence Natives', *Norfolk Journal and Guide*, September 1945, B16.
73 Carruthers, *Good Occupation*, 296.
74 Ollie Stewart, 'Nuernberg GIs Excited as Pal Marries Fraulein', *Baltimore Afro-American*, 26 June 1948, 1.
75 Ibid.
76 Ibid.; on the history of respectability politics and 'racial uplift', see Jacqueline M. Moore, *Booker T. Washington, W.E.B. Du Bois, and the Struggle for Racial Uplift* (Wilmington: Scholarly Resources, 2003).
77 For multiple complaints by soldiers who were denied a marriage license by their commanders, see Library of Congress, NAACP Papers, Group II, Box G 15, Veterans Affairs, Soldier Marriage, 1944–9; on the ongoing (violent) discrimination of black and white couples both at the hands of white American and German authorities and individuals, see Fehrenbach, *Race after Hitler*, chs 1 and 2; Schroer, *Recasting Race*, ch. 3.
78 Stewart, 'Nuernberg GIs Excited as Pal Marries Fraulein', *Afro-American*, 26 June 1948, 1.
79 'Social equality' was a common expression meaning cross-racial intimacy and sexual acts; on the term, see, for instance, Anthony S. Chen, *The Fifth Freedom: Jobs, Politics, and Civil Rights in the United States, 1941–1972* (Princeton and Oxford: Princeton University Press, 2009), 65.
80 William J. Maxwell, *F.B. Eyes: How J. Edgar Hoover's Ghostreaders Framed African American Literature* (Princeton and Oxford: Princeton University Press, 2016).
81 Lilo Engelmann, 'I Am a German War Bride', *Tan Magazine*, October 1953, 54; Kate A. Baldwin, *The Racial Imaginary of the Cold War Kitchen: From Sokol'niki Park to Chicago's South Side* (Lebanon, NH: Dartmouth College Press, 2016); 'Life with Daughter of Nazi Isn't Bad, Cincinnati Ex – GI Declares', *Chicago Defender*, 31 December 1949, 5; Alvah, *Unofficial Ambassadors*.

11

Shared Spaces: Social Encounters between French and Germans in Occupied Freiburg, 1945–55

Ann-Kristin Glöckner

After the Second World War, sixteen-year-old Margrit lived in Freiburg im Breisgau in the French Zone of occupation. In 1946, she attended the fiftieth birthday party of a neighbour, who had also invited two French soldiers of Moroccan descent. In her diary, Margrit described the two men as very generous, noting that they liked to play football with the children: 'They both liked to be in familial surroundings and were very polite human beings – something you couldn't say about all of them'.[1] When Hadu, one of the Moroccans, found out that Margrit was originally from the city of Karlsruhe, he got excited because he was looking for his girlfriend Hannelore, whom he had met there. He showed Margrit a photo of his girlfriend but she did not know her. Margrit's father, who was also present at the event, eyed them critically and watched them closely. Hadu brought Margrit a baguette, chocolates and cookies, all of which were products she had not tasted for a long time. Her father, however, was displeased with the situation and wanted his daughter to leave the party.[2] A few days later, Margrit saw the young woman from Hadu's photo sitting at the victory monument in Freiburg. It turned out that Hannelore had come to the city in order to look for Hadu but had got lost. Margrit helped the young couple find each other and was overwhelmed by their gratitude. Later, when Hadu's unit was sent back to Morocco, Hannelore left the country with him.[3]

This story provides a colourful first impression of several different aspects of personal 'encounters' in occupied Germany. The following chapter examines other similar everyday interactions between Germans and French in the city of Freiburg and explores, in particular, the role played by gender and race. Starting from an understanding of occupation as a dynamic social process in which roles and power relations are in a constant process of negotiation and redefinition, the chapter examines personal and social interactions by analysing the spaces where encounters between occupiers and occupied took place. In doing so, it draws on approaches from gender studies, notably on intersectional theory.[4] The chapter is based on an analysis of a broad range of sources from daily life, including letters and diaries. It takes into account both German and French sources in order to assess the experience of occupation from the perspective of both the occupiers and the occupied, while also considering official documents from the French Military Government.

There has been less research on the French Zone than on the other two western zones.[5] Before the Occupation Archives were opened in Colmar in 1986,[6] the official documents of the French Military Government remained inaccessible for historians. Until then, the occupation was generally remembered in Germany as the *düstere Franzosenzeit* (dark time of the French) contributing towards a tendency to ignore or simply condemn what occurred in the French Zone and concentrate on the presumably more 'benign' developments in the two other western zones.[7] This is one reason for the widespread perception of the French Zone as an *Ausbeutungskolonie* (colony of exploitation), a term notably used by Theodor Eschenburg, one of the leading German political scientists of the post-war period.[8] Generally speaking, therefore, in the 1980s it was still the case, as the pioneering historian of the French Zone, F. Roy Willis, had written in 1962, that 'the history of the French Zone has, for the most part, been written by its critics'.[9] Research from the early 1990s, however, led by a new generation of researchers from Freiburg, including Edgar Wolfrum, Peter Fäßler and Reinhard Grohnert followed Rainer Hudemann's pioneering approach to examine French politics in Germany from a much more nuanced perspective.[10] Through their archival work, these more recent historians corrected the earlier, predominantly negative view of French policy and emphasized that a committed policy of renovation, reform and institutional democratization had been promoted by the French authorities, motivated mainly by their security interests and concerns.[11]

Yet while historians have now arrived at a more balanced understanding of French occupation policy, research on the French Zone has so far primarily focused on political history and international relations,[12] with people's daily experiences of occupation having been largely neglected.[13] The studies that have explored everyday life have described it in very general terms without looking in detail at individual perceptions or social interactions.[14] Similarly, historians have rarely used approaches from gender studies to analyse encounters between occupiers and occupied in the French Zone, though this has recently started to change.[15]

To understand the complexities of daily life under occupation and the multiple processes of negotiation that took place within a changing power framework, the field of gender studies provides us with a range of tools to analyse struggles around power, domination and control.[16] Following the main tenet of the intersectional approach, however, gender needs to be regarded as only one aspect of people's identity and cannot be analysed without considering other coexisting and interconnected axes of identity. The interactions between the occupiers and the occupied were shaped by the Military Government's official guidelines as well as by social, cultural, and personal norms and backgrounds. In the French Zone, different people met and mingled: they had different ethnic origins, nationalities, genders, ages and social backgrounds. All these interrelated axes of personal identity influenced not only people's perception of themselves, but also their awareness of others. At the same time, these vectors of personal identity need to be seen as more than just the characteristics of individuals.[17] They are social structures, 'constructed through social interactions and manifested in the institutions of society, interpersonal interactions, and the minds and identities of those living in social orders'.[18]

This chapter focuses on the factors that were most influential in shaping people's everyday experience during the French occupation, in particular gender and race. The significance and complexity of those two categories and their interrelationship becomes apparent when they are explored through examining everyday encounters between Germans and French. Those encounters happened in certain spaces, such as the street, the pub, buses and trams, or the home, which thereby acquired additional meaning and significance through the social interactions which took place in them. Space is therefore understood as a relational, a social as well as a physical category; in other words, to quote the German sociologist Martina Löw: 'space arises from the activity of experiencing objects as relating to one another'.[19] Such a conception of space is intimately related to questions of power and social hierarchies. Social spaces are gendered and structured, and therefore different spaces determine how women and men can act in them. At the same time, these spaces are still produced by human beings, so they also 'reflect and affect the ways in which gender is constructed and understood' by the women and men arriving, departing, staying, interacting or living in them.[20]

From the nineteenth century onwards, with increasing industrialization and mass production, spaces have increasingly been separated between the public and the private spheres, leading to a gradual division between spaces for living and working. Together with a tendency to distinguish between masculine and feminine in many areas of life, spaces have also been coded as either the one or the other. Pierre Bourdieu has argued that the private home became connected to the female sphere of household and child care, while the public sphere became a male space connected to education and property.[21] Access to spaces is not only dependent on gender though, but also on class, race, social status, physical appearance and other personal characteristics. When viewed in this way therefore, the issue of how public and private spaces were used, who was permitted to enter them, and on what terms, was strongly connected to questions of power and participation, which were highly significant in the post-war period, when relationships between occupiers and occupied were both unequal and highly contested.

Franco-German encounters in Freiburg

At the end of the war, in April 1945, Freiburg im Breisgau was still quite a densely populated city, with almost 60,000 inhabitants. By December 1947, the population had already grown to 100,000.[22] During the war, the city had endured severe air raids, with almost the entire old town left in ruins, except for the cathedral, which surprisingly remained mostly intact.[23] Housing was also hit hard by aerial bombardment; of 30,000 flats, only 8,000 remained undamaged.[24] On 21 April 1945, French troops invaded Freiburg, marking the beginning of the occupation of the city. The troops were part of the *Première armée française* (First French Army) that had been formed in the part of northern Africa not occupied by the Germans. It was composed of French citizens who had fled from the German occupation and escaped to the French colonies as well as of colonial soldiers from northern Africa. After the First Army's landing in France, they were joined by resistance fighters from the *Forces Françaises de l'Intérieur* (FFI).[25]

From 1946 to 1952, Freiburg was the capital of the newly founded state of (South) Baden and therefore gained considerably in political significance. It also housed one of the biggest garrisons in the French Zone, which therefore made it a focal point in the zone for interactions between occupiers and occupied. About 5,000–7,000 members of the *Forces Françaises en Allemagne* (FFA) were stationed in the city,[26] including professional soldiers, conscripts, civil servants and family members who had followed their relatives.[27] The age of the military personnel had a significant impact on how they experienced their time in Germany, together with if they had seen active duty in battles or, in the case of some older men, if they had been stationed in Germany during the occupation of the Rhineland after the First World War. Many were young men who were seeing a foreign country for the first time in their lives, and for whom the occupation of their own country by Germany was a formative experience. Thus, a nineteen-year-old French lieutenant, for example, described how 'the liberation of France represented the first step of our big dream but the privilege of entering this country which had occupied us and to become, on our part, the vanquishers and the occupiers, exceeded all our expectations. The very young combatants especially felt this quite notably.'[28]

When the people of Freiburg saw the French troops arriving in the streets, their impressions and expectations were very diverse. Seventeen-year-old Lilo Neumeier recorded in her diary that she mostly saw Moroccans arriving in Freiburg and noted down the 'black faces, that awed us. As we soon found out for a reason because rumours of rapes rose.'[29] Heinz Hummel, then ten years old, also remembered in 2005 the colonial soldiers who occupied Freiburg: 'Suddenly tanks arrived from the direction of Zähringen, behind them foot soldiers. A lot of coloured soldiers, Moroccans, Senegalese. They were the first coloured people I had ever seen. My amazement was endless.'[30] During the occupation, another woman from Freiburg wrote in a letter to Emmanuel Mounier, the editor of the French journal *Esprit*, that she had expected many positive things from the French occupiers: 'You [the French] had big chances because many, many Germans saw you as liberators. Many of us admired your country, your culture, your democracy! – Which was something they desperately longed for.'[31]

Although it can be assumed that this woman did not speak for as 'many Germans' as she claimed, she certainly represented one group in German society that shared a rather positive idea of France. Especially among intellectual and anti-National Socialist circles, the French were admired as *la grande nation*.[32] Yet it is also evident from the young woman's letter that her high expectations were deeply disappointed, prompting the question of why this should have been so.[33] In the following sections, everyday life experiences are examined using a spatial approach, focussing on some of the most significant public, semi-public and private locations where Germans and French met in Freiburg. These were the locations where people worked together, where they drank, where they fell in love, where they debated, got into fights and where friendships began. Exploring the relationship between occupiers and occupied in this way demonstrates that interactions were very diverse, ranging from violence, rejection and indifference to sympathy and intimacy, and the balance of power could shift subtly over time and from place to place.

Public spaces

The street

The street is the most public place discussed in this chapter. It is a space that, at least in theory, everyone can enter. Although there were curfews at the beginning of the occupation,[34] the streets were still a space that was open to the general public during daytime. Nevertheless, this space was shaped decisively by the occupation regime, and it was here that direct encounters between the occupiers and the occupied were almost inevitable. In public, the occupiers were not only recognizable by speaking French but also because they were dressed in khaki-coloured uniforms, which even the civil personnel of the Military Government were required to wear.[35] To make quite sure that they could distinguish themselves from the local population and to assert their authority as occupiers, the French Military Government did not allow Germans to wear khaki clothes.[36]

The French implemented several such symbolic policies aiming to showcase the new hierarchy in public and demonstrate visibly who was in charge. Every male German civilian, for example, had to salute Allied officers on the street,[37] and the French flag was displayed prominently in public places. Such emphatic demonstrations of power could occasionally lead to friction with the local population. In the night of 16 February 1947, for instance, the French Tricolour in front of the sergeants' accommodation in the *Basler Straße* was pulled down and torn to pieces. Since the offenders could not be found, the German *Oberbürgermeister* (mayor), Wolfgang Hoffmann, following orders of the Military Government, instructed former Nazis who lived close by to guard the newly flown French flag for the following eight nights.[38] In doing so, Hoffmann adopted the role of a mediator, trying to calm down the local French troop commander who was considering a much more severe punishment.

The streets were therefore one notable space in which conflicts between the occupiers and the occupied took place, though it was also a space in which the occupiers were bound by certain rules and expected forms of behaviour. In December 1945, for example, a young French soldier was sentenced to twenty days in prison because a patrolling officer had caught him by surprise with a German woman. He had fled the scene but had forgotten to take his trousers with him. Later, a patrol found him in a drunken state.[39] He was not the only French man who attracted the authorities' attention by dating a German woman. In the same month, several soldiers were sentenced to ten to twenty days in prison because they had been seen walking arm in arm with German women in the streets of Freiburg, at a time when French regulations forbade such activities.[40] Comparing the sentences to other offences committed by soldiers, however, such as not wearing a tie (punished with six days in prison) or having a hand in their pocket and reading a magazine on the street (eight days in prison), shows that it appears to have been classified as a minor offence. Displaying a romantic relationship with a German woman openly on the street was the most highly visible way for a member of the occupying force to demonstrate that they were engaged in this form of fraternization.[41] It provoked reactions from the local German population as well as from their French military superiors, although in this case it was the women who were criticized rather than the men. Various poems such as the following were circulated among the population:

> Der Mann liegt im Soldatengrab,
> Die Frau in Negerbetten.
> Der Mann gab sich fürs Vaterland,
> die Frau für Zigaretten.[42]

This poem articulated a common contemporary reproach from a male perspective, claiming that German men had fought as soldiers for their country and risked being killed, while women were 'having a good time' and only thinking about their own interests, instead of considering the higher good of the nation.[43] Germans also often complained in their diaries about German women's 'lack of dignity'.[44] Many German men seem to have felt inferior vis-à-vis the victors and thought their own masculinity was being questioned when they saw German women publicly dating French men. In short, as Uta Poiger has argued, German conceptions of masculinity were in a state of crisis after the Second World War, as they had not only been defeated in battle, but were also no longer able to fulfil the traditionally male roles of protector and provider. Highly visible romantic relationships between the occupiers and the occupied on the streets of German cities served to reinforce their apparent inferiority compared to the French occupiers.[45]

In particular, as illustrated by the reference in the poem to women lying in *Negerbetten*, the idea that German women might have sexual relationships with black soldiers seems to have terrified a lot of men. Such racist patterns of thinking were influenced by earlier propaganda of the *Schwarze Schmach* (Black Shame) that emerged after the First World War during the Allied occupation of the Rhineland, when colonial soldiers constituted one-third of the French occupation troops.[46] The German press ran a sophisticated campaign between 1920 and 1932, spreading fears about colonial soldiers who were, according to this propaganda, giving their sexual instincts free rein with the permission of their superiors. This racist narrative claimed that such relationships were a deliberate political strategy devised by the French authorities to produce a *Mulatisierung* (mulatto-ization) of the German population, contaminating the 'German race' and spreading diseases.[47] In the last year of the Second World War, the fear of 'the black soldier' was further stoked by Nazi propaganda, which warned of a 'black invasion' should Germany lose the war.[48]

There were, in fact, many different types of relationships between German women and French men. Besides romantic relationships, there was also (hunger-) prostitution, and grey areas between the two. During the war and its immediate aftermath, women were more or less on their own in terms of supporting their children and themselves while their male partners were away from home.[49] Large numbers of men had been killed during the war or were still in captivity, which meant that there were 50 per cent more women than German men living in Freiburg in 1947.[50] In the summer of 1946, the average food ration in the French Zone was less than 1,000 calories per person per day, representing roughly half of what an adult requires to preserve their body weight.[51] French soldiers, by contrast, were much better provisioned with food and other necessities.[52] This disparity could explain why some women became involved with French men who were better fed, appeared physically more attractive and often had a surplus of food and luxuries such as cigarettes they could offer as gifts. In these circumstances, relationships may have combined elements of compulsion, seduction, convenience and true affection.[53] In the words of historian Hanna Schissler, 'whatever the nature of these relationships, they deeply hurt German men's self-esteem. German men felt cheated, hurt and humiliated. For the returning soldiers, women's independence and autonomy (including sexual autonomy) became a huge problem.'[54]

Such relationships between French men and German women were not always consensual, but often marked by violence. Immediately after the invasion of Freiburg, the rape of German girls and women by French soldiers appears to have been a common occurrence. The exact number is not known, since many of these crimes were never reported. There are, however, reports of at least sixty women who were registered in Freiburg because they were raped after the invasion of the city and became pregnant.[55] Even after May 1945, however, rape continued to occur.[56] In many cases, French army officers distanced themselves from these crimes and capitalized on existing racial anxieties by claiming that the rapes were only committed by colonial soldiers.[57] In a monthly report from Freiburg, written in November 1945 by Lieutenant Colonel Montel, the chief of the Military Government in Freiburg, 'the Moroccans' are characterized as 'brutally virile', 'naive', 'simple' and 'infantile'. According to him, one consequence of their character and behaviour towards women was a surge in venereal diseases.[58] Such statements reinforced the German population's prejudices, although there is no evidence that French soldiers from North Africa were more likely to rape German women than their fellow soldiers from France.[59] Nevertheless, among the German public, the stereotype of the 'potent black beast'[60] found its way into the diaries of several citizens of Freiburg. One of them was Luise H., who recorded rumours that circulated shortly after the invasion and was concerned for her daughter: 'Now it becomes generally known that two young women were raped by a Negro in *Schwarzwaldstraße*, who is supposed to have been shot by his superior afterwards. I watch my girl anxiously … We will go to bed early again.'[61] For this woman, as for many others at the end of the war, the street therefore became a public place associated with fear and danger.[62] The consequence was, at least during the initial period of occupation, a retreat into the home. Luise H. did not want to leave the house and therefore hid out with her daughter in their home. Hers was not an isolated case: a lot of women acted like this during the invasion and in the direct aftermath of the war, with many sources documenting how some of them hid in the attic or under their parents' beds.[63]

While the women may have felt safer at home, it was not necessarily the case that they were protected from attacks there. French soldiers raped women both on the street and in private houses. Immediately after the invasion, most rapes were committed spontaneously and in an uncoordinated manner, and happened most often in public spaces during daytime. After the Military Government had established itself in Germany, rapes became increasingly premeditated, occurring in the secrecy of darkness and in places hidden from public view.[64] It would appear that at the end of the war, the French authorities were either unable to control or else tolerated rapes committed by their troops in public spaces, which could be seen as a highly visible display of power by the victors and a means of humiliating the vanquished.[65] While the military authorities later attempted to control the soldiers' behaviour, rapes continued nevertheless in secrecy, away from public view.

In the streets of Freiburg, violent encounters did not only happen between German women and French men but also between German and French men, although they were of a different nature: police records contain numerous reports of street brawls. Both Germans and French were the instigators of such fights, but at the beginning of the occupation, there were more attacks on Germans by French military men than the other way around. An examination of the police records of the French Gendarmerie in Freiburg would suggest that the number of violent attacks committed on the street were the highest compared to any other space, such as in shops and pubs or on buses and trams.[66] During the night of 4 August 1947, for example, two drunken white French soldiers left their home with the intention of beating up Germans in the street. While drifting through the city, they started to punch pedestrians *en passant*, not realizing that they were also hurting fellow Frenchmen. When they noticed their mistake, they started to ask the passers-by about their nationality before hitting them.[67] Seventeen-year-old Walter Oskar D. described the incident: 'About two hundred meters from the first houses of the old town, I encountered two drunk French soldiers; one was quite tall and the other one rather small. When they arrived, those military men asked if I was French and after my response that I was German they kicked me.'[68] Such activities were indicative of the power that some French soldiers felt they possessed in their position as occupiers. Although the French military tribunal later condemned the beatings, these men were able to exercise their power over the occupied as they pleased, at least for a short time. The Military Government, however, examined the case closely and the Delegate of the District of Freiburg, Lieutenant-Colonel Marcellin, wrote a letter to the Freiburg garrison commander, expressing his concerns about the harmful consequences that incidents like this had 'on the moral interests of the occupying power'.[69] Clearly, it was not in the interest of the French authorities to antagonize the local population and risk a decline in their moral as well as in their physical authority, which might lead to further conflict.

There are many other examples in police records where French soldiers harassed Germans on the street.[70] In July 1948, for instance, six young soldiers wanted to celebrate the end of their period of military service and met up with two French women at the *Foyer militaire* where they drank two bottles of wine. Later, they all proceeded to a German *Gasthaus* where they had more drinks. At about 10:00 p.m., they left the establishment singing and chanting and headed in the direction of the *Schwabentor*. Without any apparent reason, one of the men proclaimed 'Let's hit Germans' and punched an old man who fell down on the street. The soldier went on kicking his victim until he became unconscious. Seventy-two-year-old Emil G. was seriously injured and taken to hospital, where he remained in a coma for twelve hours. The group of soldiers continued their route and attacked other passers-by. The two French women accompanying them – one of whom, according to the police report on the incident, worked for the Military Government – tried to stop them. Yet 'because Germans were the victims' they were not very persistent with their attempt to interrupt the beatings, as the police interrogation report noted.[71]

The available evidence would suggest that most brawls and violent attacks on the streets were initiated by the French. Nevertheless, there were a few incidents during which Germans acted violently. Most of these cases appear to have occurred in the later period of occupation, when the balance of power had started to shift. On the night of 17 April 1955, for example, four French soldiers were attacked by about twenty young Germans. The French were on their way back home after they had been to the cinema in the old town, when the Germans blocked their path close to *Martinstor* and started to hit them without any provocation from their part. The soldiers were so seriously injured that they could not work for several days. A few days later, Colonel Dupont of the Third Division wrote a letter about the incident to the mayor of Freiburg: 'In general, I believe that the French soldiers in the city of Freiburg behave very respectably. But it is difficult, if an incident like this recurs, to expect from our young twenty-year old men to keep cool and to prevent them from calling their comrades to the scene in order to take revenge.'[72] A similar incident in which three French servicemen were hit by Germans on motorcycles had taken place just a few weeks earlier.[73] Generally speaking, however, there were fewer attacks initiated by German men against French men on the streets. This reflected the fact that at the beginning of the occupation, the French seem to have been noticeably present as occupiers on the streets, exercising control over the Germans and showcasing who was in charge. While brawls between French and Germans continued to take place in the 1950s, by that time most of the attacks were committed by Germans. It would appear that, by then, Germans felt less inferior to the French as well as generally less intimidated. The foundation of the Federal Republic of Germany (FRG) and the regaining of national sovereignty was reflected in everyday interactions and a changing balance of power between occupiers and occupied on the streets.

Semi-public spaces

The pub

Unlike the street, the pub is not accessible for everyone, though it is a place in the public sphere. In order to enter, people have to be of age and need to have enough money to pay for the drinks they consume. Some pubs are also highly selective in who they allow to be 'regulars', or so-called *Stammgäste*. In the post-war period, women were not welcomed into every pub, while French soldiers sometimes had trouble getting accepted as customers, all of which renders the pub a semi-public space.

Like the street, pubs were a site of brawls. In August 1948, two French servicemen were attacked by the drunken German Marc M. in the café *Schiff* in Freiburg. M. said to them: 'Why did you come to occupy Germany? You should better have stayed at home. But luckily, in six months you won't be here anymore.'[74] He underlined his statement with the gesture of pulling the trigger of a gun. Marc M., who was working as a translator for the Military Government, was arrested and taken to prison. Similarly, on the night of 27 June 1954, four French soldiers went to a restaurant to drink beer. The owner of the establishment refused to serve them, under the pretext of being about to close. Since the other German customers were still sitting at their tables drinking, the soldiers protested. A German guest then intervened by punching one of the officers from the group in the face, and then fled the scene.[75]

Such cases demonstrate how Germans occasionally tried to maintain control over 'their' traditional social spaces. A pub or restaurant owned by Germans could become a hostile place for the French who entered it. They could be excluded from the collective experience of drinking together in a bar because the German customers (and sometimes the owners) barred them from being part of it. Those who decided to react aggressively towards French people intruding in such spaces risked being punished by the occupiers but usually the perpetrators fled the scene quickly. As late as the 1950s, Germans who attacked French people could still expect long prison sentences. This is demonstrated, for example, by the case of the truck driver Franz N. from Freiburg, who in 1951 killed a French serviceman in a traffic accident. The Military Government classified the accident as an 'attack on a member of the occupying power', and he was sentenced by the *Tribunal Supérieur* (higher military court) in Rastatt to fifteen years in prison.[76]

Despite the threat of severe punishment, some German men seem to have felt that in semi-public spaces such as a pub they were in a stronger position than the occupiers, and they appear to have been more willing to fight the occupiers openly there than in public spaces such as the streets. The customers in a German pub were, especially when they were regulars, a close-knit community. It was not easy for anyone to enter these establishments as an outsider and be accepted as part of the group, least of all for the French. At the same time, it was often an emphatically male space. It became a place where husbands and fathers 'got away from it all', and where women were not necessarily accepted.[77] In this sense, the *Stammgäste* tried to preserve their haven from various intruders, of which the occupiers were but one type.

For the period between 1947 and 1955, French police records document thirteen brawls taking place in pubs or restaurants initiated by Germans and two started by French people; in four cases, it was not clear who was the initiator.[78] The pub was primarily the site of conflicts between men, and women were hardly ever involved.[79] In some cases there were specific causes for such conflicts, such as particular arguments that provoked a row, or fights over women.[80] In other cases, however, it was simply open resentment against the occupiers that motivated such activities and the pub provided a space where the power struggle for male predominance inherent in military occupation found open expression instead of being repressed or concealed.

The tram

The tram can also be defined as a semi-public space. It is a form of public transportation that in theory everyone can use, but passengers must meet the requirement of being able to buy a ticket and they have to obey certain legal and behavioural rules. During the time of occupation, the ultimate arbiter and body responsible for enforcing these rules was the French Military Government.

On the tram, many conflicts took place between German ticket inspectors and French passengers. Most of the time, the reason for these disputes was that the French passenger had not bought a ticket and did not think they should be reprimanded for it by a German. According to French Military Government regulations, the French did indeed enjoy priority over Germans in the use of trams. If a tram was crowded and French people wanted to get on, the German passengers had to leave to make space for the French.[81] Nevertheless, French passengers still had to buy tickets, and when they did not do so there were inevitable frictions. One such case occurred in December 1948, when the ticket inspector Franz H. demanded to see the ticket of a French civilian. This was observed by twenty-year-old sergeant Raymond D., who became very angry, punched H. on the chest, dragged him out of the tram, and hit him again. When interrogated by French military police, D. denied having attacked the ticket inspector physically but stated: 'However, I have to specify that the result of this incident was provoked by my enragement because the ticket inspector wanted to kick me out and for that reason hassled me. In this moment, I thought about the bad treatment my family had to suffer during the German occupation of France and that made me lose it.'[82] This case may serve as one example for how the experience of the German occupation of France may have influenced the behaviour of the French occupiers in Germany, though D. might also just have used this particular excuse to defend his behaviour.

Whatever the real motivations behind such violence, cases such as this did put the French Military Government in a difficult position. In this particular instance, the mayor of Freiburg wrote to Colonel Monteux, the chief of the Military Government in Freiburg, demanding punishment because employees of the tram company were regularly being attacked by the French: 'From events like these severe incidents can result, since, as I know, the people of Freiburg are agitated due to these repeated incidents to such an extent that they won't keep calm anymore'. Seeking to placate such German concerns and keep order within their zone, the French police started investigations and eventually punished Sergeant D. with a harsh penalty.[83] That German demands met with such an accommodating response by the occupiers was possible because at local government level, the relations between German and French officials were quite respectful and constructive, with German mayors describing the cooperation with French commanders in very positive terms. Mayor Hoffman, for instance, sang the praises of Colonel Monteux, who in his opinion neither behaved as a victor nor ever said a word about the Germans out of hatred.[84]

In April 1947, the *Délégation Supérieure* (provincial Military Government) noted in a report that 'after a quite calm era', attacks against German civilians had started again: 'On the tram, it happens frequently that French soldiers intentionally block the entrance of the trams so that the German passengers can't get on. If they insist, they are maltreated or even punched and then forced to leave the tram immediately.'[85] As a result of these violent incidents, the tramway employees decided that they needed to issue a strong message to the occupiers and went on strike in June 1948 to protest against the behaviour of French military staff using public transport in Freiburg.[86] In doing so, they tried to regain power over the public space of the tram by using the classic instrument of protest available to workers: they stopped working. The trade union agreed to support the strike but the Military Government was not included in the decision-making process. Although the French criticized the reaction of the tramway employees, on the same day that the strike took place the Military Government expelled from the French Zone a French serviceman who through his violent actions had been the immediate cause of the strike.[87] Yet again, therefore, it would seem that at the highest levels of the French Military Government there was a tendency to try to contain confrontation with the local population and respond to their demands in order to keep the zone calm. Violent attacks by individual members of the occupation forces were clearly counterproductive and not conducive to the broader goal of stabilizing the occupation.

Private spaces

The home

The home is the most private and intimate space considered in this chapter. And yet, during the time of occupation, it was also a place over which the Military Government was able to exercise control because of the lack of housing space after the war. Requisitions were one of the main reasons for conflict between the German population and the Military Government.[88] Germans and French people were forced to live together in close proximity as neighbours, creating interactions that could be the beginning of both friendships and conflicts. Especially at the beginning of the occupation, housing space in Freiburg was in very short supply. In September 1946, there were 2,540 flats with 5,600 rooms occupied by the French. This meant that 11 per cent of the still existing living space in the city was claimed by the French authorities.[89] German families who were living in houses or big flats had to share their accommodation with the occupiers. This billeting policy was different from requisitioning in the US and British Zones, where the occupiers had determined that their troops had to be housed separately from the German population, and the previous occupiers were evicted from requisitioned properties. According to French regulations, houses and flats belonging to former members of the Nazi Party (NSDAP) were supposed to be requisitioned first. In practice, however, this was not always the case, consequently provoking considerable resentment among the population of Freiburg.[90]

Cohabitation and sharing the same property could lead to problems for the occupiers, especially when people had to live together in a relatively small space. In July 1947, for instance, a forty-five-year-old Frenchman reported at the local police station that he and his children were being harassed by their German landlady and her daughter. According to their report, the landlady and daughter would wait for the French children in the kitchen and then hit them. They also threatened them verbally, yelling: ‘Go away, this is not your home … Go back to France’.[91] The landlady and her daughter denied the abuse and stated that the French children were quite noisy and broke rules all the time, such as by mixing dirty and clean laundry. She stated that they had already requested another lodger at the housing office because they did not want to live with 'these French people' anymore. As late as 1950, several French tenants pressed charges against their German landlords because they expressed Francophobe attitudes and spoke of 'dirty French people' who should leave Germany.[92]

Germans, for their part, also complained about their French neighbours, and about what they saw as the rude and inconsiderate behaviour of the victors. One of those who protested vociferously was Otto Vielhauer, a member of the *Landtag* (regional parliament) of Baden-Württemberg,[93] who wrote directly to the mayor complaining about the French family Chadron living in the flat above him. Monsieur Chadron had previously worked as a *gendarme* in a French colony, and Vielhauer referred to this in his complaint: 'These people act utterly against cultural norms … like in an African colony … where the Mister Gendarme has operated before! – Above me it is often so noisy … that you can neither work nor rest. My previous attempts to end this mischief were unsuccessful … I even have the feeling that those "victors" were acting out of bad faith.'[94] This letter was forwarded to the superior of the gendarme Chadron. Since Vielhauer did not hear from the Mayor for two weeks, he wrote to him again, citing once more that his neighbour was behaving unduly in the manner of a 'victor'. By using the word 'victor' ironically and in quotation marks, he distanced himself from accepting the French army as rightful occupiers and combined this with the stereotype of uncivilized conditions in Africa. Vielhauer's particular phraseology as well as his persistence in pursuing his complaint lends this quarrel between neighbours a political dimension although this was never stated explicitly. Conflicts emerging from the occupation of the local population's private sphere allowed Germans to articulate broader critiques of the occupation and its legitimacy, shrouded as supposedly apolitical complaints about daily life.

For others, however, the experience of living together resulted in a rapprochement with the occupiers. French and Germans sometimes lived together in harmony, even if they were initially forced to do so against their will. One might take again the case of Luise H. as an example. She noted in her diary in July 1945 that a French sergeant was accommodated in the room previously occupied by her daughter and described him as 'a very nice, decent man. We respect him highly.'[95] Another German woman had similarly positive memories of her new French housemate:

> One room of our three-room-apartment was requisitioned. My granny had to move to the living room. After anxious waiting it was not a soldier who arrived but a woman. She was the girlfriend of an officer: 'Denise'. After initial strangeness and scepticism on both sides she turned out to be an Alsatian and spoke more and more German with us. At the end a pleasant relationship was established, and we sunbathed together on our balcony.[96]

There are other notable examples of female solidarity between German and French women. In 1955, for example, a German housemaid was attacked in her room by a man who tried to rape her. She escaped and fled to the French family she was working for downstairs. Her female employer accompanied her to the police office to file charges.[97]

When it comes to gender, however, there are interesting distinctions that can be drawn within German–French relations. French women in particular were often remembered negatively by Germans, especially by men. One German said in an interview in 1982: 'Of all occupants, the French women were the worst. Arrogant, demanding – former housemaids wanting to be addressed as "Madame la Colonelle" – we didn't miss that whole rigmarole, but we feared to say anything because we were very hungry and we even accepted to work for them.'[98] For him and for many other Germans, it was disturbing to see women in the powerful position of the occupier. This challenged post-war conceptions of femininity which revolved around notions of women as the 'weaker sex' that their powerful position as occupiers clearly challenged.

Conclusion

Here, we must return to the story with which this chapter started. The German teenager Margrit clearly had prejudices when it came to colonial soldiers. She did not expect them to be friendly and polite, but when she met two of them in the familial surroundings of her neighbour's home, she became friends with them. Direct encounters in the private space made her change her opinion, so that, in this case, Nazi propaganda and earlier stereotypes dating back at least to the interwar period were superseded by her personal experience. It is also a story of a relationship between a male occupier and a female member of the occupied population, representing a rather typical role allocation in terms of gender. Finally, Margrit's father represents the critical perception of such relationships by public opinion, as he clearly did not want his daughter to be seen with a French colonial soldier.

The stories of German–French encounters in everyday life described in this chapter show, however, how diverse those interactions were. Quite often, they were part of a broader power struggle in which the occupiers, despite their presumed monopoly of force, were not necessarily in the stronger position. All public, semi-public and private spaces were affected by the various regulations issued by the French Military Government, though to a different extent, and what occurred on the ground was often as much determined by the individual responses of both the occupied and the occupiers as it was by broader French policies dictated from above.

In the case of public spaces, the various examples of street brawls illustrate how the shift in the broader political situation triggered by the foundation of the FRG was reflected in everyday life, at a time when the roles of occupiers and occupied were already starting to change. In the 1950s, German men appeared to be more willing to start a fight with the occupiers openly on the street, than they had been in the early phases of the occupation. The relationship towards public spaces, however, differed markedly among men and women. For women, the public space in the initial period of the occupation was strongly associated with the danger of being raped, and the violent actions of some of the victors against the population shaped the long-term image of the French occupation among the German public. It supported the idea of particularly violent occupiers, which was first framed by Nazi propaganda at the end of the war. After the early period of occupation, however, everyday life slowly began to revert to safer and more predictable patterns, with more friendly and romantic relationships developing between the occupiers and the occupied population.

In semi-public spaces, even in the earlier period of the occupation, Germans tried to preserve control over 'their' spaces by different means: in pubs, they fought the occupiers openly, while in the case of conflicts on the trams, German workers went on a strike in an attempt to force the French to change their practices. In the private space, direct encounters could lead to conflicts as well as rapprochement, as the case of Margrit well demonstrates.

While there were numerous instances of frictions and conflicts in everyday life between German and French people, at the higher levels of the French Military Government there was an increasing desire, often motivated by pragmatic reasons of efficiency and considerations about how to run a stable occupation, for a rapprochement between the occupiers and the occupied. The violent attacks carried out by some of the French occupiers challenged this rationale and conflicted with the Military Government's interest in creating a positive image of the occupation troops among the population. Broadly speaking, at local government level, cooperation between the City Council and the local Military Government worked quite well, and it was characterized by a respectful, cordial relationship and a joint effort to reconstruct the city.

Examining occupation from a spatial perspective reveals how the occupiers shaped spaces in everyday life and how this influenced social interactions with the occupied population. Combining an analysis of spaces, such as the street, the pub, the tram and the home, with categories such as gender and race reveals that spaces are represented and understood in different ways so that they restrict or facilitate certain activities and can exclude or include certain groups. The experience of personal encounters and everyday life under occupation in the French Zone cannot therefore be described in simplistic terms of occupiers imposing their unconstrained will and might, and the powerless occupiers merely submitting to superior force. Conversely, the experience of both occupiers and occupied was often ambiguous, multifaceted, highly gendered and ultimately situational, depending on who interacted with whom, and contingent on the public, semi-public and private spaces where the encounters took place.

Notes

1 Deutsches Tagebucharchiv (DTA, German Diary Archives) 2019-1, 96. All quotations were translated from German or French into English by the author.

2 Ibid.

3 Ibid., 96–100.

4 For an overview on intersectionality, see Leslie McCall, 'The Complexity of Intersectionality', *Signs* 30, no. 3 (2005): 1771–800.

5 Stefan Martens, 'Zwischen Demokratisierung und Ausbeutung: Aspekte und Motive der französischen Deutschlandpolitik nach dem Zweiten Weltkrieg', in *Vom, 'Erbfeind' zum 'Erneuerer': Aspekte und Motive der französischen Deutschlandpolitik nach dem Zweiten Weltkrieg*, ed. S. Martens, Beihefte der Francia 27 (Sigmaringen: Jan Thorbecke Verlag, 1993), 9.

6 In 2010, *Les archives de l'occupation française en Allemagne et en Autriche* were transferred from Colmar to the Diplomatic Archives located in La Courneuve, near Paris.
7 Edgar Wolfrum, *Französische Besatzungspolitik und deutsche Sozialdemokratie: Politische Neuansätze in der 'vergessenen Zone' bis zur Bildung des Südweststaates 1945–1952* (Düsseldorf: Droste, 1991), 20. On the notion of 'benign' occupations, see the chapter by Peter Stirk in this volume.
8 Theodor Eschenburg, *Jahre der Besatzung, 1945–1949* (Stuttgart: Deutsche Verlags-Anstalt, 1983), 96.
9 F. Roy Willis, *The French in Germany 1945–1949* (Stanford: Stanford University Press, 1962), vi.
10 Wolfrum, *Französische Besatzungspolitik und deutsche Sozialdemokratie*, 21; Peter Fäßler, *Badisch, christlich und sozial: Zur Geschichte der BCSV/CDU im französisch besetzten Land Baden (1945–1952)* (Frankfurt a.M.: Peter Lang, 1995); Reinhard Grohnert, *Die Entnazifizierung in Baden 1945–1949: Konzeptionen und Praxis der 'Epuration' am Beispiel eines Landes der französischen Besatzungszone* (Stuttgart: Kohlhammer, 1991); Rainer Hudemann, 'Frankreichs Besatzung in Deutschland: Hindernis oder Auftakt der deutsch-französischen Kooperation?' in *Von der Besatzungszeit zur deutsch-französischen Kooperation: De la période d'occupation à la coopération franco-allemand*, ed. J. Jurt (Freiburg i.Br.: Rombach, 1993), 237–54.
11 Edgar Wolfrum, 'Französische Besatzungspolitik', in *Deutschland unter alliierter Besatzung 1945–1949/55: Ein Handbuch*, ed. W. Benz (Berlin: Akademie-Verlag, 1999), 61.
12 Karen H. Adler, 'Selling France to the French: The French Zone of Occupation in Western Germany, 1945–c. 1955', *Contemporary European History* 21, no. 4 (2012): 576.
13 Detlef Grieswelle, 'Vorwort', in *Alliierte Truppen in der Bundesrepublik Deutschland*, ed. D. Grieswelle and W. Schlau (Bonn: Köllen, 1990), 5.
14 Edgar Wolfrum, '"Jammert im Leid der Besiegte, so ist auch der Sieger verloren". Kollektive Alltagserfahrung in der französischen Besatzungszone nach 1945', in *Die 'Franzosenzeit' im Lande Baden von 1945 bis heute: Zeitzeugnisse und Forschungsergebnisse = La présence française dans le pays de Bade de 1945 à nos jours*, ed. J. Jurt (Freiburg i.Br.: Rombach, 1992), 21–38.
15 See the ongoing research project by Karen H. Adler (University of Nottingham) on 'France in Germany: A Social and Cultural History of Occupation'.
16 Gudrun-Axeli Knapp, '"Intersectionality" – ein neues Paradigma feministischer Theorie? Zur transatlantischen Reise von "Race, Class, Gender"', *Feministische Studien* 23 (2005): 68–81; Gabriele Winkler and Nina Degele, *Intersektionalität: Zur Analyse sozialer Ungleichheiten* (Bielefeld: Transcript, 2009), 9–24.
17 Candace West and Sarah Fenstermaker, 'Doing Difference', in *Race, Class, & Gender: Common Bonds, Different Voices*, ed. E. Ngan-Ling Chow, D. Wilkinson and M. Baca Zinn (Thousand Oaks, London and New Delhi: SAGE, 1996), 370.
18 Margaret L. Andersen, 'Foreword', in *Race, Class & Gender*, ix.
19 Martina Löw, 'The Constitution of Space: The Structuration of Spaces through the Simultaneity of Effect and Perception', *European Journal of Social Theory* 11, no. 1 (2008): 26.
20 Doreen Massey, *Space, Place and Gender* (Cambridge: Polity Press, 1994), 179.
21 Pierre Bourdieu, *Die männliche Herrschaft* (Frankfurt am Main: Suhrkamp, 2005), 57.

22 Max Bruecher, *Freiburg im Breisgau 1945: Eine Dokumentation* (Freiburg i.Br.: Rombach, 1980), 8.
23 Gerd R. Ueberschär, *Freiburg im Luftkrieg 1939–1945* (Freiburg: Ploetz, 1990), 242; Christof Strauß, 'Freiburg im Breisgau als Hauptstadt des Landes Baden – der Not geschuldet, die Not verwaltend', in *Die Zeit nach dem Krieg: Städte im Wiederaufbau*, ed. K. Moersch and R. Weber (Stuttgart: Kohlhammer, 2008), 64.
24 Peter Fäßler et al., 'Hauptstadt ohne Brot: Freiburg im Land Baden (1945–1952)', in *Geschichte der Stadt Freiburg: Von der Badischen Herrschaft bis zur Gegenwart*, ed. H. Haumann and H. Schadeck, 2nd edn (Stuttgart: Theiss, 2001), 378.
25 Gerd R. Ueberschär, 'Eroberung und Besetzung Südwestdeutschlands durch die Alliierten 1945', in *Südbaden unter Hakenkreuz und Trikolore: Zeitzeugen berichten über das Kriegsende und die französische Besetzung 1945*, ed. B. Serger, K.-A. Böttcher and G. R. Ueberschär (Freiburg i.Br.: Rombach, 2006), 21–2.
26 Norbert Ohler, 'Franzosen in Deutschland – Freiburg als Beispiel', in *Die 'Franzosenzeit'*, 65–6.
27 Marc Hillel, *L'occupation française en Allemagne (1945–1949)* (Paris: Balland, 1983), 182.
28 Ibid., 42–3.
29 Bernd Serger and Karin-Anne Böttcher, 'Der Einmarsch der Alliierten', in *Südbaden*, 315.
30 Ibid., 274.
31 Emmanuel Mounier (ed.), *Anthologie der deutschen Meinung: Deutsche Antworten auf eine französische Umfrage* (Konstanz: Amus, 1948), 145. Mounier, a French journalist, travelled through Germany after the war and tried to record as many different opinions as possible. He was not working for the French government, although it supported him financially. He claimed, however, that this did not influence his findings. (6ff)
32 The expression *la grande nation* is – although it seems to be a French term – primarily used in German-speaking countries to describe the grandeur of the French nation.
33 A priest from St. Märgen, a small community in the Black Forest (close to Freiburg), described similar expectations and disappointments. Cf. Jürgen Wolfer, *Ein hartes Stück Zeitgeschichte: Kriegsende und französische Besatzungszeit im mittleren Schwarzwald: Zwischen 'Werwölfen', 'Kränzlemännern' und 'schamlosen Weibern'* (Hamburg: Kovac, 2012), 219.
34 Stadtarchiv Freiburg (StAFr), D.Aö. 1/53.
35 Willis, *The French in Germany*, 67.
36 StAFr, K1/44-921.
37 Fäßler et al., *Hauptstadt ohne Brot*, 394.
38 StAFr, C5/39.
39 Centre des Archives Diplomatiques (CAD) Paris-La Courneuve, 7BAD/5, H 1.103/1.
40 Ibid.
41 The Supreme Headquarters, Allied Expeditionary Force (SHAEF) stipulated a non-fraternization ban for the soldiers of all nations during the invasion. Nevertheless, the French military command rejected this isolation of the troops as 'antithetical to the French character'. However, non-official contacts, including handshakes, visits, gifts and dates, remained prohibited until late 1945. Marriages between French soldiers and German women were not allowed until August 1948, and even then, they needed official permission. Cf. Rainer Hudemann, 'Heimliche Liebe: Französische Soldaten

und deutsche Frauen', in *Es begann mit einem Kuss: Deutsch-Alliierte Beziehungen nach 1945* (*It Started with a Kiss: German-Allied Relations after 1945 = Tout a commencé par un baiser: Les relations germano-alliées après 1945*), ed. F. Weiß (Berlin: Jaron, 2005), 28–37; Willis, *The French in Germany*, 248; Fabrice Virgili, *Naître ennemi: Les enfants de couples franco-allemands nés pendant la seconde guerre mondiale* (Paris: Payot: 2009), 301.

42 Literal translation: The man is lying in a soldier's grave / The woman is lying in negros' beds / He gave himself for the fatherland / She gave herself for cigarettes. Cf. Mounier, *Anthologie der deutschen Meinung*, 19.

43 This was also the case in the US Zone; see Susanne zur Nieden, 'Erotic Fraternization: The Legend of German Women's Quick Surrender', in *Home/Front: The Military, War, and Gender in Twentieth-Century Germany*, ed. K. Hagemann and S. Schüler-Springorum (Oxford and New York: Berg, 2002), 302–5.

44 For example, DTA, 699-10, 8.

45 Uta G. Poiger, 'Krise der Männlichkeit: Remaskulinisierung in beiden deutschen Nachkriegsgesellschaften', in *Nachkrieg in Deutschland*, ed. K. Naumann (Hamburg: Hamburger Edition, 2001), 227–63; Sandra Maß, *Weiße Helden, schwarze Krieger: Zur Geschichte kolonialer Männlichkeit in Deutschland 1918–1964* (Köln: Böhlau, 2006), 314.

46 Maß, *Weiße Helden, schwarze Krieger*, 4.

47 Jean-Yves Le Naour, *La honte noire: L'Allemagne et les troupes coloniales françaises 1914–1945* (Paris : Fayard, 2003), 8–9.

48 Maß, *Weiße Helden, schwarze Krieger*, 309–10.

49 Patrick Farges and Elissa Mailänder, 'Des "conditions masculines" au sortir de la Seconde Guerre Mondiale: Perspectives transnationales', in *La 'condition féminine': Feminismus und Frauenbewegung im 19. und 20. Jahrhundert/Féminismes et mouvements de femmes aux XIXe-XXe siècles*, ed. F. Berger and A. Kwaschik (Stuttgart: Franz Steiner Verlag, 2016), 159.

50 Fäßler et al., *Hauptstadt ohne Brot*, 377.

51 Werner Köhler, *Freiburg i. Br. 1945–1949: Politisches Leben und Erfahrungen in der Nachkriegszeit* (Freiburg i. Br.: Verlag Stadtarchiv Freiburg im Breisgau, 1987), 98.

52 StAFr, C5/1421.

53 Helke Sander, 'Erinnern/Vergessen', in *BeFreier und Befreite: Krieg, Vergewaltigung, Kinder*, ed. H. Sander and B. Johr (München: Kunstmann, 1992), 13.

54 Hanna Schissler, '"Normalization" as Project: Some Thoughts on Gender Relations in West Germany during the 1950s', in *The Miracle Years: A Cultural History of West Germany, 1949–1968*, ed. H. Schissler (Princeton: Princeton University Press, 2001), 361.

55 Ohler, *Franzosen in Deutschland*, 69.

56 La Courneuve CAD 7BAD/5, H 0.004/2; La Courneuve CAD 7BAD/20, H 1.278; Christine Eifler, 'Nachkrieg und weibliche Verletzbarkeit: Zur Rolle von Kriegen für die Konstruktion von Geschlecht', in *Soziale Konstruktionen: Militär und Geschlechterverhältnis*, ed. Ch. Eifler and R. Seifert (Münster: Westfälisches Dampfboot, 1999), 164.

57 Rainer Gries, 'Les enfants d'État : Französische Besatzungskinder in Deutschland', in *Besatzungskinder: Die Nachkommen alliierter Soldaten in Österreich und Deutschland*, ed. B. Stelzl-Marx and S. Satjukow (Wien: Böhlau, 2015), 387. On German priests'

perceptions of rapes committed by occupation troops in Freiburg and neighbouring areas, see the chapter by Johannes Kuber in this volume.
58 CAD La Courneuve 7BAD/13, H 1.106/1.
59 Gries, *Les enfants d'État*, 389–91.
60 Maß, *Weiße Helden, schwarze Krieger*, 311.
61 DTA, 1226-1.
62 Atina Grossmann, 'A Question of Silence: The Rape of German Women by Occupation Soldiers', *October* 72 (1995): 58.
63 Ute Bechdolf, 'Den Siegern gehört die Beute: Vergewaltigungen beim Einmarsch der Franzosen im Landkreis Tübingen', *Geschichtswerkstatt* 16 (1988): 31.
64 Gries, *Les enfants d'État*, 388–9.
65 Birgit Beck, 'Vergewaltigung von Frauen als Kriegsstrategie im Zweiten Weltkrieg?', in *Gewalt im Krieg: Ausübung, Erfahrung und Verweigerung von Gewalt in Kriegen des 20. Jahrhunderts*, ed. A. Gestrich (Münster: Lit., 1996), 39.
66 For this chapter, I analysed police records and reports on incidents between French military men and the German population from 1947 to 1955. I found records of thirty-two brawls which took place on the street and nineteen which took place in a pub. It has to be borne in mind, however, that police records are not continuously archived and that there are gaps of several months.
67 CAD La Courneuve 7BAD/5, H 0.004/3.
68 Ibid.
69 CAD La Courneuve 7BAD/5, H 0.004/3.
70 See, for instance, CAD La Courneuve 7BAD/5, H 0.004/2; 7BAD/5, H 0.004/3; 7BAD/20, H 1.278.
71 CAD La Courneuve 7BAD/5, H 0.004/2.
72 StAFr, C5/38.
73 CAD La Courneuve 7BAD/20, H 1.278.
74 CAD La Courneuve 7BAD/5, H 0.004/2.
75 CAD La Courneuve 7BAD/20, H 1.278.
76 Landesarchiv Baden-Württemberg, Staatsarchiv Freiburg, F 176/1 no. 3.
77 Franz Dröge and Thomas Krämer-Badoni, *Die Kneipe: zur Soziologie einer Kulturform oder 'Zwei Halbe auf mich!'* (Frankfurt a.M.: Suhrkamp, 1987), 236.
78 CAD La Courneuve 7BAD/ H 0.004/3; H 1.201; H 1.271; H 1.274; H 1.278; H 1.279.
79 CAD La Courneuve 7BAD/15, H 1.201; 7BAD/20, H 1.278.
80 CAD La Courneuve 7BAD/20, H 1.278.
81 StAFr, C5/39.
82 CAD La Courneuve 7BAD/5, H 0.004/2.
83 Ibid.
84 Fäßler et al., *Hauptstadt ohne Brot*, 397.
85 CAD La Courneuve 7BAD/5, H 0.004/3.
86 CAD La Courneuve 7BAD/21, H 2.001.
87 Ibid.
88 This was not only the case in the French Zone. For a detailed study on this topic in the British Zone, see the chapter by Bettina Blum in this volume.
89 Köhler, *Freiburg i.Br. 1945–1949*, 38.
90 Ibid., 35.
91 CAD La Courneuve 7BAD/5, H 0.004/2.
92 CAD La Courneuve 7BAD/16, H 1.271/3.

93 Köhler, *Freiburg i. Br. 1945–1949*, 279.
94 StAFr, C5/39.
95 DTA, 1226-1.
96 Serger and Böttcher, *Der Einmarsch der Alliierten*, 347–8.
97 CAD La Courneuve 7BAD/20, H 1.274/2.
98 Hillel, *L'occupation française en Allemagne*, 191.

12

'Gosh … I Think I'm in a Dream!!': Subjective Experiences and Daily Life in the British Zone

Daniel Cowling

Most historical assessments of Europe in the aftermath of the Second World War conjure up images of utter misery, desolation and dislocation. Tony Judt, for one, notes that contemporary photographs and films leave us with the inescapable sense that 'everyone and everything' was 'worn out, without resources, exhausted'. To this picture of abject despair there was, we are told, one exception: those 'well-fed Allied occupation forces' now tasked with 'winning the peace'.[1] Yet, as Susan L. Carruthers has recently observed, while we have come to know a good deal about the citizens of continental Europe who experienced the chaos and wretchedness of those tumultuous years, we understand much less about the way in which occupiers embraced their new found supremacy in the post-war world.[2] Scholars have, for instance, seldom considered the experiences of the thousands of British civilians and soldiers who relocated to Germany as members of the Control Commission for Germany (British Element) (CCG (BE)) or British Army of the Rhine (BAOR).[3] In particular, British women who worked for the CCG (BE) have received very little attention in historical accounts of the immediate post-war period.[4] The following chapter draws upon the private letters and photographs of two women who served in the Control Commission, revealing their personal perceptions and representations of everyday life as a victor alongside 'a defeated people'.[5] These subjective accounts provide a penetrating insight into the lived experience of occupation, documenting how the social history of post-war Europe was perceived and memorialized by its own participants.

We have no accurate statistics for the total number of women employed in the British Zone, although they certainly made up a sizeable proportion of the CCG (BE)'s staff, which numbered around 26,000 in 1946.[6] While the majority took up jobs in offices as typists or personal assistants, there were also opportunities to work in the various sections of the Control Commission and deal with issues as diverse as education, welfare or the law.[7] The richly detailed and broadly complementary accounts provided by two of these women, Edna Wearmouth and Mary Bouman, are particularly valuable case studies. Their letters and photograph albums offer colourful and reflective descriptions of the experiences of British women at the lower end of the CCG (BE)'s administrative hierarchy in post-war Germany.

Edna Wearmouth was aged just 21 when she joined the CCG (BE) in 1946 and found herself whisked off from North East England to Bletchley Park for a crash course on all things German. Edna came from relatively modest origins, with her father having worked at the Montagu View Colliery in Northumberland, and she had no experience of foreign travel. This was to change in the spring of 1947 when, after taking a temporary posting with the Forestry Commission in London, Edna finally achieved what she described as her 'life's ambition' of seeing Germany first-hand.[8] The story of this young woman's time as a clerk in T-Force, the division tasked with recovering scientific and technological assets from Germany, was meticulously recorded in the seventy-five letters and numerous photographs that flooded back to her father over the next year. She enthusiastically took up German lessons, relishing the opportunity for exploring this former enemy nation and getting to know its people first-hand. Edna also savoured the bounties of life as an occupier: 'Gosh … I think I'm in a dream!!', she exclaimed in the summer of 1947, 'candies, biscuits, tinned fruit and chocolate – well again, I can only say it's a dream! If I could only send it home'.[9]

In January 1946, Mary Bouman arrived in Germany at the age of 38 and began work as a translator in the Legal Division of the Zonal Executive Offices at Herford, a position she would retain until the end of 1949. She was the daughter of an Associated Press correspondent and had briefly lived in both Paris and Berlin before the war. Now, as a fluent German speaker, Mary returned to Germany, recording her experiences as part of the Control Commission in ninety-three letters sent back home to her parents in London.[10] In this correspondence, we see her appreciation of the generous supplies of food and alcohol, the lavish parties and the chances to travel around Germany and Europe that were on offer during her time as a member of the CCG (BE). At the same time, Mary came to resent the culture of excessive paternalism that she perceived to be rampant among members of the British staff:

> Two new young women, civilians like myself, have arrived in our Mess. They are trying to take the food in hand and invade the kitchen trying to show the Germans how to make things … They don't like how the toast is done, why no grill or toast racks. In vain I'll try to explain to them that the Germans don't know much about the art of making toast … But they say they must learn.[11]

These subjective visions 'from below' provide an enlightening window onto the intricacies of European history in the immediate post-war period. The two collections of letters and photographs are categorized here as ego documents, autobiographical sources in which the 'I', their author, remains continuously present as the writing and describing subject.[12] Through this conceptual framework, which prioritizes focusing on assembled sets of sources in their entirety, we can more easily acquire a privileged insight into the 'self' of their authors and their personal representation of historical events. This focus on the 'structures and subjectivities' of past events, as Mary Fulbrook and Ulinka Rublack have pointed out, helps to bring forth new avenues of investigation.[13]

Despite their contrasting backgrounds, Edna and Mary shared many of the same experiences and perceptions of life in post-war Germany. Both quickly became immersed in the social life of the British occupation forces, taking advantage of the material benefits available to members of the occupation staff. Their testimonies illustrate that while a culture of pleasure seeking and paternalism did exist in the British Zone, time spent as part of the Control Commission could also be an edifying and genuinely transnational experience. In addition, Edna and Mary's vibrant personal depictions of life in the British Zone exemplify the significance of gender as a framework for understanding the history of the Allied occupation. The reconstruction of mentalities from such intimate first-hand accounts therefore reveals some of the ways in which British occupiers saw themselves and their place in the world during a time of extraordinary transformation at home and abroad.[14]

A tale of two civvies

The earliest correspondence that Edna and Mary sent home from post-war Germany reflected their unease at the destruction they had encountered. Although both women now assumed an honorary military rank, along with its many privileges, they arrived as members of the civilian staff that made up the CCG (BE). As such, while reports in the British media had undoubtedly acquainted them to some extent with the devastation waiting for them in Germany, these first-hand encounters with ruined towns and cities inspired a profound sense of distress and incredulity. Edna Wearmouth, despite arriving almost two years after the end of the war, was taken aback at the level of damage she witnessed in Cologne, where over 60 per cent of the city had been destroyed.[15] Evidently sensing that words could only convey so much, she compiled a photo collage in order to truly capture its overwhelming scale.[16] Here, Edna purposefully juxtaposed her personal images of the ruins with an accompanying set of pictures, mainly shop-bought photographs and postcards, which depicted the city in its pre-war splendour.[17]

Mary Bouman was also troubled by the heavily bombed towns and cities that she came across in the British Zone, writing to her parents in the spring of 1946 of her sympathy for 'poor old Hamburg'.[18] What concerned her was not just the 'terrible sight' of the ruins, 'which are on too vast a scale to cope with', but also the plight of the city's inhabitants who, though 'quite respectably clad', were seen 'poking into refuse bins hoping to pick up something or other. It is all so tragic.' The hardships that Mary witnessed also inspired irritation at the perceived obliviousness of people back in Britain, becoming particularly incensed when one friend, residing in a small Yorkshire town that had emerged from the war largely unscathed, wrote to her requesting a chrome watch:

> Does she think one can just go into a shop here and buy a watch? ... She should come from pretty little Pickering [that] she so despises and see the utter ruin and destruction and grim conditions out here. She is a foolish woman and doesn't know anything. There is no place in the world for such people nowadays.[19]

Mary, now living and working amid such overwhelming destruction, also expressed astonishment at the prevailing culture of the British occupation, where she felt opulent luxuries available only to occupiers coexisted awkwardly alongside the housing shortages and hunger facing most Germans: 'it is a strange feeling to pass from utter desolation to the soft carpets, comfortable chairs, spacious restaurants and luxurious bedroom fittings of the modern hotel', she wrote, 'it is like passing into another world'.[20]

But, like it or not, both women now were part of the exclusive domain of lavish and, at times, distasteful indulgence afforded to British occupiers. It was, in fact, not long before their depictions of occupation life began to focus more on day-to-day experiences than the turmoil of post-war Germany. They were soon recounting in prodigious detail the manifold opportunities for luxury consumption and socializing that they came to enjoy during their time as part of the CCG (BE), emphasizing the camaraderie that had developed among members of the British staff.

There was, most notably, an interminable interest in the quality, variety, and availability of food, which, according to Mary Bouman, had become 'almost as international a means of understanding between the nations as music and the arts'.[21] Both Edna and Mary described in great detail the fluctuating assortment of foodstuffs now available to them in messes and requisitioned hotels and clubs.[22] We learn, for instance, of a visit to the Lemgo Club where diners were treated to shrimp cocktail, roast chicken with sauté potatoes, champignons and grilled tomatoes, and *ananas à l'américaine* with ice cream, all accompanied with brandy, wine, and coffee.[23] While a meal of such extravagance may not have been an everyday occurrence, items such as fruit and fresh cream seldom obtainable in Britain were now commonly available to members of the CCG (BE). Indeed, while there were occasional grumbles, including Mary's complaints that too much mess food came out of tins and that 'we never see any green salad or such fresh things at all', there was an underlying sense of satisfaction at the ease of attaining enjoyable and nourishing meals: 'THE FOOD?!!! It's amazing!!', Edna exclaimed, 'in England, before the war, we never had anything like this'.[24]

It is hardly surprising, given the turmoil and destruction that both women had witnessed first-hand, to find a degree of incredulity alongside this sense of gratitude: 'I just can't believe it', Edna remarked upon finding fresh white bread, 'if it weren't for the names on all the places, I'd never believe I was in Germany'.[25] This astonishment at the privileges afforded to them was augmented by the obvious discrepancies in terms of food provision between occupiers and occupied. The German people faced near starvation in the earliest years of the occupation, as Mary acknowledged in her first letter home when describing 'a defeated looking lot of people' who appeared 'cold and hungry'.[26] By the time Edna arrived in Germany the food situation had improved somewhat, although there remained a marked inequality in the size and variety of the allocations provided to the Germans and the British. She was even moved to try and redress the imbalance herself, telling her father that she had 'taken to pinching bits and pieces from our mess to feed some of the people'.[27]

The allocation of food in post-war Germany undoubtedly reinforced the power dynamics of the occupation, ensuring the physical and psychological supremacy of the Allied occupiers. Edna even wondered whether it was a conscious attempt by the British authorities to 'show the Germans they were wrong when they broadcast that we were starving' during the war.[28] Moreover, both women were plainly aware that the material advantages available to them in Germany were exceptional. Mary acknowledged that she was 'one of the very lucky ones' who did not 'have to think what the next meal will consist of' or 'worry about the countless other difficulties connected with keeping house today'.[29] Likewise, Edna recognized that her good fortune contrasted sharply not only with the German people, but also friends and family back home in 'austerity Britain':

> You know dad I cannot help but feeling how lucky I am. I'm out here just when things are short at home and I'm getting all the best of everything ... I have the feeling that I must make the most of every bit of my time out here for I'll never be so well off again. Life may bring me now some very hard times, but I can always think back on the things I had out here.[30]

Another topic of considerable, and often expressly approving, interest was the seemingly unceasing flow of inexpensive or free alcohol in the British Zone. In the spring of 1946, when Germany faced an impending famine, Mary Bouman remarked that 'the only commodity of which there seems no lack is drink. We may have to starve at some future date but it hardly seems likely that we will go thirsty'.[31] The pervasive drinking culture of the British Zone was most palpable at the parties and dances that CCG (BE) and BAOR personnel held with an astonishing regularity in their exclusive clubs, hotels and messes. Edna Wearmouth's experience suggests that avoiding alcohol was more of a challenge than acquiring it. She had arrived in Germany resolutely teetotal, facing much jovial derision as a result, but before long the conviviality of her new environment had enticed her to sample the luxurious libations on offer:

> I had my first sip of champagne. They got a bottle and I had to have a little sip, just to say I'd tasted it. I didn't like it very much – it tasted rather like cider but I expected it to be marvellous but I thought it like Andrews liver salts!! Have you tasted it? I'll never make a booser [*sic*], will I?[32]

The abundance of alcohol helped to fuel a sexually permissive culture within the British Zone. It is well documented that relationships between British men and German women were commonplace during the occupation, ranging from casual sex to more serious encounters. The latter resulted in an estimated 10,000 German 'war brides' emigrating to the UK between 1947 and 1950.[33] While British women seldom engaged in such Anglo-German affairs, impeded not only by official strictures but also the threat of moral censure, many of them did partake in amorous interactions with other members of the Allied occupation authorities. Edna, for instance, seems to have received a great deal of attention from colleagues, with 'the men at the office' assuring her that she 'could have more escorts than Princess Elizabeth'.[34] In the spring of 1947, she developed a close relationship with a corporal in the BAOR named Bill who bought her flowers, accompanied her on drives and walks through the countryside, helped her send packages home and went dancing with her.[35] Yet their courtship came to an end after only a few months when Edna decided that she 'didn't want to go out with him any more ... because although he's so very nice and all the girls love him, I don't like him enough'.[36]

It is notable that Mary, whether due to her age and superior social standing, her lack of enthusiasm for parties and dances, or perhaps simply because she was writing to her parents, made almost no allusions to the subject of sex and relationships. On the other hand, Edna's correspondence suggests that her time in occupied Germany was, to some extent, shaped by the gendered atmosphere of permissiveness and sexual liberation she had encountered there. She regularly criticized colleagues in the CCG (BE) and BAOR for getting 'rolling drunk' at every opportunity and creating an unwelcoming and, at times, uncomfortable atmosphere.[37] On one occasion, Edna described a 'usual do' during which, as ever, drunkenness and unruly behaviour were rife: 'I do wish they were different for I love dancing, and I often wish I could go to a nice dance out here, but I cannot stand these men'.[38] Her memoir is even more forthright, explaining how she and other women were subject to lurid tales and sexual advances from their male colleagues:

> I was getting less innocent by the day. In the office, especially since the arrival of beautiful Enid, Bert was chagrined to find that neither of us fell for his hunky handsomeness and he took a daily delight in trying to shock us by regaling us with tales of his sexual exploits and his various German mistresses who, he said, fell at his feet … He was a walking Kama Sutra.[39]

Another consequence of the generous ration of alcohol (and cigarettes) made available to British personnel was its function as currency on post-war Germany's ubiquitous black market. This opened up an array of otherwise unobtainable goods and services to members of the CCG (BE) and BAOR. Mary Bouman seems to have been fairly reticent about engaging in such dealings, indicative of the perceived immorality of black market activities in post-war Britain.[40] She was nevertheless willing to stock up on coffee 'which one can barter for eggs, milk, vegetables etc' in preparation for a forthcoming trip to Bavaria. 'I know it sounds very like Black Market', Mary noted with some reluctance, 'but it isn't as though one makes a practice of it. It is just for pure convenience in my case.'[41] Edna Wearmouth, on the other hand, seems to have partaken in the barter economy with a much greater regularity, procuring laundry services (ten cigarettes) and packs of writing paper (twenty cigarettes) as well as various postcards, souvenirs, and other luxuries.[42] These small-scale trades, though strictly prohibited, became a widely practiced and sometimes unavoidable part of life as an occupier.

There were, however, also examples of more sinister large-scale profiteering in the British Zone. This was, Edna Wearmouth explained to her father, an infuriating and unwelcome feature of the military occupation:

> A most objectionable young man came in to disturb our quiet. I shall never forget that man. He boasted about all the money he's making out here, changing cigarettes for German marks and selling them for English money … He said he'd never go back to UK for he was having the time of his life out here. Never did a stroke of work, plenty of money, everything on the Black Market, plenty of drinks, plenty of parties – how Enid and I kept our mouths shut and refrained from spitting at him, I cannot imagine!!![43]

Likewise, Mary Bouman condemned the 'strange life out here' where trading surplus cigarettes provided some with an opulent lifestyle 'sometimes quite devoid of reality' and augmented the segregation between rulers and ruled. This rift, she suggested, was also partly the responsibility of the ex-imperial staff working in the CCG (BE), who seemed to regard Germany 'as a sort of British colony and the Germans as a species of rather inferior natives'.[44]

It is of little surprise that the boisterous and, at times, sensational social environment of occupied Germany met with some rebuke in the British media, with numerous correspondents sounding alarm at the 'public exhibitions of drunkenness', 'horrid examples of carnal lust', and 'corrupt practices' they had come across.[45] The British occupiers, rather than being lauded for leading by example in the effort to 're-educate' German society, were accused of running amok in their 'Black Zone'. The written press, purportedly seeking to safeguard Britain's national interest, suggested that this wayward conduct was endangering a hard-fought peace: an article in the *Daily Mirror*, for example, claimed the CCG (BE) cost British taxpayers as much as £160 million per year to 'teach the Germans to despise us'.[46] This public denigration of the occupation staff reached its height in September 1947 when the *Daily Express* published a particularly incendiary exposé labelling the 'corrupt' and 'lazy' occupation staff as 'spivs' who 'discredit our rule' and should be brought home immediately.[47]

It therefore appeared to many in Britain that the occupation was epitomized by a marked separation between Allied occupiers, enjoying the best of times, and occupied Germans, subject to the worst. We have, however, seen the ways in which Edna and Mary's accounts contest this black-and-white portrayal of life in post-war Germany. They had been consistently mindful to differentiate themselves, and most of their colleagues, from what they believed to be a disorderly minority giving the CCG (BE) a bad name. This tendency only grew stronger in the face of public criticism, which both women felt had produced a misleading picture of the British Zone. Edna, for instance, made a conscious effort to defend the occupation staff when describing a dance she had recently attended in Oberursel: 'I never saw the bar and certainly *no one* got drunk, so you see you cannot ever say that *ALL* CCG are alike.'[48] Moreover, the offending articles were themselves pilloried, with personal correspondence providing a means for both women to set the record straight. Mary complained that the *Daily Express*'s labelling of the occupation staff as 'spivs' was a 'scurrilous attack' bereft of humour or nuance.[49] She suggested that while 'there are some pretty useless types' in Germany this was no different than you would find in any profession in Britain and, moreover, that 'as well as indulging in parties ... people here also work quite hard'.[50]

It seems clear, in fact, that both women felt a great deal of pride and satisfaction in their work, personally identifying with their organization and its larger mission in Germany. This was, in part, a consequence of the changes to the British labour market that accompanied the end of the war: the demobilization of the armed forces reduced the number of jobs available to women.[51] Thus, the chance for professional advancement that life as an occupier offered to its female participants represented a major incentive. Edna's service history is a case in point: starting out as a typist in Herford, she was quickly offered a promotion to become personal assistant to a senior officer.[52] It was not long before Edna was asked to go on a special assignment for the

CCG (BE) in Frankfurt am Main, located in the US Zone. Her colleagues assured her that this was 'a great honour' and, despite recognizing that it was 'a big step' to 'go so far away by myself', she accepted on the grounds that 'opportunity only knocks once' and 'we must all learn to be brave'.[53] Here, Edna was placed in charge of a pool of typists, marking her ascent within the administration while also prompting a sense of unease at the power she now wielded as part of an occupying force: 'they are all German and I am in charge of them. I don't like it. It's not fair somehow, but I'll bide my time'.[54]

'Like walking through a fairy tale'

Edna and Mary's subjective accounts depict occupied Germany as an extraordinary social milieu where constructive transnational exchanges between occupiers and occupied transpired. There were, for all the stories of wanton excess and the segregation between rulers and ruled, frequent opportunities for the British to rewardingly engage with Germans, German culture and their new environment. In this sense, Edna and Mary's representations of their daily lives reveal how the social worlds of former enemies became unavoidably entangled amid the disorder and uncertainty of post-war Europe.

The beauty and curiosity of unfamiliar physical surroundings was the subject of profound fascination. The chance to explore Germany and Europe was particularly appealing, with both women taking advantage of a generous allowance of leisure time and their newfound sense of independence. They visited towns, cities, and landmarks throughout the country, including Altenau, Cologne, Goslar, Oldenburg, Hamburg, Garmisch-Partenkirchen, the Möhne Dam, Berchtesgaden and Berlin, as well as making longer excursions to Paris, Brussels and Stockholm.

Edna Wearmouth, who had never been abroad before, was adamant that she would 'make the most of every minute' of her time away and greeted the opportunity to explore the countryside with a particular enthusiasm.[55] Her photograph albums of natural landmarks were often excitably captioned with historical information or local legends, such as the Pied Piper.[56] The notion of Germany as a place of natural beauty or, to quote one caption, 'like walking through a fairy tale' was unexpected and challenged the preconception that this was a land of bombed-out ruins and concentration camps.[57] 'I can never rave enough about the beauty of Germany', Edna wrote to her father, 'you will wonder, I've no doubt, at the way I tell you that every place is lovely – but it's true. There are so many lovely places.'[58] Moreover, her description of finding 'the most wonderful cemetery you can imagine' encapsulates the way in which Germany's physical characteristics could influence attitudes towards the country and its people more generally:

> I've never seen anything like it. It is in among the wood and like a huge garden of remembrance … It's so hard to describe but if you can imagine a lovely park and a cemetery which is very well cared for and massed with flowers and nearby, away among the trees, separate graves with huge rocks as gravestones and flowers planted everywhere, you can get an idea of what it's like … I really felt that a race of people who can be so sentimental and create something so lovely, cannot be bad at heart.[59]

Mary Bouman, better acquainted with Europe from before the war, revealed a quasi-anthropological interest in her new environment that was facilitated by her status as an occupier. She explained to her parents that a favourite pursuit while travelling through Germany was 'going into these once private houses and sniffing around', on occasion receiving 'pleasant little shocks' such as 'solid looking candelabra vases with branches of fir stuck in them'.[60]

Local customs also inspired much warm-hearted puzzlement, be it regarding strange foods, unusual weather or peculiar festivities. Mary embraced the traditions and unabashed enthusiasm associated with the Christmas season in Germany, having a 'Christmas with an English and German flavour' during which 'the fir garlands with *Lametta* made by the German staff vie with the garish paper decorations supplied by NAAFI'.[61] She exchanged presents with local residents, gifting them alcohol, crayons and cocoa, and, in her self-appointed role as an unofficial cultural ambassador, even sought to introduce the peculiarly British culinary customs of Christmas cake and mince pies to Germany.[62] Children's Christmas parties were another site of cross-cultural exchange, as Mary explained to her parents:

> The Germans I don't think ever went in for children's Christmas parties as we know them. Their idea is to sit round a table ... and sing carols over and over again with serious solemn faces and then get up and recite long intricate verses to Father Christmas. Any idea of a good romp or games seems unknown. But how they loved it when we showed them the way.[63]

Edna and Mary's explorations of Germany, along with its culture and traditions, were facilitated through regular and predominantly positive interactions with the German people. In her first letter home, Edna had declared that she was 'just dying to learn German and be able to speak to them'.[64] This was something she pursued upon arriving in Herford, where she took language lessons with Hans Thol, the former resident of her lodgings who now lived in the cellar of the house along with his wife Anneliese and their four-year-old son.[65] In time, Edna grew more comfortable conversing with the Germans she met in the course of her work and travels, photographing many of the people she had befriended.[66] These pictures, full of smiles and usually featuring Edna or one of her colleagues posing alongside newfound friends or jovial strangers, project a sense of warmth and companionship rather than apprehension or estrangement (see Figure 12.1).[67]

Mary Bouman, on the other hand, remained more mindful of her sense of duty as a representative of the CCG (BE): 'it is very good to mix as much as possible with the Germans', she suggested, 'if only to correct some very erroneous ideas they seem to have about things in general and in particular about affairs in the outside world'.[68] Moreover, her letters often took on an anthropological guise, as exemplified by her first recorded impressions of the German people:

> So far I have seen no aggressive Germans, only depressed, suppressed and furtive ones. Here they don't look quite so thin or cold but they certainly seem subdued and SO QUIET. We know how noisy Germans can be. I believe, however, that the attitude differs in the various parts due to a variety of reasons. Here in Lübbecke the Nazis had a very strong hold.[69]

Figure 12.1 Edna Wearmouth with German friends, ca. 1947. © Imperial War Museum, London.

This inquisitive and paternalistic outlook, undoubtedly inspired in part by the discussion of 're-educating' Germans that had been commonplace in wartime Britain, was most certainly encouraged by senior officials in the CCG (BE). That said, we have already seen how Mary, whose language skills facilitated in-depth exchanges on a daily basis, also had more kindly interactions with local people.

It was, in fact, not uncommon for either Mary or Edna to accompany German friends and acquaintances on trips across the country, not least because their knowledge of the country and array of local contacts made them particularly useful travelling companions. These informal arrangements offered the opportunity to see new sides to Germany, gaining novel first-hand perspectives on a people who only a few years earlier had been regarded as the enemy. Edna made one memorable visit to Fulda, staying in the family home of her German friend Günther, a university student. They were accompanied on this weekend of sightseeing and rambling by Edna's CCG (BE) colleagues Jackie and Enid, Günther's friend and fellow student Harald, and Mac, an American who worked with the United Nations Relief and Rehabilitation Administration (see Figure 12.2).[70] Edna recounted how during the journey, which was taken on public transport, they had been 'chatting away to all the Germans and before long we had the whole blinking bus talking to us. Everyone was roaring and laughing at our broken German, but we carried on a lively conversation all the way.'[71] This motley crew, with ample provisions of food in hand, arrived to a warm welcome

Figure 12.2 Edna Wearmouth with friends during a trip to Fulda, July 1947. © Imperial War Museum, London.

and a cup of '*Kaffee*', which, she explained to her father, was what Germans had when 'we drink tea'. There were, however, also more familiar traditions:

> On Sunday in Germany they have exactly the same customs as in England. Everyone dresses in their best to go to Church and there is an air of peace everywhere. They all go for walks and have the same meals. Not like the Americans with cinemas and their jiving etc.[72]

In the first months of the occupation, with lingering fears of so-called werewolf attacks from fanatical Nazis and a widely held conviction that occupiers should act sternly towards the Germans, all unnecessary contact with locals was strictly forbidden. This rather impracticable directive was regularly disobeyed, for means both fair and foul, and soon 'fraternization' became something of a public sensation. In Britain, the mainstream media and church leaders were among those who expressed their concern at the supposed improbity of British personnel alleged to be getting far too up-close and personal with their former enemies. This commotion soon subsided, and, in turn, regulations were relaxed in September 1945, although some restrictions remained, including a ban on overnight stays in German residences.[73] It is noteworthy, then, that Edna and her group of friends came under the scrutiny of senior officers, who took to arranging cars and drivers for their regular outings 'to discourage us from fraternising and from using German transport'.[74] At the beginning of 1948, long after fraternization restrictions had been lifted, Edna began to organize a trip to Bavaria with a German typist from her office named Emmi. These plans were held up by the recalcitrance of her superiors, who were, she recalls in her memoir, 'aghast that I should be considering travelling along with a German girl who was "quiet and dull" (in their opinion)' and concerned that 'I would have to travel, at my own risk, on a German train and make my own arrangements.' Edna, undaunted, 'did just that'.[75]

Edna and Mary's experiences highlight the enduring – if largely unexploited – potential of the CCG (BE) as a tool of person-to-person reconciliation. The censure of such sincere, not to mention successful, attempts at integration, even as Anglo-German rapprochement became a political priority, appears in hindsight to be something of a contradiction. It is, moreover, impossible to escape the conclusion that the admonition of Edna's interactions with Germans arose from gendered expectations of her conduct in post-war Germany: moralistic opposition to 'fratting' remained, even after official restrictions were lifted, and the higher-ups of the CCG (BE) felt compelled to 'protect' their young female colleagues. It is conspicuous that Mary Bouman does not appear to have come across the same patriarchal supervision, perhaps a consequence of her status as an older, middle-class woman fluent in the local language.

These subjective reflections on life as an occupier portray the opportunity for transnational interactions with Germany and Germans as a memorable, enlightening and altogether rewarding experience. The prospects for personal fulfilment and the positive exchanges with Germany described in these letters are a world away from the drunken debauchery commonly associated with the British Zone. Above all, the occupation was, it seems, a much more multifaceted social experience than has often been recognized, providing at least some of its participants not only with opportunities for amusement and socializing but also uniquely transnational interactions with this former enemy nation and its people. The personal letters and photographs that these two women sent home to family members offered an alternative portrayal of life in post-war Germany, contributing to popular understandings of the occupation and its subsequent memorialization in Britain.

'Concentration camps, atrocities, persecutions, war, where were they all'

In these optimistic accounts of life as a British occupier we see unconscious echoes of the admiring rhetoric that we most readily associate with Anglo–German relations of the nineteenth century. It is intriguing, considering the divisive tensions that had existed between the two nations since 1914, that both Edna and Mary favoured more hopeful visions of a country and people they had come to hold in high regard, generally eschewing any reference to the Nazi past.

Edna Wearmouth rarely mentioned the thorny issues of recent history, assuring her father in on letter that she would '*never* get into any politic [*sic*] arguments with the German people'.[76] Mary Bouman, on the other hand, was less withholding, making intermittent allusions to the Third Reich's troubling legacy. Yet she acknowledged her own inclination to uphold a more sanguine image of Germany during a trip to the Winterberg ski resort:

> Again the uncanny appeal [that] Germany can have began involuntarily to steal over me; the snow covered firs and hills outside, the skis stacked up in the wooden porch and inside the comfy rooms and plump beds ... Concentration camps, atrocities, persecutions, war, where were they all. How could they have happened. How is it possible to reconcile them with the decency, honesty and simplicity of the scene here. It is indeed difficult to understand how they can exist side by side. I suppose I was seeing Germany's other and more pleasant face.[77]

It was, however, only a few months later that Mary came across various *lieux de mémoire*[78] relating to Nazi Germany, including the Bergen-Belsen concentration camp. The account of this visit is the only extended passage referring to the Holocaust in either set of sources:

> I stopped a while and looked around me to take in the scene: the huge staked graves, the sinister barbed wire, the sad memorials, the complete sense of utter desolation in this isolated spot hemmed in as far as one could see by dense forestland, and the knowledge of what had gone on here, gave me a feeling of acute depression. Altogether you feel it is a place of grim memory and I was glad to leave it ... We passed on from flattened Belsen to ruined Hamburg – the one the cause of the other – arriving in time for tea and then drove out to the Officers Country Club on the way to Blankensee. It was a lovely evening so we strolled through the glorious grounds now brilliant with rhododendrons and azaleas and the trees too just at their best. Had Belsen just been a bad dream? Anyway the ghosts were laid here, for it was impossible to imagine that anything so vile had existed.[79]

Mary's candid disclosure of her intention to leave behind memories of this troubling place and its bleak associations provides us with a revealing insight into the post-war mentalities of British occupiers. It seems as if she, along with Edna, sought to move on from the unsettling tensions of the recent past.[80] Thus, the serene land of natural beauty and friendly people that had so enthralled them could be insulated from challenging questions of guilt and recrimination that may otherwise have plagued their interactions with Germany.

'Thank God I'm alive to see all this!'

These two case studies offer a glimpse into a huge array of source material, which offers a unique insight into the mentalities of individual British occupiers as they navigated their way through the social tapestry of post-war Germany. These subjective accounts help to uncover the multifaceted experience of occupation. Above all, Mary Bouman and Edna Wearmouth's letters and photographs illustrate that the social aspects of occupation, rather than its political significance, were of paramount importance to many in the CCG (BE). A sense of fun, optimism and exploration is palpable throughout their correspondence, while references to the Nazi past were markedly infrequent. It was novel interactions and experiences, confounding their expectations, which took centre stage, ranging from socializing and consumptive indulgence to curiosity regarding local customs, friendly interactions with Germans or astonishment at the beauty of the countryside. The hopeful excitement that characterizes Edna and Mary's accounts of their time in post-war Germany did, on occasion, even inspire optimistic visions for the future. Edna repeatedly told her father how she longed for him to see Germany, with its beautiful countryside, kindly people, cultural heritage and charming history.[81] Likewise, Mary reckoned that the quiet country towns of the British Zone where much of the CCG (BE) administration was based might be an ideal place for British retirees:

> So many people here see places they would like to retire to … You see in most of these small German towns there is almost always a good theatre and opera and other amenities that go to make up a cultural life which one misses in so many English towns and particularly in the suburbs of big cities. I myself often think how pleasant life could be, especially for retired people, in some of the places I see, that is, of course, under normal conditions – and one could always be sure of getting adequate domestic help. I often think of you and Daddy in this connection.[82]

The distinctive power dynamics of military occupation, conveying social status, privileges and a paternalistic outlook towards Germans, is certainly discernible in both sets of letters. Yet Edna and Mary's accounts of life in post-war Germany reveal that while occupiers and occupied in post-war Germany certainly inhabited distinct social worlds, their lives intertwined in all manner of ways and with all manner of results. Their letters and photographs foregrounded stories of positive exchanges and interactions with Germany and Germans, conveying a sense of camaraderie as former enemies became friends. These representations of the occupation portrayed it as an occasion for exploration and reconciliation in a strange but welcoming country, rather than simply a chance to enjoy the fruits of victory. There was a palpable sense of awe and enchantment as both women travelled through the lush countryside, encountering charming local traditions and kindly residents. This was not, it seems, a straightforward relationship between rulers and ruled, but rather a more nuanced and adaptable relational paradigm that took root amid the insecurities of post-war Europe.

It is evident that gender was a particularly significant framework in shaping Edna and Mary's time as occupiers, as the gendered power differentials witnessed across British society in the late 1940s coalesced with the unusual power dynamics of military occupation. Thus women could be ostracized by the sexualized atmosphere of British-only social events and admonished by male colleagues for their interactions with the local populace, while also enjoying the material and psychological advantages that came with life as an occupier. Moreover, finding work in post-war Germany as part of the occupation authorities represented a potentially valuable opportunity for professional advancement. In hindsight, it is also reasonable to suggest that it was the women of the CCG (BE) who most eagerly embraced the opportunities for an enhanced sense of independence, finding personal fulfilment as British occupiers in post-war Germany.[83]

Edna and Mary, despite their contrasting ages and social standing, both savoured the chance for socializing and exploration that came their way, looking back upon their time with much fondness. 'I shall be most sorry to leave', wrote Mary in the autumn of 1949, 'I shall miss my independence, the service, the friends who remain, the ease of entertaining and the odd glass of sherry or liqueur'.[84] Edna, in anticipation of her return home, reflected upon the edifying and enriching quality of her life in Germany: 'I have you to thank for all this lovely experience which has come my way dad. For being so un-selfish and letting me travel and see and learn so much.'[85]

In addition, Edna and Mary were clearly mindful of the audience to whom they sent their numerous letters and photographs. Hence, their accounts were marked with a strong compulsion to convey a sense of 'the real German' and 'the real Germany' to an audience they believed to have been misinformed by the mass media. The intimate character of quotidian practices such as letter writing and amateur photography certainly furnished Edna and Mary's correspondence with a considerable, if admittedly unquantifiable, impact upon its readership. The diffusion of these letters and photographs across networks of family, friends and acquaintances further augmented this influence: Edna Wearmouth was, for example, astonished to find one of her letters published in the local church gazette, while Mary Bouman insisted that her father use this collection of letters to 'give Auntie Dora a vivid account of my life out here and thus absolve me from having to enter into long details of the set-up … and the kind of life one leads'.[86] Through their subsequent preservation or, in the case of photographs, curation, these collections became depositories of memory that recalled post-war Germany, offering a window onto the past for family, friends and even their author's future selves. Thus, these letter compilations and photograph albums, which recounted the findings from personal discoveries in narrative form, were some of the earliest attempts to historicize the occupation.

These case studies caution against painting the post-war period in black and white, even if it has often seemed like the most appropriate colouration.[87] The stark divergence of wartime quickly broke down into a much more complex and nuanced picture, one in which there was room for flashes of colour and vibrancy amidst the extensive turmoil. While the experiences of British occupiers in post-war Germany could starkly contrast with the destruction and distress surrounding them, the two worlds of occupier and occupied were not hermetically sealed from one another nor inherently oppositional. The letters and photographs sent home from occupied Germany reveal with a captivating warmth the multiplicity of interactions, exchanges, antagonisms and friendships that emerged during an exceptional time of Anglo-German interaction. For Edna and Mary, the Allied occupation was foremost a time of exhilarating adventures and enchanting memories, an experience that they would certainly never forget:

> You have no idea how lovely it is here. I just cannot find words to describe it … How could they ever want to go to war?? … Monday night one of the motor cyclists took me pillion riding all over the country. It was great. The girls howled at me in riding breeches, and a crash helmet?!!! … Passing through some glorious scenery on the back of the motor cycle, I felt that I wanted to shout out loud 'Thank God I'm alive to see all this!'[88]

Notes

1 Tony Judt, *Postwar: A History of Europe since 1945* (London: Vintage, 2010), 13.
2 Susan L. Carruthers, *The Good Occupation: American Soldiers and the Hazards of Peace* (Cambridge, MA: Harvard University Press, 2016), 14.
3 This scarcity of research is all the more surprising when one considers the numerous memoirs and personal accounts which have been published: these include Michael Howard, *Otherwise Occupied: Letters Home from the Ruins of Nazi Germany* (Tiverton: Old Street, 2010); Harry Leslie Smith, *Love Among the Ruins: A Memoir of Life and Love in Hamburg, 1945* (London: Icon Books, 2015); Noel Annan, *Changing Enemies: The Defeat and Regeneration of Germany* (New York and London: HarperCollins, 1996); George Clare, *Before the Wall: Berlin Days 1946–1948* (New York: Dutton, 1989). The only studies of everyday life in the British Zone are: Roy Bainton, *The Long Patrol: The British in Germany since 1945* (Edinburgh: Mainstream, 2003), an interesting set of personal testimonies which offers little in the way of historical analysis; Patricia Meehan, *A Strange Enemy People: Germans under the British, 1945–1950* (London: Peter Owen, 2001), which primarily relies on oral history interviews recorded several decades later; and Peter Speiser, *The British Army of the Rhine: Turning Nazi Enemies into Cold War Partners* (Urbana: University of Illinois Press, 2016), which includes no personal accounts. Christopher Knowles, *Winning the Peace: The British in Occupied Germany, 1945–1948* (London and New York: Bloomsbury Academic, 2017), a biographical history of the occupation, is a valuable recent contribution to this historiography.
4 The only significant work on the subject is Ruth Easingwood, 'British Women in Occupied Germany: Lived Experiences in the British Zone 1945–1949' (PhD diss., University of Newcastle Upon Tyne, 2009). This scarcity of research contrasts with the large body of literature on the experience of German women in the aftermath of the Second World War, including Sibylle Meyer and Eva Schulze, *Wie wir das alles geschafft haben: Alleinstehende Frauen berichten über ihr Leben nach 1945* (München: Beck, 1984); Elizabeth Heineman, *What Difference Does a Husband Make? Women and Marital Status in Nazi and Postwar Germany* (Berkeley and Los Angeles: University of California Press, 1999).
5 *A Defeated People* was the title of an official CCG (BE) documentary film about conditions in Germany, directed by Humphrey Jennings and released in 1946.
6 Quoted in Meehan, *A Strange Enemy People*, 14.
7 There were also numerous positions in the Women's Affairs Section; see Denise Kathrin Tscharntke, 'Educating German Women: The Work of the Women's Affairs Section of the British Military Government 1946–1951' (PhD diss., Durham University, 2001).
8 Edna Wearmouth to her father, 15 March 1947, France/Germany, Private Papers of Miss E Wearmouth, Documents.5413, Imperial War Museum Archive.
9 Edna Wearmouth to her father, 17 June 1947, Frankfurt, Wearmouth Papers.
10 'Obituary: John A. Bouman', *Standard-Sentinel* (5 November 1958): 36.
11 Mary Bouman to her parents, 4 March 1946, Lübbecke, Private Papers of Miss M Bouman, Documents.16779, Imperial War Museum Archive.
12 Mary Fulbrook, *Dissonant Lives: Generations and Violence through the German Dictatorships* (Oxford: Oxford University Press, 2011), 16–8, 477–80; Mark Hewitson, '"I Witnesses": Soldiers, Selfhood and Testimony in Modern Wars', *German History* 28, no. 3 (1 September 2010): 310–25.

13 Mary Fulbrook and Ulinka Rublack, 'In Relation: The "Social Self" and Ego-Documents', *German History* 28, no. 3 (1 September 2010): 263.
14 Carruthers, *The Good Occupation*, 14.
15 Jeffry M. Diefendorf, *In the Wake of the War: The Reconstruction of German Cities after World War II* (New York and Oxford: Oxford University Press, 1993), 126.
16 On the use of personal photography as a source for twentieth-century German history, see Elizabeth Harvey and Maiken Umbach, 'Introduction: Photography and Twentieth-Century German History', *Central European History* 48, no. 3 (2015): 287–99.
17 Edna Wearmouth, 'Köln on the Rhein', photograph album, June 1947, Wearmouth Papers.
18 Mary Bouman to her parents, 25 April 1946, Herford, Bouman Papers.
19 Mary Bouman to her parents, 29 November 1947, Herford, Bouman Papers.
20 Mary Bouman to her parents, undated letter 'Bummel in Hamburg', Hamburg, Bouman Papers.
21 Mary Bouman to her parents, 20 February 1946, Lübbecke, Bouman Papers.
22 Mary Bouman to her parents, 29 January 1946, Lübbecke, Bouman Papers; 9 October 1946, Herford, Bouman Papers.
23 Mary Bouman to her parents, 13 June 1949, Herford, Bouman Papers.
24 Edna Wearmouth to her father, 17 June 1947, Frankfurt, Wearmouth Papers; Mary Bouman to her parents, 19 May 1947, Herford, Bouman Papers.
25 Edna Wearmouth to her father, 15 March 1947, France/Germany, Wearmouth Papers.
26 Mary Bouman to her parents, 9 January 1946, Lübbecke, Bouman Papers.
27 Edna Wearmouth to father, 11 May 1947, Herford, Wearmouth Papers.
28 Edna Wearmouth to her father, 18 March 1947, Herford, Wearmouth Papers.
29 Mary Bouman to her parents, 29 January 1948, Herford, Bouman Papers.
30 Edna Wearmouth to her father, 16 October 1947, Frankfurt, Wearmouth Papers.
31 Mary Bouman to her parents, 4 March 1946, Lübbecke, Bouman Papers.
32 Edna Wearmouth to her father, 27 March 1947, Herford, Wearmouth Papers.
33 Inge Weber-Newth and Johannes-Dieter Steinert, *German Migrants in Post-War Britain: An Enemy Embrace* (London and New York: Routledge, 2006), 163; Inge Weber-Newth, 'Bilateral Relations: British Soldiers and German Women', in *Gendering Migration: Masculinity, Femininity and Ethnicity in Post-War Britain*, ed. Louise Ryan and Wendy Webster (Aldershot: Ashgate, 2008), 53–70.
34 Edna Wallace (née Wearmouth), 'Bound for Germany' (unpublished manuscript, undated), Wearmouth Papers; Edna Wearmouth to her father, 29 March 1947, Herford, Wearmouth Papers.
35 Edna Wearmouth to her father, 29 March 1947, 17 April 1947, 21 April 1947, Herford, Wearmouth Papers.
36 Edna Wearmouth to her father, 11 May 1947, Herford, Wearmouth Papers.
37 Edna Wearmouth to her father, 1 November 1947, Winterberg, Wearmouth Papers.
38 Edna Wearmouth to her father, 19 September 1947, Frankfurt, Wearmouth Papers.
39 Edna Wallace (née Wearmouth), 'Bound for Germany' (unpublished manuscript, undated), Wearmouth Papers.
40 The public perception of the black market as a moral category, as opposed to an economic or legal one, is discussed in Mark Roodhouse, *Black Market Britain, 1939–1955* (Oxford: Oxford University Press, 2013).
41 Mary Bouman to her parents, 1 June 1948, Herford, Bouman Papers.

42 Edna Wearmouth to her father, 27 March 1947, 24 March 1947, 27 April 1947, Herford, Wearmouth Papers.
43 Edna Wearmouth to her father, 1 November 1947, Winterberg, Wearmouth Papers.
44 Mary Bouman to her parents, 2 August 1946, 20 August 1946, Herford, Bouman Papers.
45 'Scandal in Germany', *New Statesman*, 9 November 1946; 'Retired for Bribery', *Daily Worker*, 3 November 1947; 'Black Zone', *Daily Mirror*, 9 July 1946; Rev. Geoffrey Druitt quoted in 'Conduct of British in Germany – Chaplain's Criticism', *The Times*, 9 August 1946, 3.
46 '£160 Million a Year – To Teach the Germans to Despise Us', *Daily Mirror*, 8 July 1946, 2.
47 J. D. Potter, 'Germany: A Report on the British Zone', *Daily Express*, 4 September 1947, 2.
48 Edna Wearmouth to her father, 17 November 1947, Frankfurt, Wearmouth Papers.
49 Mary Bouman to her parents, 11 September 1947, Herford, Bouman Papers.
50 Mary Bouman to her parents, 11 September 1947, Herford, Bouman Papers; 29 January 1946, Lübbecke, Bouman Papers.
51 The impact of the Second World War upon the position of women in Britain is the source of much discussion; see Caitriona Beaumont, 'The Women's Movement, Politics and Citizenship, 1918–1950s', in *Women in Twentieth-Century Britain*, ed. Ina Zweiniger-Bargielowska (Harlow: Longman, 2001), 264–77; and Lucy Noakes, 'War and Peace', in *Women in Twentieth-Century Britain*, 307–20.
52 Edna Wearmouth to her father, 21 May 1947, Herford, Wearmouth Papers.
53 Edna Wearmouth to her father, 23 May 1947, Herford, Wearmouth Papers.
54 Edna Wearmouth to her father, 13 October 1947, Frankfurt, Wearmouth Papers.
55 Edna Wearmouth to her father, 31 July 1947, Frankfurt, Wearmouth Papers.
56 Edna Wearmouth, 'Partnachklamm', photograph album, 1948, Wearmouth Papers.
57 Edna Wearmouth, 'Hameln', photograph album, May 1947, Wearmouth Papers; Edna Wearmouth, 'Reifenberg am Taunus', photograph album, October 1947, Wearmouth Papers; Edna Wearmouth, 'Garmisch-Partenkirchen', photograph album, March 1948, Wearmouth Papers; Edna Wearmouth, 'Partnachklamm', photograph album, March 1948, Wearmouth Papers.
58 Edna Wearmouth to her father, 28 July 1947, Frankfurt, Wearmouth Papers.
59 Edna Wearmouth to her father, 11 May 1947, Herford, Wearmouth Papers.
60 Mary Bouman to her parents, 20 January 1946, Lübbecke, Bouman Papers.
61 Mary Bouman to her parents, 27 December 1946, Herford, Bouman Papers.
62 Ibid.
63 Mary Bouman to her parents, 31 December 1948, Herford, Bouman Papers.
64 Edna Wearmouth to her father, 15 March 1947, France/Germany, Wearmouth Papers.
65 See Bettina Blum's chapter in this volume for more on British requisitioning policy.
66 Edna Wearmouth, 'Saying Goodbye to Fatherly Driver', photograph album, undated, Wearmouth Papers; Edna Wearmouth, 'Garmisch-Partenkirchen', photograph album, March 1948, Wearmouth Papers.
67 Edna Wearmouth, 'With Irmgard, Me, Ilse', photograph album, undated, Wearmouth Papers.
68 Mary Bouman to her parents, 6 August 1947, Herford, Bouman Papers.
69 Mary Bouman to her parents, 9 January 1946, Lübbecke, Bouman Papers.
70 Edna Wearmouth, 'Walking in the Rhön with Günther Jackie and Harald', photograph album, undated, Wearmouth Papers.

71 Edna Wearmouth to her father, 14 July 1947, Frankfurt, Wearmouth Papers.
72 Ibid.
73 The National Archives, FO 1056/30, letter from Chief Administrative Officer, 10 January 1947, cited in Knowles, *Winning the Peace*, 170.
74 Edna Wallace (née Wearmouth), 'Bound for Germany' (unpublished manuscript, undated), Wearmouth Papers.
75 Ibid.
76 Edna Wearmouth to her father, 8 April 1947, Herford, Wearmouth Papers.
77 Mary Bouman to her parents, 18 March 1946, Lübbecke, Bouman Papers.
78 Pierre Nora, 'Between Memory and History: Les Lieux de Mémoire', *Representations*, Special Issue: Memory and Counter-Memory 26 (1989): 7–24.
79 Mary Bouman to her parents, 28 May 1946, Lübbecke (Visit to Belsen), Bouman Papers.
80 This distancing of the Nazi past was another manifestation of the collective amnesia regarding the Holocaust that historians have identified as an emergent phenomenon in post-war Britain; see Tony Kushner, *The Holocaust and the Liberal Imagination: A Social and Cultural History* (Oxford: Blackwell, 1994).
81 Edna Wearmouth to her father, May 1947, Herford, Wearmouth Papers.
82 Mary Bouman to her parents, 10 June 1948, Herford, Bouman Papers.
83 The enhanced sense of independence and responsibility that came with moving abroad and participating in occupation life is also evident in the letters sent home by younger men in the CCG (BE) and BAOR; see Howard, *Otherwise Occupied*. Yet the extent to which this feature characterized the letters of these two women is striking, especially when one considers that Mary Bouman was an older woman with considerable experience of travel abroad.
84 Mary Bouman to her parents, 2 October 1949, Herford, Bouman Papers.
85 Edna Wearmouth to her father, 1 November 1947, Winterberg, Wearmouth Papers.
86 Edna Wearmouth to her father, 10 July 1947, Frankfurt, Wearmouth Papers; Mary Bouman to her parents, 26 October 1949, Herford, Bouman Papers.
87 There are numerous prominent examples in the vast literature on Europe in the immediate post-war period which seem to suggest this was primarily a time of suffering, disruption and chaos, including Keith Lowe, *Savage Continent: Europe in the Aftermath of World World II* (London: Viking, 2012) and Ian Buruma, *Year Zero: A History of 1945* (London: Atlantic Books, 2013).
88 Edna Wearmouth to her father, May 1947, Herford, Wearmouth Papers.

Part Five

Mediating Occupation: Interactions, Intermediaries and Legacies

13

'We Are Glad They Are Here, But We Are Not Rejoicing!': The Catholic Clergy under French and American Occupation

Johannes Kuber

Despite the toxic competition from twelve years of National Socialism, religion still played an important role in many people's lives at the end of the Second World War; 95 per cent of Germans were official members of one of the two big denominations,[1] and 45 per cent of German Catholics went to church regularly in 1946.[2] While most other ideological and institutional structures that had shaped everyday life during the preceding twelve years had disintegrated by the end of the war, for many Germans personal faith and religious institutions remained a significant influence on their daily lives.

To assess the impact of the occupation upon religious life in Germany we need to consider those who were most closely involved, most notably, the German priests. While the role of the churches and their members during the Third Reich has been controversially discussed for decades,[3] there is little disagreement among scholars about the Christian clergy's role in the period following the Second World War. According to a wide-ranging historiographical consensus, the Christian churches – especially the Catholic Church – were the only institutions to survive National Socialism in working order, were regarded by the Allies as key partners for reconstruction and democratization, and consequently quickly took over a range of important sociopolitical functions in occupied Germany.[4]

Closer investigation, however, reveals a major research gap. First, this broader narrative has become so commonplace that it is mostly alluded to in passing but hardly ever corroborated by evidence. Second, in the few available studies that do go into detail, it is almost exclusively the role and attitude of high-ranking Church dignitaries (such as the bishops and the pope) that are taken into account and simplistically equated with 'the' Catholic Church in its entirety.[5] By contrast, the history of the Church at the grassroots level of parishes and local priests has been mostly ignored by historians.[6] Thus, apart from the occasional claim that priests had a major influence on the occupiers' appointment of new mayors, the role of the parish clergy has been largely neglected in works on the early post-war period.[7]

Figure 13.1 Archbishop Conrad Gröber in Walldürn, 1947 (photo by Peter Nagel; courtesy: Archives of the Archbishopric of Freiburg, EAF Nb 8/151).

This is all the more surprising as in 1945 Catholic priests were still accepted by many Germans as influential authorities and had a significant impact on public opinion in their parishes, especially in rural Catholic areas.[8] After the collapse of the German government and the immediate ban of Nazi organizations, they were often the only figures of authority left at the local level to whom Germans could turn for consolation and guidance. After two and a half years of occupation, the intelligence department of the French police in Württemberg therefore came to the conclusion that particularly in the countryside, the Catholic priests were omnipotent: 'The priest is practically the chief of the community ... "The priest said it, therefore it is true!" is the general view'.[9] This social position made them natural contact persons for the Allies, who were looking for German social intermediaries through which to interact with the population and collect information about local conditions.

The following chapter analyses the role of the Catholic clergy as a local elite and some aspects of their mentalities, interests and actions in 1945 by looking at their responses to the German defeat and occupation and their interactions with the occupiers. It explores the priests' perception of French and American troops, how their image of the Allies was formed, their role as social intermediaries in the local context and their personal motivation. My analysis of these questions relies primarily on nearly 400 reports by Catholic parish priests from the Archdiocese of Freiburg in southwest Germany, a diocese covering a territory that transcended the zonal boundaries established by the Allies and was occupied by French troops in the south and by American troops in the north.[10] On 17 May 1945, only nine days after the German surrender, Freiburg's Archbishop Conrad Gröber[11] asked his clergy to submit reports about the last weeks of the war and the first weeks of occupation.

This led to the production of almost one thousand reports, submitted mostly in the summer of 1945 by nearly every Catholic parish in this large archdiocese, which comprised a population of around 2.6 million people, 1.6 million of which were Catholic.[12] The unusually high number of reports and the large geographical area covered make these letters an invaluable source for exploring the German clergy's perception of the events that were unfolding before them in the immediate post-war period.[13]

The priests' perception of the occupation and the occupiers

When the war ended, the clergy's feelings, like those of many Germans, seem to have been dominated by what one might describe as 'sad relief'. Despite the impact of the war and their general reservations against National Socialism, the Catholic priests, many of whom had fought in the First World War, were politically conservative, held staunchly patriotic views and were deeply troubled by their country's total defeat. At the same time, they were relieved because they no longer had to fear Allied air strikes or the Nazis' arbitrary measures against the Church.

To be sure, the attitudes of the Catholic clergy and the Nazis had overlapped in some areas, such as the fight against Bolshevism, and priests rarely engaged in active resistance.[14] In their post-war reports, however, the clerics from the Archdiocese of Freiburg depicted National Socialism as an ideology contrary to the teachings of the Catholic Church and as a threat to the free practice of religion. Time and again, the reports described the key elements of the Third Reich as 'godlessness'[15] and 'anti-clericalism';[16] other components of National Socialism seemed barely worth mentioning. This was in line with the widespread notion within the Catholic milieu that National Socialism was, in the end, just another consequence of the moral disorientation of the modern world caused by the secularization of society, collectivism and the general acceleration of life[17] – or, as one priest complained, by how 'humanity has been chased into a really tremendous speed – railway, bicycle, car, aeroplane, V1, 2, atomic bomb, marching … boxing, football, sports of all sorts, dancing and God-knows-what – just not a single minute of quiet in the world any more to think and recollect oneself!'[18] These assumptions corresponded with broader attitudes within the German episcopate and among Catholic journalists that sidestepped questions of guilt for the crimes of National Socialism and presented the Catholic Church and its followers as a unified stronghold of resistance against the Nazi regime.[19]

During April and the early days of May 1945, relief from the dual threats of Nazi rule and, just as importantly for the clerics, from the constant fear of air strikes, came to the archdiocese in the form of Allied soldiers. The expression used almost unanimously by the clergy to describe their own feelings and those of their communities in the face of occupation was that of *aufatmen*: the proverbial 'sigh of relief'. Accordingly, almost all German attempts at defence were condemned not only as futile, but above all as 'foolish if not criminal', given the danger they entailed for civilians.[20]

This did not mean, however, that the priests welcomed the Allied soldiers with open arms. Even though some clergymen used the controversial word 'liberation'[21] or called the Allies 'the saviour from the Nazi yoke',[22] almost all of them initially kept a critical distance from the occupiers, motivated by feelings of national loyalty. A day before the occupation of the Black Forest village of Buchenbach, for example, the local priest reminded his congregation from the pulpit 'to meet the approaching enemy with manly earnestness, as it befits every Christian who loves his fatherland even in the greatest adversity'.[23] Generally speaking, the priests were thankful that the occupiers brought the cessation of hostilities and returned to Germans their religious freedoms. At the same time, however, they also regarded the occupiers as 'the enemy' that had brought 'our troops' and the clergy's beloved fatherland to its knees. These deeply conflicted feelings found apt expression in one priest's short remark: 'The Americans are here: we are glad they are here, but we are not rejoicing!'[24]

While such general attitudes were widespread, the clergy's verdict on the occupiers differed from parish to parish, ranging from downright condemnation to more ambivalent and nuanced judgements, including explicit praise for the occupiers' well-mannered and cooperative behaviour. American soldiers were often described as 'decent', 'correct' and 'disciplined', and were generally greeted with much more sympathy than the French. A close study of the reports indicates that the priests' differing perceptions of the French and American troops were determined by at least four factors: their understanding of how many German women were raped by Allied soldiers; the frequency of lawful and unlawful acts that caused hardship for the German population; the occupiers' religious policies and their local implementation; and the Allied soldiers' personal religiosity.

Within the area examined, the priests reported around 1,700 cases of sexual violence.[25] Fewer than 5 per cent were recorded as occurring in the US Zone, which suggests that the priests probably under-reported sexual crimes committed by Americans. Reports from cities that were first occupied by French troops and then handed over to the Americans confirmed the priests' impression that many more rapes were committed by the French. One cleric from Karlsruhe, for instance, wrote: 'Lootings and rapes were the order of the day. 115 cases of rape have become known … Ever since the Americans have been occupying Karlsruhe, no case of looting or rape has become known'.[26] Aside from sexual and other violence, most priests also complained about offences against private property. While requisitioning, together with eviction in the US Zone and billeting in the French Zone, were generally seen as hard but unavoidable consequences of the war, arbitrary theft and robbery committed by individual soldiers had a significantly negative impact on the priests' perception of the occupiers. This, too, was recorded much more frequently in the French Zone.[27] The negative first impression of the French occupiers even prompted some clerics to draw direct comparisons with the 'terror' of the Nazis.[28]

The priests' records are in line with numerous other local reports that depict the French soldiers as more violent than their American counterparts.[29] Historical research, too, has long been dominated by the image of the French Zone as a mere 'colony of exploitation'. Although this simplistic image has been corrected by more recent studies,[30] the amount of corroborating evidence from contemporary German sources suggests that the priests' accusations against the French occupiers were at least partly justified. Nonetheless, this widespread German perception was undoubtedly distorted by preconceived notions about 'the French' and 'the Americans'. The image of France in Germany had been dominated by the narrative of the 'hereditary enmity' between Germans and French, the humiliating experience of the lost First World War and the collective memory of the ensuing French occupation of the Rhineland.[31] At the same time, Nazi propaganda had failed to completely reshape a positive German image of the United States, influenced by centuries of transatlantic exchange, together with the attraction of more recent American popular culture.[32]

In addition to generally favouring Americans and denigrating the French, the priests tended to racialize sexual violence against German women as a crime typically committed by soldiers of colour. Although more recent research has shown that both white and black French and American troops committed numerous acts of sexual violence,[33] the priests often blamed French colonial and African American soldiers for all cases of rape, with frequent references to a presumed causal connection between skin colour and sexual crime. One priest, for instance, noted: 'Now groups of black soldiers marched through, who, thank God, did not stop to rest here. Therefore there were no rapes here from this side'.[34] In other cases, clergymen made more subtle causal connections between skin colour and sexual crime, writing, for instance: 'although the village was occupied for weeks, also by coloured troops, rapes have not become known'.[35] This distorted perception was strongly related to the collective memory of the 'black shame' after the First World War, when French colonial troops stationed in the Rhineland had been discursively constructed as brutal, uncivilized sexual predators.[36]

As shown below, the clergy's attitude towards the occupiers was also shaped by broader Allied policies towards the Catholic Church and its practices, representatives and property. More generally, however, the priests were used to judging their fellow human beings by the quantity and quality of their public religious practice. For instance, they consistently portrayed particularly vicious Nazis as anti-religious, while often defending 'ordinary' party members by reference to their religiosity.[37] They applied the same logic to the occupiers: the more piety the latter displayed (mostly measured by the number of soldiers visiting church and their behaviour during mass), the more the priests were inclined to forget other points of criticism and view them favourably. Moreover, when the occupiers and the occupied observed shared religious practices and beliefs, such as when American soldiers handed out rosaries to German children in a small Catholic village, their common faith was conducive to mutual respect and understanding: the 'Other' quickly lost part of its otherness.[38] Several priests from both occupation zones reported that looting soldiers left religious objects such as paintings and crucifixes untouched, and spared houses that were recognizable as inhabited by Catholics.[39]

On the other hand, several priests made disparaging remarks about the religious attitude of Allied, and particularly French troops, sometimes deliberately using the occupiers' presumed lack of faith as a means to reassert their own moral legitimacy: Germany may have lost the war, but the occupiers' alleged ignorance of religion allowed the priests to feel morally superior. Complaining about the French soldiers' weak display of piety, one priest, for instance, remarked: 'I believe that the southern French bishop who has called for a prayer crusade for the Germans should first of all ask people to pray for the members of his own diocese!'[40]

That the priests almost exclusively reacted in such a way in areas occupied by the French, while often praising the predominantly Protestant Americans for their deep faith and regular church attendance, may to some extent be explained by fewer nationalist prejudices against the Americans and their perceived better conduct, but a shared faith and displays of piety seem generally to have been welcomed by the priests, regardless of denominational differences. Although France was an overwhelmingly Catholic (albeit officially secular) country, the *Première armée française* that occupied the area consisted of a conglomerate of different combat groups, including many Muslim colonial troops and also communist *Résistance* fighters.[41] Both of these groups were met with particular suspicion by the priests. It is notable, however, that in contrast to their scorn for the 'faithless knaves'[42] from metropolitan France, the clergy's discourse about the colonial troops, mostly lumped together as 'Moroccans', was dominated by racist, but not religious stereotypes; disparaging remarks about their mainly Muslim faith are hard to find. Some priests accused colonial soldiers of destroying Christian symbols,[43] but in general, their faith was not used to explain their behaviour. One cleric even wrote that the North African troops in his town 'were … popular with the population because of their friendliness, their decency and also their Mohammedan piety. Quite a few of us could have learned a lesson from the prayer exercises of the sons of the desert.'[44] A different faith, it seems, was still better than none at all.

Between cooperation and protest: How the priests interacted with the occupiers

The Catholic clergy's conflicted attitudes about German defeat had a significant impact on their interactions with the occupiers. Their feelings of loyalty towards the German nation mostly prevented them from forging close bonds with Allied soldiers. At the same time, however, they considered it their duty to avert further hardship for the population and make the transition to peace as smooth as possible. They were therefore prepared to cooperate as well as protest, whenever they considered it necessary. Archbishop Gröber, in two letters to his clergy anticipating the end of the war, had refrained from giving any instructions about the priests' appropriate conduct in the case of occupation, apart from ordering additional church services and prayers, and reminding them of their 'holy duty to unswervingly stay with the flock entrusted to them as a brave shepherd'.[45] As we will see, this allowed the parish priests to be flexible in their daily encounters with the Allies.

In some rare cases, priests wrote about their attempts to facilitate a peaceful occupation of their parishes, such as by crossing the enemy lines and reporting to the Allied troops that the German military had already left the area.[46] In their entirety, however, the priests' own accounts of the end of war do not corroborate the claim, made in various historical studies, that the clergy frequently played an important role in the peaceful surrender of their parishes.[47] Nevertheless, contacts between the occupying forces and the local clergy were usually established soon after the occupation, with many Allied commanders immediately visiting the parish houses and demanding information, such as the relative proportions of Protestants and Catholics in the local communities. The occupiers also asked many priests for recommendations for the replacement of Nazi mayors, local governments and civil servants.[48] In a few cases, clergymen were appointed by the Military Governments as interim mayors or temporarily took on leadership roles on their own initiative, seeking to fill the power vacuum that emerged at the local level.[49]

The official policy on the treatment of the German churches by the Allies was based on the US directive JCS 1143 and publicly announced by General Eisenhower in May 1945.[50] According to these guidelines, the German people had the right to practice religion freely as long as religious assemblies were not used for political purposes.[51] Although the Americans were aware of nationalist and anti-democratic tendencies among the clergy, they regarded the churches as important allies for the stabilization of German society. Accordingly, they generally treated them with goodwill and followed a strict policy of non-intervention in ecclesiastical matters.[52] In Württemberg-Baden, for example, 'it became the policy of the Religious Affairs Branch … to interfere with the work of the churches as little as possible … and to insist within the area as a whole, upon the most tolerant acceptance of religious freedom'.[53] The French, who had been promised their own occupation zone only in February 1945, had not made plans for a distinct religious policy and initially largely followed the US directives.[54] Yet due to their more frequent, though inconsistent[55] censorship of political sermons and pastoral letters as well as other restrictive measures,[56] mainly motivated by French security interests, the priests and the broader population generally perceived French religious policy as anti-clerical.[57]

In general, both the French and the Americans granted the Catholic Church several privileges during the initial period of the occupation that they did not extend to other institutions: church services were the only public assemblies permitted;[58] religious literature was allowed to be published much earlier than other writings;[59] and while schools were only reopened in the autumn of 1945, religious education was permitted immediately. This enabled the Catholic Church to take over a range of functions within different levels of society and gain not only a publicity lead, but also an organizational and political advantage over other institutions and social groups.

The clergy was well aware of the sympathetic American guidelines regarding the churches. One priest, for instance, noted rather happily that the French commander in his village 'accurately obeyed Eisenhauer's [*sic*] order that the accommodation of soldiers in the parish house is not allowed',[60] while the vicar general protested that a

Figure 13.2 An Allied soldier contemplates a ruined church in Cologne, 1945 (Getty Images).

French decree regarding religious education 'stands in stark contrast to Eisenhauer's [*sic*] guarantee … concerning free practice of religion'.[61] In most places, though, the clerics seem not to have had any reason to complain. Usually, they perceived the occupiers' attitude towards them and their institution as exceptionally respectful and benevolent. Some priests even mentioned their 'friendly relationship'[62] with Allied commanders or military chaplains, some of whom were accommodated in their parish houses. In contrast to regular residential homes, however, the occupiers largely exempted the priests' lodgings from house searches, requisitioning, looting, eviction and billeting. Sometimes, the Military Governments visibly placed the priests' homes under official protection by posting signs that read 'Off limits'[63] or 'Requisition interdite'.[64] Even in communities that suffered heavily from looting, the parish houses usually remained untouched. As the writer of an anonymous letter to Archbishop Gröber stressed, 'clergymen are the only officials who are somewhat protected against the excesses by virtue of their vestment'.[65] As we will see, this gave the priests a special social position that had a major impact on their interactions with the occupiers. The sacredness of churches was largely respected, too, and religious practice including church service, processions and religious education could once again unfold without hindrance. As one priest noted with relief, 'the occupation force does not interfere in church life, religious instruction etc., but lets us work freely in this field, for which we are already quite grateful after the conditions of the last decade'.[66]

In general, the French and American commanders seem to have followed official directives. There were exceptions, of course, especially in the French Zone. Some local commanders, for instance, were unable to keep their troops from pillaging parish houses. French soldiers might have been harder to control because, in contrast to their American allies, many of them had personally suffered under German occupation.[67] When one priest, for example, complained because the French had taken away his typewriter, he was told 'that German soldiers had done much worse, chased women and children into the streets and then burned the houses, and also that "as a cleric" I should be "above material things" '.[68] Another priest reported that in his village, the French troops declared that he, together with the mayor and the police officers, would be shot as hostages in case not everybody turned in their weapons or reported their party membership.[69]

Such exceptions from the generally favourable treatment of the Catholic Church and its clergy suggest that local commanders were able to act on their own initiative and, if they wished to do so, partly ignore official directives to treat the Catholic Church favourably. At the same time, however, there are also examples of officers who used their personal authority to tone down official measures they considered too strict. For instance, after the French Military Government had banned priests from giving religious lessons to children over ten years old, one well-meaning member of the local commander's office in Constance gave the vicar general 'the non-binding advice to call the religious education of older age groups "church service" '[70] and so evade the ban. The same strategy was also successfully applied in Karlsruhe.[71]

Especially during the first weeks of occupation, the American and French occupiers often relied on the clergy's support. For instance, local commanders enlisted the priests' services as intermediaries by asking them to announce Allied regulations concerning curfew hours or the surrender of weapons during church service. In Constance, after some official notices had been torn down, the priests agreed to read a declaration admonishing the population to preserve public peace and warning youths against further mischief.[72] Similarly, an American officer, admitting that he was aware of the risks of 'severe excesses through excessive drinking of alcohol, rape etc.', tried to use the local priest to enforce order and asked him 'to point out most urgently that all inhabitants, especially young girls, were expected to exercise the strongest restraint towards the soldiers'.[73]

Most clerics willingly complied with these requests, seeing their role as intermediaries as natural. In a report for the French Military Government, the priest of a village near Karlsruhe declared: 'We, the priests, we will always stay here to help, assist and comfort people. In case the authorities must complain about the population, we kindly ask to let us know, and we will do everything in our power to influence the population and to work on good terms with the authorities'.[74] However, when several

French commanders demanded that priests read from the pulpit a proclamation about the German massacre in Oradour-sur-Glane (10 June 1944), reminding the Germans of their guilt and contrasting the crime with the benevolence of the French occupiers,[75] reactions were mixed. While one priest obeyed 'so as not to cause more severe treatment of the population',[76] his colleague from a nearby village refused, justifying his decision with the ban on reading aloud in church anything not related to church matters. The French commander responded by publicly announcing 'that due to the lack of cooperation by the priest … the community would in future no longer be treated with cooperation' from his troops, such as helping to transport sick persons from the village to the nearest hospital at Sigmaringen.[77] This case illustrates the priests' difficult balancing act between cooperation with the occupiers, concern for their communities and loyalty to their official duties.

Apart from the priests' role as intermediaries during the initial period of occupation, both the French and the Americans also considered them potentially helpful in the re-education of the German population. This found its main expression in Allied support for the reactivation of Catholic youth groups, a policy from which the clergymen quickly tried to capitalize. Thus, in a letter to the Military Government, four priests in Constance pleaded for a shorter curfew by underlining the importance of their own educational work intended to 'counter the corruptive influence of Hitler Youth'.[78]

Soon, it was the priests who took the initiative in the communication between the occupiers and the clergy, primarily to call attention to problems of the occupation and present themselves as advocates for the interests of the German population. Especially in smaller villages, the priests were well informed about the local goings-on and were often confronted by crimes carried out by the occupiers such as by witnessing looting or acting as confidants for the victims of rapes, their relatives and local doctors. They reacted in different ways. Many opened up the clergy houses as night shelters for local women.[79] Some also described how they themselves came to the aid of harassed women, for instance, by calling Allied officers for help, in one case allegedly even by single-handedly disarming a French soldier. Writing about himself in the third person, one cleric boasted that 'with his vigorous appearance, prelate Dr. Föhr managed to chase the soldiers out of the house and even take the revolver off one of them, which, offering his apologies, he had to pick up at the clergy house the next morning'.[80] The most widespread reaction among the clergy, however, was to issue verbal and written complaints at the local headquarters, pleading for tighter controls by appealing to the commanders' sense of decency and justice.[81] In an impassioned letter to the local French commander, a cleric from Badenweiler, an idyllic health resort at the edge of the Black Forest, wrote:

> I know very well that the guilt account of the Germans under the National Socialist regime is very big. But I also know that the Allies have declared in the proclamations signed by General Eisenhower that they came 'as conquerors, but not as oppressors' … Didn't you come to put an end to injustice once and for all? If you want to exact vengeance, however: is violence and rape, mostly committed against innocent persons, the right way? … Herr Kommandant! Help immediately! Otherwise these methods will drive the population to desperation.[82]

It is noticeable that while all these clerical interventions were targeted at preventing further sexual violence, not a single priest mentioned any possible support for those women who had already been raped; on the contrary, the discourse in the reports was often one of trivialization or even victim blaming.[83]

As self-appointed intermediaries, many priests, according to an American report, took 'an active interest in the fate of their people who come under the Denazification rule'.[84] Similarly, priests supported German prisoners of war and internees, not only through pastoral care and food collections,[85] but also by appealing for the release of individual parishioners. Although the Allied commanders were often annoyed by the extent of the clergy's interference,[86] various accounts of prisoner releases in the clerical reports suggest that at the local level, the clergy's intervention could very well be rewarded with success. One priest, for instance, prided himself to have convinced the French *Capitaine* to set free about ten German soldiers and all forty to fifty members of the local *Volkssturm*;[87] another claimed to have achieved the symbolic release of fourteen political internees on the occasion of Bastille Day on 14 July 1945.[88] Admittedly, such reports must be taken with a grain of salt, given that the Catholic priests had an obvious interest in claiming such successes as their own achievements, which allowed them to portray themselves as protectors of the population.

Quite how much of the clerics' interaction with the occupiers was driven by a strategic agenda to broaden the social profile of the church, however, can only remain a matter of speculation. What the priests' reports do show is a feeling of pastoral responsibility towards their communities, with charity considered an integral part of pastoral care.[89] The priests did not take on this role unexpectedly: during the last months of war, the range of their activities had already grown in many places, for instance when they gave first aid after airstrikes, accommodated bombed-out parishioners, and collected food, clothing and money for them.[90] After the occupation, the priests further expanded their charity work. They intensified their donation campaigns for the homeless,[91] organized temporary housing space for those whose homes had been confiscated[92] and quickly turned into contact persons for all kinds of requests, from forwarding letters to helping with the search for missing persons.[93] Spiritual welfare was in similar demand: while the last years of war had already seen an increase in church attendance, the end of the war and the following period of hardship and uncertainty brought another (temporary) revival with full churches and high participation in processions and pilgrimages.[94]

The Catholic clergy under occupation: Local and long-term impact

Historians have hitherto paid little attention to the role of local representatives of the Catholic Church in the aftermath of the Second World War. Although in most cases the priests did not exercise a significant influence upon Allied commanders, they were a force not to be underestimated in the complex web of relationships between the occupiers and the occupied. The combination of the priests' status within local power structures, Allied directives that were sympathetic to the cause of the churches and the capacity of religion to function as a bridge between occupiers and occupied allowed them to position themselves as 'first responders' and intermediaries in their communities. The priests might only have been able to react to the occupiers and were far from setting the agenda, but through personal encounters and interventions in their parishes they could be of vital importance for people threatened by rape, imprisonment or loss of property. In many places, thus, the local clergy seem to have been essential for the making of stability in the immediate post-war period. This was so not only through their advocacy for the population and their role as intermediaries, but also through their proactive welfare activities and, as a 'bearer of continuity',[95] their commitment to the maintenance of an orderly church life, which offered their communities familiar rituals and a sense of normality in times of upheaval.

Since the First World War, the Catholic clergy had increasingly been reduced to the ecclesiastical sphere and lost a number of its former functions, a development that had reached its climax during the Third Reich.[96] In the immediate post-war period, this trend came to a momentary halt and was even reversed. Of course, that reversal was only temporary: as German authorities took up their work again, relief organizations were founded and parties, trade unions and other interest groups rebuilt, the priest, once again, became one of various local actors competing for social influence and power. The 'religious spring' of the immediate post-war period, too, seemed to come to an end as soon as the worst hardships had been overcome, as expressed in many a disillusioned clergyman's complaint.[97] Yet in a long-term perspective, church attendance in West Germany still remained surprisingly stable until the mid-1960s,[98] and the churches remained important voices in German society, intervening frequently in political, social and cultural debates.[99] This is also true for the Catholic parish priest who, at least for some years and particularly in rural areas, retained his traditional standing as an important local authority. In January 1948, the French *délégué* of Kreis Neustadt reported: 'The influence of the clergy remains crucial. On the local level, it manifests itself in the political, social, cultural area through political parties, relief organizations, youth movements'.[100]

The situation of change and uncertainty after the Allied occupation of Germany enabled the Catholic parish priests to temporarily pause a long-term trend of decreasing social significance. By positioning themselves as spiritual mentors, practical helpers and persistent conflict managers, they managed to fill a gap that had been opened by the downfall of the Nazi regime, its governmental structures and its ruling ideology. This made a lasting impression on large parts of German society, lending greater legitimacy to the Catholic clergy's intervention in public life and underlining their claim as a force to be reckoned with.

Notes

1 Armin Nolzen, 'Nationalsozialismus und Christentum: Konfessionsgeschichtliche Befunde zur NSDAP', in *Zerstrittene 'Volksgemeinschaft': Glaube, Konfession und Religion im Nationalsozialismus*, ed. Manfred Gailus and Armin Nolzen (Göttingen: Vandenhoeck & Ruprecht, 2011), 154.

2 Antonius Liedhegener, 'Nachkriegszeit (1945–1960)', in *Handbuch der Religionsgeschichte im deutschsprachigen Raum: 20. Jahrhundert – Epochen und Themen*, ed. Volkhard Krech and Lucian Hölscher, vol. 1 (Paderborn: Schöningh, 2015), 141.

3 For a brief but balanced overview, see Olaf Blaschke, *Die Kirchen und der Nationalsozialismus* (Stuttgart: Reclam, 2014).

4 For a recent example, see Kristian Buchna, *Ein klerikales Jahrzehnt? Kirche, Konfession und Politik in der Bundesrepublik während der 1950er Jahre* (Baden-Baden: Nomos, 2014), 37–41.

5 See, for example, Konrad Repgen, 'Die Erfahrung des Dritten Reiches und das Selbstverständnis der deutschen Katholiken nach 1945', in *Die Zeit nach 1945 als Thema kirchlicher Zeitgeschichte: Referate der internationalen Tagung in Hünigen/ Bern (Schweiz) 1985*, ed. Victor Conzemius, Martin Greschat and Hermann Kocher (Göttingen: Vandenhoeck & Ruprecht, 1988).

6 Damian van Melis, '"Strengthened and Purified Through Ordeal by Fire": Ecclesiastical Triumphalism in the Ruins of Europe', in *Life after Death: Approaches to a Cultural and Social History of Europe during the 1940s and 1950s*, ed. Richard Bessel and Dirk Schumann (Cambridge: Cambridge University Press, 2003), 232.

7 The only notable exception is Werner K. Blessing, '"Deutschland in Not, wir im Glauben …": Kirche und Kirchenvolk in einer katholischen Region 1933–1949', in *Von Stalingrad zur Währungsreform: Zur Sozialgeschichte des Umbruchs in Deutschland*, ed. Martin Broszat, Klaus-Dietmar Henke and Hans Woller, 3rd edn (München: Oldenbourg, 1990).

8 Ibid., 109.

9 'Le curé est pratiquement le chef de la commune … "Le prêtre l'a dit, donc c'est vrai!" est la pensée générale', in 'Etude sur les religions dans le Wurtemberg', November 1947, Tübingen, cited in Hellmuth Auerbach, 'Französische Besatzungsmacht, Katholische Kirche und CDU in Württemberg-Hohenzollern 1945–1947: Schwierigkeiten mit Bildungsreform und Demokratisierung', in *Von der Besatzungszeit zur deutsch-französischen Kooperation*, ed. Joseph Jurt (Freiburg: Rombach, 1993), 143–6.

10 Berichte über Kriegsereignisse, 1945–7, EAF (Erzbischöfliches Archiv Freiburg) B2-35/147–52. One hundred and eleven of these reports are from the deaneries of Tauberbischofsheim, Walldürn, Lauda, Mannheim and Heidelberg, occupied by American troops; 267 are from the deaneries of Bretten, Karlsruhe, Pforzheim, Achern, Offenburg, Waldkirch, Freiburg, Breisach, Neuenburg, Wiesental, Konstanz, Sigmaringen and Veringen, occupied by French troops. (Karlsruhe and Pforzheim were later allocated to the US Zone.) The reports were written in German; all following quotations are my translation.

11 A controversial figure, Gröber was a supporting member of the SS before distancing himself from and publicly criticizing National Socialism from the mid-1930s onwards, while still occasionally using anti-Semitic language in public sermons. See www.freiburg.de/pb/site/Freiburg/get/params_E-874030221/1028363/Strassennamen_Abschlussbericht.pdf (accessed 5 June 2017).

12 Erzbischöfliches Ordinariat Freiburg, Runderlass an die Dekanate, 17 May 1945, EAF B2-35/152. Martin Furtwängler, 'Bevölkerungsstatistik', in *Handbuch der baden-württembergischen Geschichte. Band 5. Wirtschafts- und Sozialgeschichte seit 1918 – Übersichten und Materialien – Gesamtregister*, ed. Hansmartin Schwarzmaier and Gerhard Taddey (Stuttgart: Klett-Cotta, 2007).

13 While the documents from Freiburg constitute by far the most extensive collection, some other bishops commissioned similar reports. For an overview, see Thomas Forstner, 'Zu Entstehung und Einordnung der Berichte katholischer Geistlicher über das Kriegsende 1945 und den Einmarsch der Amerikaner', in *Das Ende des Zweiten Weltkriegs im Erzbistum München und Freising: Die Kriegs- und Einmarschberichte im Archiv des Erzbistums München und Freising*, ed. Peter Pfister (Regensburg: Schnell + Steiner, 2005).

14 For the archdiocese of Freiburg, see Roland Weis, *Würden und Bürden: Katholische Kirche im Nationalsozialismus* (Freiburg: Rombach, 1994).

15 Report by Joseph Fischer, Weingarten bei Offenburg, 1 February 1947, EAF B2-35/150.

16 Report by Wilhelm Fertig, Ersingen, 29 July 1945, EAF B2-35/150.

17 See Liedhegener, 'Nachkriegszeit (1945–1960)', 136, 139.

18 Fridolin Mayer, Pfarrchronik von Bombach vom 15. April 1942 – 15. April 1947, EAF PfA Bombach 341.

19 See Christian Schmidtmann, '"Fragestellungen der Gegenwart mit Vorgängen der Vergangenheit beantworten": Deutungen der Rolle von Kirche und Katholiken in Nationalsozialismus und Krieg vom Kriegsende bis in die 1960er Jahre', in *Zwischen Kriegs- und Diktaturerfahrung: Katholizismus und Protestantismus in der Nachkriegszeit*, ed. Andreas Holzem and Christoph Holzapfel (Stuttgart: Kohlhammer, 2005), 167–201. Kristine Fischer-Hupe, 'Der Kirchenkampfdiskurs nach 1945: Wie katholische und evangelische Theologen in der frühen Nachkriegszeit über den Kirchenkampf der Jahre 1933–1945 sprachen', *Kirchliche Zeitgeschichte* 15, no. 2 (2002): 467–75.

20 Report by Joseph Fischer, Weingarten bei Offenburg, 1 February 1947, EAF B2-35/150.

21 See, for example, the report by Hermann Stiefvater, Inzlingen, 22 August 1945, EAF B2-35/151.

22 Report by Kilian Gehrig, Boxtal am Main, 8 March 1946, EAF B2-35/150.

23 Report by Albert Seifried, Buchenbach, 29 July 1945, EAF B2-35/147.

24 'Die Ami sind da: wir sind froh, dass sie da sind, aber wir freuen uns nicht, dass sie da sind!', report by Joseph Merk, Leutershausen, 8 March 1946, EAF B2-35/148.

25 This number is a modest estimate and does not include the numerous cases of attempted rape.

26 Report by Erwin Ostermann, Karlsruhe Heilig Geist (Daxlanden), 10 April 1946, EAF B2-35/148. On sexual violence committed by the occupiers, see Silke Satjukow and Rainer Gries, *'Bankerte!': Besatzungskinder in Deutschland nach 1945* (Frankfurt and New York: Campus, 2015), 34–7, 42–6, and Miriam Gebhardt, *Als die Soldaten kamen: Die Vergewaltigung deutscher Frauen am Ende des Zweiten Weltkriegs* (München: DVA, 2015).

27 Seventy-five per cent of the reports from the French Zone, but only forty per cent of the reports from the US Zone, mention property crime.

28 See, for example, the letter by Adolf Futterer, Achkarren, to Archbishop Gröber, 10 May 1945, EAF B2-1945/2101.

29 Klaus-Dietmar Henke, 'Politik der Widersprüche: Zur Charakteristik der französischen Militärregierung in Deutschland nach dem Zweiten Weltkrieg', *Vierteljahrshefte für Zeitgeschichte* 30, no. 3 (1982), 505.

30 Edgar Wolfrum, 'Die französische Politik im besetzten Deutschland: Neue Forschungen, alte Klischees, vernachlässigte Fragen', in *Deutsche und*

Franzosen im zusammenwachsenden Europa 1945–2000, ed. Kurt Hochstuhl (Stuttgart: Kohlhammer, 2003), 61–72.

31 Edgar Wolfrum, 'Die Rache der Franzosen', *Die Zeit*, 18 May 2000. Available online: www.zeit.de/2000/21/Die_Rache_der_Franzosen (accessed 5 June 2017); Satjukow and Gries, *'Bankerte!'*, 32–4.

32 Petra Goedde, *GIs and Germans: Culture, Gender, and Foreign Relations, 1945–1949* (New Haven and London: Yale University Press, 2003), 24–40; Klaus-Dietmar Henke, *Die amerikanische Besetzung Deutschlands*, 2nd edn (München: Oldenbourg, 1995), 87–93.

33 Satjukow and Gries, *'Bankerte!'*, 34–7; J. Robert Lilly, *Taken by Force: Rape and American GIs in Europe during World War II* (Basingstoke and New York: Palgrave Macmillan, 2007), 117–8.

34 Report by Bernhard Kaiser, Tiergarten, undated, EAF B2-35/147.

35 Report by Edmund Beuchert, Krensheim, 17 July 1945, EAF B2-35/149.

36 See, for example, Christian Koller, 'Enemy Images: Race and Gender Stereotypes in the Discussion on Colonial Troops. A Franco-German Comparison, 1914–1923', in *Home/Front: The Military, War and Gender in Twentieth-Century Germany*, ed. Karen Hagemann and Stefanie Schüler-Springorum (Oxford and New York: Berg, 2002); Julia Roos, 'Nationalism, Racism and Propaganda in Early Weimar Germany: Contradictions in the Campaign against the "Black Horror on the Rhine"', *German History* 30, no. 1 (2012). Johannes Kuber, '"Frivolous Broads" and the "Black Menace": The Catholic Clergy's Perception of Victims and Perpetrators of Sexual Violence in Occupied Germany, 1945', in *War and Sexual Violence:* ed. Sarah K. Danielsson and Frank Jacob (Paderborn: Schöningh, forthcoming).

37 Johannes Kuber, 'Die Pfarrer und das Kriegsende: Kontinuitäten im Denken und Handeln katholischer Geistlicher 1945', in *Deutsche Kontinuitäten? Beiträge zur interdisziplinären studentischen Tagung an der Universität Hannover im März 2016*, ed. Lisa Dopke et al. (Hannover: scius, 2016), 39–40.

38 Report by Wilhelm Schumacher, Dittwar, 8 March 1946, EAF B2-35/150.

39 See, for example, the reports by Theodor Renner, Unterbalbach, after 18 June 1945, EAF B2-35/149, or Ernst Grieshaber, Karlsruhe Heilig Kreuz, 1 May 1946, EAF B2-35/148.

40 Report by Josef Siebold, St. Märgen, 16 May 1945, EAF B2-35/147. He probably alluded to bishop Pierre-Marie Théas of Montauban, co-founder of a 'Crusade of Prayers for the Conversion of Germany', a campaign that soon came to prominence under the name of Pax Christi.

41 F. Roy Willis, *The French in Germany 1945–49* (Stanford: Stanford University Press, 1962), 67–70.

42 'Glaubenslose Gesellen', report by unidentified priest, Hausen am Andelsbach, 11 March 1946, EAF B2-35/151.

43 See, for example, the report by Andreas Seiler, Oberwinden, 18 June 1945, EAF B2-35/151.

44 Heinrich Roth, Waldkircher Erlebnisse aus den Kriegsjahren, EAF Na45-5. Published in Heinrich A. Roth, 'Waldkircher Erlebnisse aus den Kriegsjahren 1939–1945: Erinnerungen eines Seelsorgers', in *Heinrich A. Roth: Waldkircher Erlebnisse aus den Kriegsjahren 1939–1945*, ed. Josef Dosch and Wolfram Wette (Waldkirch: Waldkircher Verlag, 1989), 43.

45 Archbishop Conrad Gröber to his clergy, Freiburg, 5 and 9 April 1945, EAF B2-NS/147.

46 See, for example, the report by Joseph Zapf, Ödsbach (Renchtal), 26 March 1946, EAF B2-35/150.

47 See, for example, Edgar Wolfrum, 'Von der Gewaltherrschaft zur Besatzungsherrschaft: Politisches Handeln und Erfahrungen im Jahr 1945', *Zeitschrift für die Geschichte des Oberrheins* 143 (1995): 379; Peter Fäßler, '"Umkehr durch Verchristlichung": Die Kirchen als Ordnungsfaktor', in *Krisenjahre und Aufbruchszeit: Alltag und Politik im französisch besetzten Baden 1945–1949* (München: Oldenbourg, 1996), 75; Karl-Heinz Braun, *Die Erzdiözese Freiburg: Von der Gründung bis zur Gegenwart* (Strasbourg: Ed. du Signe, 1995), 38.

48 See, for example, the report by Eugen Mogg, Hofweier, 3 September 1945, EAF B2-35/150.

49 See, for example, the reports by Max Ruh, Oberkirch, 14 May 1945, EAF B2-35/150; by Franz Schmal, Todtnauberg, 18 March 1946, EAF B2-35/151; and by Viktor Burkart, Einhart, 30 June 1945, EAF B2-35/151.

50 Cited in Armin Boyens, 'Die Kirchenpolitik der amerikanischen Besatzungsmacht in Deutschland von 1944 bis 1946', in Armin Boyens et al., *Kirchen in der Nachkriegszeit: Vier zeitgeschichtliche Beiträge* (Göttingen: Vandenhoeck & Ruprecht, 1979), 68–9.

51 'Bekanntmachung des Obersten Befehlshabers der alliierten Streitkräfte, General Eisenhower', published in the Allied news bulletin *Die Mitteilungen* 4 (5 May 1945), cited in Gerhard Besier, Jörg Thierfelder and Ralf Tyra (eds), *Kirche nach der Kapitulation. Vol. 1: Die Allianz zwischen Genf, Stuttgart und Bethel* (Stuttgart, Berlin and Köln: Kohlhammer, 1989), 87.

52 See Michael Lingk, *Amerikanische Besatzer und deutsche Kirchen 1944–1948: Eine Studie zu Kirchenbild und Kirchenpolitik der amerikanischen Besatzungsmacht unter besonderer Berücksichtigung Württemberg-Badens und Bayerns* (Tübingen: UVT, 1996), 33–75.

53 History of Military Government in Land Wuerttemberg-Baden to 30 June 1946, OMGUS (National Archives Washington, RG 260/OMGUS, microfiches in Hauptstaatsarchiv Stuttgart) 12/1-1/32/4 of 5.

54 See Jörg Thierfelder, 'Die Kirchenpolitik der Besatzungsmacht Frankreich und die Situation der evangelischen Kirche in der französischen Zone', *Kirchliche Zeitgeschichte* 2, no. 1 (1989): 221–5.

55 The sermons of Archbishop Gröber, for instance, were often authorized despite their highly political character so as not to antagonize the population of Baden. See Christophe Baginski, *Frankreichs Kirchenpolitik im besetzten Deutschland 1945–1949* (Mainz: Gesellschaft für Mittelrheinische Kirchengeschichte, 2001), 34–43, 127–58.

56 For example, catechetical instruction was only allowed for pupils up to 10 years old (Gouvernement Militaire, Détachement de Bade, Note de service, 14 May 1945, Archives de l'occupation française en Allemagne et en Autriche, Archives diplomatiques, La Courneuve [hereafter AOFAA] 1BAD-2037), and a popular catechism was prohibited due to its allegedly one-sided paragraph on the French Revolution (Gouvernement Militaire, Détachement de Bade, Général Morlière, 6 June 1945, AOFAA 1BAD-2034).

57 Christophe Baginski has shown, however, that in reality the French occupiers respected the pre-existing structures of the German churches and did not seek to introduce the French model of laicism. See Baginski, *Frankreichs Kirchenpolitik*, 55–94, 263–6.

58 Hermann Ehmer, 'Der Neubeginn in Parteien, Gewerkschaften und Kirchen', in *Der deutsche Südwesten zur Stunde Null: Zusammenbruch und Neuanfang im Jahr 1945 in Dokumenten und Bildern*, ed. Hansmartin Schwarzmaier (Karlsruhe: Generallandesarchiv Karlsruhe, 1975), 210.

59 Doris von der Brelie-Lewien, *Katholische Zeitschriften in den Westzonen 1945–1949: Ein Beitrag zur politischen Kultur der Nachkriegszeit* (Göttingen: Muster-Schmidt, 1986), 9–10, 48–9. In Freiburg, for instance, the first post-war issue of the official gazette of the archdiocese was published on 12 May 1945, while the daily newspaper *Freiburger Nachrichten* was only authorized in September; see Heiko Haumann, 'Sorge ums Überleben – wenig Zeit für Politik: Probleme der ersten Nachkriegsjahre in Freiburg', in *Alltagsnot und politischer Wiederaufbau: Zur Geschichte Freiburgs und Südbadens in den ersten Jahren nach dem 2. Weltkrieg*, ed. Arbeitskreis Regionalgeschichte Freiburg (Freiburg: Schillinger, 1986), 13–4.

60 Report by Christoph Eichenlaub, Ebersweier, 13 December 1946, EAF B2-35/150.

61 Vicar general Adolf Rösch to Erzbischöfliches Ordinariat Freiburg, Aussprache mit Major d'Alouzier, Stadtkommandant in Konstanz am 2. Juni 1945, EAF B2-35/149.

62 See, for example, the reports by Richard Anton Hund, Waldkirch, undated, EAF B2-35/151, or by Anton Schmid, Schutterwald, 8 January 1947, EAF B2-35/150.

63 Report by Franz Rudolf, Heidelberg St. Vitus, 7 March 1946, EAF B2-35/148.

64 Report by Nikolaus Maier, Gammertingen, 20 June 1945, EAF B2-35/151.

65 Anonymous letter to Archbishop Conrad Gröber, Badenweiler, 1 May 1945, EAF Nb8/110.

66 Report by Karl Gnädinger, Schopfheim, 3 June 1945, EAF B2-35/151.

67 Satjukow and Gries, *'Bankerte!'*, 34–5.

68 Report by Alban Hils, Feldkirch, 11 November 1945, EAF B2-35/149.

69 Report by Hermann König, Todtnau, 11 July 1945, EAF B2-35/151.

70 Vicar general Adolf Rösch to Erzbischöfliches Ordinariat Freiburg, Aussprache mit Major d'Alouzier, Stadtkommandant in Konstanz am 2. Juni 1945, EAF B2-35/149.

71 Report by Albert Rüde, dean of Karlsruhe, Karlsruhe, 8 August 1945, EAF B2-35/148.

72 Vicar general Adolf Rösch to Erzbischöfliches Ordinariat Freiburg, Die Besetzung der Stadt Konstanz, Konstanz, 19 May 1945, EAF B2-35/149.

73 Report by Lorenz Henn, Bretzingen, 20 June 1945, EAF B2-35/151.

74 Karl Riehle, Rapport sur la situation de l'église catholique à Malsch, 1 May 1945, AOFAA 1BAD-2034.

75 Oradour was frequently brought up by the French occupiers as a symbol of German terror; see Marc Hillel, *L'occupation française en Allemagne 1945–1949* (Paris: Balland, 1983), 125–6.

76 Joseph Rager, dean of Veringen, to Erzbischöfliches Ordinariat Freiburg, Hettingen, 22 June 1945, EAF B2-35/142.

77 Report by Leo Rager, Feldhausen, 11 July 1945, EAF B2-35/151.

78 Ernst Kuenzer, Joseph Dreher, Hermann Steiert, and Franz Huber to the Military Government of Constance, 22 May 1945, AOFAA 1BAD-2045.

79 See, for example, the reports by Hermann Ruf, Dekanat Achern, 13 July 1945, EAF B2-35/147, or by Franz Schurr, Wöschbach, 31 July 1945, EAF B2-35/147.

80 Report by Ernst Föhr, Freiburg St. Johann, 24 June 1945, EAF B2-35/148.

81 See, for example, the reports by Ernst Grieshaber, Karlsruhe Heilig-Kreuz (Knielingen), 1 May 1946, EAF B2-35/148, or by Franz Herr, Seebach (Baden), 10 June 1945, EAF B2-35/147.

82 Clemens Tetzlaff to the French commander, Badenweiler, 30 April 1945, EAF B2-1945/2107 (emphasis in original).
83 See Kuber, 'The Catholic Clergy's Perception of Victims and Perpetrators of Sexual Violence in Occupied Germany'.
84 OMGWB, Education and Cultural Relations Division, weekly report, 22 September 1945, OMGUS 12/87-3/8/7 of 8.
85 See, for example, the report by Josef Siebold, St. Märgen, 16 May 1945, EAF B2-35/147.
86 See, for example, Gouvernement Militaire, Détachement d'Emmendingen, Capitaine Chervy, Rapport hebdomadaire, 28 May–5 June 1945 and 4–10 June 1945, AOFAA 1BAD-128.
87 Report by Franz Schmal, Todtnauberg, 18 March 1946, EAF B2-35/151.
88 Report by Ernst Kuenzer, Konstanz Münsterpfarrei, after 20 January 1946, EAF B2-35/149.
89 See, for example, the minutes of the autumn conference 1945 of the deanery of Endingen, 26 November 1945, EAF Dek. Endingen 128.
90 Kuber, 'Die Pfarrer und das Kriegsende', 25–6.
91 See, for example, the report by Max Kölmel, Königshofen, summer/autumn 1945, EAF B2-35/149.
92 See, for example, the report by Richard Dold, Karlsruhe St. Bonifatius, 19 June 1945, EAF B2-35/148.
93 See, for example, Pfarrarchiv Lörrach St. Bonifatius, Schrank A, Vermisste/Krieg, and Schrank 1, Zeugnisse und Empfehlungen.
94 See, for example, the report by Erich Weick, Tauberbischofsheim, 3 June 1945, EAF B2-35/150.
95 Thomas Großbölting, *Der verlorene Himmel: Glaube in Deutschland seit 1945* (Göttingen: Vandenhoeck & Ruprecht, 2013), 73.
96 Thomas Forstner, *Priester in Zeiten des Umbruchs: Identität und Lebenswelt des katholischen Pfarrklerus in Oberbayern 1918 bis 1945* (Göttingen: Vandenhoeck & Ruprecht, 2014), 290–2.
97 See, for example, report by Joseph Ludwig Saur, Heidelberg St. Raphael, 11 March 1946, EAF B2-35/148.
98 Detlef Pollack and Gergely Rosta, *Religion in der Moderne: Ein internationaler Vergleich* (Frankfurt and New York: Campus 2015), 119.
99 Ibid., 158–9.
100 Gouvernement Militaire, Cercle de Neustadt, Délégué Vittecoq, Rapport annuel 1947, AOFAA 1BAD-243.

14

From Denazification to Renazification? West German Government Officials after 1945

Dominik Rigoll

At the Potsdam Conference in July and August 1945, Clement Attlee, Josef Stalin and Harry S. Truman decided not only that 'all members of the Nazi Party who have been more than nominal participants in its activities and all other persons hostile to Allied purposes' were to be 'removed from public and semi-public office, and from positions of responsibility in important private undertakings'. They also agreed that those dismissed were to 'be replaced by persons who, by their political and moral qualities, are deemed capable of assisting in developing genuine democratic institutions in Germany'.[1] Even though the Potsdam Agreement thus explicitly linked denazification and the recruitment of trustworthy staff as two sides of the same coin, we still know relatively little about how staff were recruited by the Western Allies to replace those 'denazified'. To be sure, when historians started working on the post-war occupation of Germany in the 1970s, they did not ignore that, at least in the West German case, *Säuberung* (purge) and *Rehabilitierung* (rehabilitation) went hand in hand.[2] However, apart from a very few exceptions,[3] this first generation of historians did not analyse in a systematic way when, how and why people were recruited as officials in local, regional and, from 1949, federal administrations. In particular, they rarely confronted the question of how high-ranking civil servants who had worked throughout the Third Reich were able to return to public office, often in their original positions, after having been formally 'denazified'.

The historiographical situation started to change in the 1990s, with the publication of major studies on the 'politics of amnesty and integration' in the early Federal Republic.[4] More recently, much attention has been given to the question of how many 'former Nazis' were recruited to work in West German government agencies after 1949, with investigations undertaken by academic research groups formed as a result of political pressure.[5] This chapter is based on data collected by a research group exploring the Ministry of the Interior.[6] It focuses on the career paths of the forty-one highest-ranking ministry officials (*leitende Beamte*) and the two ministers who were active during the first two years of the Ministry's existence, in 1949 and 1950. At first sight this might appear to be a very narrow sample, considering that about 55,000 civil servants were discharged in 1945 pending denazification proceedings. By 1950, when denazification had officially ended, less than 2,000 of those dismissed in the preceding five years were still considered as too compromised to hold public office. Around 53,000 'denazified' civilians (and 190,000 professional soldiers) were then entitled to return into the civil service or to draw a pension, though not all of them chose to do so.[7]

On the other hand, however, the careers of the two ministers and forty-one government officials can reveal a great deal about the recruitment of staff not only after 1949, but also after 1945. Their personnel files not only inform us about their careers in the Third Reich and the Federal Republic, but also about what happened during the military occupation: When, by whom and for what reasons were they hired into the civil service? Were they considered to be anti-Nazi or were they 'denazified' before re-recruitment? To what extent could the Allies influence an official's career? Did various groups of individuals follow distinct career patterns? Did the widespread relaxation of denazification during the Cold War – the 'depurge'[8] – lead to a 'renazification' of the civil service, as claimed at the time by some German and Allied observers?[9]

Recent studies on the staff of West German state institutions generally do not address these questions systematically. They are mostly interested in the extent of involvement or 'incrimination' (*Belastung*) members of staff had with the Nazi regime, and in how the federal institutions dealt with the past of their officials.[10] This focus is problematic. First, many of the political quarrels of the early Federal Republic can only be understood against the backdrop of the military occupation after 1945, which, when the High Commissioners replaced the Military Governors in 1949, had created a legacy of international, political, social, economic and cultural structures and institutions which influenced the future development of the two German states, to a degree comparable with the legacy of the Third Reich or the Weimar Republic. Second, when the Federal Republic of Germany (FRG) was founded in 1949, most of the key political, social and cultural positions were filled by so called '45ers': people who had been hired into administrative or political positions immediately after the war by the Allies or by Germans working under Allied supervision, either after a very brief period of exclusion from office in 1945 or having experienced no exclusion at all.

In the Ministry of the Interior, half of the top positions in 1949 and 1950 were occupied by 45ers – among them the first two ministers, the state secretary (the most senior civil servant in the ministry) and five out of six heads of department. At the same time, however, only a tiny minority were former opponents or victims of Nazism. Most of them had already been high-ranking civil servants between 1933 and 1945. Yet, for reasons presented in the second part of this chapter, the Allies considered them, in the words of the Potsdam Agreement of 1945, as 'capable of assisting in developing genuine democratic institutions'. In the first part of this chapter, I will explore how the question of the 45ers has been treated in public debate, in the social sciences and in the historiography, both in West Germany and the United States, before the issue disappeared from public view in the 1980s and 1990s. This disappearance is astonishing and needs further explanation. The 45ers played a crucial political role not only during the period of occupation and direct Allied rule before the founding of the Federal

Republic in 1949, but also during the time of limited German sovereignty under the Occupation Statute between 1949 and 1955.

The original 45ers: The story of a disappearance

In the late 1940s and the early 1950s, a heated debate took place in the Federal Republic about the Allied occupation and its political legacy. A majority of the population had a negative opinion about the years between the end of the war and the start of the 'economic miracle' in the 1950s, after the so-called Korea boom. In 1951, according to public opinion polls, 80 per cent of West Germans considered the period from 1945 to 1948 as 'the worst of the century', closely followed by the years 1949–51. The year 1937, on the other hand, was widely thought of as an *annus mirabilis*, despite the fact that by then democratic parties had already been banned for four years and racist laws prohibiting marriages between Jews and Germans had recently been passed.[11] Besides the majority that held this view, there was, however, a minority who identified with some of the Allied reform projects, such as thorough denazification, democratization and long-term demilitarization. When these projects were gradually relaxed after the beginning of the Cold War and then largely abandoned by Konrad Adenauer's conservative coalition governments, critics, especially on the Left, but also among liberal and conservative opponents to Nazism, complained about the 'restoration' of the power of social elite groups, such as industrialists, businessmen, bourgeois politicians, army officers and senior civil servants who, in many cases, had contributed to the rise of Hitler and supported the Nazi regime throughout the war.[12]

Another critical expression used at the time was that of the 'renazification' (*Renazifizierung*) of German politics and society. Eugen Kogon, a Buchenwald survivor and author of the US-sponsored study *Der SS-Staat*, warned in 1947 that an unjust denazification would lead to 'renazification' as it encouraged anti-Allied resentments among the population.[13] Gustav Heinemann, who would later become the first Federal Minister of the Interior, also used the term in 1947 to warn about the dangers inherent in an excessive denazification and claimed that denazification should instead focus on the removal of 'dangerous National Socialists'.[14] In 1949, the American occupiers also started to talk of 'renazification', although in this case they feared it might arise from insufficient or incomplete denazification. James Newman, the Land Commissioner of Hesse, noted that in his region as well as elsewhere in the FRG, 'Nationalism is resurgent', and that 'many former Nazis are being restored to or turning to positions of power, influence and prominence in government, politics and the more public professional and industrial fields', and consequently:

> The combination of the two trends above mentioned, based, as they seem to be, upon the fostering of the old traditions, customs and teachings in and of institutions, antedating Hitler and the Third Reich, still remaining in Germany, creates an atmosphere and a fertile field in which National Socialism or some

> similar autocratic, dictatorial and undemocratic regime could find life and come into being and control.[15]

Both Heinemann and Newman agreed that, to minimize the risk of renazification, at least the key political positions should be kept free from returning functional elites. From the beginning of the occupation, these positions were generally occupied by so-called *45er* or *1945er.* These were the names given to those who had been appointed to public office by the Allies or under Allied supervision in the immediate post-war period, in order to replace the approximately 55,000 officials who had lost their positions. As will be shown in the second part of this chapter, however, while some of those appointed by the Allies had opposed or had been dismissed by the Nazis, many others among the so-called 45ers had themselves held senior public office throughout the Third Reich. In the German language, labelling a political group with a specific year is quite common. For instance, the failed German revolutionaries of 1848 are called *48er* and the students who participated in the protests of 1968 are commonly labelled *68er*. However, in contrast to the 68ers and the bourgeois revolutionaries of 1848, the 45ers were a very diverse group, including people of all ages, and from different political and social backgrounds, from communist workers to reactionary bourgeois. Women were also to a limited extent present among the 45ers, although very few were employed as civil servants in 1949.[16]

In the political discourse of the 1950s and 1960s, the name '45er' could have different meanings. In a very general way, the term implied not only that someone actively participated in post-war reconstruction after 1945, but also that they had a more or less strong anti-Nazi record. In this vein, '45er' could designate politicians who had started their career before 1933 and had a comeback in 1945, after having been excluded from power by the Nazis. In his book *Männer, die für uns begannen* (*Men Who Started for Us*), published in 1961, the journalist Hermann Behr, for example, used the term '45er' to describe leading political figures of the immediate post-war period such as Konrad Adenauer, Kurt Schumacher and Theodor Heuss.[17] A second meaning of the term was broader, focusing not so much on elected politicians but more on state institutions and on society in general, describing civil servants, managers and journalists who were permitted by the Allies to retain their existing positions in 1945 or quickly re-employed. Eugen Kogon, for example, who in the meantime had been appointed professor of political sciences in Darmstadt, had not only politicians in mind, but also these functional elites, when in 1954 he famously lamented the 'defeat of the 45ers' by the '131ers'.[18]

In terms of career paths, the 131ers may indeed be seen as the antagonists of the 45ers. In the words of the political scientist Lewis J. Edinger, the 131ers were the 'totalitarian elite' to which the 45ers represented a 'political antithesis' and 'potential counter-elite'.[19] This does not imply that all 131ers had been convinced Nazis, but that, broadly speaking, they had been part of the Nazi regime through their work as government officials or in the military. Initially, the term designated people purged from the state or military apparatus in 1945 and granted the right to return if not to their previous post to their previous rank, thanks to Article 131 of the Basic Law of 1949 and the federal '131er-law' of 1951. More generally, however, the term 131er designated former functional elites of the Third Reich who, after a relatively short period of professional and political marginalization, managed to start a second career thanks to the Cold War and the founding of two antagonistic German states.

If Kogon is considered today as a moral founding father of the FRG, he was a political and intellectual outsider when he first wrote about the marginalization of 45ers by 131ers and the 'restoration' of functional elites who had served under the Nazis. In the early post-war period, the whole subject was highly taboo and it was not a coincidence that, when social scientists discovered the problem of elite change and continuity after 1945, Edinger, the first scholar to publish on the topic, was the son of a German-Jewish refugee who had fled to the United States after 1933. In 1965, Wolfgang Zapf, a young sociologist, continued Edinger's work by publishing a study on *Wandlungen der deutschen Elite*. Zapf came from West Germany, but as a student and later research assistant of Ralf Dahrendorf, he was strongly influenced by US and British liberal elite theory. Dahrendorf, in turn, cited Zapf's results in his famous book on *Gesellschaft und Demokratie in Deutschland* (Society and Democracy in Germany) published in 1968.[20] Zapf's chapter on the occupation period is tellingly entitled *Männer, die für uns begannen*, recycling the phrase coined by Behr in his 1960 book.[21] Edinger, Zapf and Dahrendorf, however, did not find many imitators. One of the reasons for this might be that their topic – continuity and change among West German elites – became highly controversial again in the late 1960s, when the so-called brown books were published in the German Democratic Republic (GDR) 'outing' hundreds of civil servants in the FRG as 'Fascists', while left-wing students, sometimes with the help of 45ers, rediscovered 'restoration' as a catchword for anti-establishment mobilization.[22]

West German historiography discovered the 45ers in the 1970s, when Lutz Niethammer's innovative research on denazification in Bavaria again highlighted the question of continuity and change in West German society. Niethammer argued that in the war's immediate aftermath, the 45ers obtained their positions in local and regional administrations as a direct result of Allied intervention. The origins of this post-war elite, he contended, lay in the *Auftragsverwaltungen*, the administrations working under the direct orders of the occupiers at 'the intermediate level of the occupation dictatorship' (*Besatzungsdiktatur*). According to Niethammer, the 45ers became 'pacemakers of westernization' (*Schrittmacher der Orientierung der Westdeutschen auf das westliche System*), reorienting politics and society towards a liberal constitution and preparing and legitimizing integration within an international order dominated by the United States. In doing so, the 45ers had to walk a tightrope between democratic protest against 'restoration' of the old order, by those who considered they had been 'liberated' from the Nazis at the end of the war, and nationalist protest from those who considered they had been defeated. Because Niethammer believed that the 45ers played such a decisive role both during the occupation and in the early Federal Republic, he suggested that historians should not only undertake a quantitative analysis of the group ('names, positions, background'), but also shift their focus from the national to the transnational perspective, by analysing 'the interaction between occupied and occupiers'.[23]

This call to action never materialized. In the 1980s and 1990s, historians published many studies on the occupation period, but they did not follow Niethammer's transnational agenda. The idea that there once was a group called 45ers seems to have been largely forgotten. In the 2000s, the old meaning of the label was superseded by a completely different definition, namely that 45ers were an entire 'generation' born in the 1920s who, just like the original 45ers, became pacemakers of democratization but took on this role only much later, in the 1960s and 1970s.[24] Many historians today do not associate the term any more with the Allied occupation, but rather with the 'Hitler Youth Generation' (*HJ-Generation*).[25] In this chapter, I propose to follow Niethammer's proposal and reconsider the role, the influence and the legacy of what one might describe as the 'original' 45ers, taking the officials at the top of the Ministry of the Interior as an example (see Figure 14.1).

The occupation as decelerator and stepping stone: Career patterns

In 1950, forty-three officials occupied the fifty-six highest positions in the ministry, with some officials occupying two positions at the same time. These numbers include the two ministers, who succeeded each other in October 1950, the ministers' personal advisers, the heads of department (*Abteilungsleiter*), the division chiefs (*Referatsleiter*) and one administrative assistant (*Sachbearbeiter*). Twenty-two of these forty-three officials, a little over half, can be considered as 45ers. They had been recruited into public office between 1945 and March 1946, when in the US Zone, the 'Law for Liberation from National Socialism and Militarism' gradually placed responsibility for denazification proceedings (and thus for the recruitment of officials) in German hands. Most 45ers were 'not affected' (*nicht betroffen*) by the Law for Liberation (*Befreiungsgesetz*) because, after having been screened by the Allies in 1945, they were either considered to be anti-Nazis or, alternatively, not especially compromised by their membership of Nazi organizations or through being part of the functional elites of the Reich. A minority was recruited while their denazification was still pending. Hans Globke, for example, co-author of the official commentary to the 1935 Racial Laws and Adenauer's State Secretary until 1963, was only 'denazified' in 1947, after having worked as an advisor to the Western Allies in 1945 and then becoming city treasurer of Aachen in 1946.[26] By 1950, the 45ers had not only 'proven' themselves in the eyes of the Allies, but had also generally regained the rank they had held in 1945, or even obtained higher positions. Their further career was therefore not dependent on the '131er law', which regulated the recruitment and promotion of officials and professional soldiers who had been dismissed from office in 1945 and not reinstated until later, often in more junior positions.

The twenty-two 45ers who were part of the senior staff of the Ministry of the Interior are highlighted in grey on the chart shown as Figure 14.1. They occupied twenty-seven of fifty-six positions. At the very top level – including ministers, state secretaries and heads of department – there is a high proportion of 45ers, occupying eight out of nine positions. At the lower levels – among the divisional chiefs and the minister's personal

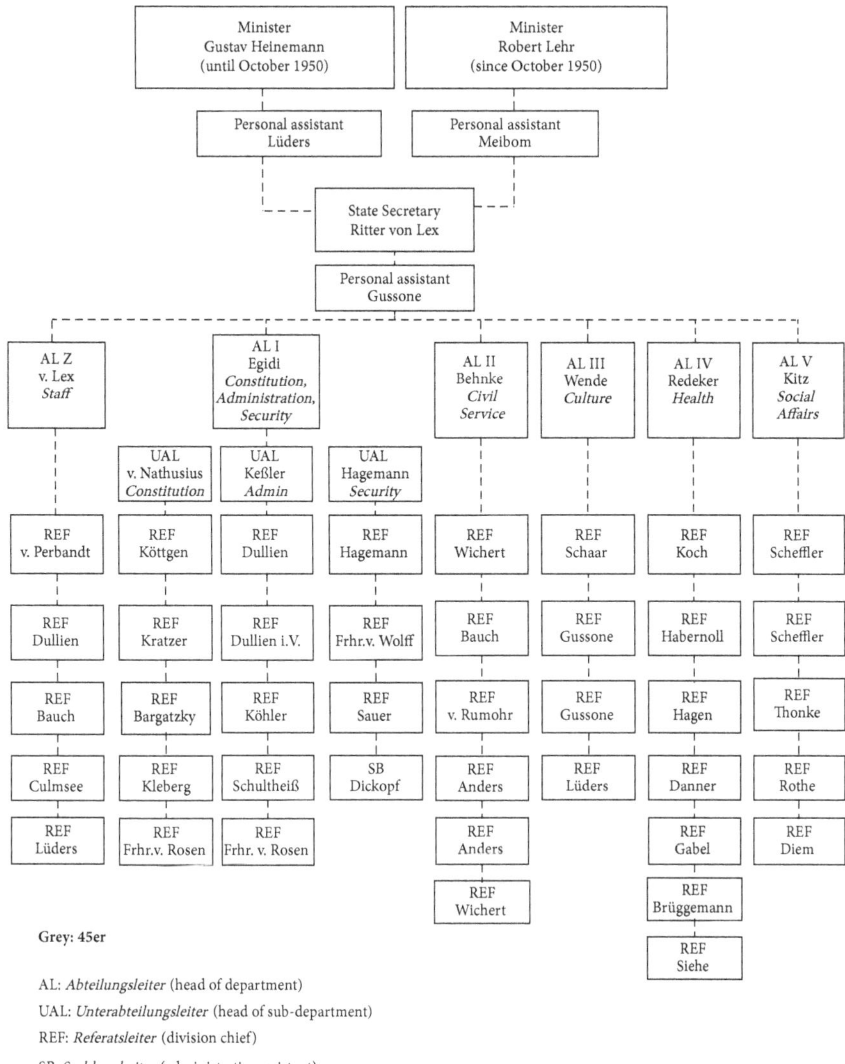

Figure 14.1 Organizational chart of the Federal Ministry of the Interior, 1950.[27]

advisers – their share drops to sixteen out of forty-one. Here, individuals who had been dismissed from public office in 1945 and re-recruited only much later, between March 1946 and May 1950, held most positions. For these 131ers, the occupation functioned as a career decelerator, which also explains why there was only one 131er among the heads of department out of a total of six, and none among the other top positions.

How did the 45ers reach the positions they held in 1950? The two ministers, Gustav Heinemann (1899–1976) and Robert Lehr (1883–1956), were 45ers of the 'Adenauer type'. Like the first Chancellor of the Federal Republic, who was appointed mayor

Figure 14.2 Gustav Heinemann helping with restoration work as mayor of Essen, 1946–9 (courtesy: German Press Agency).

(*Oberbürgermeister*) of Cologne by the Americans in 1945, both Heinemann and Lehr started their post-war careers by being selected by the occupiers for top positions at local or regional level. Before and during the war Heinemann was a commercial lawyer and director of the *Rheinische Stahlwerke*, a large steel, mining and engineering company.

Until 1933 he was a member of a small protestant religious party and a supporter of the Weimar Republic, but not actively engaged in politics. In 1945, the British appointed him deputy mayor (*Bürgermeister*) of Essen. He had to fill out a questionnaire (*Fragebogen*), but had little difficulty convincing the occupiers that he had opposed the Nazi regime due to his Christian and liberal principles: 'During the *Kirchenkampf* (struggle in the church against NSDAP influences)', Heinemann wrote in English, 'I held numerous speeches and lectures at synods and at meetings of the parish'. At one of the synods 'the Deutsche Christen (Nazi-Christians) made tumultuous attacks against me when I declared that even decrees given out by Hitler would not sanction the violation of church law by the Nazis. This lecture was published in the printed report on this synod page 34/35'. He also added that a 'number of pamphlets … are bearing my name'.[28] This appears to have convinced the British occupiers of his anti-Nazi credentials, with the responsible British Public Safety Officer concluding that Heinemann 'may retain present position' as a lawyer and director of a coalmine, without undergoing extensive denazification measures.[29] From 1946 to 1949, Heinemann was elected mayor (*Oberbürgermeister*) of Essen. From 1948, he served as Minister of Justice of North Rhine-Westphalia. In addition, he was an active member of the Council of the evangelical church in Germany.[30]

Lehr's post-war career started when the British appointed him First Minister (*Oberpräsident*) of the North Rhine region in 1945. A year later, he was elected to the regional parliament of the newly created *Land* of North Rhine-Westphalia, where he became leader of the Christian Democratic Union (CDU) group. Like Adenauer, Lehr was an elected member of the Parliamentary Council, the constituent assembly that drafted and adopted the Federal Republic's constitution.[31] Lehr had been mayor of the city of Düsseldorf from 1924 until he was dismissed by the Nazis in 1933, and a leading politician in the *Deutschnationale Volkspartei*, a reactionary and anti-Semitic party. Despite their political differences, Lehr and Heinemann had much in common. Like Adenauer, they were both founding members of the CDU in 1945. They were also trained lawyers and had administrative skills and experience – Lehr as long-time mayor, Heinemann as director of a mining company. After 1933, their opposition to the new regime was evident, albeit not to the same extent. In contrast to Heinemann, Lehr had not spoken out in open opposition to the Nazis, but after having been arrested briefly in 1933, he retreated into private life and held no official position.

Heinemann's personal assistant, Carl Lüders (1913–2006), represents a rare type of 45er: the defector or *Überläufer*. Lüders was fourteen years younger than his superior and had started his career only after 1933. He also trained as a lawyer but, as a convinced National Socialist, he had been a Hitler Youth functionary responsible for ideological training. In 1939, he joined the army. Captured by the British in 1944, he switched sides and collaborated by delivering BBC broadcasts targeting German soldiers. He returned to Germany in October 1945. In Hamburg, the British first appointed him assistant judge, then president of the Central Legal Office *(Zentraljustizamt)* of the British Zone. He also worked as a journalist at *Nordwestdeutscher Rundfunk*, the main German broadcasting corporation for the British Zone.[32]

Lüders claimed that the German Army had initiated a legal case against him because of his defection (*Wehrkraftzersetzung*). It is not clear from the available sources whether he was actually prosecuted; he was in Britain, not in Germany at the time, so there would have been little point in doing so. But what is perhaps more significant is that he evidently wanted people to think that he had been persecuted by the Nazis. Being a 45er was therefore not only about specific experiences before 1945. Rather, it was also about publicly claiming and expressing certain allegiances and commitments after the war.[33] The 45ers represented a group of people with shared experiences, who together formed an imagined – and to a certain extend invented – community. People chose to be part of the group or to leave it, and for that purpose they could modify their CVs in accordance with their respective choices. Adenauer was a 45er, too. Yet, like many other 45ers in important positions, he was careful not to style himself in this fashion. In post-war western Germany an individual's personal past was in many respects a taboo subject. This was true not only for those who had supported the Nazis, but also for those who were regarded, or regarded themselves, as anti-Nazis. Talking too much about the past might threaten Germany's democratic new beginning. As Heinemann put it in May 1950: 'If we start throwing accusations around, we won't get anywhere'.[34]

A third group of 45ers were senior civil servants of what one could describe as the 'Hans Globke type'. In 1950, they represented the most important group at the top of the ministry – both in terms of numbers (nine out of forty-three), and in terms of influence: Hans Ritter von Lex, Hans Egidi, Erich Wende, Wilhelm Kitz, Max Hagemann, Sklode von Perbandt, Walter Bargatzky, Karl Sauer and Herbert Freiherr von Wolff. They held almost all key positions in the second rank behind the minister, including that of State Secretary, five of the six posts of heads of department, one of the three heads of sub-departments, and all positions of Public Security division chiefs.[35] As in Globke's case, which remains highly controversial,[36] the war and post-war careers of these officials were more ambivalent than those of Heinemann, Lehr and Lüders. Two of them (Bargatzky and von Wolff) had joined the Nazi party, but later argued (more or less convincingly) that they had been close to the military opposition. The others, like Globke, had never joined the NSDAP. Egidi, von Lex, Wende and Sauer had been close to national liberal or Catholic parties before 1933. Like Globke, they had also all remained high-ranking civil servants between 1933 and 1945. As such, they were an integral part of the Nazi regime and faced automatic dismissal in 1945. Very quickly after the war, however, they were re-recruited by the occupiers. This owed much to their professional expertise which was in great demand during the period of reconstruction. At the same time, their return into office was only possible because the occupiers were prepared to trust people like them who declared repeatedly that they had not been 'real Nazis' at all, merely 'apolitical officials'. Egidi, von Lex and Wende were classified by the occupiers as 'not affected' (*nicht betroffen)* by denazification and so never formally assessed. Kitz, Bargatzky, Hagemann, Sauer and von Wolff, were only subjected to a denazification procedure much later, when criteria were far less strict than they were in 1945 and early 1946.

Perhaps the most interesting – and certainly the most influential – member of this third group was Hans Ritter von Lex. Much like Globke, who headed the Chancellor's Office until Adenauer's retirement in 1963, von Lex dominated the Ministry of the Interior until his own retirement in 1960, serving three different ministers over the years. Like Globke, von Lex was involved in all important personnel and security decisions as well as in negotiations with the Allies.[37] Also like Globke, von Lex had been a high-ranking civil servant in the Ministry of the Interior of the Reich and had some skeletons in his closet. In 1936, he had been responsible for the organization of the Olympic Games, helping to construct a façade that would hide what was happening in Germany, namely the persecution of political opponents and Jews. Earlier, in March 1933, von Lex had met with Hitler and the Nazi Minister of the Interior, Wilhelm Frick, to discuss an alliance between von Lex's Bavarian Peoples Party (BVP) and the NSDAP. After the meeting, he wrote down a record of his conversation with Hitler which illustrates some of his broader attitudes. In particular, von Lex noted how he had assured the Führer that

> The Bavarian Peoples Party agrees that Marxism should be destroyed, but this must be done in ways that conform to Christian moral law. As regards Communism … the Bavarian Peoples Party can accept to the greatest possible extent whatever is proposed [by the Nazi Party]. Liberating the German people

> from this contamination through the application of the strictest methods has been the joint demand in all patriotically minded circles. Social Democracy [on the other hand] is a strand of Marxism against which one should apply less of a strategy of physical extermination, but rather use spiritual measures to ensure its defeat.[38]

Like Globke, Hans Ritter von Lex was arrested in 1945 – and quickly transferred to the Ministerial Collecting Center (MCC), where the British and the Americans 'exploit[ed] German ministerial personnel and documents' in a joint operation with the codename 'Goldcup'.[39] At the MCC, Ritter von Lex wrote studies on federalism, the democratization of the administration and denazification.[40] He did not, however, stay long at the MCC as he was needed to head up the newly established Ministry of the Interior in the State of Bavaria. Von Lex was personally known to the Prime Minister (*Ministerpräsident*) of the *Land*, Fritz Schäffer, who had been appointed in 1945 by the Americans but was dismissed shortly afterwards on account of alleged Nazi sympathies. As a US Military Government official explained to his superiors, von Lex had been the object

> of a widespread search for some weeks. The position of Minister of the Interior has been held vacant pending the results of the search for it can only be successfully handled by a person of von Lex's qualifications. It is requested that facilities be placed at the disposal of von Lex to permit him to reach Munich, that he may take up the duties of this important post with the least possible delay.[41]

There were a number of obstacles though. The first problem, according to another US official, was that von Lex was committed at Goldcup to work with the British as well as with the Americans. Still, the official continued, the 'primary objective' was 'to get the man'.[42] While the British apparently did not object to his removal, when Schäffer tried to install von Lex as his Minister of the Interior, social democrats and communists opposed the nomination of this 'notorious reactionary' (*berüchtigter Reaktionär*).[43] Some weeks later, Schäffer himself was relieved of his post by General Eisenhower for having hired too many former Nazis. (Between 1949 and 1957, Schäffer served, however, as the first Federal Minister of Finance and helped organize the reinstatement of the 131ers in the ministry.) Von Lex, on the other hand, was not dismissed in 1946, but continued to play an important role despite being relegated to the second rank at the Bavarian Ministry of the Interior. In 1949, Adenauer appointed a commission presided by Heinemann and Schäffer, in which Globke and von Lex wrote recommendations setting out who should be employed at the federal ministries. The commission recommended von Lex as the first State Secretary of the newly formed Federal Ministry of the Interior.[44] Like Globke and many other former Nazi officials who had been in close contact with the Americans since 1945, he continued to advocate a policy favouring the return of dismissed officials into the government bureaucracy, while painting a nightmarish scenario if too many opponents of Nazism, namely social democrats and communists, were recruited in their place.[45] Long before the Cold War had started, these conservative 45ers exploited anti-Communist and

Figure 14.3 Hans Ritter von Lex (second from right) at the tenth anniversary parade of the *Bundesgrenzschutz* (German Federal Border Guard), 1961 (courtesy: German Federal Archives).

conservative prejudices among the Allied officials they dealt with, not least in order to secure their own future in the German civil and military services.

In some way or another, this was also true for a fourth group of 45ers, namely officials with special technical skills. In the Ministry of the Interior, one can find them in the Department for Public Health: Franz Redeker, Friedrich Koch, Arnold Habernoll, Wilhelm Hagen, Heinrich Danner, Bernward Gabel, Konrad Brüggemann and Kurt Siehe. They could continue working in 1945 with even less trouble than von Lex because the Allies considered their professions 'apolitical'. Hans Redeker, for instance, head of the public health department until 1953, was recruited in 1945 to restore the health care system in the British Zone, even though – or probably because – this tuberculosis expert had been a senior official in the Berlin Police until 1945.[46]

The fifth and last group of 45ers that can be identified are civil servants who were forced to retire during the Third Reich and then resumed their career in 1945. Wilhelm von Nathusius, for example, occupied one of the three posts of heads of sub-departments; these were important posts, but certainly no top positions.[47] As a social democrat, he was forced to retire in 1933 as chief administrative officer of a district (*Landrat*). He worked for an insurance agency until 1945. After the war, he entered the administration of the Soviet Zone for some months but then fled to the US Zone in

1946 where he entered the Hessian Ministry of Agriculture, eventually becoming the mayor of Wiesbaden in 1948. Similarly, Ernst Wichert, who had joined the NSDAP in 1933, was forced to retire in 1939 after having married the ex-wife of a Jew. In January 1946, he was able to rejoin the civil service as an official in the provincial government of Westphalia in the British Zone, before being appointed to the Federal Ministry of the Interior in 1949.

Paul Dickopf, finally, represents a special, yet noteworthy case. His name did not appear on the official ministerial organizational chart of senior civil servants in 1950 because, technically, he was only an administrative assistant (*Sachbearbeiter*). Dickopf had also been recruited in 1945, though in Switzerland, rather than in Germany. He had been working as a spy there, employed by the *Abwehr,* one of the secret intelligence services of the German military. In 1939, after completing his training as a police detective, he had briefly joined the SD, the secret intelligence service of the SS. In 1945, the Office of Strategic Services (OSS), the US military secret service responsible for covert anti-Nazi operations in Europe during the war, recruited him as an agent. The OSS station chief in Switzerland at the time was Allen W. Dulles, later appointed director of the US Central Intelligence Agency (CIA) and the brother of John Foster Dulles, US Secretary of State from 1953 to 1959. Like von Lex, Dickopf wrote reports and studies for his new employers, in particular on issues of internal security.[48] In the 1960s, he became one of the central figures of the West German security state, both as president of the Federal Criminal Police Office and as a CIA agent.[49]

Although Dickopf was recruited in 1945, he was no 45er. Rather, he can be considered as a security official of the Gehlen type. Reinhard Gehlen was a *Wehrmacht* top spy whom the OSS recruited together with hundreds of his comrades in the post-war period, even though – or rather because – many had played a crucial role in the war of destruction against the USSR and had fought against the Resistance in western Europe. In 1948, even though Dickopf was formally 'denazified' and the Americans supported him with certificates (*Persilscheine*), he was rejected when he applied for a position as a police criminal investigation officer in Hesse, because of his former SS membership. To the annoyance of his American liaison officer, Heinemann hesitated to hire him for a position in the Federal Ministry of the Interior in 1949.[50] When Ritter von Lex finally informed Dickopf about his recruitment as *Sachbearbeiter* in May 1950, the State Secretary stressed that all future remunerations or promotions would depend on the planned '131er law'.[51]

Conclusion and outlook

While the process of denazification in Western Germany has been studied extensively by historians, its counterpart and logical continuation, the recruitment of trustworthy staff to work in local, regional and state administrations in the early post-war period, has remained largely unexplored until very recently. To be sure, in the 1950s and 1960s, at a time when certain aspects of the occupation period were still a taboo subject in Germany, a small number of intellectuals and social scientists started to research a group of people whom they called 'the men who started for us' (*Männer, die für uns begannen*), sometimes using the terms 'anti-totalitarian counter-elite' or '45ers' to describe them. In the 1970s, the historian Lutz Niethammer claimed that the '45ers' should be studied both from a quantitative and qualitative perspective, because in his view they had been the 'pacemakers' of democracy building in the immediate post-war era. Niethammer was certainly correct, at least to some extent. Politicians considered today as founding fathers of the Federal Republic (and, it should be noted, of Austria too)[52] were mostly 45ers, including Konrad Adenauer, Willy Brandt, Gustav Heinemann and many others. The 'Mothers of the Basic Law' were also part of this counter-elite put in place during the early days of the occupation, such as Helene Wessel, Helene Weber, Elisabeth Selbert and Frieda Nadig.[53]

The example of Brandt, who died in 1992, shows that 45er politicians shaped the FRG not only in the 1950s and 1960s, but also continued to do so in the 1970s and in the 1980s. Can the same be said of the officials in the Ministry of the Interior who had been recruited in the immediate post-war period? When it comes to the ministry itself, the 45ers doubtlessly left an imprint in the first decade of its existence, with a peak in their influence in the early 1950s. Ritter von Lex stayed until 1960, when Josef Hölzl replaced him. Hölzl was a former municipal official and NSDAP *Blockleiter* who had been forced to leave his post and work in the construction industry between 1945 and 1947.[54] Most 45ers retired from office in the course of the 1950s. In contrast to the East German Ministry of the Interior, however, where a much younger cohort came into positions of responsibility from the early 1950s onwards, the western 45ers were generally replaced by 131ers who were now in their forties and fifties. In the first half of the 1960s, 131ers dominated the whole institution, providing the minister, the two state secretaries and all heads of department. Broadly speaking, their reign ended in the course of the 1970s, when they were replaced by members of the Hitler Youth generation.[55]

Does this mean that the FRG was 'renazified' in the 1950s and 1960s? To some extent this was certainly the case, as the denazification measures implemented in 1945 and 1946 were almost completely undone, especially, but not exclusively, in the civil service. Generally speaking, with the exception of former state secretaries or heads of department, most government officials of the Third Reich could continue in some way or another as civil servants. For this majority, whom contemporaries called '131ers' or *die Ehemaligen*, the occupation therefore represented only an interruption to their careers, not its end. A minority made up of the 45ers, by contrast, experienced the occupation as stepping stone that allowed them to continue and, in many cases progress further in their previous careers largely uninterrupted. By 1949, though already outnumbered by the 131ers, they still held many of the most senior positions, not least because of Allied support.

Considering that opponents and victims of Nazism were a minority even among these 45er officials, one can argue that the 'restoration in the civil service'[56] did not start with the Cold War, but rather began in the very first moments of the occupation. In the final analysis, the term restoration, or rather the notion of a 'restoration of the personnel',[57] seems better than the concept of 'renazification' for capturing what was occurring in western Germany and for analysing career patterns in the ministry. Clearly, the swift undoing of denazification did not lead to a Fourth Reich. As Edinger already pointed out in 1960, if the Western Allies were incorrect in claiming that there had been an 'artificial revolution' after 1945, in which a totalitarian elite was replaced by an anti-Nazi counter elite,[58] it is also true that generally 'no major Nazi figure', such as top functionaries of the NSDAP or senior officials involved in the Nazi apparatus of political and racial persecution, 'held an important public or private position' after 1945.[59] Furthermore, if victims of Nazism and proven anti-Nazis were a tiny minority in the state and military apparatus of the Federal Republic as well as among western Germany's economic and business elites, they were present in local and regional administrations, in the political parties and trade unions, especially among social democrats, socialists and communists, as well as in the media and in intellectual life. Heinemann is a case in point. On the one hand, he left the ministry in protest in 1950 because he feared that an all too quick 'remilitarization' would lead to a 'renazification'.[60] On the other hand, he continued to be politically active as member of the Bundestag and in civil society, defending socialists, pacifists and communists in court. When a new generation contributed to the electoral victories of Brandt's SPD, Heinemann even managed to regain public office between 1966 and 1974, first as Federal Minister of Justice, then as Federal President.

Assessing the legacy of the 45ers is not straightforward. Heinemann, for example, was a pacemaker of liberal democratization at different crucial junctures of the early Federal Republic. This included his role during reconstruction in the immediate post-war period, acting as a liberal spokesperson in the 'cold civil war'[61] during the 1950s, and finally as a senior politician in the period of broader democratization during the 1960s and 1970s.[62] This pattern, however, is not representative for all 45ers, as only few of them advocated liberal democracy. Lehr, for example, who succeeded Heinemann in 1950 as Minister of the Interior, was in favour of a very conservative, if not authoritarian democracy. Following Niethammer, one might argue that the 45ers were torn between the expectations of those who felt defeated in 1945 on the one hand, and those who felt liberated and hoped for comprehensive reforms on the other.[63] Of course, 45er politicians and officials who wanted to hold on to their posts and have a successful career had to take into account the 'defeated' who represented a majority among the German population. Some, such as Heinemann, however, were more open to the demands of the 'liberated' while others, such as Adenauer, paid more attention to the demands of the 'defeated' with the aim of stabilizing the FRG.

Given these circumstances, 45er officials of the 'Globke type' had a key role to play. As the case of Ritter von Lex demonstrates, from 1945 officials of this type tended to advocate a policy which, on the one hand, accepted Allied supremacy, while simultaneously seeking to diminish the impact of democratization, denazification, demilitarization and decartelization. Just like conservative politicians of the Adenauer type, these senior civil servants justified their actions by the need to secure the cooperation of former functional elites of the Third Reich, and so minimize the threat of social upheaval and communist revolution. In short, in their view, democratization had to be limited to protect democracy, or rather to shield a specific kind of authoritarian democracy in which communists were outlaws and liberals like Heinemann had to adapt to the ruling political order. Thus, German officials were anticipating the Cold War even before it reached a global scale. They did so not only out of ideological conviction, but also because the anti-Communist turn both in West Germany and among the Western Allies helped them to justify their own re-recruitment and disguise their failures before and after 1933. In doing so, they not only implemented Allied policies, but also strongly influenced them from the start of the occupation. At the same time, these 45ers functioned as role models for the 131ers, who after having been dismissed by the Allies in 1945 and not reinstated until 1949 or later, were in even greater need of legitimization. Until the 1960s, 45ers of the 'Globke type' in conjunction with the 131ers entirely dominated the state apparatus of the Federal Republic. Taken together, they certainly did not act, to use the phraseology of Till van Rahden, as 'clumsy democrats'[64], but rather as self-confident pacemakers of an authoritarian democracy, which shaped the political culture of the FRG throughout its existence, from the 1950s through to the 1970s and beyond.[65]

Notes

1 Foreign Relations of the United States, 1945, II, 1482.

2 See, for example, Lutz Niethammer, *Entnazifizierung in Bayern. Säuberung und Rehabilitierung unter amerikanischer Besatzung* (Frankfurt am Main: Fischer, 1972); Clemens Vollnhals (ed.), *Entnazifizierung. Politische Säuberung und Rehabilitierung in den vier Besatzungszonen 1945–1949* (Munich: dtv, 1991).

3 Falco Werkentin, *Die Restauration der deutschen Polizei: Innere Rüstung von 1945 bis zur Notstandsgesetzgebung* (Frankfurt am Main: Campus, 1984); Henric L. Wuermeling, *Die weiße Liste. Umbruch der politischen Kultur in Deutschland 1945* (Frankfurt am Main: Ullstein, 1988).

4 Norbert Frei, *Adenauer's Germany and the Nazi Past. The Politics of Amnesty and Integration* (New York: Columbia University Press, 2002); Ulrich Brochhagen, *Nach Nürnberg. Vergangenheitsbewältigung und Westintegration in der Ära Adenauer* (Berlin: Ullstein, 1999).

5 For an overview, see Christian Mentel and Niels Weise, *Die zentralen deutschen Behörden und der Nationalsozialismus. Stand und Perspektiven der Forschung* (Munich and Potsdam, 2016).

6 See the preliminary study: Frank Bösch and Andreas Wirsching (eds), *Die Nachkriegsgeschichte des Bundesministeriums des Innern (BMI) und des Ministeriums des Innern der DDR (MdI) hinsichtlich möglicher personeller und sachlicher Kontinuitäten zur Zeit des Nationalsozialismus* (Munich and Potsdam, 2015).

7 Statistische Berichte, Arb. Nr. VII/7/2, 10 June 1950, ed. Statistisches Amt des Vereinigten Wirtschaftsgebietes, 3–5; see also Frei, *Adenauer's Germany*, 69–71.

8 This term has been derived from the French term 'désépuration'. On the latter, see Alain Bancaud and Marc Olivier Baruch, 'Vers la désépuration? L'épuration devant la juridiction administrative, 1945–1970', in *Une poignée de misérables. L'épuration de la société française après la Seconde Guerre mondiale*, ed. Marc Olivier Baruch (Paris: Fayard, 2003), 480–512.

9 On the renazification problem, see Dominik Rigoll, *Staatsschutz in Westdeutschland. Von der Entnazifizierung zur Extremistenabwehr* (Göttingen: Wallstein, 2013), 33–75.

10 Dominik Rigoll, 'Das Gründungspersonal der Bonner Bundesbehörden. Über Karriere- und Rekrutierungsmuster nach 1945', *ZeitRäume* (2016): 55–72.

11 Michael Geyer, 'Der Kalte Krieg, die Deutschen und die Angst. Die westdeutsche Opposition gegen Wiederbewaffnung und Kernwaffen', in *Nachkrieg in Deutschland*, ed. Klaus Naumann (Hamburg: Hamburger Edition, 2001), 283–4.
12 Claudia Fröhlich, 'Restauration. Zur (Un-)Tauglichkeit eines Erklärungsansatzes westdeutscher Demokratiegeschichte im Kontext der Auseinandersetzung mit der NS-Vergangenheit', in *Erfolgsgeschichte Bundesrepublik? Die Nachkriegsgesellschaft im langen Schatten des Nationalsozialismus*, ed. Stephan Alexander Glienke et al. (Göttingen: Wallstein Verlag, 2008), 17–46; Christoph Kleßmann, *Die doppelte Staatsgründung. Deutsche Geschichte 1945–1955* (Bonn: BPB, 1991), 11–4, 296–302.
13 Eugen Kogon, 'Das Recht auf den politischen Irrtum', *Frankfurter Hefte* 2 (1947): 641.
14 Landtag Nordrhein-Westphalen, 9 December 1947, 43–4, 49.
15 Newman to McCloy, Subject: Renazification, 24 October 1949, National Archives and Records Administration (hereafter NARA), RG 466/A1/267/1.
16 Dominik Rigoll, 'Wenn Pazifistinnen den inneren Frieden stören: Sicherheit, Generation und Geschlecht in der frühen Bundesrepublik', *Ariadne* 66 (2014): 43–5.
17 Hermann Behr, *Vom Chaos zum Staat: Männer, die für uns begannen, 1945–1949* (Frankfurt am Main: Frankfurter Bücher, 1961), 313, 315–6.
18 Eugen Kogon, 'Beinahe mit dem Rücken zur Wand', *Frankfurter Hefte* 9 (1954): 641.
19 Lewis J. Edinger, 'Post-Totalitarian Leadership: Elites in the German Federal Republic', *American Political Science Review* 54 (1960): 58.
20 Ralf Dahrendorf, *Gesellschaft und Demokratie in Deutschland* (Munich: dtv, 1972), 233–64.
21 Wolfgang Zapf, *Wandlungen der deutschen Elite. Ein Zirkulationsmodell deutscher Führungsgruppen 1919–1961* (München: Piper, 1965), 145–51; see also, with case studies on both the FRG and the GDR, Wolfgang Zapf (ed.), *Beiträge zur Analyse der deutschen Oberschicht*, 2nd edn (Munich: Piper, 1965).
22 Rigoll, *Staatsschutz*, 178–207.
23 Lutz Niethammer, 'Einleitung', in *Inspektionsreisen in der US-Zone. Notizen, Denkschriften und Erinnerungen aus dem Nachlass*, ed. Walter Louis Dorn (Stuttgart: Deutsche Verlags-Anstalt, 1973), 7–8.
24 Joachim Kaiser, 'Phasenverschiebungen und Einschnitte in der kulturellen Entwicklung', in *Zäsuren nach 1945. Essays zur Periodisierung der deutschen Nachkriegsgeschichte*, ed. Martin Broszat (Munich, Oldenbourg, 1990), 73; Joachim Kaiser, 'Ich bin ein Alt–45er', *Süddeutsche Zeitung*, 15 March 2008; Dirk Moses, 'Die 45er: Eine Generation zwischen Faschismus und Demokratie', *Neue Sammlung* 40 (2000).
25 See, for instance, Ulrich Herbert, 'Drei politische Generationen im 20. Jahrhundert', in *Generationalität und Lebensgeschichte im 20. Jahrhundert*, ed. Joachim Reulecke (Munich: Oldenbourg, 2003), 95–114.
26 Erik Lommatzsch, *Hans Globke (1898–1973). Beamter im Dritten Reich und Staatssekretär Adenauers* (Frankfurt am Main and New York: Campus, 2009), 104–59.
27 The date quoted in the file is May 1950, except for the ministers and their assistants. Siegfried Fröhlich (ed.), *Das Bonner Innenministerium. Innenansichten einer politischen Institution* (Bonn: Osang, 1997), 391.
28 Anlage I zum Personalfragebogen, 30 May 1945, Landesarchiv Nordrhein-Westfalen (hereafter LA NRW), NW 1005-G40/71/072.
29 Fragebogen Work Sheet, 1946–1948, LA NRW, NW 1005-G40/71/072.

30 Thomas Flemming, *Gustav W. Heinemann. Ein deutscher Citoyen* (Essen: Klartext, 2014), 93–183.
31 Eleonore Sent, 'Dr. Robert Lehr (20.8.1883–13.10.1956)', *Düsseldorfer Jahrbuch* 78 (2008).
32 Stefanie Palm, 'Kultur, Medien, Wissenschaft und Sport', in Bösch and Wirsching, *Nachkriegsgeschichte*, 84.
33 Rigoll, *Pazifistinnen*, 44.
34 Heinemann to Zimmermann, 3 May 1950, Archiv der sozialen Demokratie, Heinemann I/27–29 (editors' translation); on the limits of what could be said about one's own biography, see Dominik Rigoll, 'Grenzen des Sagbaren. NS-Belastung und NS-Verfolgungserfahrung bei Bundestagsabgeordneten', *Zeitschrift für Parlamentsfragen* (2014): 128–40.
35 Tagebuch Hans Ritter von Lex, Bundesarchiv (hereafter BArch), N 1147/16; Hans Egidi, BArch, DOl/DOK-P/12338; Erich Wende, BArch, Pers 101/49323; Wilhelm Kitz, BArch, PERS 101/49730; Karl Sauer, BArch, Pers 101/54814, Walter Bargatzky, BArch, B 126/16934; Herbert Freiherr von Wolff, BArch, Pers 101/52437. On Hagemann, see Horst Albrecht, *Im Dienst der inneren Sicherheit. Die Geschichte des Bundeskriminalamtes* (Wiesbaden: BKA, 1988), 86–9. I am grateful to Stefanie Palm, Maren Richter, Irina Stange and Frieder Günther for sharing their biographical data with me.
36 Compare, for example, Lommatzsch, *Hans Globke*, and Jürgen Bevers, *Der Mann hinter Adenauer. Hans Globkes Aufstieg vom NS-Juristen zur Grauen Eminenz der Bonner Republik* (Berlin: Christoph Links, 2009).
37 See, for instance, the negotiations on the West German Security Service in BArch, B136/4367.
38 Quoted after Wolfgang Dierker, '"Ich will keine Nullen, sondern Bullen". Hitlers Koalitionsverhandlungen mit der Bayerischen Volkspartei im März 1933', *Vierteljahrshefte für Zeitgeschichte* 50 (2001): 139.
39 Lester K. Born, 'The Ministerial Collecting Center Near Kassel, Germany', *American Archivist* 13 (1950): 245–6, 238, 246.
40 Personalbogen Hans Ritter von Lex, BArch, PERS 101/49835, PERS 101/49838.
41 Hirtle to Commanding General, 27 June 1945, NARA, RG 260/OMGUS/771.
42 Smith to Brentnall, 17 July 1945, NARA, RG 260/OMGUS/771.
43 Field intelligence study No. 24, 27 September 1945, in Ulrich Borsdorf and Lutz Niethammer (eds), *Zwischen Befreiung und Besatzung. Analysen des US-Geheimdienstes über Positionen und Strukturen deutscher Politik 1945* (Weinheim: Beltz Athenäum, 1995), 193.
44 Udo Wengst, *Staatsaufbau und Regierungspraxis 1948–1953. Zur Geschichte der Verfassungsorgane der Bundesrepublik Deutschland* (Droste: Düsseldorf, 1984), 135–85.
45 Lutz Niethammer, *Die Mitläuferfabrik. Die Entnazifizierung am Beispiel Bayerns* (Dietz: Berlin, 1982), 165–98.
46 Maren Richter, 'Gesundheits- und Sozialwesen', in Bösch and Wirsching, *Nachkriegsgeschichte*, 66–79.
47 Wilhelm von Nathusius, BArch, PERS 101/52167; Ernst Wichert, BArch, B 126/17057; R 9361-I/41065.
48 Dieter Schenk, *Die braunen Wurzeln des BKA* (Frankfurt am Main: Fischer, 2003), 84–8.
49 Baumann et al., *Schatten*, 69–78.

50 Aktennotiz Dickopf, 12 January 1950, BArch, N 1265/35.
51 Ritter von Lex to Dickopf, 16 May 1950, BArch, N 1265/11. On Dickopf and the broader recruitment of former members of the Gestapo, SS and *Abwehr* by the Allied secret services, see the chapter by Michael Wala in this volume.
52 Austrian historians speak of the '45er-Generation': Manfried Rauchensteiner, *Die Zwei. Die große Koalition in Österreich 1945–1966* (Wien: Österreichischer Bundesverlag, 1987), 185, 360; Herwig Wolfram, *Österreichische Geschichte 1890–1990. Der lange Schatten des Staates* (Wien: Ueberreuter, 1994), 448.
53 Behr, *Männer, die für uns begannen*; Carmen Sitter, *Die Rolle der vier Frauen im Parlamentarischen Rat. Die vergessenen Mütter des Grundgesetzes* (Münster: LIT, 1995).
54 Josef Hölzl, BArch, Pers 101/49409, Pers 101/49408.
55 Dominik Rigoll, '"Ein Sieg der Ehemaligen": Beamtenrechtliche Weichenstellungen für "45er" und "131er"', in *Hüter der Ordnung. Die Innenministerien in Bonn und Ost-Berlin nach dem Nationalsozialismus*, ed. Frank Bösch and Andreas Wirsching (Wallstein Verlag: Göttingen, 2018).
56 Kleßmann, *Staatsgründung*, 251–6.
57 Jürgen Kocka, 'Neubeginn oder Restauration?', in *Wendepunkte deutscher Geschichte 1848–1945*, ed. Carola Stern and Heinrich August Winkler (Frankfurt am Main: Fischer, 1979), 154.
58 See, for instance, John D. Montgomery, *Forced to Be Free* (Chicago: Chicago University Press, 1957).
59 Edinger, *Post-Totalitarian Leadership*, 65. To be sure, more junior officials involved in these crimes, such as Dickopf and many others, were employed in the police and secret intelligence services until the 1960s and 1970s, as discussed in the chapter by Michael Wala in this volume.
60 Rigoll, *Staatsschutz*, 84–94.
61 Patrick Major, *The Death of the KPD: Communism and Anti-Communism in West Germany, 1945–1956* (Oxford: Clarendon Press, 1998), especially 294–304.
62 Rigoll, *Staatsschutz*, 87–94, 113–4, 135–44, 200–42, 361, 390, 433–4.
63 Niethammer, 'Einleitung', 8.
64 Till van Rahden, 'Clumsy Democrats: Moral Passions in the Federal Republic', *German History* 29 (2011): 485–504.
65 See, for instance, Dominik Rigoll, 'Stabilsierungspolitik'; 'Kampf um die innere Sicherheit: Schutz des Staates oder der Demokratie?', in *Hüter der Ordnung*, ed. Bösch and Wirsching.

15

The Value of Knowledge: Western Intelligence Agencies and Former Members of the SS, Gestapo and Wehrmacht during the Early Cold War

Michael Wala

'The Red Orchestra is not dead, and I know this because Western intelligence services are interested in it.'[1] This 1950 statement by Alexander Kraell, a lawyer, former Nazi Party member and high court judge during the Third Reich, at first glance hardly seems very spectacular. A closer look, however, points to a number of important questions about the relationship between the American, British and French secret services and former members and supporters of the Nazi regime. It also reveals some of the methods by which both sides acquired, transferred and sometimes invented knowledge and secret information after the war. In 1942, Kraell had presided over the Nazi *Reichskriegsgericht* (military high court) trials of a group of individuals opposed to National Socialism, many of whom were condemned to death and executed. The Gestapo had lumped them all together, claiming that they were members of an organization called the 'Red Orchestra' (*Rote Kapelle*). In 1950, eight years later, Kraell was a witness for the defence in the trial of Manfred Roeder, another lawyer, who had been a judge advocate in the 1942 Red Orchestra trial, responsible for investigating and prosecuting suspects, but was now himself in the dock, accused of having permitted the use of torture and committing crimes against humanity.

The most important question implied in Kraell's statement is why were Western intelligence organizations interested in the so-called Red Orchestra in 1950 at all? The organization that the Gestapo called the *Rote Kapelle* had actually been a group of mostly unconnected anti-Nazi resistance fighters in Germany, together with members of Soviet espionage rings operating in German-occupied Europe and Switzerland. The *Rote Kapelle* was basically a Nazi invention, a story spun in 1942 to enable the Gestapo to ferociously hunt down any opponents of the Nazi regime, across the whole of German-occupied Europe. How did Kraell 'know' that Western intelligence services were still interested in the Red Orchestra in 1950, and what did this have to do with Roeder and others who had been involved in killing supposed Soviet agents or prosecuting them in court and sending them to the gallows? Was hunting the Red Orchestra after 1945, as has been argued again recently, not simply the paranoid brainchild of the German secret service and the *Bundesnachrichtendienst* chief, Reinhard Gehlen, and so perhaps disruptive but of no great significance?[2]

A closer look at what lies behind Kraell's statement and an exploration of what drove the interest in the Red Orchestra among Western secret services after 1945 sheds light on an overlooked but nonetheless highly significant dimension of information exchange and knowledge acquisition during the occupation of Germany by the Western Allies. Moreover, the story of the Red Orchestra played an important part in creating what Michael Herman has recently called the 'state of mind of the Cold War'.[3] This process was closely intertwined with the changing relationship between British, French and American intelligence organizations on the one side and former members of the Gestapo, SS and *Wehrmacht* on the other. It was critical in forming Western European and transatlantic intelligence cooperation during the early Cold War, when an ally became the enemy and a former enemy a (semi-)trusted ally.

It is easy to assume that all of a sudden, right at the end of the Second World War, the Cold War broke out, just like the flu. That historians have to dig deeper to find satisfactory answers as to what processes contributed to the beginning of the Cold War is self-evident and does not need to be argued. A conventional diplomatic history approach that analyses what US Secretary of State George C. Marshall said to Soviet Minister of Foreign Affairs Molotov on this or that occasion is clearly not sufficient and needs to be complemented with approaches from cultural and social history. At the same time, the history of secret intelligence has only recently moved to the centre of historiographical attention.[4] This chapter argues that the increasingly close individual and organizational relationships between Western intelligence officers and former members of the Gestapo and SS, that resulted from their working together in hunting the Red Orchestra, played a significant role in the formation of early Cold War attitudes among both Western Allied and German intelligence communities. This process can be illustrated by a few examples of the activities of British, French and American intelligence organizations in post-war Germany, who were trying to gather information on what they considered to be a potential Soviet threat by working together with former members of criminal Nazi Organizations, the Gestapo and SS, as well as erstwhile Wehrmacht military intelligence (*Abwehr*) officers.

The starting point of the post-war hunt for the Red Orchestra appears to have been in late May 1945, when the British captured and interned Horst Kopkow, a former SS *Sturmbannführer* (major).[5] Kopkow had been in charge of the *Sonderkommission Rote Kapelle*, a special team established by the Nazi regime within the *Reichssicherheitshauptamt* (Reich security office) to investigate the supposed group. He soon supplied British and Allied intelligence services not only with information about his former colleagues in the SS and the SD (the *Sicherheitsdienst*, which acted as the intelligence arm of the SS), but also succeeded in planting among his captors the first seeds of interest in the Red Orchestra.[6]

Kopkow's and other Gestapo, SS and SD members' cooperation with their former enemies was grounded in two overarching goals they all shared after 1945: first, avoiding prosecution for their activities during the Third Reich and second, achieving rehabilitation together with financial, social and personal security for themselves as individuals. Many lived under false names and so avoided denazification. For Kopkow, and all those who had been involved in hunting members of the German and Soviet-led opposition to the Nazi regime, it was thus essential to convince the Allies that the supposed members of the Red Orchestra they had persecuted, arrested, interrogated, tortured, killed or sentenced to death, were not resistance fighters at all, but rather spies, who were exclusively interested in financial gains and morally corrupt. The obvious benefit of convincing the Western Allies of this claim was that it would help them portray their own actions during the Third Reich in a more favourable, or at least a less incriminating, light. If successful, this alone might have enabled Kopkow and his colleagues to achieve their primary aims of avoiding prosecution and starting along the road to personal rehabilitation. But they soon realized that they could also acquire bargaining power and even agency if they were able to convince the Allied intelligence officers that these alleged German and Soviet spies and their supposed network had not been entirely destroyed but was still active and dangerous, now working against the Western Allies. Allied intelligence officers, however, were initially suspicious of such claims. Kopkow's British interrogators in 1945, for instance, were actually well aware that he was trying to plant seeds of distrust, remarking in an internal report that 'a conflict between the USSR [and the Western Allies] would suit him down to the ground'.[7]

However, as tensions between the members of the anti-Hitler coalition increased in early 1946,[8] Kopkow's warnings about Soviet spies, previously regarded by the British as what they actually were, namely not more than self-serving pretensions of knowledge to endear him to his captors, were taken more seriously. In March 1946, the British Joint Intelligence Committee agreed with their American counterparts that the Soviet Union would not initiate any military confrontation over the next few years.[9] Nonetheless, an American memorandum was concerned that we 'possess virtually no intelligence in Russia, nor have we set the machinery in motion to remedy this deficiency'.[10] It could thus be seen as a logical step to turn to former members of the German intelligence community, who claimed to have expert knowledge about the USSR and Communist espionage. The fortunes of Kopkow and his colleagues therefore saw a rapid and dramatic shift, with their presumed expertise on Soviet intelligence activities now increasingly in demand by the Western Allies.

If what Kopkow told his interrogators was true, this would have been evidence for Soviet double-dealing, so even the unproven possibility that he might be telling the truth made him a valuable asset. Kopkow thus emerged as one of the key experts on the Soviet spy system first interrogated and subsequently used by the British. Most notably, British intelligence officers protected him from certain prosecution in Germany by evacuating him to England and then declaring that he had become ill and died of pneumonia before he could be fully interrogated – before sending him back to Germany under an alias and with false documents.[11]

Records in British, American and German archives document a large number of similar cases that reveal how, in the early Cold War, a shift took place among all three of the Western Allies from initial suspicion, to using such people for information gathering, eventually leading to their being held in high regard as knowledgeable experts on Soviet espionage. Another example is the case of SS *Hauptsturmführer* (captain) Heinrich Reiser, who was part of the Paris branch of the *Sonderkommission*

Rote Kapelle. He was interrogated by the French in Freiburg in 1947 and 1948, as was Walter Klein, a minor Gestapo member, who after March 1951 was paid by the French *Sûreté* to locate additional members of the *Sonderkommission* and so gather as much information as possible about the Red Orchestra.[12]

Richard Gerken, a former military intelligence captain based at Münster and responsible for countering sabotage and disruption, was another case in point. He had mainly worked in the Netherlands, Belgium and France during the war. When caught by the Allies, he was extremely cooperative, revealing arms caches, reporting what he knew about the structure and staff of the *Abwehr* (the military intelligence branch of the German army) and naming fellow officers who had been with the SD at the *Reichssicherheitshauptamt*.[13] To gain favour with the British, he submitted plans for a new German political structure in a short essay on fighting Bolshevism in the western zones of Germany. Unsurprisingly, his political ideas were not quite in tune with the Western Allies' various public pronouncements on democracy, a fact which, it would seem, did not cause him much concern. Using a formula current in the 1940s among conservative and often undemocratic political groups, he recommended that 'the Political-Party State should be supplanted by the Corporate State' (*An die Stelle des Parteien-Staates tritt der Ständestaat*). At the same time, and somewhat paradoxically, he advocated the creation of a new political party with an integral political intelligence service (as the SD had been for the Nazi Party).[14]

Gerken's attempts at impressing the Allies were not entirely successful. His British interrogators' verdict was harsh, writing in October 1947:

> Gerken is a hypocrite and an opportunist. Chameleon-like, he is capable of changing his political colour at will … [W]ere the Russians to enter this Zone, he would no doubt become an ardent and assiduous promoter of Communism. Gerken gives himself out as an anti-Nazi … but investigations of this office have revealed him as one using the Party [NSDAP] for the furtherance of his own ambitions … were Gerken to be employed in any capacity by Intelligence, he could not be trusted, either to remain loyal or to supply bona-fide information.[15]

Concealing his past membership of the Nazi Party, Gerken succeeded in obtaining a temporary internal security position in North Rhine-Westphalia in 1947, but had to leave when his superiors discovered he had been a party member. In 1950, he was successful in his application to join the information and intelligence department of the Ministry of the Interior in Lower Saxony, despite all candidates having to be vetted by the British occupation authorities. By now, despite the blunt assessment by his interrogators in 1947, he was acting as an agent for the British secret services, and also provided them with information on the newly formed German intelligence services. In 1952, Gerken moved to the *Bundesamt für Verfassungsschutz*, a federal institution founded in 1950, similar to the British MI5. Here, he headed the counter espionage department. Although the Western Allies were adamant that no former member of the Gestapo should be employed by the *Bundesamt*, they evidently looked the other way and made no objections when Gerken hired a large number of nominally freelance staff who had exactly that personal background. Despite their supposedly unofficial ties with the *Bundesamt*, some of them nonetheless had offices at the organization's headquarters and became an integral part of the agency, often dealing with foreign intelligence services.[16]

One of these freelancers was former SS *Obersturmführer* (lieutenant) Johannes Strübing, who had worked with Kopkow at the *Sonderkommission*. He had lived under a false name until 1949 when he was arrested by the US Counter Intelligence Corps (CIC). Strübing soon realized that in addition to asking questions about his own conduct, such as whether he had tortured prisoners and if his victims had been resistance fighters, his American interrogators were also keen to obtain information on the Red Orchestra. Although he must have been quite certain that all those he had captured and interrogated during the war as supposed *Rote Kapelle* members were no longer alive, he began to claim that some may have survived and furthermore, were still active, adding that there was no doubt that they really were Soviet spies.[17]

It was Strübing who launched a full-scale operation hunting the supposedly still active Red Orchestra members, in an operation that extended beyond Germany to include other Western intelligence agencies. The result was a list of initially nearly two thousand potential spies supposedly roaming Germany and Western Europe. Among the suspects were resistance fighters who had escaped the Nazis, such as Adolf Grimme (the first post-war Minister of Culture of Lower Saxony, who was appointed by the British in 1948 as the first German manager of the broadcaster NWDR), others who had fled Germany, such as Otto John (the first president of the *Bundesamt*), or the children or relatives of those who had been killed by the Nazis. One of the suspects, for example, was the diplomat Hartmut Wolfgang Schulze-Boysen, brother of resistance fighter Harro Schulze-Boysen, who had been murdered in 1942. According to Strübing, 'quite reliable' sources 'knew' that he and his wife were Communists. The evidence provided for this damning accusation was that the couple knew a woman who, it was said, had, after her divorce, been romantically involved with a man whose father was a Communist, and this was proof enough of 'a well-established Communist link into the Foreign Office'. As part of the inquiry, Strübing contacted the supposedly deceased Kopkow who, however, rather than confirming that Schulze was a Communist, exonerated him because he 'knew' that he had not been involved in his brother's activities. It is clear from such interactions that former members of the Gestapo were well connected, exchanged information, coordinated and sometimes modified their strategies to persuade and convince Allied intelligence services about their 'knowledge' that the Red Orchestra was still active.[18]

SS *Standartenführer* (colonel) Walter Huppenkothen, responsible for the death of Dietrich Bonhoeffer and other resistance fighters, worked along similar lines. He acted as an agent for the CIC under the cover name 'Fidelio', telling them what he 'knew' about the Red Orchestra. Others, such as SS *Sturmbannführer* (major) Walter Klein, wrote long reports for the French *Sûreté*, while Manfred Roeder similarly provided the CIC as 'Othello' with what he 'knew'. The cumulative effect of the presentation of all this supposedly objective knowledge was that it finally convinced the reluctant Americans that the Red Orchestra did in fact still exist. Consequently, with the assistance of these former Nazi officials, an eighty-three-page list naming all presumed survivors of the group was compiled, and they were placed under observation.[19]

Seasoned Western intelligence officers therefore went from treating what these people told them as 'information', something that had to be critically weighed and analysed, to regarding it as verified 'knowledge', even though it was confirmed only by other former members of the Gestapo. What now served as the foundation for operations against these supposed spies was hardly objective data or information, but nevertheless allowed former Gestapo members to continue tainting as spies people who had opposed or resisted the Nazi regime, in order to further their own personal goals and careers in the immediate post-war period.

In the early 1950s, the Americans and British began to exchange details of what they had heard from Kopkow, Strübing and others among each other and with other European services. They also circulated old Gestapo documents that had survived the war. Soon the French were involved together with the Dutch and the Swiss. Intelligence agents from all these countries were hunting for members of a spy organization that, in reality, did not exist, that had been invented by former Gestapo members, and was nothing more than an imaginary threat to their individual and collective national security. After the early 1950s, the German *Bundesamt für Verfassungsschutz* took a lead in fostering cooperation between American and British services and their Swiss, Dutch and French counterparts. Strübing at the *Bundesamt* was the major driving force in this, traveling to the Netherlands and to Switzerland under the codename of 'Stahlmann' and meeting with American and British intelligence officers. It must have been an open secret among most of those he worked with who he really was; at least the CIA knew his real name and background. His counterparts in the Netherlands were former members of the Dutch resistance and it is hard to imagine that they were deceived for long. Collaboration with Dutch intelligence services in searching for members of the Red Orchestra was particularly strong. This may have been because the former Gestapo officers' attitudes towards Soviet agents coincided with those of many of the Dutch officials. Strübing was given a set of guidelines in 1958 by his Dutch colleagues which stated that: 'a man who once has worked for a Soviet espionage service [during the war] should be regarded as a potential [Soviet] agent [after the war] until this is absolutely proven to not be the case'. We can be certain that Strübing would have subscribed to every single word of this statement.[20]

As late as 1956, *Verfassungsschutz* officers returned from a meeting with the French security agency, the *Direction de la Surveillance du Territoire,* with information about large numbers of documents on the Red Orchestra. The French also informed them that they were eager to cooperate closely as 'what had happened in the past had to be overcome … cooperation … in fighting the Communists is of the highest importance'.[21] Similarly, Strübing continued to keep in close contact with his Dutch colleagues, traveling to The Hague to check old Gestapo files the Dutch had received from the British. Later, he provided his Dutch counterparts with documents he had acquired from an informant who previously had worked for the Gehlen Organization in Germany.[22] Another lively exchange took place with the Swiss intelligence service. At the end of November 1958, for example, Strübing travelled to Switzerland under his well-used alias 'Stahlmann'. Through tactics such as these, the former Gestapo officers, now employed at the *Verfassungsschutz,* kept the fires burning as long as they could, but in 1963 their past in the Gestapo was revealed in the press and scandalized. As a result, they had to leave the *Verfassungsschutz*, and without them as a driving force, the hunt for the Red Orchestra soon petered out.[23]

In addition to hunting the Red Orchestra, Western intelligence services used former members of the Gestapo, *Abwehr* and SS in other roles and to perform other functions during the period of the early Cold War. After the start of the Korean War in 1950, former members of the Wehrmacht and Waffen-SS were sought to staff and shape covert 'stay-behind' operations established in Germany by the CIA and other Western intelligence services. Rather than being asked to provide information on potential Soviet spies, as Kopkow and Strübing were doing, these former SS and Wehrmacht members were considered to be military experts on guerrilla warfare, needed in case of what many Western intelligence officers believed was a danger of an imminent attack by the Red Army. One of those employed by the CIA in this context was Walter Kopp, a former colonel of the German Wehrmacht. His American handlers believed that he could be trusted because of his staunch anti-Communism, and they were willing to overlook, or at least mitigate, the obvious Nazi nostalgia and outright racist attitudes in his thinking. Thus, even when he told his CIA contacts that he believed that 'the fight of the white races against the colored races can only be won with American aid, and that the fight against Communism is mainly a fight between the white and the colored races' they were not deterred from employing him. 'Subject is a German Army officer through and through', a US report concluded after Kopp was asked to take a polygraph (lie detector) test. In a striking assessment that says as much about the attitudes towards race of the American intelligence officers conducting the proceedings as it does about Kopp, the report continued:

> Racial fanaticism is present in his thinking to a staggering degree. It is present in a positive rather than negative sense, in that he does not condemn one race, but during the interview said many times that the white race must win out over the yellow or Asiatic races. America must unite with England, France, Germany, Italy, etc., in fighting the menace from Asia.

Not surprisingly, Kopp was found to be anti-Semitic but, the CIA officers concluded, 'not rabidly so', adding that he was not a Nazi and had to join the SS against his will, apparently accepting without question the story presented to them by Kopp himself.[24]

This peculiar understanding shown by his US interrogators of what constitutes 'positive' racism as well as their differentiation of degrees of anti-Semitism, suggests that there was a high degree of racial prejudice and anti-Semitism among the CIA officers with whom Kopp was in touch. Despite their evaluation of Kopp as a racist, they claimed that his 'loss would have serious repercussions'. We can assume that Kopp was but one example among many, and their evaluation of him and others like him is an indication of the uncritical proximity that had developed between the United States and other Western agencies and former SS, Gestapo and Wehrmacht intelligence officers. Many CIA officers shared not only their German colleagues' information, but at least some aspects of their anti-Semitic or racist mental attitudes and evaluations. A common outlook helped to facilitate the close working relationships, the uncritical reliance on the information provided and the supposed positive knowledge acquired from their German colleagues. There is ample evidence in the documents that this process was not particular to the Americans, differing only in degrees from other Western intelligence agencies and their members working on the ground in Germany.[25]

This was the context in which all West German Federal security institutions, not only the *Bundesamt für Verfassungsschutz*, were established after the war. For the *Bundeskriminalamt* (BKA), the German federal police, Paul Dickopf was the willing tool employed by the American services. Dickopf, a former member of the SS and the SD, worked for the *Abwehr* and was sent to Switzerland in 1943 to infiltrate either Swiss intelligence or the American OSS. By 1948, he had returned to Germany as an American agent. Regarded as trustworthy, he was helped by the Americans in his denazification process and was supported in penetrating the newly re-established German police.[26] At first, the Americans used him to acquire information about former members of the SD and the *Abwehr*. The shift from supplier of raw information to an expert providing supposedly valuable knowledge about an area that was actually not his real expertise was swift. He had been based in Stuttgart at the start of the war, before going to France and Belgium in 1942, but now in 1948, realizing quickly what type of information was deemed valuable by Western intelligence agencies, he styled himself as an expert on police and intelligence organizations in Russia and Eastern Germany and supplied the Americans with lengthy evaluations and reports. Dickopf's knowledge, in conjunction with his credentials as a staunch anti-Communist, was considered so valuable for the process of recruiting staff to reconstruct the West German federal police, that he was asked to draft the organizational structure of the future BKA in 1948, and was later able to implement this in his position as a senior official in the Federal Ministry of the Interior.

After 1950 Dickopf became responsible for setting up the BKA, which he later led, first as vice president, and then, after 1965, as president. It is indicative of the Americans' trust in his supposed knowledge and expertise that they did not prevent him from hiring a large number of former members of the SS. Among those was former SS *Hauptsturmführer* (captain) and war criminal Theodor Saevecke, who became a member of the BKA's *Sicherungsgruppe* (security group) that was responsible for espionage cases uncovered by the *Verfassungsschutz*, because the *Bundesamt* did not have legal powers to interrogate and arrest suspects. Saevecke's unaltered sympathies for Nazi ideas were not only known to the Americans, but the Ministry of the Interior, the superior authority to the BKA, had few qualms too. When allegations about Saevecke's war crimes in Italy first surfaced in 1954, he was protected by the deputy minister, State Secretary Hans Ritter von Lex.[27] Former members of the SS soon made up 70 per cent of the upper echelons in the BKA, while Dickopf remained on the CIA payroll at least until 1967.[28]

In the uneasy setting of the post-war period, former members of the Gestapo and the SS acquired significant agency using their supposed expertise to construct an imagined enemy out of the remains of the Red Orchestra. Selling their presumed knowledge about Soviet spies and Communist intelligence activities paid off for most, at least in terms of their financial and job security. More importantly, by the late 1950s, their success in planting among Western intelligence groups the idea that the Red Orchestra was still active had fundamentally changed the intelligence landscape, leading to

Western European and transatlantic intelligence cooperation. Based on knowledge that had been constructed during the war when the influence of the Gestapo was at its height, its former members reconstructed and reinvented the Soviet threat to fit their personal goals. They made it into a commodity that was shaped according to the value placed on it and ascribed to it by US, British and French security services.

The 'knowledge' these men supplied arguably had an impact on political decision-makers, particularly in Great Britain and the United States. The Red Orchestra may never have existed after 1945, but it nonetheless turned out to have an important role in shaping a transatlantic intelligence community in the post-war period. It altered both the attitudes of the Western Allies towards West Germany and the attitudes of the West German political elite towards the Western Allies' occupational regime. By the mid-1960s, when interest had faded, hunting the Red Orchestra had already played out its part in helping to create European and transatlantic cooperation. Former Gestapo, SS, SD and Wehrmacht officials succeeded in reconstructing their knowledge acquired during the Third Reich for a sellers' market of information, of knowledge, and of meaning, to fit the political reality of the early Cold War period, when the Western Allies were highly suspicious of Soviet intentions and activities in Germany and Western Europe, and were desperate to know more about them.

The Red Orchestra turned out to be a valuable commodity that altered the attitudes of people on the ground, by redefining who was the enemy. It persuaded US, British and French intelligence officers that the Gestapo's old enemy still existed, was still active and potentially dangerous, and was identical to the new and now common enemy, Soviet communism. The activities of the individuals discussed in this chapter in perpetuating what might be termed the post-war myth of the Red Orchestra's continued existence therefore supported the Adenauer government's goal to become a trusted ally and integral part of a Western Alliance in the early Cold War. It was also convenient for the Western Allies' security services, anxious to justify their own existence in the changed international order after the end of the wars against Germany and Japan. The Federal Republic's security organizations may have been only half-trusted by their new allies, but one of the surprising legacies of occupation was that despite, or perhaps because they were staffed by former members of the SS and Gestapo and military intelligence officers, they were accepted by and fully embedded into the Western Cold War intelligence community.

Notes

1 Statement by Dr Alexander Kraell, 14 March 1950, Bundesamt für Verfassungsschutz Archives (ZAW) 255, microfilm, 596.

2 Most recently: Gerhard Sälter, *Phantome des Krieges. Die Organisation Gehlen und die Wiederbelebung des Gestapo-Feindbildes 'Rote Kapelle'* (Berlin: Ch. Links Verlag, 2016).

3 Michael Herman, 'What Difference did It Make? Cold War Intelligence from a Todays' Point of View', paper presented at conference *Creating and Challenging the Transatlantic Intelligence Community* (30 March 2017). Available online: www.c-span.org/video/?426220–2/cold-war-intelligence-gathering-training (accessed 30 September 2017).

4 For example, see Constantin Goschler and Michael Wala, *'Keine neue Gestapo'. Das Bundesamt für Verfassungsschutz und die NS-Vergangenheit* (Reinbek bei Hamburg: Rowohlt, 2015); Richard J. Aldrich, *The Hidden Hand: Britain, America, and Cold War Secret Intelligence* (London: John Murray, 2002); Christopher Andrew, *The Defence of the Realm: The Authorized History of MI5* (London: Allen Lane, 2009); Sarah-Jane Corke, *US Covert Operations and Cold War Strategy: Truman, Secret Warfare and the CIA* (London: Routledge, 2008).

5 SS ranks have been followed by their approximate British/US equivalents in the text.

6 Subject: Kopkow, Horst, to SHAEF CI War Room, July 3, 1945, The National Archives, Kew (TNA), KV 2-1500.

7 Special Points. Secret, Kopkow, Horst., undated, TNA, KV 2–1500.

8 On increasing tensions among the Allies, see, for example, Anne Deighton, *The Impossible Peace: Britain, the Division of Germany and the Origins of the Cold War* (Oxford: Clarendon Press, 1990); for a US perspective, see Carolyn Eisenberg, *Drawing the Line: The American Decision to Divide Germany, 1944–1949* (Cambridge, New York and Melbourne: Cambridge University Press, 1996).

9 Donald C. Watt, 'Die Sowjetunion im Urteil des britischen Foreign Office 1945–1949', in *Der Westen und die Sowjetunion: Einstellungen und Politik gegenüber der UdSSR in Europa und in den USA seit 1917*, ed. Gottfried Niedhart (Paderborn: Schöningh, 1983), 247ff, citing Roberts to Foreign Office, 20 March 1946, TNA, FO 371/56831.

10 Matthew M. Aid, 'A Tale of Two Countries: U.S. Intelligence Community Relations with the Dutch and German Intelligence and Security Services, 1945–1950', in *Battleground Western Europe: Intelligence Operations in Germany and the Netherlands in the Twentieth Century*, ed. Beatrice de Graaf, Ben de Jong and Wies Platje (Amsterdam: Het Spinhuis, 2007), 102, citing Memorandum, G. A. L. to Hull, Intelligence on Russia, 22 March 1946, National Archives, College Park (NACP) RG 319, Entry 154 OPD TS Decimal File 1946–1948, Box 75, File P&O 350.05 TS (Section I) Cases 1–44.

11 Sarah Helm, 'The Gestapo Killer Who Lived Twice', *Sunday Times*, 7 August 2005.

12 Translations of German Police (BKA) interrogations of former officers of RK Sonderkommission (1951), NACP RG 263, ZZ-18, Box 107, Reiser, Heinrich Josef. For Reiser and Klein, see Norman J. Goda, 'Tracking the Red Orchestra: Allied Intelligence, Soviet Spies, Nazi Criminals', in *U.S. Intelligence and the Nazis*, ed. Richard Breitman et al. (Cambridge and New York: Cambridge University Press, 2005), 307.

13 Sgt. Richard R. C. Cooke to OC No 59 FS Section, Subject: Gerken, Richard – Abwehr Agent (Personality List), 14 May 1945, TNA, WO 208/5211.

14 Gerken, 'Bekämpfung des militärischen und ideologischen Bolschewismus durch Massnahmen in den westlichen Sektoren Deutschlands', undated, TNA, WO 208/5211.

15 8 Area Intelligence Office and Headquarters, Intelligence Division, 22 October 1947, TNA, WO 208/5211.

16 Arrested, Gerken, Richard @ Dr. Miller, @ R. H. Gaelen @ Gahrken, Capt. @Gehrken, Capt @ Gerlach, Hpm., undated, TNA, WO 208/5211; H. M. Askew, Regional Intelligence Office Hannover to Security Directorate, *Rusty* Penetration of BfV, 18 February 1952, TNA, WO 208/5211; Goschler and Wala, *'Keine neue Gestapo'*, 61–6.

17 Available BDC Information, NACP RG 263, Entry ZZ-16, Box 51, File Struebing, Johannes; Bundesbeauftragter für Stasi Unterlagen Archiv Berlin (BStU), Ministerium für Staatssicherheit, HA, IX11, PA 2952.

18 II/G-a-3, note for the file, subject: Harmut Wolfgang Schulze-Boysen, 12 June 1954, ZAW 227; OTTO (Organization Gehlen) to BfV III/41, 24 August 1953, ZAW 227; BfV, III, to OCA Liaison Office, Mr. Hughes, 18 December 1954, ZAW 227.

19 Agent Report, Proposed Use of Former Gestapo Personnel to Combat Present Day Illegal KPD Activities, undated, NACP RG 319, A1-134-B, B321, XE003856, Huppenkothen, Walter; The Case of the 'Rote Kapelle': Second Report, NACP RG 65, A1-136Z, B44, 'Rote Kapelle'; Bruno C. Richter, Special Agent CIC, Subject 'Rote Kapelle', 13 May 1948, NACP RG 319, A1-134-A, B62, ZA020253, Red Orchestra ('Rote Kapelle'); Personality Reports of R/K Survivors, undated, NACP RG 263, ZZ-18, Box 108, Roeder, Manfred.

20 Translation, vom holl. Dienst übergeben, Strübing, 1958, ZAW 227.

21 Günther Nollau, note for the file: Verbindungen zur französischen Sureté, 2 June 1956, ZAW 553; Nollau, Aktennotiz, July 27, 1956, ZAW 553; Memorandum, undated ZAW 553; Nollau to VP/P (vice president/president), 13 September 1956, ZAW 553.

22 The Gehlen Organization was the precursor of the West German federal secret foreign intelligence agency. It was founded in 1946 in the US Zone by the German Second World War general Reinhard Gehlen, in collaboration with US occupation authorities.

23 Goschler and Wala, *'Keine Neue Gestapo'*, 228–38.

24 Polygraph Examination of KIBITZ-15 (Kopp); Com – 241, 20 January 1953, NACP, RG 263, ZZ-18, Box 68, Kopp, Walter.

25 See also Chief of Mission, Frankfurt, Review of KIBITZ-15 Net, 19 January 1953, NACP, RG 263, ZZ-18, Box 68, Kopp, Walter.

26 For Dickopf's appointment as an official in the German Federal Ministry of the Interior, see the chapter by Dominik Rigoll in this volume.

27 Imanuel Baumann et al., *Schatten der Vergangenheit. Das BKA und seine Gründungsgeneration in der frühen Bundesrepublik* (Köln: Luchterhand, 2011), 219–37. For more on von Lex's personal background and appointment as State Secretary at the German Federal Ministry of the Interior, see the chapter by Dominik Rigoll in this volume.

28 *Caravel* (CIA cover name for Dickopf), Frankfurt (COS), undated, NACP RG 263, Entry ZZ-18, Box 24, Dickopf, Paul; *Caravel*, 16 March 1950, NACP RG 263, Entry ZZ-18, Box 24, Dickopf, Paul; Chief, Foreign Branch M, Chief of Station, Karlsruhe, *Hathor* (CIC cover name for Dickopf) Progress Report, 23 December 1948, NACP RG 263, Entry ZZ-18, Box 24, Dickopf, Paul.; Memorandum for the Record. Subject: Meeting with *Caravel*, 30 December 1968, NACP RG 263, Entry ZZ-18, Box 24, Dickopf, Paul .

Select Bibliography

Adler, Karen H. 'Selling France to the French: The French Zone of Occupation in Western Germany, 1945–c. 1955'. *Contemporary European History* 21, no. 4 (2012): 575–95.

Ahrens, Michael. *Die Briten in Hamburg. Besatzerleben 1945–1958*. Munich and Hamburg: Dölling und Galitz, 2011.

Aid, Matthew M. 'A Tale of Two Countries: U.S. Intelligence Community Relations with the Dutch and German Intelligence and Security Services, 1945–1950'. In *Battleground Western Europe: Intelligence Operations in Germany and the Netherlands in the Twentieth Century*, edited by Beatrice de Graaf, Ben de Jong and Wies Platje, 95–122. Amsterdam: Het Spinhuis, 2007.

Arai-Takahashi, Yutuka. *The Law of Occupation*. Leiden: Martinus Nijhoff, 2009.

Baginski, Christophe. *Frankreichs Kirchenpolitik im besetzten Deutschland 1945–1949*. Mainz: Gesellschaft für Mittelrheinische Kirchengeschichte, 2001.

Bainton, Roy. *The Long Patrol: The British in Germany since 1945*. Edinburgh: Mainstream, 2003.

Baumann, Imanuel, Herbert Reinke, Andrej Stephan and Patrick Wagner. *Schatten der Vergangenheit. Das BKA und seine Gründungsgeneration in der frühen Bundesrepublik*. Cologne: Luchterhand, 2011.

Beattie, Andrew H. 'Die alliierte Internierung im besetzten Deutschland und die deutsche Gesellschaft: Vergleich der amerikanischen und der sowjetischen Zone'. *Zeitschrift für Geschichtswissenschaft* 62, no. 3 (2014): 239–56.

Beattie, Andrew H. '"Lobby for the Nazi Elite"? The Protestant Churches and Civilian Internment in the British Zone of Occupied Germany, 1945–1948'. *German History* 35, no. 1 (March 2017): 43–70.

Beck, Birgit. 'Vergewaltigung von Frauen als Kriegsstrategie im Zweiten Weltkrieg?'. In *Gewalt im Krieg: Ausübung, Erfahrung und Verweigerung von Gewalt in Kriegen des 20. Jahrhunderts*, edited by Andreas Gestrich, 34–50. Münster: Lit. 1996.

Beetham, David. *The Legitimation of Power*. 2nd ed. Basingstoke: Palgrave Macmillan, 2013.

Benvenisti, Eyal. *The International Law of Occupation*. Oxford: Oxford University Press, 2012.

Benz, Wolfgang. *Auftrag Demokratie: Die Gründungsgeschichte der Bundesrepublik und die Entstehung der DDR 1945–1949*. Berlin: Metropol-Verlag, 2009.

Berghahn, Volker. *The Americanisation of West German Industry, 1945–1973*. Cambridge and New York: Cambridge University Press, 1986.

Bessel, Richard. *Germany 1945: From War to* Peace. London: Simon & Schuster, 2009.

Bessel, Richard, and Dirk Schumann (eds). *Life after Death: Approaches to a Cultural and Social History of Europe during the 1940s and 1950s*. Cambridge: Cambridge University Press, 2003.

Biddiscombe, Perry. *The Denazification of Germany: A History 1945–1950*. Stroud: Tempus, 2007.

Biddiscombe, Perry. *Werwolf! The History of the National Socialist Guerrilla Movement, 1944–1946*. Cardiff: University of Wales Press, 1998.

Biess, Frank, and Robert G. Moeller (eds). *Histories of the Aftermath: The Legacies of the Second World War on Europe*. New York and Oxford: Berghahn Books, 2010.

Blaschke, Olaf. *Die Kirchen und der Nationalsozialismus*. Stuttgart: Reclam, 2014.

Boehling, Rebecca. *A Question of Priorities: Democratic Reform and Economic Recovery in Postwar Germany*. Providence and Oxford: Berghahn Books, 1996.

Bösch, Frank, and Andreas Wirsching (eds). *Die Nachkriegsgeschichte des Bundesministeriums des Innern (BMI) und des Ministeriums des Innern der DDR (MdI) hinsichtlich möglicher personeller und sachlicher Kontinuitäten zur Zeit des Nationalsozialismus*. Munich and Potsdam: 2015. Available online: www.ifz-muenchen.de/fileadmin/user_upload/Neuigkeiten%202015/BMI_Abschlussbericht%20der%20Vorstudie.pdf (accessed 18 August 2017).

Broszat, Martin, Klaus Dietmar Henke and Hans Woller (eds). *Von Stalingrad zur Währungsreform: Zur Sozialgeschichte des Umbruchs in Deutschland*, 3rd ed. Munich: R. Oldenbourg, 1990.

Brüggemeier, Franz-Josef, Mark Cioc and Thomas Zeller (eds). *How Green Were the Nazis? Nature, Environment and Nation in the Third Reich*. Athens: Ohio University Press, 2005.

Buchna, Kristian. *Ein klerikales Jahrzehnt? Kirche, Konfession und Politik in der Bundesrepublik während der 1950er Jahre*. Baden-Baden: Nomos, 2014.

Carruthers, Susan L. *The Good Occupation: American Soldiers and the Hazards of Peace*. Cambridge, MA: Harvard University Press, 2016.

Certeau, Michel de. *The Practice of Everyday Life*. Berkeley: University of California Press, 1988.

Conway, Martin. 'The Rise and Fall of Western Europe's Democratic Age, 1945–1973'. *Contemporary European History* 13, no. 1 (2004): 67–88.

Conway, Martin, and Peter Romijn (eds). *The War for Legitimacy in Politics and Culture 1936–1946*. Oxford and New York: Berg, 2008.

Defrance, Corine. *La politique culturelle de la France sur la rive gauche du Rhin, 1945–1955*. Strasbourg: Presses universitaires de Strasbourg, 1994.

Deighton, Anne. *The Impossible Peace: Britain, the Division of Germany and the Origins of the Cold War*. Oxford: Clarendon, 1990.

Dichter, Heather L. 'Sporting Relations: Diplomacy, Small States, and Germany's Postwar Return to International Sport'. *Diplomacy & Statecraft* 27, no. 2 (2016): 340–59.

Dinstein, Yoram. *The International Law of Belligerent Occupation*. Cambridge: Cambridge University Press, 2009.

Dixon, John G. 'The Founding of the Cologne Sporthochschule'. *Sports International* 6 (1982): 14–20.

Doering-Manteuffel, Anselm. *Wie westlich sind die Deutschen? Amerikanisierung und Westernisierung im 20. Jahrhundert*. Göttingen: Vandenhoeck & Ruprecht, 1999.

Dorn, Walter Louis. *Inspektionsreisen in der US-Zone. Notizen, Denkschriften und Erinnerungen aus dem Nachlass*, edited by Lutz Niethammer. Stuttgart: Deutsche Verlags-Anstalt, 1973.

Dower, John W. *Embracing Defeat: Japan in the Aftermath of World War* II. London: Penguin, 2000.

Edinger, Lewis J. 'Post-Totalitarian Leadership: Elites in the German Federal Republic'. *The American Political Science Review* 54, no. 1 (1960): 58–82.

Elster, Jon. *Closing the Books: Transitional Justice in Historical Perspective*. Cambridge: Cambridge University Press, 2004.

Elster, Jon (ed.). *Retribution and Reparation in the Transition to Democracy*. New York: Cambridge University Press, 2006.

Eschenburg, Theodor. *Jahre der Besatzung: 1945–1949*. Geschichte der Bundesrepublik Deutschland 1. Mannheim: Deutsche Verlagsanstalt; Brockhaus, 1983.

Evans, Richard. *Rituals of Retribution: Capital Punishment in Germany, 1600–1987*. Oxford: Oxford University Press, 1996.

Fäßler, Peter, Reinhard Grohnert, Joachim Haug, Heiko Haumann and Edgar Wolfrum. 'Hauptstadt ohne Brot: Freiburg im Land Baden (1945–1952)'. In *Geschichte der Stadt Freiburg: Von der Badischen Herrschaft bis zur Gegenwart*, edited by Heiko Haumann and Hans Schadeck, 371–427. Stuttgart: Theiss, 2001.

Fehrenbach, Heide. *Race after Hitler: Black Occupation Children in Postwar Germany and America*. Princeton: Princeton University Press, 2007.

Feigel, Lara. *The Bitter Taste of Victory*. London: Bloomsbury, 2016.

Foschepoth, Josef (ed.). *Kalter Krieg und deutsche Frage: Deutschland im Widerstreit der Mächte 1945–1952*. Göttingen, Zurich: Vandenhoeck & Ruprecht, 1985.

Fox, Gregory H. *Humanitarian Occupation*. Cambridge: Cambridge University Press, 2008.

Frei, Norbert. *Adenauer's Germany and the Nazi Past: The Politics of Amnesty and Integration*. New York: Columbia University Press, 2002.

Friedmann, Wolfgang. *The Allied Military Government of Germany*. London: Stevens & Sons, 1947.

Fulbrook, Mary. *Dissonant Lives: Generations and Violence through the German Dictatorships*. Oxford: Oxford University Press, 2011.

Fulbrook, Mary, and Ulinka Rublack. 'In Relation: The "Social Self" and Ego-Documents'. *German History* 28, no. 3 (September 2010): 263–72.

Gebhardt, Miriam. *Als die Soldaten kamen: Die Vergewaltigung deutscher Frauen am Ende des Zweiten Weltkrieges*. Munich: Deutsche Verlags-Anstalt, 2015.

Gedenkstätte Berlin-Hohenschönhausen (ed.). *Speziallager – Internierungslager: Internierungspolitik im besetzten Nachkriegsdeutschland*. Berlin: Gedenkstätte Berlin-Hohenschönhausen, 1996.

Gildea, Robert, Olivier Wieviorka and Anette Warring (eds). *Surviving Hitler and Mussolini: Daily Life in Occupied Europe*. Oxford and New York: Berg, 2006.

Gimbel, John. *A German Community under American Occupation*. Stanford: Stanford University Press, 1961.

Glienke, Stephan Alexander, Volker Paulmann and Joachim Perels. *Erfolgsgeschichte Bundesrepublik? Die Nachkriegsgesellschaft im langen Schatten des Nationalsozialismus*. Göttingen: Wallstein Verlag, 2008.

Goda, Norman J. W. *Tales from Spandau: Nazi Criminals and the Cold War*. Cambridge: Cambridge University Press, 2007.

Goda, Norman J. W. 'Tracking the Red Orchestra: Allied Intelligence, Soviet Spies, Nazi Criminals'. In *U.S. Intelligence and the Nazis*, edited by Richard Breitman, Norman J. W. Goda, Timothy Naftali and Robert Wolfe, 293–316. Cambridge and New York: Cambridge University Press, 2005.

Goedde, Petra. *GIs and Germans: Culture, Gender and Foreign Relations, 1945–1949*. New Haven and London: Yale University Press, 2003.

Goschler, Constantin, and Michael Wala. *'Keine neue Gestapo': Das Bundesamt für Verfassungsschutz und die NS-Vergangenheit*. Reinbek bei Hamburg: Rowohlt, 2015.

Graber, Doris. *The Development of the Law of Belligerent Occupation 1863–1914. A Historical Survey*. New York: AMS Press, 1949.

Graham-Dixon, Francis. *The Allied Occupation of Germany: The Refugee Crisis, Denazification and the Path to Reconstruction*. London and New York: I.B. Tauris, 2013.

Graml, Hermann. *Die Alliierten und die Teilung Deutschlands: Konflikte und Entscheidungen, 1941–1948*. Frankfurt a. M.: Fischer, 1988.

Grossmann, Atina. 'A Question of Silence: The Rape of German Women by Occupation Soldiers'. *October* 72 (Spring 1995): 42–63.

Grossmann, Atina. *Jews, Germans and Allies: Close Encounters in Occupied Germany*. Princeton: Princeton University Press, 2007.

Hagemann, Karen, and Stefanie Schüler-Springorum (eds). *Home/Front: The Military, War and Gender in Twentieth-Century Germany*. Oxford and New York: Berg, 2002.

Harvey, Elizabeth, and Maiken Umbach. 'Introduction: Photography and Twentieth-Century German History'. *Central European History* 48, no. 3 (2015): 287–99.

Hechter, Michael. *Alien Rule*. Cambridge: Cambridge University Press, 2013.

Henke, Klaus-Dietmar. 'Politik der Widersprüche: Zur Charakteristik der französischen Militärregierung in Deutschland nach dem Zweiten Weltkrieg'. *Vierteljahrshefte für Zeitgeschichte* 30, no. 3 (1982): 500–37.

Henke, Klaus-Dietmar. *Die amerikanische Besetzung Deutschlands*. 2nd ed. Munich: R. Oldenbourg, 1995.

Herbert, Ulrich (ed.). *Wandlungsprozesse in Westdeutschland: Belastung, Integration, Liberalisierung 1945–1980*. Göttingen: Wallstein Verlag, 2002.

Hersey, John. *A Bell for Adano*. New York: Alfred A. Knopf, 1944.

Herzog, Dagmar. *Sex after Fascism: Memory and Morality in Twentieth-Century Germany*. Princeton: Princeton University Press, 2005.

Hewitson, Mark. '"I Witnesses": Soldiers, Selfhood and Testimony in Modern Wars'. *German History* 28, no. 3 (September 2010): 310–25.

Hillel, Marc. *L'occupation française en Allemagne 1945–1949*. Paris: Balland, 1983.

Hiller, Hubertus. *Jäger und Jagd: Zur Entwicklung des Jagdwesens in Deutschland zwischen 1848 und 1914*. Münster: Waxmann Verlag, 2003.

Hodenberg, Christina von. 'Of German Fräuleins, Nazi werewolves and Iraqi insurgents'. *Central European History* 41 (2008): 71–92.

Höhn, Maria. *GIs and Fräuleins: The German-American Encounter in 1950s West Germany*. Chapel Hill: University of North Carolina Press, 2002.

Höhn, Maria, and Martin Klimke. *A Breath of Freedom: The Civil Rights Struggle, African American GIs, and Germany*. New York: Palgrave Macmillan, 2010.

Horn, Christa. *Die Internierungs- and Arbeitslager in Bayern 1945–1952*. Frankfurt am Main: Peter Lang, 1992.

Hudemann, Rainer. *Sozialpolitik im deutschen Südwesten zwischen Tradition und Neuordnung 1945–1953. Sozialversicherung und Kriegsopferversorgung im Rahmen französischer Besatzungspolitik*. Mainz: von Hase & Koehler, 1988.

Hüser, Dietmar. *Frankreichs 'doppelte Deutschlandpolitik': Dynamik aus der Defensive – Planen, Entscheiden, Umsetzen in gesellschaftlichen und wirtschaftlichen, innen- und außenpolitischen Krisenzeiten, 1944–1950*. Berlin: Duncker & Humblot, 1996.

Hüser, Karl. *'Unschuldig' in britischer Lagerhaft? Das Internierungslager No. 5 Staumühle 1945–1948*. Cologne: SH-Verlag, 1999.

Huster, Ernst-Ulrich, Gerhard Kraiker, Burkhard Scherer, Friedrich Karl Schlotmann and Marianne Welteke. *Determinanten der westdeutschen Restauration*. Frankfurt: Suhrkamp, 1972.

Jackson, Simon A., and Dirk Moses. 'Transformative Occupations in the Middle East'. *Humanity* 8, no. 2 (Summer 2017): 231–46.

Jarausch, Konrad. *After Hitler, Recivilizing Germans, 1945–1995*. Oxford: Oxford University Press, 2006.

Judt, Tony. *Postwar: A History of Europe since 1945*. London: Vintage, 2010.

Jurt, Joseph (ed.). *Die 'Franzosenzeit' im Lande Baden von 1945 bis heute: Zeitzeugnisse und Forschungsergebnisse = La présence française dans le pays de Bade de 1945 à nos jours*. Freiburg i. Br.: Rombach, 1992.

Kalshoven, Frits. *Belligerent Reprisals*. Leyden: Sijthoff, 1971.

Kater, Michael H. *Hitler Youth*. Cambridge, MA: Harvard University Press, 2004.

Kellermann, Henry J. *Cultural Relations as an Instrument of U.S. Foreign Policy: The Educational Exchange Program between the United States and Germany, 1945–1954*. Washington, DC: Government Printing Office, 1978.

Kleßmann, Christoph. *Die doppelte Staatsgründung. Deutsche Geschichte 1945–1955*. Bonn: Bundeszentrale für politische Bildung, 1991.

Knapp, Gudrun-Axeli. '"Intersectionality" – ein neues Paradigma feministischer Theorie? Zur transatlantischen Reise von "Race, Class, Gender"'. *Feministische Studien* 23 (2005): 68–81.

Knigge-Tesche, Renate, Peter Reif-Spirek and Bodo Ritscher (eds). *Internierungspraxis in Ost- und Westdeutschland nach 1945*. Erfurt: Gedenkstätte Buchenwald, 1993.

Knowles, Christopher. *Winning the Peace: The British in Occupied Germany 1945–1948*. London: Bloomsbury Academic, 2017.

Kocka, Jürgen. '1945: Neubeginn oder Restauration'. In *Wendepunkt deutsche Geschichte 1848–1945*, edited by Carola Stern and Heinrich A. Winkler, 141–90. Frankfurt a. M.: Fischer, 1979.

Kogon, Eugen. 'Beinahe mit dem Rücken zur Wand'. *Frankfurter Hefte* 9 (1954): 641–5.

Köhler, Werner. *Freiburg i. Br. 1945–1949: Politisches Leben und Erfahrungen in der Nachkriegszeit*. Freiburg i. Br.: Verlag Stadtarchiv Freiburg im Breisgau, 1987.

Kronenbitter, Günther, Markus Pöhlmann and Dierk Walter (eds). *Besatzung: Funktion und Gestalt militärischer Fremdherrschaft von der Antike bis zum 20. Jahrhundert*. Paderborn: Schöningh, 2006.

Kuber, Johannes. '"Frivolous Broads" and the "Black Menace": The Catholic Clergy's Perception of Victims and Perpetrators of Sexual Violence in Occupied Germany, 1945'. In *War and Sexual Violence*, edited by Sarah K. Danielsson and Frank Jacob. Paderborn: Schöningh, forthcoming.

KZ-Gedenkstätte Neuengamme (ed.). *Beiträge zur Geschichte der nationalsozialistischen Verfolgung in Norddeutschland*, vol. 12: *Zwischenräume: Displaced Persons, Internierte und Flüchtlinge in ehemaligen Konzentrationslagern*. Bremen: Edition Temmen, 2010.

Le Naour, Jean-Yves. *La honte noire: L'Allemagne et les troupes coloniales françaises 1914–1945*. Paris: Fayard, 2003.

Levy, Alexandra F. 'Promoting Democracy and Denazification: American Policymaking and German Public Opinion'. *Diplomacy & Statecraft* 26, no. 4 (2015): 614–35.

Lilly, J. Robert. *Taken by Force: Rape and American GIs in Europe during World War II*. Basingstoke and New York: Palgrave Macmillan, 2007.

Lingk, Michael. *Amerikanische Besatzer und deutsche Kirchen 1944–1948: Eine Studie zu Kirchenbild und Kirchenpolitik der amerikanischen Besatzungsmacht unter besonderer Berücksichtigung Württemberg-Badens und Bayerns*. Tübingen: UVT, 1996.

Long, Bronson. *No Easy Occupation: French Control of the German Saar, 1944–1957*. Rochester: Camden House, 2015.

Löw, Martina. 'The Constitution of Space: The Structuration of Spaces through the Simultaneity of Effect and Perception'. *European Journal of Social Theory* 11, no. 1 (2008): 25–49.

Maß, Sandra. *Weiße Helden, schwarze Krieger: Zur Geschichte kolonialer Männlichkeit in Deutschland 1918–1964*. Cologne: Böhlau, 2006.

Maelstaf, Geneviève. *Que faire de l'Allemagne? Les responsables français, le statut international de l'Allemagne et le problème de l'unité allemande (1945–1955)*. Diplomatie et histoire. Paris: Direction des Archives Ministère des Affaires Étrangères, 1999.

Maier, Charles S. 'The Two Postwar Eras and the Conditions for Stability in Twentieth-Century Western Europe'. *American Historical Review* 86, no. 2 (1981): 327–52.

Mayne, Richard. *In Victory, Magnanimity in Peace, Goodwill: A History of Wilton Park*. London: Frank Cass, 2003.

Mazower, Mark, Jessica Reinisch and David Feldman (eds). *Post-War Reconstruction in Europe: International Perspectives, 1945–1949*. Oxford: Oxford University Press, 2011.

Meehan, Patricia. *A Strange Enemy People: Germans under the British, 1945–1950*. London: Peter Owen, 2001.

Mentel, Christian, and Niels Weise. *Die zentralen deutschen Behörden und der Nationalsozialismus. Stand und Perspektiven der Forschung*. Munich and Potsdam: Institut für Zeitgeschichte, 2016.

Meyer, Kathrin. *Entnazifizierung von Frauen: Die Internierungslager der US-Zone Deutschlands 1945–1952*. Berlin: Metropol, 2004.

Moeller, Robert G. *War Stories: The Search for a Usable Past in the Federal Republic of Germany*. Berkeley, Los Angeles and London: University of California Press, 2001.

Möhler, Rainer. *Entnazifizierung in Rheinland-Pfalz und im Saarland unter französischer Besatzung von 1945 bis 1952*. Mainz: von Hase & Koehler, 1992.

Naumann Klaus (ed.). *Nachkrieg in Deutschland*. Hamburg: Hamburger Edition, 2001.

Niethammer, Lutz. 'Alliierte Internierungslager in Deutschland nach 1945: Vergleich und offene Fragen'. In *Von der Aufgabe der Freiheit: Politische Verantwortung und bürgerliche Gesellschaft im 19. und 20. Jahrhundert, Festschrift für Hans Mommsen zum 5. November 1995*, edited by Christian Jansen, Lutz Niethammer and Bernd Weisbrod, 469–92. Berlin: Oldenbourg Akademieverlag, 1995.

Niethammer, Lutz. *Die Mitläuferfabrik: Die Entnazifizierung am Beispiel Bayerns*. Berlin: J.W.H. Dietz, 1982.

Niethammer, Lutz. *'Hinterher merkt man, daß es richtig war, daß es schief gegangen ist': Nachkriegserfahrungen im Ruhrgebiet*. Berlin: Dietz, 1983.

Niethammer, Lutz, Ulrich Borsdorf and Peter Brandt (eds). *Arbeiterinitiative 1945: Antifaschistische Ausschüsse und Reorganisation der Arbeiterbewegung in Deutschland*. Wuppertal: Hammer, 1976.

Overy, Richard. *Interrogations: Inside the Minds of the Nazi Elite*. London: Penguin, 2001.

Paterson, Sarah. '"Operation Union": British Families in Germany, 1946'. *Imperial War Museum Review* 10 (1995): 74–83.

Poiger, Uta G. *Jazz, Rock, and Rebels: Cold War Politics and American Culture in a Divided Germany*. Berkeley: University of California Press, 2000.

Pronay, Nicholas, and Keith M. Wilson (eds). *The Political Re-education of Germany and Her Allies after World War II*. London: Croom Helm, 1985.

Puaca, Brian M. *Learning Democracy: Education Reform in West Germany, 1945–1965*. New York: Berghahn Books, 2009.

Radkau, Joachim. *Wood: A History*. Cambridge: Polity Press, 2012.

Rauh-Kühne, Cornelia. 'Die Entnazifizierung und die deutsche Gesellschaft'. *Archiv für Sozialgeschichte* 35 (1995): 35–70.

Reinisch, Jessica. *The Perils of Peace: The Public Health Crisis in Occupied Germany*. Oxford: Oxford University Press, 2013.

Rempel, Gerhard. *Hitler's Children: The Hitler Youth and the SS*. Chapel Hill: University of North Carolina Press, 1989.

Rigoll, Dominik. 'Das Gründungspersonal der Bonner Bundesbehörden. Über Karriere- und Rekrutierungsmuster nach 1945'. *ZeitRäume* (2016): 55–72.

Rigoll, Dominik. *Staatsschutz in Westdeutschland. Von der Entnazifizierung zur Extremistenabwehr*. Göttingen: Wallstein, 2013.

Rosenberg, Jonathan. *How Far the Promised Land? World Affairs and the American Civil Rights Movement from the First World War to Vietnam*. Princeton: Princeton University Press, 2005.

Rösener, Werner. *Die Geschichte der Jagd. Kultur, Gesellschaft und Jagdwesen im Wandel der Zeit*. Düsseldorf: Artemis & Winkler, 2004.

Rubin, Gerry R. 'British Military and Government Lawyers on the Defeat of Nazi Germany'. *Military Law and Law of War Review* 47 (2008): 97–137.

Ruhm von Oppen, Beate (ed.). *Documents on Germany under Occupation, 1945–1954*. London: Oxford University Press, 1955.

Rüther, Martin, Uwe Schütz and Otto Dann (eds). *Deutschland im ersten Nachkriegsjahr: Berichte von Mitgliedern des Internationalen Sozialistischen Kampfbundes (ISK) aus dem besetzten Deutschland 1945/46*. Munich: K.G. Saur, 1998.

Sälter, Gerhard. *Phantome des Krieges. Die Organisation Gehlen und die Wiederbelebung des Gestapo-Feinbildes 'Rote Kapelle'*. Berlin: Ch. Links Verlag, 2016.

Satjukow, Silke, and Rainer Gries. *'Bankerte!': Besatzungskinder in Deutschland nach 1945*. Frankfurt and New York: Campus, 2015.

Schildt, Axel. 'The Long Shadows of the Second World War: The Impact of Experiences and Memories of War on West German Society'. *German Historical Institute London Bulletin* 29, no. 1 (May 2007): 28–49.

Schissler, Hanna. '"Normalization" as Project: Some Thoughts on Gender Relations in West Germany during the 1950s'. In *The Miracle Years: A Cultural History of West Germany, 1949–1968*, edited by H. Schissler, 359–75. Princeton: Princeton University Press, 2001.

Schmidt, Eberhard. *Die verhinderte Neuordnung 1945–1952: Zur Auseinandersetzung um die Demokratisierung der Wirtschaft in den westlichen Besatzungszonen und in der Bundesrepublik Deutschland*. Theorie und Praxis der Gewerkschaften. Frankfurt a. M.: Europäische Verlags-Anstalt, 1970.

Schmidt, Ute, and Tilman Fichter. *Der erzwungene Kapitalismus: Klassenkämpfe in den Westzonen 1945–1948*. Rotbuch 27. Berlin: Wagenbach, 1971.

Schroer, Timothy L. *Recasting Race after World War II: Germans and African Americans in American-Occupied Germany*. Boulder: University of Colorado Press, 2007.

Schwarz, Hans-Peter. *Vom Reich zur Bundesrepublik: Deutschland im Widerstreit der außenpolitischen Konzeptionen in den Jahren der Besatzungsherrschaft 1945–1949*, 2nd ed. Stuttgart: Klett-Cotta, 1980.

Seipp, Adam. *Strangers in the Wild Place: Refugees, Americans, and a German Town, 1945–1952*. Bloomington: Indiana University Press, 2013.

Serger, Bernd, and Karin-Anne Böttcher. 'Der Einmarsch der Alliierte'. In *Südbaden unter Hakenkreuz und Trikolore: Zeitzeugen berichten über das Kriegsende und die französische Besatzung 1945*, edited by Bernd Serger, Karin-Anne Böttcher and G. R. Ueberschär, 242–329. Freiburg i. Br.: Rombach, 2006.

Sharples, Caroline. 'Burying the Past? The Post-Execution History of Nazi War Criminals'. In *A Global History of Execution and the Criminal Corpse*, edited by Richard Ward, 249–71. Basingstoke: Palgrave Macmillan, 2015.

Sharples, Caroline. *Postwar Germany and the Holocaust*. London: Bloomsbury Academic, 2016.

Sollors, Werner. *The Temptation of Despair: Tales of the 1940s*. Cambridge, MA: The Belknap Press of the University of Harvard, 2014.

Speiser, Peter. *The British Army of the Rhine: Turning Nazi Enemies into Cold War Partners*. Urbana: University of Illinois Press, 2016.

Stirk, Peter. *A History of Military Occupation from 1791 to 1914*. Edinburgh: Edinburgh University Press, 2016.

Stirk, Peter. *The Politics of Military Occupation*. Edinburgh: Edinburgh University Press, 2009.

Strauß, Christof. 'Freiburg im Breisgau als Hauptstadt des Landes Baden – der Not geschuldet, die Not verwaltend'. In *Die Zeit nach dem Krieg: Städte im Wiederaufbau*, edited by K. Moersch and R. Weber, 58–82. Stuttgart: Kohlhammer, 2008.

Tent, James. *Mission on the Rhine: Reeducation and Denazification in American-Occupied Germany*. Chicago: University of Chicago Press, 1982.

Turner, Ian D. (ed.). *Reconstruction in Post-War Germany: British Occupation Policy and the Western Zones, 1945–55*. Oxford: Berg, 1989.

Tusa, Ann, and John Tusa. *The Nuremberg Trial*. London: Macmillan, 1983.

Uekoetter, Frank. *The Green and the Brown: A History of Conservation in Nazi Germany*. Cambridge: Cambridge University Press, 2006.

Vollnhals, Clemens (ed.). *Entnazifizierung: Politische Säuberung und Rehabilitierung in den vier Besatzungszonen 1945–1949*. Munich: Deutscher Taschenbuch Verlag, 1991.

Warde, Paul. *Ecology, Economy, and State Formation in Early Modern Germany*. Cambridge: Cambridge University Press, 2006.

Webster, Ronald. 'Opposing "Victors' Justice": German Protestant Churchmen and Convicted War Criminals in Western Europe after 1945'. *Holocaust and Genocide Studies* 15, no. 1 (2001): 47–69.

Welch, David. 'Citizenship and Politics: Legacy of Wilton Park for Post-War Reconstruction'. *Contemporary European History* 6, no. 2 (1997): 209–14.

Wember, Heiner. *Umerziehung im Lager: Internierung und Bestrafung von Nationalsozialisten in der britischen Besatzungszone Deutschlands*. Essen: Klartext, 1991.

Wildt, Michael. *Der Traum vom Sattwerden*. Hamburg: VSA, 1986.

Willard-Foster, Melissa. 'Planning the Peace and Enforcing the Surrender'. *Journal of Interdisciplinary History* 40 (2009): 33–56.

Willett, Ralph. *The Americanization of Germany, 1945–1949*. London: Routledge, 1992.

Willis, F. Roy. *The French in Germany, 1945–1949*. Stanford: Stanford University Press, 1962.

Willoughby, John. *Remaking the Conquering Heroes: The Social and Geopolitical Impact of the Post-War American Occupation of Germany*. New York and Basingstoke: Palgrave, 2001.

Woite-Wehle, Stefanie. *Zwischen Kontrolle und Demokratisierung: Die Sportpolitik der französischen Besatzungsmacht in Südwestdeutschland 1945–1950*. Schorndorf: Hofmann, 2001.

Wolfrum, Edgar. *Französische Besatzungspolitik und deutsche Sozialdemokratie: Politische Neuansätze in der 'vergessenen Zone' bis zur Bildung des Südweststaates 1945–1952*. Düsseldorf: Droste, 1991.

Wolfrum, Edgar. 'Von der Gewaltherrschaft zur Besatzungsherrschaft: Politisches Handeln und Erfahrungen im Jahr 1945'. *Zeitschrift für die Geschichte des Oberrheins* 143 (1995): 353–84.

Wright, Lord. 'The Killing of Hostages as a War Crime'. *British Yearbook of International Law* 25 (1948): 296–310.

Zapf, Wolfgang. *Wandlungen der deutschen Elite. Ein Zirkulationsmodell deutscher Führungsgruppen 1919–1961*. Munich: Piper, 1965.

Index

Lightning Source UK Ltd.
Milton Keynes UK
UKHW021531030320
359688UK00005B/192